Series Editors:
Steven F. Warren, Ph.D.
Joe Reichle, Ph.D.

**Communication
and Language
Intervention
Series**

Volume 1

Causes and Effects in Communication and Language Intervention

Communication and Language Intervention Series

Volume 1

Causes and Effects in Communication and Language Intervention

Edited by

Steven F. Warren, Ph.D.
Professor of Special Education and Psychology
Department of Special Education
George Peabody College
Vanderbilt University
Nashville, Tennessee

and

Joe Reichle, Ph.D.
Professor of Communication Disorders
Department of Communication Disorders
University of Minnesota
Minneapolis, Minnesota

PAUL·H· BROOKES PUBLISHING CO.   Baltimore • London • Toronto • Sydney

Paul H. Brookes Publishing Co.
P.O. Box 10624
Baltimore, Maryland 21285-0624

Typeset by The Composing Room of Michigan, Inc., Grand Rapids, Michigan.
Manufactured in the United States of America by
The Maple Press Company, York, Pennsylvania.

Library of Congress Cataloging-in-Publication Data
Causes and effects in communication and language intervention / edited
    by Steven F. Warren and Joe Reichle.
        p.   cm.—(Communication and language intervention series; 1)
    Includes bibliographical references and index.
    ISBN 1-55766-075-1
    1. Language disorders in children.   2. Speech therapy for children.   I.
Reichle, Joe (Joe Ernest), 1951–   .   II. Warren, Steven F.   III. Series.
    [DNLM: 1. Language Disorders—diagnosis.   2. Language Disorders—
in infancy & childhood.   3. Language Therapy.   WL 340 C376]
RJ496.L35C38   1992
618.92′855—dc20
DNLM/DLC
for Library of Congress   91-15659
                                                                              CIP

This book is dedicated to
Richard L. Schiefelbusch in recognition of
the extraordinary contributions that he has made
to the development of the field of
communication and language intervention.

Contents

Series Preface

THE PURPOSE OF THE *Communication and Language Intervention Series* is to provide meaningful foundations for the application of sound intervention designs to enhance the development of communication skills across the life span. We shall endeavor to achieve this purpose by providing readers with presentations of state-of-the-art theory, research, and practice.

In selecting topics, editors, and authors, we shall not attempt to limit the contents of this series to those viewpoints with which we agree or which we find most promising. We shall be assisted in our efforts to develop the series by an editorial advisory board consisting of prominent scholars representative of the range of issues and perspectives to be incorporated in the series.

We trust that the careful reader will find much that is provocative and controversial in this and future volumes. This will be necessarily so to the extent that the work reported is truly on the so-called cutting edge, a mythical place where no sacred cows exist. This point is demonstrated time and again throughout this volume as the conventional wisdom is challenged (and occasionally confirmed) by various authors.

Readers of this and future volumes are encouraged to proceed with healthy skepticism. In order to achieve our purpose, we shall need to take on some difficult and controversial issues. Errors and misinterpretations will inevitably be made. This is normal in the development of any field, and should be welcomed as evidence that the field is moving forward and tackling difficult and weighty issues.

Well-conceived theory and research on development of both children with and children without disabilities is vitally important for researchers, educators, and clinicians committed to the development of optimal approaches to communication and language intervention. For this reason, each volume in this series will include chapters pertaining to both development and intervention.

The content of each volume will reflect our view of the symbiotic relationship between intervention and research: demonstrations of what may work in intervention should lead to analyses of promising discoveries and insights from developmental work that may in turn fuel further refinement and development by intervention researchers.

An inherent goal of this series is to enhance the long-term development of the field by systematically furthering the dissemination of theoretically and empirically based scholarship and research. We promise the reader an opportunity to participate in the development of this field through the debates and discussions that occur throughout the pages of the *Communication and Language Intervention Series*.

Editorial Advisory Board

Foreword

THE PAST SEVERAL YEARS HAVE extended the work of the various disciplines in the language intervention field. It is time now for a new burst of effort and a new commitment to language intervention. In this new series we can expect to make further gains in consensus building regarding theory, strategy, and anticipated outcomes.

This consensus is likely to develop in part from the quality and the cogency of this book series. The books will integrate, combine, and interpret an extensive body of knowledge. In addition, at least three favorable conditions can be observed in the current literature that auger for success in building this consensus. First, there is an increasing interdisciplinary exchange among scientists from relevant sectors. This means that there is a community of scholarship that supports language intervention. Second, the intervention field is moving toward the creation of natural conditions and contexts in which children learn or are taught their language skills. There is now congruence between the data on language acquisition that developmental psycholinguists collect and the data about taught language that intervention specialists collect. As these data are acquired, the theories and the supporting data from the two groups can be interpreted from a common frame of reference. Finally, since the conditions devised by language intervention specialists are recorded along with the outcome data, there is an experimental character to the work of interventionists that adds richness and confirmation to the descriptive data of acquisition studies. Both research groups share an important purpose, which is to explain how language is acquired.

The aim of the series will be to enhance the long-term development of the language intervention field. It is a great privilege for me to commend this well-conceived new series, which will help move us toward disciplinary status for speech, language, and communication.

Richard L. Schiefelbusch, Ph.D.
Schiefelbusch Institute for Life Span Studies
University of Kansas
Lawrence, Kansas

Volume Preface

THIS VOLUME CONSISTS OF 14 chapters reflecting in many ways the richness and diversity of the communication and language intervention field. The title of the book, *Causes and Effects in Communication and Language Intervention*, represents a theme that underlies most of the chapters. Our purpose is to provide the reader with a state-of-the-art overview of research and development in the emerging field of communication and language intervention. We have chosen topics that we feel represent a cross-section of issues that are important to practitioners as well as researchers in the areas of communication and language intervention, development, and assessment. Each contributor was chosen based on the importance of his or her research. Each chapter is intended to stand on its own, and need not be read in conjunction with other chapters. Each concludes with a discussion of the educational and clinical implications of the work described, and an examination of directions for future research.

This book begins with an essay by Warren and Reichle on the emerging field of communication and language intervention. Warren and Reichle argue that although the field of communication and language intervention is inherently transdisciplinary, the need now exists for it to become more clearly identified in its own right. One purpose of this essay is to set forth the larger agenda for the *Communication and Language Intervention Series*.

During the 1980s, a number of studies reported on the effects of various milieu language intervention strategies. For both theoretical and philosophical reasons, these more naturalistic intervention approaches have had wide appeal. In Chapter 2, Kaiser and her colleagues critique the empirical support for these procedures. Their analysis suggests both strengths and limitations of these procedures.

Like milieu teaching, training parents to facilitate the language development of their children has received substantial attention in recent years. In Chapter 3, Tannock and Girolametto provide a critical review of parent-focused language intervention programs that use the Interactive Model of facilitation. Their review suggests that this approach may enable parents to motivate and enhance children's *use* of existing communicative and linguistic abilities, but may not enhance children's *acquisition* of new linguistic structures. The limitations identified in both chapters may be more apparent than real in that they may reflect inadequate measurement of the appropriate dependent variables rather than inherent limitations of these intervention models.

In Chapter 4, Goldstein and Kaczmarek move the focus beyond language per se to examine the relationship between communicative skills and social competence. After establishing the crucial nature of this relationship, they discuss a wide range of techniques and approaches that applied researchers have studied for promoting communicative interaction in integrated early intervention settings.

Chapters 5, 6, and 7 address issues related to severe communication disabilities. In Chapter 5, Romski and Sevcik report the results of a longitudinal study of communication acquisition in children with severe retardation who were provided with

appropriate augmented communication devices. In contrast to a great volume of literature that has argued that children with severe mental retardation need high levels of
prompting and massed practice in order to learn language, Romski and Sevcik's data
suggest that what these children may really need are "relevant moments" within the
natural course of everyday augmented communicative interaction. That is, like other
children, they may learn more efficiently and successfully via a relatively small number of contextually appropriate, embedded teaching incidents.

In Chapter 6, Reichle and his colleagues examine current issues facing interventionists who serve learners who might benefit from the use of augmentative or alternative communication systems. This chapter focuses on making decisions regarding the
initial selection and implementation of graphic mode (communication board) and
gestural mode (natural gestures/sign) programs.

One of the most severe communication disorders—and historically one of the
most resistant to effective remediation—is autism. In Chapter 7, Klinger and Dawson
report compelling evidence that certain socially based intervention techniques may be
more effective with young children with autism because of the apparently inherent
tendency of these children to respond poorly to unpredictable, noncontingent social
situations. Klinger and Dawson conclude their chapter with a discussion of specific
techniques that should be effective given this tendency.

In Chapter 8, Olswang and her colleagues offer a decidedly different perspective
on the role of assessment with children with language impairments or mild developmental disabilities. Working from a Vygotskian perspective, Olswang and her colleagues examine the conditions under which a child is ready to benefit from one
intervention approach versus another. They argue that by identifying a child's "zone of
proximal development" via dynamic assessment, the efficacy of the intervention process can be optimized by matching specific intervention approaches to the child's level
of skill mastery.

Continuing a focus on assessment, in Chapter 9, Wetherby and Prizant offer a
broad-based examination of the clinical issues pertaining to the assessment and early
identification of communication disorders. They review the literature exploring the
emerging communication and language patterns of children with communicative impairments, then present a model of communication assessment that profiles the communicative, social-affective, and symbolic abilities of young children from prelinguistic development through early linguistic development.

In Chapter 10, Yoder and his colleagues move the focus from assessment toward a
common theme among all types of language disorders and delays: how to get young
children with developmental disabilities to talk more with adults. They review the
support for three conversational recruiting strategies—topic continuations, questions,
and verbal routines. One important conclusion they reach is that adult questions are an
excellent conversational eliciting technique with children who exhibit low rates of
talking and are just beginning to acquire basic vocabulary. This finding supports the
appropriate use of modestly intrusive teaching procedures, such as those used in milieu
language teaching.

Young children who show signs of expressive language delay but appear to be
normal in other ways present an enigma to researchers and clinicians. Based on their
research, Whitehurst and his colleagues argue in Chapter 11 that intervention with
these children may be unnecessary since most seem to reveal normal language development by age 6 whether they receive intervention or not.

Several chapters identify problems with measures used to document language
growth and intervention effects and point out how these limitations affect what we
really know about the remediation of these deficits. In Chapter 12, Klee explores

several methods used in research and clinical practice to quantify and evaluate the spontaneous language production of young children. This chapter will be of particular interest to researchers who base their analysis on naturalistic speech samples.

In Chapter 13, Abbeduto and Rosenberg examine how adults with mental retardation function as speakers and listeners in their social interactions. They summarize the research on this issue and discuss the implications for assessment and intervention. Their review focuses primarily on the knowledge and skills that underlie the acts of speaking and listening, rather than on ways that the environment contributes to problems in linguistic communication.

In the final chapter of the book, Bricker takes on the formidable task of integrating the preceding 13 chapters. As one of the original contributors to the field of early communication and language intervention, and one of the foremost scholars in the field today, Bricker has a unique vantage point from which to critique this body of work. She offers the reader an insightful synthesis of the contents of this volume placed in the context of the broader themes that must drive research if the field of language intervention is to make further progress.

Contributors

The Editors

Steven F. Warren, Ph.D., Professor of Special Education and Psychology, George Peabody College, Vanderbilt University, Nashville, TN 37203. Dr. Warren is also Associate Director of the John F. Kennedy Center for Research on Education and Human Development at Vanderbilt University, and Co-Director of the Center's Mental Retardation Research Training Program. His research has focused on language generalization and milieu language intervention approaches.

Joe Reichle, Ph.D., Professor of Communication Disorders and Educational Psychology, University of Minnesota, Minneapolis, MN 55455. Dr. Reichle has published extensively in the area of communication and language intervention and is actively involved in the preparation of speech-language pathologists and special educators. He serves as the chair of the publication board of The Association for Persons with Severe Handicaps and as a reviewer and editorial consultant to various scholarly journals.

The Chapter Authors

Leonard Abbeduto, Ph.D., Associate Professor of Educational Psychology, University of Wisconsin, Madison, WI 53706. Dr. Abbeduto is also an investigator at the Waisman Center on Mental Retardation and Human Development. His research has focused on the nature, causes, and consequences of language and communication problems in persons with mild and moderate mental retardation.

David S. Arnold, M.A., Doctoral Student, Department of Clinical Psychology, State University of New York at Stony Brook, Stony Brook, NY 11794-2500.

Barbara A. Bain, Ph.D., Associate Professor of Speech Pathology and Audiology, Idaho State University, Pocatello, ID 83209. Dr. Bain's research has focused on treatment efficacy with children with phonological and language disorders.

Kerri Bishop, M.Ed., Research Assistant and Doctoral Student, Department of Special Education, George Peabody College, Vanderbilt University, Nashville, TN 37203.

Diane Bricker, Ph.D., Professor of Special Education and Communication Disorders and Sciences, University of Oregon, Eugene, OR 94503. Dr. Bricker is also Director of the Early Intervention Area of the Center on Human Development, the University of Oregon's University Affiliated Program. Her research has focused on the development of effective early intervention programs for at-risk and disabled infants and young children and their families, and on the development of communication intervention procedures that focus on the use of child-directed activities.

Betty Davies, M.A., Research Associate, the John F. Kennedy Center for Research on Education and Human Development, Vanderbilt University, Nashville, TN 37203.

Geraldine Dawson, Ph.D., Professor of Psychology, University of Washington, Seattle, WA 98195. Dr. Dawson is Director of the Child Psychology Program at the University of Washington. She has published widely in the area of autism, examining brain–behavior relationships, social and cognitive development, and early intervention strategies. Her current research focuses on the effectiveness of child-directed play strategies for promoting early social and communicative development, and on the diagnosis of autism in infancy.

Janet E. Fischel, Ph.D., Associate Professor, Department of Pediatrics, School of Medicine, State University of New York at Stony Brook, Stony Brook, NY 11794-8111. Dr. Fischel is Director of Medical Education and Associate Director of Residency Training for the Department of Pediatrics at the State University of New York at Stony Brook. Her research has focused on childhood disorders of elimination and on infants at risk for poor developmental progress. In collaboration with Grover Whitehurst and the Stony Brook Language Project, she is studying the relationship between early language disorders and developmental/cognitive consequences, and the impact of strategies of early reading on language development in 2- to 4-year old children.

Luigi Girolametto, Ph.D., Clinical Researcher and Speech-Language Pathologist, The Hospital for Sick Children, Toronto, Ontario M5G 1X8, Canada. Dr. Girolametto is also Assistant Professor in the Graduate Department of Speech Pathology at the University of Toronto. His research has focused on the application and efficacy of the interactional model of language intervention with high-risk infants and preschool children with developmental delays. He is the coauthor, with I. Ushycky, of *Talking to Baby: Parent-Infant Early Communication Program.*

Howard Goldstein, Ph.D., Associate Professor of Communication and Psychiatry, University of Pittsburgh, Pittsburgh, PA 15260. Dr. Goldstein's research has examined various aspects of language development in children with developmental disabilities. In particular, he has worked on identifying conditions that facilitate generalized language learning. He is currently studying classroom-based interventions for enhancing the communication skills of young children with disabilities.

Glenn A. Johnson, M.A., Doctoral Student, Department of Speech and Hearing Sciences, University of Washington, Seattle, WA 98195.

Susan Johnston, B.A., Doctoral Student, Department of Communication Disorders, University of Minnesota, Minneapolis, MN 55455.

Louise Kaczmarek, Ph.D., Assistant Professor of Psychiatry, University of Pittsburgh, Pittsburgh, PA 15213. Dr. Kaczmarek is also a staff member of the Child Language Intervention Program at the University of Pittsburgh. Her principal research interests focus on developing language and communication intervention strategies for use with learners with severe disabilities, preparing personnel to work in early intervention, and transdisciplinary consultation. She is currently the principal investigator on a project examining the spontaneous communication of preschool children with severe disabilities and coprincipal investigator for an inservice training project for related service personnel in early intervention.

Ann P. Kaiser, Ph.D., Professor of Special Education and Psychology and Human Development, George Peabody College, Vanderbilt University, Nashville, TN 37203. Dr. Kaiser's research has focused on early language intervention, parents as facilitators of their children's language development, and the ecological analysis of language learning environments. In conjunction with the Milieu Teaching Group at Vanderbilt, she has recently completed a series of studies comparing the effects of alternative language interventions on the language development of young children with disabilities. She is the editor of the *Journal of The Association for Persons with Severe Handicaps*.

Anne Keetz, M.S., Doctoral Student, Department of Special Education, George Peabody College, Vanderbilt University, Nashville, TN 37203.

Thomas Klee, Ph.D., Associate Professor of Speech-Language Pathology and Audiology, University of Wyoming, Laramie, WY 82071-3311. Dr. Klee's research interests include the application of clinical linguistics in the evaluation of child language disability and the problems of language acquisition in children with specific language impairment. He is the editor of the computer applications section of *Child Language Teaching and Therapy* and the former associate editor for child language of the *Journal of Speech and Hearing Research*.

Laura Grofer Klinger, B.A., Doctoral Student, Department of Psychology, University of Washington, Seattle, WA 98195.

Peggy Locke, Ph.D., Project Coordinator, Department of Communication Disorders, University of Minnesota, Minneapolis, MN 55455.

Christopher J. Lonigan, Ph.D., Postdoctoral Fellow, John F. Kennedy Center for Research on Education and Human Development, Vanderbilt University, Nashville, TN 37203. Dr. Lonigan's research interests include language and behavior disorders of childhood and early intervention.

Pat Mirenda, Ph.D., Associate Professor of Special Education and Communication Disorders, University of Nebraska-Lincoln, Lincoln, NB 68583-0732. Dr. Mirenda's primary areas of research are severe intellectual disabilities, autism, augmentative communication, and nonaversive behavior management. She is particularly interested in developing strategies for integrating students with severe disabilities into regular classrooms, and in studying the attitudes of such students' peers without disabilities toward the augmentative and alternative communication systems of their classmates.

Lesley B. Olswang, Ph.D., Professor of Speech and Hearing Sciences, University of Washington, Seattle, WA 98195. Dr. Olswang's clinical experience, teaching, and research focus primarily on language in children functioning below the developmental age of 5. She is currently the principal investigator of a National Institutes of Health research grant exploring the language acquisition process and evaluating the efficacy of direct clinical treatment for children with language impairments.

Laura Piché, M.A., Doctoral Student, Department of Communication Disorders, University of Minnesota, Minneapolis, MN 55455.

Barry M. Prizant, Ph.D., Professor, Division of Communication Disorders, Emerson College, Boston, MA 02116. Dr. Prizant's primary research and clinical work has been with children with autism and severe social-communication disorders and with at-risk infants and preschool children.

Mary Ann Romski, Ph.D., Associate Professor of Communication and Psychology, Georgia State University, Atlanta, GA 30303. Dr. Romski is also affiliated with the Language Research Center of Georgia State and Emory Universities. Her research has focused on studying the language acquisition process of nonspeaking children with mental retardation.

Sheldon Rosenberg, Ph.D., Professor of Psychology and English and Research Professor in Developmental Disabilities, University of Illinois at Chicago, Chicago, IL 60680. Dr. Rosenberg's research has focused on language development in people with mental retardation. He is the founder of the journal *Applied Linguistics*.

Rose A. Sevcik, Ph.D., Research Associate, Language Research Center, Georgia State University, Atlanta, GA 30303. Dr. Sevcik's research interests include language and communication acquisition and impairments, mental retardation, neuropsychology, and nonhuman primate behavior.

Rosemary Tannock, Ph.D., Behavioral Scientist, The Hospital for Sick Children in Toronto, Toronto, Ontario, M5G 1X8 Canada. Dr. Tannock is also Lecturer in the Department of Psychiatry at the University of Toronto. Her research has focused on the early effects of early parent–child interaction on children's development of communicative and linguistic abilities and on the effectiveness of parent-focused language intervention programs for preschool children with developmental delays. She is currently investigating the nature and treatment of language disorders in children with Attention Deficit Hyperactivity Disorder.

Amy M. Wetherby, Ph.D., Associate Professor of Communication Disorders, Florida State University, Tallahassee, FL 32306-2007. Dr. Wetherby's research has focused on communicative and cognitive-social aspects of language problems in children with autism and on the early identification of children with communication impairments. She is the coauthor, with Barry Prizant, of the *Communication and Symbolic Behavior Scales* (1990).

Grover J. Whitehurst, Ph.D., Professor of Psychology and Pediatrics, State University of New York at Stony Brook, Stony Brook, NY 11794-2500. In recent years, Dr. Whitehurst's research has shifted from basic to applied work, and he has studied the causes and effects of expressive language delay in preschool children and the effects of shared picture book reading on the development of language and preliteracy skills in day care settings and in the home. Since 1981, he has been the editor of *Developmental Review*.

Paul J. Yoder, Ph.D., Research Assistant Professor of Special Education, George Peabody College, Vanderbilt University, Nashville, TN 37203. Dr. Yoder is also an investigator at the John F. Kennedy Center for Research on Education and Human Development at Vanderbilt University. His research has focused on the social influences of language use and development in children with and children without disabilities. He is currently working on developing and testing the relative efficacy of language and prelinguistic communication interventions with preschool children with mental retardation.

Acknowledgments

W E WISH TO ACKNOWLEDGE the influence of Jon Miller of the University of Wisconsin on the organization of this volume. Jon, a member of the Editorial Advisory Board of the *Communication and Language Intervention Series*, noted that current intervention strategies are often influenced significantly by earlier empirical work that describes typical as well as atypical development. Consequently, it makes sense first to describe validated practice based on empirically derived developmental data and then to describe new foci of study that at some future point may affect intervention practice. Although we have not adhered religiously to this organizational framework, we believe that it offers a fresh perspective on the relationship between descriptive research and intervention research and practice. Thus, the chapters of this volume are organized along a continuum from intervention to development, instead of the more typical reverse ordering.

We would also like to acknowledge the contributions made by Barbara S. Karni, who served as our technical editor, and Melissa Behm, Vice President of Paul H. Brookes Publishing Co. By being a rigorous and insightful editor and timely prompter, Barbara made our jobs far easier, and much more pleasant. Melissa's contributions to all facets of this volume and to the development of the *Communication and Language Intervention Series* reflect the dedication of Brookes Publishing to the development of this series, and, more importantly in our minds, to the substantive development of the field.

Causes and Effects in Communication and Language Intervention

1

The Emerging Field
of Communication and
Language Intervention

Steven F. Warren and Joe Reichle

THE PURPOSE OF THIS BOOK is to provide a state of the art overview of research and development in communication and language intervention. This purpose assumes the existence of a communication and language intervention field. Does such a field exist separate from such disciplines as special education, speech-language pathology, developmental psychology, and so forth? Are there special qualities of intervention research that support the establishment of a distinct discipline? Or should intervention remain an "area of interest" embedded within the larger context of the social and health sciences and services?

THE TRANSDISCIPLINARY AND TRANSPARENT
NATURE OF COMMUNICATION AND LANGUAGE INTERVENTION

Communication and language play central roles in human development and behavior across the life span. The broad, pivotal role of communication and language means that communication and language intervention must be transdisciplinary. Being transdisciplinary can have many drawbacks. The foremost problem is that a transdisciplinary field can be viewed as transparent—difficult to see, difficult to grasp, and, to a certain extent, difficult to conceptualize.

An array of evidence leads us to characterize the field of communication and language intervention as transparent. First, there is no journal devoted primarily to research on communication and language intervention, although

We would like to acknowledge the thoughtful input of Howard Goldstein and Paul Yoder on an earlier draft of this chapter.

many journals publish occasional articles on the subject, or deal broadly with communication development and disorders. Thus, to uncover literature on language and communication intervention, one must search across the scientific journals of many related fields. Goldstein and Hockenberger (in press) have noted the relative paucity of articles on intervention in the journals in which one might most expect them—those published by the American Speech-Language-Hearing Association (ASHA). In a survey of 17 journals between 1978 and 1988, they found that only 17% of child language intervention studies (approximately two and a half per year) had been published in ASHA journals. Most of the work they surveyed had been published by researchers working in related disciplines, such as special education and psychology.

Second, practitioners in this field are spread out. Language intervention issues are included under the purview of many professional organizations, and relevant work is carried out by professionals from a wide range of backgrounds. This is positive in that it ensures rich, multidisciplinary input into theory, research, and practice. But this diffusion also leads to dissolution and lack of focus. How many practitioners can keep up with 17 different journals, regularly attend meetings by multiple professional groups, and in general manage to keep up with a field that has no center?

Third, the complexity and ubiquity of human language and communication strongly encourages conceptual and clinical fragmentation. The human communication "system" builds on the complexity of sensorimotor, phonological, semantic, syntactic, and pragmatic subsystems influenced by both genetic and environmental forces, and is embedded in human social behavior and culture. This inherent complexity naturally spawns scientists and clinicians who are expert in only one of these many interacting systems, and lack a perspective on how their particular component fits into the overall development of the system.

Nowhere has this fragmentation been more obvious than in theories of language acquisition among children without disabilities. Since the 1970s, much progress has been made in identifying the basic puzzle pieces necessary to construct a picture of this process. But despite some recent congruence on a general level (within a broadly defined social-cognitive perspective), the study of language development in children without disabilities remains a confusing morass of theories, subtheories, minitheories, ideas, perspectives, concepts, and critiques. In terms of Kuhn's four-stage schemata for the development of a scientific paradigm, the field seems to be entering stage two, in which many paradigms (partial and complete) vie simultaneously for the attention of the field's scientific community (Kuhn, 1970). (This same observation probably holds for the behavioral and social sciences in general.) Kuhn argues that this is a normal and healthy progression for any field. But it often stifles communications among scientists, educators, and others, and tends to perpetuate fragmentation and resistance to new fields that evolve out of old ones.

In addition to these factors, some intervention research has been poorly received by the scientific community. Some behavioral scientists have argued that our knowledge of development is too rudimentary to support anything but crude, ill-defined intervention efforts (see Baer, Wolf, & Risley, 1987). Intervention research has often been referred to pejoratively as "lacking in theory" or "unscientific," and frequently equated with antiquated views of behaviorism (Baer et al., 1987; Goldstein, 1990). Despite these criticisms and the problems associated with being an inherently transdisciplinary field, communication and language intervention research has progressed, if not prospered, since the 1970s. The field is becoming increasingly sophisticated, theory driven, intellectually intriguing, and important. In short, despite its transdisciplinary nature and all the other problems it confronts, research on communication and language intervention is blossoming in many ways. First, the field has accumulated a substantial data base. For example, Goldstein and Hockenberger (in press) identified 151 peer-reviewed child language intervention studies published between 1978 and 1988. Second, the published research of the field is becoming increasingly sophisticated (Goldstein, 1990; Warren, in press). For instance, the vast majority of research published in recent years has included analyses of generalization (see Chapter 2). Impressive results have been demonstrated by some early language intervention approaches (see Warren & Kaiser, 1988). New developments, such as augmentative communication approaches and devices (see Chapter 6) and sophisticated, ecologically valid prelinguistic assessments (see Chapter 9) have emerged. Third, substantial progress has been made in identifying specific variables that may contribute to the development of language delays and disorders. These include studies of the likely sources of specific language delays (see Chapter 11); studies of the inability of children with autism to process complex, novel stimuli (see Chapter 7); and studies of expressive language delay in children with Down syndrome (Miller, 1987). Some of these problems may be amenable to intervention.

Finally, despite the field's lack of cohesion and focus, the outlines of a discipline of communication and language have existed since the early 1970s. The origin of the field might be traced to the 1972 Chula Vista Conference on Language Intervention sponsored by the National Institute of Child Health and Human Development. This conference spawned the famous "red book" edited by Richard Schiefelbusch and Lyle Lloyd (Schiefelbusch & Lloyd, 1974), and led to the development of the Language Intervention Series edited by Schiefelbusch and published by University Park Press until 1985.

Since the 1970s many intervention-focused grants have been funded, books published, conferences held, and special interest groups formed within larger associations. A loose network of language and communication intervention researchers can be identified. Still, as of this writing, there is no formal association of communication and language intervention researchers, and no discipline can be clearly defined.

What will move the field toward full disciplinary status? How will such a discipline be defined? Should the field emerge as a full-fledged discipline? How would such a discipline differ from the present field of communication disorders? Prior to answering these questions, we need to examine the unique value and qualities of intervention research.

THE CHALLENGES OF INTERVENTION RESEARCH

As more variables are identified and explicated, as more specific hypotheses are developed, and as better measures are created and validated, the scientific as well as the clinical and educational value of intervention research will increase enormously. The need for high-quality intervention research has never been greater: in the United States, an increasing number of young children are developmentally at risk due to growing poverty and the associated "new morbidity" (Baumeister, Kupstas, & Klindworth, 1990). In the meantime, the void between the need for intervention and the existence of intervention approaches that have been scientifically validated is being filled by an ever increasing number of treatment techniques and programs with no empirical support whatsoever (Goldstein, 1990).

Despite the growing sophistication of and need for intervention research, such research remains a poor cousin of descriptive and basic research in the lofty intellectual circles of academia. This is true even within a substantial portion of the speech and hearing sciences research community. For intervention research truly to emerge as a highly regarded discipline, this must change. For that to occur, stereotypes about intervention research need to be reconsidered. That is, the intellectual challenge and value of intervention research needs to become fully appreciated.

In our view, good intervention research represents one of the highest forms of human endeavor. It is the result of bringing to bear reductive, ecological, and creative thinking in order to solve a problem (Turner, 1989).

The reductive mode of thinking is essentially analytic. Its purpose is to take the object of study apart to see what it is made of and how it works. Its goal is to tease out the operations of a system into a single line of logic. Much of developmental psychology and most basic research are replete with examples of reductive thinking. Indeed, this form of thinking has much to recommend it, including the qualities of demonstrability, communicability, and repeatability. But it has deficiencies, too. Primary among these is that it is deterministic: since the outcome is always inherent in the origin, it can only look backward into the past. Had Columbus taken a reductive approach, he would never have discovered America, or even tried to do so (Bannister, 1970, as cited by Goldstein, 1990).

Creative thinking, by way of contrast, proceeds in the same direction as evolution—from the simple to the complex; from the past to the future; from origins to new, unpredictable outcomes. It is the mode of thought that encompasses progress, construction, synthesis, and invention. It is through the creative mode that science, so often dominated by reductive thinking, is transformed into technology. Yet the creative mode has serious limitations. Primary among these is that it tends to value things most for what they may become, not for what they are. This lack of appreciation for and even impatience with the past and present can cause creative thinking, on its own, to create wasteful and unnecessary, even harmful, technology, as well as the occasional masterpiece.

Ecological thinking reflects the recognition that all is system, that we are, or at least should be, equal and interdependent participants in the world, and that all systems must work in some type of balance and harmony. This type of thinking has many virtues. Foremost among them is its devotion to a nonhierarchical view of living beings, and a recognition of the concept of the "common good." It focuses on neither the downward vertical relations of a system to its past roots and internal components, nor its upward evolving relation to its future, but concerns itself only with present horizontal relations within systems. Taken by itself, ecological thinking minimizes any differences in value between things, because to do so would implicitly create a hierarchy, which is the antithesis of pure ecological thinking. Yet despite the appeal of this nonhierarchical view, it also represents a serious limitation. Because of the hierarchical implications, pure ecological thinking is inherently hostile to any kind of innovation, intervention, or change to make something "better." Indeed, from a radical ecological perspective, "better" does not exist. The old adage of early medicine to "let nature take its course" represented a type of ecological thinking (or perhaps just an excuse for the lack of progress yet to be spawned by reductive and creative thinking) that often had predictable—and fatal—results.

It should be obvious that none of these modes of thought, taken alone, can produce an effective intervention approach; each suffers from inherent limitations. However, history suggests that when all three forms of thinking are simultaneously applied to a problem—such as putting a man on the moon—successful outcomes are often achieved. What a scientist conducting a meaningful program of intervention or problem-driven research is really trying to do is to create the future, not merely study the past or the present. But to be successful at such an ambitious enterprise, he or she must wisely bring together the reductive or analytic approach, creative abilities and insights, and knowledge of the ecosystems in which the intervention results must survive and prosper. Can there be a more intellectually challenging and intriguing process?

Communication and language intervention research is fundamentally problem-driven research. By remaining focused on the goal of developing effective, ecologically and socially valid interventions, it is possible for areas of research within the field to move ahead without getting bogged down in the shifting sands of theory. Yet it is essential to use and contribute to theory lest we risk developing approaches that are narrow, poorly conceptualized, and ultimately doomed to fail. The Wright brothers may not have been particularly interested in aerodynamic theory, but they needed to know something about it to build a machine that would fly. At the same time, we must keep in mind that a process that seems to be relatively important in normal development— or, alternatively, to play only a bit part in it—may be vitally important when reconfigured and used wisely in intervention. Finally, if some technique or approach really works—that is, leads to meaningful change and generalization—then theory will eventually catch up with it. Theory must conform to new evidence, not vice versa (Kuhn, 1970).

Intervention research must be informed by descriptive studies that shed light on underlying problems and processes that may be amenable to intervention. Thus, work that attempts to determine the causes of specific language delays in children with normal intelligence (see Chapter 11), to identify the specific cognitive constraints and characteristics that affect communication development in children with autism (see Chapter 7), or to delineate the characteristics of linguistic development in children with mental retardation (see Chapter 13) complements intervention research in that it may directly contribute to the development of treatments for these disorders. However, the formalization of a field of communication and language intervention research implies a maturing of our knowledge about general and specific disabilities to the extent that the field is more or less ready to move beyond its historic (and reductive) emphasis on the description and documentation of problems toward an increasing emphasis on intervention and treatment research. We believe that the field is ready for this new emphasis, and that its byproducts will include many unpredictable theoretical and technological spin-offs and breakthroughs.

WHY MUST A SEPARATE DISCIPLINE BE CONCEIVED?

Why should this discipline emerge? The discipline of communication and language intervention should continue to evolve and coalesce for moral as well as scientific reasons. We have a moral imperative to help people with communication and language disorders and delays by perfecting and then implementing effective prevention and intervention approaches. Science is a tool with which to understand and solve empirical problems. As science develops, it spawns technologies that can be applied to real-world problems. Evolution of a field toward an increasing emphasis on intervention is thus a sign of maturation and should be supported.

WHAT WILL MOVE THE FIELD TOWARD DISCIPLINARY STATUS?

On one level, the field of language and communication intervention will move toward disciplinary status by the creation of the symbols of any discipline (e.g., high-profile journals, books, regular conferences). The more tangible— and probably more important—development will be the increase in professional respect for intervention research within the scientific community, which should occur as intervention research is increasingly seen to inform and test theories.

As we noted early in this chapter, the field of communication and language intervention both suffers from the drawbacks and enjoys the benefits of being transdisciplinary. On the surface, one might think that the field is a natural subdiscipline of speech and hearing sciences, perhaps best represented within the disciplinary confines of the American Speech-Language-Hearing Association. There are several reasons this has not worked. First, as we have noted, much of the relevant work has been done by researchers whose primary affiliation is with other disciplines (e.g., developmental disabilities, child development, early intervention). Second, as research has increasingly shown, classroom education represents a critical element in the treatment of many communication and language problems. Given ASHA's commitment to the profession of speech-language pathology, effective approaches to communication and language may occasionally create a conflict of interest between the profession and the demands of optimal intervention. Third, all of the existing disciplines are too large, too entrenched, too wrapped up in their own agendas to serve as the locus of the transdisciplinary field of communication and language intervention.

HOW WILL SUCH A DISCIPLINE BE DEFINED?

The new discipline should be broadly defined, rather than defined by any particular methods or theory. It should encompass the experimental methods of group and single-subject designs. It should investigate which interventions are appropriate for which goals with people with various disabilities. As the discipline develops, it will likely include an increasing neuroscience emphasis congruent with the striking theoretical and technological developments expected to occur in neuroscience (itself a transdisciplinary spin-off of psychology, cell biology, and pharmacology). The discipline will be fundamentally problem driven, and characterized by researchers who apply reductive, creative, and ecological thinking.

CONCLUSION

The full development of the discipline of communication and language intervention will require that researchers, with all their varied backgrounds; educators; speech-language pathologists; and others come together in a context that allows them to transcend their social and professional histories and focus on the development of optimally effective intervention approaches, strategies, and techniques for the myriad of communication and language problems that exist. To the extent that this fails to happen, people with potentially preventable or treatable disorders or delays will suffer needlessly. Conversely, full development of the discipline could result in unprecedented advances in the area of communication and language intervention.

REFERENCES

Baer, D.M., Wolf, M.M., & Risley, T.R. (1987). Some still-current dimensions of applied behavior analysis. *Journal of Applied Behavior Analysis, 20*, 313–328.
Bannister, D. (1970). Psychology as an exercise in paradox. In D.P. Schultz (Ed.), *The science of psychology: Critical reflections* (pp. 4–10). Englewood Cliffs, NJ: Prentice Hall.
Baumeister, A.A., Kupstas, F., & Klindworth, L.M. (1990). New morbidity: Implications for prevention of children's disabilities. *Exceptionality, 1*, 1–18.
Goldstein, H. (1990). The future of language science: A plea for language intervention research. *Asha Reports, 20*, 41–50.
Goldstein, H., & Hockenberger, E.H. (in press). Significant progress in child language intervention: An 11-year retrospective. *Research in Developmental Disabilities*.
Kuhn, T.S. (1970). *The structure of scientific revolutions*. Chicago: University of Chicago Press.
Miller, J. (1987, December). *The developmental asynchrony of language development in children with Down syndrome*. Paper presented at the National Down Syndrome Society Symposium "Psychobiology of Down Syndrome," New York.
Schiefelbusch, R.L., & Lloyd, L.L. (Eds.) (1974). *Language perspectives: Acquisition, retardation, and intervention*. Baltimore: University Park Press.
Turner, F. (1989, August). Life on Mars: Cultivating a planet and ourselves. *Harpers, 279*.
Warren, S.F., & Kaiser, A.P. (1988). Research in early language intervention. In S.L. Odom & M.B. Karnes (Eds.), *Early intervention for infants and children with handicaps: An empirical base* (pp. 89–108). Baltimore: Paul H. Brookes Publishing Co.
Warren, S.F. (in press). Early language intervention: Challenges for the 90s. In A.P. Kaiser & D. Gray (Eds.), *Enhancing children's communication: Research foundations for intervention*. Baltimore: Paul H. Brookes Publishing Co.

2

Evaluating Milieu Teaching

Ann P. Kaiser, Paul J. Yoder, and Anne Keetz

MILIEU TEACHING IS A NATURALISTIC strategy for teaching functional language skills. Included in this class of language interventions are specific teaching techniques such as incidental teaching (Hart & Risley, 1968), mand-model (Warren, McQuarter, & Rogers-Warren, 1984), time delay (Halle, Marshall, & Spradlin, 1979) and child-cued modeling (Alpert & Kaiser, in press). Several variations of naturalistic language teaching procedures containing all or some of the components of milieu teaching are also included in this class of intervention procedures. Nearly all of the elaborations and variations that comprise the literature on milieu teaching derive their basic tenets from the early work of Hart and Risley (1968, 1980) on the effects of incidental teaching with low-income preschool children. Hart and Risley's original strategies for incidental teaching were designed to give the child opportunities to practice a communication skill during the interactions between an adult and child that naturally arise in an unstructured situation such as freeplay (Hart & Risley, 1975).

Milieu teaching procedures share several common features: 1) teaching occurs following the child's lead or interest; 2) multiple, naturally occurring examples are used to teach simple, elaborated language forms; 3) child production of language is explicitly prompted; 4) consequences for child responding include those associated with the specific linguistic form and those that are natural to the context in which teaching occurs; and 5) to varying extents, the teaching episode is embedded in ongoing interactions between the milieu teacher and the student. Milieu teaching uses a basic antecedent-response-consequence paradigm that has its roots in applied behavioral interventions

Preparation of this manuscript was supported in part by Grant No. G008400663 and Grant No. H02D90071 from the Office of Special Education, Grant No. G008720107 from the National Institute for Disability and Rehabilitation Research, and Grant Nos. RR-00165 and NICHD-06-016 from the National Institutes of Health. This chapter was completed while the first author was a visiting scientist at the Language Research Center of Georgia State University and Emory University.

(Hart & Rogers-Warren, 1978). Milieu procedures differ from more traditional direct instruction in the types of antecedents (child interest versus teacher prompt) and consequences (functionally related to the response versus consistent across trials) associated with the child's response. Both environmental arrangement to provide a context for teaching and the use of a responsive interactive style in conversation with the language learning child are often described as auxiliaries to the instructional procedures.

In their 1986 review of milieu teaching research, Warren and Kaiser (1986) made a strong argument for the efficacy of milieu teaching as a language intervention technique. This argument was based on two criteria: evidence that the primary effects of the intervention (e.g., changes in targeted language skills) have been demonstrated consistently across studies, and evidence that the applications of the procedure have resulted in significant changes in the target children's general communication repertoires when measured within the training sessions. Although the review indicated that the first of these criteria was met fully and that the second was met in some studies to varying degrees, it did not examine the extent to which there was evidence that milieu teaching systematically affects children's language development when assessed outside the training session. In addition, the Warren and Kaiser review paid relatively little attention to the methodology used to assess generalized effects and the relationship between assessment methods and reported outcomes.

This chapter examines the experimental literature on applications of milieu teaching in order to assess the efficacy of this approach as a language intervention strategy. Particular emphasis is placed on evaluating evidence that milieu teaching can positively affect children's language development and evidence indicating the extent of changes in generalized language abilities resulting from milieu interventions. This review focuses on the analyses of evidence of generalization as a primary indicator of the efficacy of milieu teaching. We consider the evidence of efficacy proceeding from the weakest to the strongest evidence. Both methodology and outcomes are addressed in examining four levels of evidence: 1) primary effects within treatment settings, 2) effects that are independent of the content in which they are assessed, 3) response/recombinatory/stimulus generalization that is context independent, and 4) global language gains that are context independent.

Nineteen studies of milieu teaching conducted between 1968 and 1990 were examined (see Table 1 for a description of these studies). Studies were included in this review if: 1) at least one of the procedures used to teach new language skills was described as an incidental or milieu teaching procedure by the author, or if the procedures fit the four parameters of milieu teaching described earlier; 2) changes in children's language skills were a primary focus of the study; and 3) the children involved were considered to have a deficit in language skills or were at risk for language development. Thus, some studies that were primarily teacher-training studies were not included because data on individual children were too limited to be evaluated fully. Studies examining only environmental arrangement or responsive conversational style were not included. With one exception (Giumento, 1990), only published studies were considered.

SUBJECTS

One hundred thirty-four (134) children and adolescents received milieu teaching in these studies. Participants included preschool children from low SES communities (38), at-risk and language-delayed preschool children (14), preschool and school-age children with mild or moderate retardation (11), preschool and school-age children with autism (20), and children with moderate to severe mental retardation (6). The 35 preschool children who received milieu teaching in two-group comparison studies (Yoder, Kaiser, & Alpert, 1991; Yoder et al., 1990) were not described individually and are not included in this summary. Across all studies, participants ranged in age from 2 years, 1 month to 15 years, 7 months. All but 7 participants were primarily verbal and were trained to respond verbally. Ninety-eight children (73%) were enrolled in preschool programs.

TRAINED RESPONSES

The responses trained in these studies (Table 2) varied widely. Responses ranged from single words to multiword grammatical forms and from a single target response (e.g., "Tray, please") to multiple targets across syntactic-semantic classes (e.g., agent-action, action-object, and modifier-noun, each with multiple possible exemplars). Participants in a study frequently had different developmentally appropriate targets. More than one language skill was sometimes targeted for an individual concurrently or sequentially. Target classes (e.g., nouns or two-word relational utterances) were sometimes defined very specifically (e.g., three words— "help," "more," and "mine"— were taught) and sometimes allowed to vary (e.g., any example of the class could be taught; items were selected based on their appropriateness and immediate functionality for the child). In about half the studies, specific targets were selected for individual students based on assessment of their language skills. In studies by Hart and Risley (1968, 1974, 1975), the same class of targets was used for all children in a classroom. Halle et al. (1979), Charlop and Walsh (1986), and Giumento (1990) taught the same specific response ("Tray, please") to all participants. Other studies were designed to target general responsiveness or responsiveness to milieu teaching episodes, or to increase the appropriate functional use of language as a general class of behavior rather than to teach specific targets (e.g., Alpert & Kaiser, in press; Warren et al., 1984).

Table 1. Summary of research findings on effectiveness of milieu teaching

Study	Design	Primary measures of improvement	Study weaknesses
Alpert & Kaiser (in press)	Single subject, multiple baseline across subjects and across four milieu techniques within subjects	Total number of words produced; number of novel words produced	Variability in child effects
Carr & Kologinsky (1983)	Single subject, multiple baseline across subjects with ABC BCD reversal	Frequency of spontaneous signing; frequency of self-stimulation	—
Cavallaro & Bambara (1982)	Single subjects, alternating treatments	Frequency of two-word requests; frequency of novel two-word requests (spontaneous or prompted)	One subject Criteria for phase change, but no stable data at phase shifts
Charlop, Schreibman, & Thibodeau (1985)	Single subject, multiple baseline	Frequency of imitation of requests; frequency of spontaneous requests	Abrupt shift for 6 of 7 subjects
Charlop & Walsh (1986)	Single subject, multiple baseline across subjects and settings	Frequency of saying "I like/love you"; frequency of eye contact; frequency of social smile; frequency of approach/touch	Single-phrase target
Giumento (1990)	Single subject, alternating treatments	Frequency of use of labels	—
Halle, Marshall, & Spradlin (1979)	Single subject, multiple baseline across meals and children with a reversal	Frequency of requests for meal	Gradual rather than immediate shifts Bar graphs rather than session-by-session data Diffusion of treatments
Hart & Risley (1968)	Single subject, AABA reversal	Frequency of use of color, number, shape, size adjectives	Mean data for conditions (group data) Incomplete reversal
Hart & Risley (1974)	Single subject, multiple baseline, group as unit	Frequency of compound sentences, adjective-noun combinations, "new" adjective-noun combinations, nouns, "new" nouns	Only group averages presented
Hart & Risley (1975)	Single subject, ABAC reversal	Frequency of compound sentences	Accelerating and decelerating trends in data prior to phase changes
Hart & Risley (1980)	Group design (reanalysis of comparison data)	Frequency of words produced; frequency of novel words	No random assignment within groups

Study	Design	Dependent variables	No statistical test of differences between groups
McGee, Krantz, & McClannahan (1985)	Single subject, multiple baseline with alternating treatments	Frequency of preposition use; frequency of errors of omission and commission	—
Oliver & Halle (1982)	Single subject, multiple baseline across two activities	Frequency of child-initiated signs; frequency of prompted signs; frequency of correct/incorrect signs	—
Rogers-Warren & Warren (1980)	Single subject, multiple baseline	Frequency of total verbalizations; proportion of responsiveness; cumulative number of new words/phases	—
Warren & Bambara (1989)	Single subject, multiple baseline across subjects	Use of various functions (declaratives, requests, imitations, vocatives, protests, no response); frequency and diversity of action verb-object combinations	—
Warren & Gazdag (1990)	Single subject within subject, multiple baseline across training targets	Frequency of target use in response to training prompts; frequency of target use in nonobligatory situations; frequency of spontaneous imitation	—
Warren, McQuarter, Rogers-Warren (1984)	Single subject, multiple baseline across subjects	Frequency of subject verbalizations to teacher; rate of nonobligatory speech; responsiveness to others' initiations	—
Yoder, Kaiser, & Alpert (1991)	Group	SICD-E; SICD-R; MLU; criterion-referenced probes	No main effects for group comparison
Yoder, Kaiser, Goldstein, Mousetis, Alpert, & Fischer (1990)	Group	SICD-E; SICD-R; PPVT; EOWPVT	No main effects for group comparison Subjects not randomly assigned to treatments Post hoc matching of subjects

Note: SICD-E = Sequenced Inventory of Communication Development-Expressive Scale; SICD-R = Sequenced Inventory of Communication Development-Receptive Scale; PPVT = Peabody Picture Vocabulary Test; EOWPVT = Expressive One Word Picture Vocabulary Test.

13

Table 2. Types of responses trained in milieu teaching studies

One-word responses

Nouns/object labels
Basic lexicon/one-word appropriate verbalizations
Single signs

Two- and three-word phrases

Two-word phrases
Two-word requests
Early relational semantic forms
Adjective noun combinations
Two-sign combinations

More than three–word phrases

Sentences containing: color, shape, number adjectives, prepositions, conjunctions to
    form compound sentences

Other specific responses

"Tray, please"
"I like/love you"

Other general responses

Spontaneous speech
Functional use of known signs
Language use
Elaborated speech
Responsiveness to adult verbalizations
Responsiveness to milieu teaching episodes

AGENTS, SETTINGS, AND PROCEDURES

In most studies (16), the milieu training occurred in a setting associated with a classroom program. Frequently, training occurred outside the classroom proper or in an area apart from regular classroom activities. Although milieu training sometimes occurred as part of the classroom activities—particularly during freeplay or learning centers—only Hart and Risley (1968, 1974, 1975, 1980) and Yoder et al. (1990) appear to have integrated milieu teaching across activities throughout the daily schedule. Typically, training was conducted by either trained classroom personnel or an experimenter. Other trainers and intervention settings included residential staff at mealtimes (Halle et al., 1979) and mothers at home (Alpert & Kaiser, in press; Charlop & Walsh, 1986).

In addition to the incidental teaching described by Hart and Risley (1980), three other milieu teaching techniques have been described and investigated. These are time delay (Halle et al., 1979), mand-model (Warren et al., 1984), and child-cued modeling (Alpert & Kaiser, in press). The studies reviewed varied considerably in the number and specific selection of milieu techniques: five studies used all four techniques, six used incidental teaching, five used time delay alone, two used mand-model alone, and two used incidental teaching and mand-model in combination. The remaining study (Giumento, 1990) used a variant of milieu procedures that was conceptually similar to milieu teaching but not easily classified in terms of the four milieu techniques. Review of individual studies suggests that variability in actual implementation of the identified procedures was extensive. In almost every study, the authors describe their particular version of the milieu teaching procedures and how it resembles the procedures employed in previous studies. In some cases, the variation may have contributed to the outcomes reported for the study. For example, Warren and Bambara (1989) and Warren and Gazdag (1990) include systematic commenting to provide nonelicitive modeling of target structures for subjects. The inclusion of this modeling component may have contributed to both the frequency of use of targets in nonobligatory contexts within training and the recombinatory generalization results that were reported. In contrast, the data presented by Carr and Kologinsky (1983) represent only posttraining maintenance of child behavior using reinforcement and minimal prompting procedures as part of an application of incidental teaching and time delay.

DESIGN

Fifteen studies employed single-subject designs to evaluate the impact of milieu teaching. Twelve studies used multiple baseline designs, three studies used reversals, three studies used alternating treatment designs, and two studies used a combination of designs.

Three studies used group comparison designs. Yoder, Davies, and Bishop (see Chapter 10) randomly assigned participants to two language interventions. Yoder and Davies (1990) matched subjects from two classroom interventions to compare outcomes. Hart and Risley (1980) compared unmatched but similar children in three classrooms, one of which received a 9-month incidental teaching intervention.

METHODOLOGICAL ISSUES IN EVALUATING EFFICACY

Establishing the efficacy of an intervention on a child's language development is conceptually and methodologically challenging. The foremost standards for determining if an intervention has had an effect are those associated with the establishment of the internal validity of the study (Campbell & Stanley, 1966). What these effects represent in terms of changes in performance, generalized knowledge, and global language development are also at issue, however. Thus, the target of intervention, the extent to which performance of this target was observed to change, the extent to which this change was generalized to other stimuli and responses, and the extent to which this change affected general language development are important in determining the efficacy of an intervention.

In the following section, we first examine the relationship between changes in generalized knowledge and changes in performance, and consider how each is related to the determination that an intervention has been effective. We then deduce a set of criteria for demonstrating that changes in generalized knowledge and development have occurred and describe the methodological strategies that are required to evaluate change using these criteria. Finally, we evaluate the methods employed by studies of milieu teaching to determine whether there is evidence of change in children's generalized skills and global language development as a result of the intervention.

It is difficult to draw distinctions between development, knowledge, and performance in the area of language. These distinctions are conceptually important, however, for understanding the effects of an intervention. For purposes of this discussion, global language development refers to systematic, progressive changes in the acquisition and use of the language system beyond the changes in specific behaviors targeted by an intervention. That is, global development indicates that the child has learned or integrated information above and beyond what is being instructed.

Not all changes in language skills are manifested as changes in language development. The acquisition of specific skills may not affect scores on standardized tests or global measures of language level (e.g., MLU). Although acquisition of specific skills may be clinically important and may affect the child's functional use of language, such acquisition does not indicate that the child's global language abilities have been affected by the intervention or that the degree of delay in language has been reduced. When significant changes in measures of child language development do result from an intervention, they constitute strong evidence that the intervention has affected the child's language abilities. Failure to obtain changes on standardized tests should be interpreted cautiously, however, particularly because standardized language tests are not well suited for assessing changes in the behavior of children in the beginning stages of communication development (e.g., before 2 years developmentally).

Changes in child linguistic knowledge may be reflected in changes in global measures of development. However, significant changes in linguistic knowledge may occur although they are not readily measured by developmental assessments. Such changes may represent an intermediate stage of remediating language deficits that is nonetheless important to the child's acquisition of new communication skills. Conceptually, changes in linguistic knowledge occur when a new linguistic rule, concept, or response class has been formed. Because none of these can be observed directly, we must infer changes in knowledge from various types of generalization. In terms of generalization from training, these changes may be described as stimulus generalization; response class generalization, including recombinatory generalization; crossmodal transfer; or some combination of all of these, as has been shown in research using stimulus equivalence paradigms (e.g., Spradlin & Dixon, 1976). For example, when children are taught a set of noun-verb combinations in a milieu intervention and produce untrained noun-verb combinations during a probe session, we assume that recombinatory generalization has occurred and that the child has acquired some knowledge above and beyond the content that was taught specifically during training. This knowledge may be characterized as acquisition of a basic rule for constructing syntactic-semantic categories. Similarly, when a child is taught to produce a set of labels using milieu teaching and he or she demonstrates increased comprehension of the labels during a probe, we assume the intervention has resulted in new linguistic knowledge in the form of increased language comprehension. Accurate assessment of changes in child knowledge requires systematic examination of the child's performance outside the training setting, typically using stimuli that were not a part of the training. Carefully constructed probes may be necessary to ascertain the parameters of conceptual knowledge that have been acquired as a result of training.

Changes in child performance of the specific words, phrases, or functions that have been taught are important indicators of the primary effects of the intervention. However, these changes, particularly when they are observed within the training session, are not sufficient indicators of change in either child linguistic knowledge or global language development.

Various aspects of the interactive context may affect child language use without producing durable changes in child language knowledge or global development. The child's language performance may change as a result of the characteristics of the specific interaction between child and adult rather than as a result of changes in child skills. For example, Yoder and his colleagues found that children with developmental delays used language more often, used more diverse vocabulary, and were more intelligible to adult listeners during interactions that had a routine than they were in nonroutine interactions (see Chapter 10; Yoder & Davies, 1990). Mirenda and Donnellan (1986) reported that adolescents with mental retardation and autism produced more spontaneous comments and questions when interacting with an adult who used a responsive interaction style (i.e., followed the child's topical lead, expanded child utterances, and asked few questions) than with an adult who used a directive style.

Because of the potential influence of context, within–treatment setting data should be evaluated cautiously. Both data derived from teaching episodes and data collected outside teaching episodes but within the treatment setting may be influenced by the child's acquisition of a "therapy set." That is, the child may have learned to respond to a given interactional context (i.e., milieu teaching in the treatment setting) in a specific manner that is different from his or her responding prior to the introduction of treatment. Changes in frequency of talking, length of utterances, and diversity of utterances are commonly used measures that are particularly sensitive to contextual influences. Although these changes might be considered indicative of performance changes, they are not necessarily changes in child skill or changes in performance independent of the immediate context. To determine if these types of changes in performance are independent of the context, evidence of similar performance must be obtained in contexts that do not include the experimental intervention. Assessment of generalization across settings and trainers is used frequently in single-subject studies to determine if the changes observed in training are context independent. However, the specific interaction style of persons in the generalization setting must be described (and preferably measured) to ensure that performance was not elicited using the experimental procedures during these assessments. The same contextual issues apply in group designs.

Figure 1 summarizes the strategies that could be used to assess the effects of an intervention on performance, generalized knowledge, and global language development.

Four criteria for demonstrating the efficacy of an intervention procedure with respect to changes in performance, knowledge, and development are:

1. The study must demonstrate adequate internal validity in order to evaluate changes in the dependent variable(s) and to assess potential treatment effects. In single-subject studies, there must be either a sharp change in level and trend associated with the intervention or a sufficiently long baseline that gradual changes in level and trend indicating acquisition of a target response can be assumed to be associated with the onset of training. In group-design studies, there must be random assignment to groups and evidence that subjects in comparison groups were equal at the outset of training.
2. Assessments of generalized changes in child performance must be separated from context effects associated with training or other elicitive procedures.
3. Assessments of changes in child linguistic knowledge must specify the changes in knowledge from baseline to treatment, must assess knowledge using stimuli that are different from those used in training, and must specify the parameters of knowledge assessed and the procedures and stimuli used in the assessment.
4. Assessments of changes in child language development must use a standardized measure of development and must account for expected change during the period of development.

Satisfaction of each of these criteria would allow us to conclude that: 1) milieu teaching results in changes in specific target behaviors (dependent variables) within the treatment sessions; 2) these changes in performance generalize to interactions in which milieu teaching is not in use (i.e., outside the training

Performance	Knowledge	Global language development
Skill observed in training setting within teaching episodes	Novel examples of class of trained targets	Changes in development measured using nonstandardized measures (e.g., MLU)
↓	↓	↓
Skill observed in training sessions but outside of teaching episodes	Novel examples observed with nontraining materials outside training sessions	—
↓	↓	↓
Skill observed outside training sessions with interactor using milieu teaching or other elicitive interaction strategy	Novel examples of trained class observed using systematic probes with responses elicited	Changes in development observed on standardized tests
↓	↓	↓
Skill observed outside training setting with neutral interactor	Novel examples of class of trained targets observed in systematic but naturalistic probes (not elicited)	—

Figure 1. Conditions for assessing changes in performance, knowledge, and global language development. Representative options for assessment in each area are presented in a continuum, with the least appropriate strategies placed at the top of each column and the most appropriate strategies placed toward the bottom of the column.

setting); 3) these changes in performance are accompanied by changes in knowledge that can be described in terms of response generalization, stimulus generalization, recombinatory generalization, and/or cross-modal transfer; and 4) changes in global language development are associated with the intervention.

Criterion I: Internal Validity

Since all but one of the studies reviewed were published in peer-reviewed journals, internal validity was expected to be uniformly high. Evaluation of each study design and its relationship to the primary results reported indicated that for the most part this was true. However, internal validity related to specific results varied within studies. For example, in single-subject, multiple-baseline design studies, two of three subjects may have shown clear and immediate shifts in performance during intervention, while the third subject showed a more gradual shift, or evidenced a trend in the baseline condition. Similar variability was observed in multiple baselines across behaviors within subjects.

Among the most difficult studies to evaluate in terms of internal validity were two studies by Hart and Risley (1968, 1975). In their 1968 study, Hart and Risley employed a reversal design (AABA) with a class of children as the unit of analysis. Most of the data presented are group means per condition.

Although some individual data are presented (mean use of color adjectives per condition for individual subjects) and sample data from the median child are presented graphically, it is not possible to evaluate trends within conditions— an evaluation that is considered essential in judging the effects of an intervention using a single-subject design. Institution of a return-to-baseline condition affected five primary measures to varying extents.

In their 1975 study, Hart and Risley reported data graphically to allow assessment of trends within and across conditions, but did not report data for individual children. The reversal design (ABCA) revealed an immediate increase in compound sentences directed to the teacher when incidental teaching was introduced. Teacher-directed sentences decreased during the subsequent (C) condition when teachers prompted children to ask other children, but teacher-directed and child-directed compound sentences fell only slightly when baseline conditions were reinstated (A). In both studies, the modest reversal of the effects of training (i.e., rates did not return to baseline levels) is interpreted by the authors as evidence of the maintained effects of the intervention, rather than failure to establish control over the primary dependent variables.

Internal validity was compromised in two of the three group comparison studies because subjects were not assigned randomly to treatments. Yoder et al. (1990) matched 15 students receiving milieu teaching with 15 students receiving responsive-interaction teaching during across-the-day interventions implemented in six classrooms. Subjects were matched on 13 variables and the matching was confirmed by statistical comparisons of the two groups in the pretreatment period. Hart and Risley (1980) compared the language performance of children in three settings (the experimental incidental teaching classroom, a Head Start program enrolling children similar to those in the experimental classroom, and a university preschool class enrolling middle-class children). Overall, the experimental and Head Start groups did not differ on the observational measures of the children's language use or Peabody Picture Vocabulary Test (PPVT) scores at the onset of the study. In using a matching strategy as a basis for comparison, there is considerable risk that the participants differ on unmeasured, but relevant, variables that were not used or assessed in assembling the comparison groups. Results should be interpreted with caution because of the possibility that unknown, preexisting differences in the groups contributed to the outcomes of the study.

In addition, the experimental design used to demonstrate control over the primary dependent variable may not have been applied as rigorously in the analysis and presentation of generalization data. In some cases, generalization data were reported as a mean across several sessions, a minimum number of generalization assessments occurred during each experimental condition, or baseline data were not collected in the generalization condition. In these instances, it was impossible to determine if there were changes in trends for the generalization data. It was thus not possible to conclude if the experimental control established for the independent variable had been established for the generalization measures.

A final issue in evaluating the results of these studies is the extent to which the intervention was described and quantified. Many studies lacked measures of the independent variable in the primary setting and/or in generalization settings. This is undesirable for a number of reasons. First, the fidelity and the intensity of the intervention are unknown. It is thus impossible to determine if variability in child data either within a subject or across subjects is related to implementation factors. Moreover, in studies in which the independent variable (e.g., teaching style) was not measured in the generalization settings, there may be questions about the extent to which results for the child subjects reflect the style used by the adult during these assessments. Failure to measure the content of teaching episodes make it impossible to determine the extent to which novel words and novel combinations reported for a session were, in fact, taught during that session.

Our evaluation of the internal validity of these 19 studies generally supports the conclusion by Warren and Kaiser (1986) that there is convincing evidence of primary within-setting effects of milieu teaching across subject populations, settings, and language behaviors. Several caveats about this conclusion are discussed in the following sections.

Criterion II: Context-Independent Effects

In applying Criterion II, we asked the question "To what extent was there evidence that the changes in child performance persisted outside the context of intervention?" Child language performance, as measured by language frequency and complexity, has been shown to be uniquely influenced by contextual factors, particularly the conversational style of the partner with whom the child is interacting (see Chapter 10; Mirenda & Donnellan, 1986). In fact, milieu teaching presumes that specific changes in the behavior of the conversational partner will dependably produce changes in the child's language performance. However, it is sometimes assumed that the direct influence of milieu teaching is limited to the actual episodes in which teaching occurs, and that changes in child language performance outside of these episodes of teaching represent generalized change in child behavior. We propose a more conservative alternative explanation: changes in child performance when measured in the training setting or under conditions similar to training in generalization settings are heavily influenced by the context itself (Johnston, 1988). Data influenced by context effects must be considered as weak evidence of generalized changes in children's language performance and should be interpreted with great caution.

Within Treatment—Setting Effects

A surprising number of studies present within treatment—setting data as evidence of the general effects of milieu teaching on child performance (e.g., Alpert & Kaiser, in press; Hart & Risley, 1968, 1974, 1975, 1980; Rogers-Warren & Warren, 1980; Warren & Bambara, 1989; Warren & Gazdag, 1990; Warren et al., 1984). Changes in frequency of child utterances, responsiveness, child initiations, novel use of words, and novel combinations in multiword phrases and sentence forms are among the measures reported as potentially influenced by the teaching context and thus possibly not indicative of durable changes in child performance

In some of these studies, additional data are presented that durable changes in child behavior occurred beyond those attributable to immediate contextual influences (i.e., evidence of person, setting, and interactive style generalization). Warren and Bambara (1989) and Warren and Gazdag (1990) assessed child performance in generalization settings in which the child's classroom teacher used an interactional style for the conversational partners that was different from milieu teaching. The measures reported in assessing across-setting and across-trainer generalization are more limited than those used to assess the primary effects of the intervention. There was evidence of increases in the frequency of using the target's semantic relations in the generalization setting in response to the classroom teacher's probe questions for one subject in the Warren and Bambara study and for two subjects in the Warren and Gazdag study. However, the rates observed were lower than those observed in the training setting. Hart and Risley (1968, 1974) used a return-to-baseline reversal condition to evaluate maintenance of child performance. Moderate reductions in overall rates for all measures were observed. Children did continue to produce the target utterances, including novel types of these utterances, at rates greater than those observed in the initial baselines. Two other factors should be considered in evaluating the Hart and Risley data. First, the reversal condition occurred in the same classroom and with the same teachers. Second, no measures of teacher behavior were reported in the 1974 study and only limited measures of teacher prompting were reported in the 1968 study. Thus, some of the contextual influences responsible for the observed treatment effects may have continued during the reversal phase.

Generalization Across Settings and Trainers

Because of the potential influence of context on child language performance, measures of changes across settings and trainers are particularly important indicators of generalization. Four formats for assessing generalization across settings and trainers have been employed in studies of milieu teaching: 1) across settings, 2) across settings using probes, 3) across settings and trainers, and 4) across trainers. The four types of assessments yield evidence of generalization that varies in strength and in interpretability. Table 3 summarizes the designs and results of studies of milieu teaching that have measured generalization across settings and trainers.

Assessments across settings only and across trainers only are somewhat weaker formats than formats in which both variables are changed because one element of the training condition (either trainer or setting) remains constant and may continue to control the target child's behavior. In across-setting generalization assessments, it is critical that the trainer who has previously conducted the milieu teaching intervention not use milieu procedures during the assessment sessions.

Five studies assessed generalization across settings (Carr & Kologinsky, 1983; Charlop, Schriebman, & Thibodeau, 1985; Charlop & Walsh, 1986; Guimento, 1990; Warren et al., 1984). Four of these studies reported strong effects; a fifth study reported positive, but variable, results. Because of the assessment methods used, the results of each study should be interpreted with caution. Warren et al. (1984) assessed generalization to freeplay settings in which teachers were instructed not to use the experimental teaching procedures. The study reports measures of teacher behavior that clearly indicate that no teaching was occurring, but does not present data during baseline or the first half of the treatment condition. Guimento (1990) assessed spontaneous use during freeplay involving the same teachers and materials used in training. Variable results were obtained across the six preschool subjects. No data on teacher prompts are reported. Charlop et al. (1985) assessed generalization to a training room. The trainer presented the time-delay procedure used in training, and consequated correct requests with access to the requested object. Because only one probe session was conducted, no assessment of trend or variability is possible. Carr and Kologinsky (1983) assessed children's responses to the time delay in five different settings during generalization trials interspersed with training in the regular settings. Correct responses were not reinforced. The target children's generalization was assessed by the trainer under conditions very similar to those that prevailed during training, but in a nontraining setting. The dramatic reversals in generalization data when a different goal was being taught in the intervention sessions demonstrates the strong context effect (i.e., stimulus-control) on child use of the target. Certainly, no durable change in child behavior could be claimed. Although the results in both of these studies indicate that all subjects were able to generalize under these conditions, the similarity of the generalization assessments to the training condition constitutes a relatively weak test of generalization.

A similar caveat must be applied in considering the evidence resulting from assessments of generalization across trainers only. In each of the four

Table 3. Summary of research findings on generalization across settings and trainers

Study	Setting	Measure	Results[a]	Study weaknesses
Generalization across settings				
Carr & Kologinsky (1983, experiment II)	Five different settings	Percentage of correct use of sign in response to delay[b]	3/3	Probes interspersed in training trials but not reinforced. Context effect demonstrated by dramatic reversals
Charlop, Schreibman, & Thibodeau (1985)	Training room	Percentage of correct requests in response to delay[c]	7/7	Functional reinforcement of correct response. Only one generalization session
Charlop & Walsh (1986)	Outdoor freeplay	Percentage of correct "I like you"[c]	4/4	Only one generalization session; responses cued
Giumento (1990)	Freeplay; same teachers, same materials	Number of intervals spontaneous use of object labels	Varied 3/6 3/6	Teacher prompts not recorded
Warren, McQuarter, & Rogers-Warren (1984)	Second freeplay, same teachers	Percentage of responsiveness;[c] rate of talking;[c] number of nonobligatory verbalizations[c]	3/3	No baseline in generalization sessions. Teacher prompts not recorded
Generalization to probe settings				
Giumento (1990)	Probe trials	Percentage of correct receptive/productive labels	Receptive: 4/6 strong 2/6 moderate Productive: 3/6 strong 3/6 moderate	Maturation could account for all receptive gains and production gain in one subject.
Hart & Risley (1974)	Not described	Correct color naming	Number of colors named correctly doubled.	Probe procedures not described
McGee, Krantz, & McClannahan (1985)	Probes by teacher one-to-one freeplay	Correct use of preposition	3/3 for all uses 2/3 for novel uses	

Study	Setting	Dependent measure	Generalization effect	Notes
Warren & Bambara (1989)	Probe questions by teacher in classroom	Percentage of correct target responses	2/2	Aggregated data used in graphs. Variability of dependent variable cannot be used to infer a treatment effect. Reversal shows context-influenced data.
Warren & Gazdag (1990)	Probe questions by teacher in classroom	Percentage of correct target responses	2/3 behaviors for 1 subject 1/2 behaviors for 1 subject 1/2 behaviors for 1 subject[d]	Aggregated data presented in graphs. Reversal shows context-effect influenced data.

Generalization across settings and trainers

Study	Setting	Dependent measure	Generalization effect	Notes
Charlop, Schreibman, & Thibodeau (1985)	Unfamiliar room	Percentage correct requests using label[b]	7/7	Delay presented to prompt responses. Only one generalization session
Charlop & Walsh (1986)	Home with mother	Percentage correct "I like you"[b]	0/4	Response cued and reinforced
Halle, Marshall, & Spradlin (1979)	Meals other than those used in training with staff	Percentage correct requests	3/4	Delay presented Only one generalization session
McGee, Krantz, & McClannahan (1985)	Classroom with teachers	Percentage intervals preposition use	3/3 frequency 3/3 novel position	Environment arranged Functional reinforcement of correct response Prompts similar to Milieu
Warren & Bambara (1989)	Classroom with teachers	Frequency of target used	1/3	Mean data across sessions; no opportunity to use trend or variability to judge training effect

(continued)

Table 3. (continued)

Study	Setting	Measure	Results[a]	Study weaknesses
Warren & Gazdag (1990)	Classroom with teacher	Frequency and diversity of nonobligatory use of targets	1/x for 2 behaviors	Mean data across sessions; no opportunity to use trend or variability to judge training effect
Generalization across trainers only				
Carr & Kologinsky (1983)				
Experiment I	New trainers	Percentage of correct requests with label[b]	3/3	During maintenance condition, trainers reinforced responses.
Experiment II	New trainers with label	Percentage of correct requests[c]	1/2 strong 1/2 modest	Context effect demonstrated by dramatic reversals
Halle, Marshall, & Spradlin (1979)	New trainers	Percentage of correct meal requests	4/5	Trainers used delay procedure.
Hart & Risley (1975)	Peers	Number of compound sentences	Yes	Some prompting by teachers
Oliver & Halle (1982)	New trainers[d]	Percentage of opportunities to initiate with sign	Yes	Trainers used delay procedure.

[a]Number of subjects whose performance during treatment differed from their performance during baseline. Traditional single-subject design criteria for shifts in level and trend were applied.
[b]Milieu teaching was used during generalization.
[c]Generalization was assessed in a probe format.
[d]Number of behaviors was not clear.

studies in which generalization across trainers was assessed and positive results reported (Carr & Kologinsky, 1983; Halle et al., 1979; Hart & Risley, 1975; Oliver & Halle, 1982), the new trainer conducted the milieu teaching procedure in a manner almost identical to that of the old trainer. In the Hart and Risley (1975) study, teachers who had previously implemented the incidental teaching procedures were present and sometimes prompted the new trainers, who were their peers.

The combined assessment of generalization across settings and trainers offers a somewhat stronger test of generalization. However, the strength of the test depends on the exact characteristics of the generalization context. Five studies assessed generalization across settings and trainers combined. In three of these studies (Charlop et al., 1985; Charlop & Walsh, 1986; Halle et al., 1979), the novel trainers presented time delays in an interactional context that was similar to the training setting (e.g., at other meals, following a hug). In each case, the child's response was consequated functionally. In two of these studies (Charlop et al., 1985; Halle et al., 1979), generalization occurred readily with almost all subjects. Charlop and Walsh (1986) reported no generalization by four subjects from the classroom interactions with teachers to home interactions with their mothers prior to training in that setting. Studies by McGee, Krantz, and McClannahan (1985), Warren and Bambara (1989) and Warren and Gazdag (1990) examined generalization to the classroom setting, where untrained teachers interacted with the target children. McGee et al. arranged the environment to increase child requests of objects similar to the training stimuli, prompted elaborated requests when the child's initial request did not contain a preposition, and consequated all correct and incorrect child requests with access to the requested object. All three subjects in this study generalized the use of prepositions to the freeplay setting. Only the Warren and Bambara and Warren and Gazdag studies appear to have tested generalization in truly naturalistic conditions that differed from training in terms of the interaction style, the trainer, and the characteristics of the activity. Warren and Bambara reported modest generalization for one of their three subjects. Warren and Gazdag reported relatively strong generalization for both of their subjects.

The fourth strategy for assessing generalization in the milieu teaching studies was the assessment of generalization across settings and tasks using a probe format. Four studies presented probe trials to the target children to assess their use of the targeted behaviors under specific stimulus conditions that differed from training in terms of both setting and trainers. These studies used a probe procedure that differed from the procedures used in training. The results reported during probe conditions varied. Hart and Risley (1975) and Giumento (1990) reported positive results for children's productive labeling using color adjectives and nouns, respectively. Giumento also reported positive results for probes of children's receptive use of these labels in the probe setting.[1] Child performance on both receptive and productive probes improved across the 6-week training period. In studies by Warren and Bambara (1989) and Warren and Gazdag (1990), probes in the form of questions that could be answered using the target linguistic form were presented by teachers in the classroom generalization setting. Correct responding was low (less than 25% correct) in one case and variable across subjects and behaviors in the other. In both instances, the authors propose that the question-answering probe was a difficult test of generalization because a range of utterances could have been used to respond appropriately to the query presented by the teacher. Neither study presents generalization data in a format that allows for inspection of trends over time to determine whether child performance improved gradually as the child had more experience with the probe task.

The results of assessments of generalization across settings and trainers appear to be related to the specific type of format used to evaluate child behavior. When only one aspect of the generalization setting (i.e., setting or trainer) varied from the original training setting, generalization was typically strong. When two (setting and trainer) or three (setting, trainer, and task format) aspects were changed, child generalization was more varied. The two most difficult tests of generalization had the most inconsistent results. These were generalization to truly naturalistic interactions with untrained teachers in nontraining settings and generalization to probe formats in which alternative responses could be used to answer appropriately. When measures of general language use (e.g., rate of talking, responsiveness, frequency of nonobligatory utterances) were reported, these measures tended to show greater change than measures of target usage within and across settings. It is important to note that these measures are sensitive to contextual influences. Because none of these studies has completely controlled for context effect in generalization analyses, these results should be interpreted as weak evidence of generalization.

Criterion III: Generalized Changes in Knowledge

The third criterion addresses the issue of what new knowledge has been learned by the child during milieu teaching. Here we ask about generalized changes in child knowledge of the communication system as indicated by evidence of changes beyond the learning of specific targets. For single-word targets, evidence of: 1) generalized use of untaught words to convey correctly taught functions (e.g., red and blue are used after training even though yellow

---

[1]Changes in children's receptive language skills are not targeted directly in milieu teaching, which focuses exclusively on production. Operant training studies (e.g., Ezell & Goldstein, 1989; Guess & Baer, 1973) provided evidence that productive and receptive use of labels were independent response classes. However, it has been posited that crossmodal transfer (from comprehension to production) occurs in typical language development and is a critical process for efficient remediation of language deficits (Kaiser & Warren, 1987).

and brown are used during training), 2) crossmodal transfer (i.e., instruction involved productive training, but changes are also seen in comprehension), or 3) generalization across specific stimuli (i.e., the word "cup" is now applied correctly to a larger class of containers) indicate that the child has formed a concept or enlarged his or her existing conceptual class. For multiword targets, such as agent-action combinations, recombination of the learned grammatical categories to form novel untrained combinations suggests that the child has acquired the rule for forming such combinations and is able to use the rule to generate novel combinations to fit the communicative context.

Table 4 summarizes the measures of stimulus class (or concept generalization), response class, and recombinatory generalization used in 10 milieu teaching studies. In each case, the authors interpreted their data as positive evidence of generalization. Seven studies measured response class generalization. In all but one study (Warren & Gazdag, 1990), however, the measures were derived from data collected within the training setting. Although the measures were not taken during the milieu teaching episode, it is possible that the utterances were the result of the contextual influences related to the implementation of the teaching procedure, as discussed in Criterion II. The same concern applies to the results of assessments of recombinatory generalization.

Only studies by McGee et al. (1985) and Warren and Gazdag (1990) offer even moderate evidence of recombinatory generalization separated from potential context effects. Except for McGee et al., none of the studies presenting response class or recombinatory generalization data attempted to indicate whether any of the responses were among those that were specifically taught. Thus, it is not possible to know if the novel instances were uses of a recently prompted utterance, or representative of the child's ability to generate novel utterances without benefit of recent modeling or prompting.

Analyses of stimulus class generalization that would be indicative of possible concept formation are limited in these studies. Oliver and Halle (1982) examined child generalization across novel opportunities in which the newly trained signs would have been appropriate. Their findings of partial generalization across novel opportunities might be considered simply as across-setting generalization. Giumento (1990) presented different exemplars for noun labels during receptive and productive probes. Generalization was very strong for receptive probes and strong for production probes. Performance improved over time in both probe tasks. However, maturation is a possible alternative explanation for the receptive generalization data.

McGee et al. (1985) is the only study in which a number of stimuli were arranged to include novel and trained examples. Spontaneous and prompted uses of recombinative responses by the child were recorded separately for these two types of stimuli. Analysis by McGee et al. of the stimulus conditions under which the response occurred provides important information about

Table 4. Summary of research findings on stimulus class, response class, and recombinatory generalization

Study	Stimulus class	Response class	Recombinatory	Study weaknesses
Carr & Kologinsky (1983)	—	Number of unique signs[a,b]	—	Control via reversal suggests context effects.
Cavallaro & Bambara (1982)	—	—	Number of novel 2-word requests[a] Number of other 2-word utterances[a]	Same goals taught in both conditions; changes not durable
Charlop, Schreibman, & Thibodeau (1985)	Percentage of correct requests with novel stimuli[c]	—	—	Only two stimuli Only one generalization session
Giumento (1990)	New objects[c]	—	—	Crossmodal transfer[a] Effects are clear in production data for 2 out of 6 subjects.
Hart & Risley (1968)	—	Number of adjectives[a,d]	Number of color-noun combinations[a,d]	—
Hart & Risley (1974)	—	Number of new nouns[a,d]	Number of adjective noun combinations[a,d]	Partial reversal indicates frequency is not a good measure of recombinatory generalization.
Hart & Risley (1975)	—	Number of different verbs[a,d] Number of different nouns[a,d]	—	No baseline Weak measures

30

Study				
Hart & Risley (1980)	—	Number of total words[c,d] Number of different words[a,d]	Total number of sentences[a,d] Number of basic sentences[a,d] Number of elaborated sentences[a,d]	Same subjects as 1974 study
McGee, Krantz, & McClannahan (1985)	—	—	Number of novel preposition-noun combinations[c]	—
Oliver & Halle (1982)	Correct response to four novel opportunities[c]	—		—
Rogers-Warren & Warren (1980)	—	Cumultive novel words[a,d]	Cumulative novel phrases[a,d]	—
Warren & Bambara (1989)	—	—	Number of total plus unique action-object combinations[a,d,e]	—
Warren & Gazdag (1990)	—	Number of total plus unique nonobligatory nouns and verbs[a,c,d]	Number of total plus unique nonobligatory combinations[a,c]	Also across pragmatic functions[a]

[a]Measure derived from within—training session data.
[b]Reversible effects for generalization data suggest context effects were responsible for changes in performance in generalization setting.
[c]Measure derived from generalization session data.
[d]Authors did not report which exact forms were taught. It is thus impossible to determine the extent to which changes in this measure are directly influenced by training. Evidence for generalization should be interpreted very cautiously.
[e]Measure derived from combined within—training session data and generalization session data.

the range of knowledge acquired as a result of training on a specific target. Children in the study used trained preposition-object combinations more frequently than they used novel combinations. Two of the three subjects appeared to generalize to novel combinations.

Criterion IV: Changes on Global Language Assessments

Criterion IV poses the question "Is there evidence that milieu teaching positively affects children's general language development?" In examining studies of milieu teaching for evidence of global language development, we considered only those studies in which there were measures that could be compared to a standard for children of a similar age and for which reported and expected gains over a period of time could be compared. Two types of measures were included: standardized test scores and mean length of utterance (MLU). Although we judge standardized tests to be the more valid measure of development, MLU is a frequently used descriptor of children's language development. Based on Miller and Chapman's (1981) calculation of expected growth of 0.1 utterances per month for children with MLUs between 1.0 and 3.5, it is possible to compare actual and expected changes over the period of the intervention. This comparison is methodologically and conceptually weak, because it assumes development is linear and accurately represented by a single measure (i.e., MLU). Both of these assumptions may be false, particularly for children developing atypically. Seven of the studies reviewed included either MLU or performance on a standardized test of language among their outcome measures. Table 5 summarizes these studies. In five studies, standardized pre- and postmeasures of child language development were presented. In each study, there is modest evidence of positive development for some subjects. However, the limitations imposed by the designs of these studies and the variability of results across subjects prevent us from interpreting these outcomes as unequivocally indicating that changes in development resulted from applications of milieu teaching. Hart and Risley (1974) reported gains on the Peabody Picture Vocabulary Test (PPVT) averaging 1.8 years by disadvantaged preschool children during a 9-month intervention. While the magnitude of this change is impressive, these results should be interpreted cautiously. The design of the study (a multiple baseline across four target classes without a nonteaching baseline) does not separate the effects of the 9 months of incidental teaching intervention from the effects of participation in the classroom program, nor does it control for maturation effects in PPVT scores. Warren and Bambara (1989) and Warren and Gazdag (1990) reported greater than expected gains on the Sequenced Inventory of Communicative Development-Receptive Scale (SICD-R) and the Sequenced Inventory of Communicative Development-Expressive Scale (SICD-E) for one of three subjects and one of two subjects, respectively. While not conclusive, these findings suggest that development may be facilitated for some subjects. How-

Table 5. Global measures of language development used in studies investigating effectiveness of milieu teaching procedures

Study	Measure	Results	Possible weaknesses
Alpert & Kaiser (in press)	MLU[a]	—	No experimental design to control for maturation
Hart & Risley (1974)	PPVT Pre-Post (mean scores for group)	1.8 yr. gain during 9-mos. intervention	Results could be from preschool alone or combination with treatment.
Warren & Bambara (1989)	SICD-R	1 of 3 subjects showed gains over predicted gain	No experimental design to control for maturation
	SICD-E	1 of 3 subjects showed gains over predicted gain	No experimental design to control for maturation
	MLU[a]	Average increase .2 MLU	Not compared to control group
Warren & Gazdag (1990)	SICD-R SICD-E	1 of 2 subjects showed gains (+ 5 mos. above predicted score) on both measures	—
Warren, McQuarter, & Rogers-Warren (1984)	MLU[a]	2 of 3 subjects showed greater than predicted gains	—
Yoder & Davies (1990)	SICD-R	Treatment effect for developmentally young for SICD-R	—
	SICD-E PPVT EOWPVT MLU		
Yoder, Davies, & Bishop (see Chapter 10)	SICD-R SICD-E MLU	SICD-E above expected score Treatment effect for developmentally young for SICD-E/CA and MLU	—

Note: PPVT = Peabody Picture Vocabulary Test; SICD-R = Sequenced Inventory of Communication Development-Receptive Scale; SICD-E = Sequenced Inventory of Communication Development-Expressive Scale; EOWPVT = Expressive One Word Picture Vocabulary Test.
[a]Within—training session data.

ever, maturation was not controlled in these studies. Two studies (Yoder et al., 1990; Yoder et al., 1991) used group designs employing global language tests. These studies allowed an assessment of language gains that are not likely to be affected by context effects. One study (Chapter 10) used random assignment to create groups; the other matched subjects on 13 pretreatment variables (Yoder et al., 1990). These studies included language samples with nontraining staff members using a neutral interaction style, and criterion-referenced and standardized tests as pre- and posttreatment measures. All procedures were conducted in a room different from the therapy locale and involved only noninstructional materials.

Yoder et al. (1991) found differentially positive effects of milieu teaching for some children. Children who were developmentally young (i.e., produced less than one utterance per minute, self-initiated less than 18% of their utterances, were intelligible less than 45% of the time) showed relatively greater gains on several posttest measures (degree of expressive delay with respect to their chronological age, MLU, and number of early pronouns and morphological markers in their language samples) after treatment than did similar children taught by a didactic language intervention (i.e., Communication Training Program, Waryas & Stremel-Campbell, 1983).

Yoder et al. (1990) matched 30 children on 13 pretreatment language variables. The results were consistent with the notion that children who are developmentally young (i.e., produced about two utterances per minute, with MLUs below 1.55) learned more receptive language skills and responded to questions during neutral interaction style language samples better than did similar children taught by an alternative procedure (i.e., Responsive-Interaction). Neither of these studies had a control group. However, a control group is not necessary to infer treatment effects if the contrast language teaching procedures (i.e., Communication Training Program and Responsive-Interaction, Weiss, 1981) do not inhibit development. Logically, neither contrast treatment would inhibit development. Growth rates were at or above the estimated rate of development before treatment. The results appear to indicate that the milieu procedure did produce durable global language changes, provided the children were developmentally young (e.g., Brown's Stage I, low-frequency talkers) and/or were taught vocabulary goals.

Four of these seven studies used MLU as a metric of global child language development. Yoder et al. (in press) found that children whose type–token ratios were less than .40 had higher MLUs after treatment when taught by the milieu method than when taught by an alternative method. Three studies (Alpert & Kaiser, in press; Warren & Bambara, 1989; Warren et al., 1984) reported greater than expected changes in children's MLU during the treatment period for some subjects. The changes reported in these three studies do not constitute strong evidence of development because the comparisons are based on within–treatment session data in each case. As discussed previously, complexity is a measure of child language that is particularly sensitive to contextual factors, and changes within an intervention context may not represent changes in the child's development outside of that context.

Overall, the studies to date offer only tentative evidence that milieu teaching facilitates children's language development as measured by greater than expected changes on standardized tests. This finding is not surprising given that none of the studies included in this review was designed specifically to ask questions about changes in global development resulting from milieu teaching.

OTHER EFFECTS OF MILIEU TEACHING

In addition to evaluating the studies on milieu teaching in terms of the four criteria, we examined these studies to determine if there is evidence that milieu teaching is more effective than other language intervention strategies and if milieu teaching results in any effects other than changes in performance, knowledge, and global language development.

Comparison of Treatment Studies

Table 6 summarizes the results of five comparisons of treatment studies that included milieu teaching or its variants as one of two treatments. Three studies used alternating treatment designs; two used group comparison designs. Cavallaro and Bambara (1982) found that milieu teaching resulted in more use of the target structure ("want" + noun) and other two-word utterances than did the question plus label teaching procedure. In the other two alternating treatments studies (Giumento, 1990; McGee et al., 1985), milieu teaching and direct instruction were found to be equally effective when subjects were taught using variants of direct instruction. In both of these studies, milieu teaching was superior in facilitating some aspects of generalized use of the new skills. McGee et al. found superior generalization of spontaneous use of the newly trained structure across settings for milieu teaching as well as better performance on probes involving novel object-preposition-location stimuli. Giumento reported more spontaneous uses of the target nouns during freeplay and better performance on production probes of children's generalization of the labels. There were no clear differences in children's performance on receptive probes.

Results of the studies by Yoder and his colleagues (Yoder et al., 1990; Yoder et al., 1991) suggest that milieu teaching may be more effective than alternative treatments for children who are developmentally younger and who have language goals that are relatively early in the developmental sequence. Yoder et al. (in press) randomly assigned 40 preschool children with language delays to one of two experimental groups: milieu teaching or didactic instruction. Individual language goals were selected for each child and training was

Table 6. Design and results of major treatment studies

Study	Design	Within-session measures	Within-session effects	Generalization measures	Generalization effects	Developmental measures
Cavallaro & Bambara (1982)	Alternating treatments with reversals (1 subject)	Number of "want + noun" utterances	Milieu teaching more effective than question label.	—	—	—
		Number of novel two-word utterances	Milieu teaching more effective than question label.	—	—	—
Guimento (1990)	Alternating treatments (6 subjects)	Acquisition of labels	Direct instruction more effective than milieu teaching for 5 of 6 subjects.[a]	Use of labels	Milieu teaching more effective than direct instruction for 2 of 6 subjects, as effective as direct instruction for 3 of 6 subjects, less effective than direct instruction for 1 of 6 subjects.[b] Milieu teaching as effective as direct instruction for receptive labeling, more effective than direct instruction for production labeling.	—

McGee, Krantz, & McClanahan (1985)	Alternating treatments (3 subjects)	Percentage of correct prepositions used	Milieu teaching as effective as traditional teaching.	Spontaneous use	Milieu teaching more effective than traditional teaching across settings and across stimulus positions. Milieu teaching more effective than traditional teaching in novel sentences.	—
Yoder, Davies, & Bishop (see Chapter 10)	Group (40 subjects)	—	—	—	—	Milieu teaching as effective as dydactic teaching for groups. Milieu teaching more effective than dydactic teaching for developmentally younger learners, less effective than dydactic teaching for developmentally older learners.

(continued)

Table 6. (continued)

Study	Design	Within-session measures	Within-session effects	Generalization measures	Generalization effects	Developmental measures
Yoder & Davies (1990)	Group (30 subjects)	—	—	—	—	Milieu teaching more effective than Responsive Interaction for developmentally younger learners, less effective than responsive interaction for developmentally older learners.

[a]Naturalistic assessment during freeplay.
[b]Determined by probe assessment.

provided for 60 sessions on these goals using the assigned treatment model. No significant differences between groups were found. However, aptitude by treatment interactions indicated that the developmental gains associated with each treatment varied according to the characteristics of the subjects. A similar pattern of results was reported by Yoder et al. (1990) when milieu teaching was compared with responsive-interactive teaching. In this study, the developmental changes in 30 children who had participated in 60 sessions of milieu teaching across the day in their preschool were compared to the changes in 15 children who had received 60 sessions of across-the-day responsive-interactive teaching. Subjects in the two groups were matched on 13 pretreatment variables. Four developmentally appropriate language goals were selected for each subject at the beginning of the intervention. Developmentally younger subjects tended to benefit more from milieu teaching than from responsive-interactive teaching, while developmentally older subjects showed somewhat greater benefits from the responsive-interactive teaching. There were no overall between-group differences for treatment outcomes.

Some very modest evidence that milieu teaching can be more effective than other language intervention procedures for some children does emerge from the five comparison studies. Milieu teaching may promote generalization somewhat better than traditional instructional methods. The conclusions of the studies by Yoder and his colleagues (Yoder et al., 1990; Yoder et al., 1991) suggest that milieu teaching may be more effective than other treatments for developmentally younger children, but not necessarily better than other treatments for mid-range or developmentally older children. Alternatively, milieu teaching may be more effective for teaching language skills that are less complex and that are typically acquired earlier in the developmental sequence. Because the studies by Yoder and his colleagues do not separate the child's developmental level from the type of goal being taught, it is impossible to determine whether one or both of these factors contribute to the observed differential effects of milieu teaching.

The results reported in the single-subject studies are generally consistent with the findings reported by Yoder and his colleagues. In two studies using alternating treatment designs (Cavallaro & Bambara, 1982; Giumento, 1990), children were taught goals that were in the early portion of the developmental sequence. The subject in the Cavallaro and Bambara study was in the early stages of language development. This subject was similar to the children for whom milieu teaching was reported to be more effective in the Yoder et al. studies, and milieu teaching was consistently found to be more effective. The language skills of six children in the Giumento study are not described in sufficient detail to compare them to the subjects in the Yoder et al. studies. The subjects in the McGee et al. (1985) study were in the middle to upper ranges of the subjects in the Yoder et al. studies, and were taught a language skill that might be considered in the middle range of early language intervention targets. Interestingly, subjects in these two studies did not exhibit consistent differences in acquisition of new forms in the two teaching conditions, but generalization of forms taught via milieu teaching was better. Although limited to a very small number of subjects, these findings suggest that the effect of milieu teaching may depend on the developmental level of the child or on the language goal being taught.

Facilitation of Other Outcomes

Two other potentially important outcomes of milieu teaching have been reported. First, Rogers-Warren and Warren (1980) presented data indicating that children generalized previously trained language targets at a much higher rate during milieu teaching than during baseline conditions. Although these results were replicated across subjects, the measures are derived from within–treatment session data and may reflect contextual influences rather than durable changes in child behavior.

Warren and Bambara (1989) and Warren and Gazdag (1990) reported changes in the rate of spontaneous imitations of target level utterances by children receiving milieu teaching. They propose that these changes may represent a change in child strategy for using linguistic input along the lines described by Shatz (1985) as indicative of "bootstrapping" operations.[2] Although it has been proposed that milieu teaching could produce changes in child strategy (Warren & Kaiser, 1986), these studies are the first to attempt to provide evidence of such changes.

SUMMARY

Our evaluation of the research on milieu teaching leads to a conservative conclusion about the extent to which empirical evidence establishes the efficacy of milieu teaching. Clearly, the strength of these conclusions must be placed in the context of the methodology of the studies from which they are drawn. In general, the studies have not provided a sufficiently rigorous set of conditions for determining the effects of milieu teaching on performance outside the intervention context, on generalized knowledge, or on global language development. It is less the case that existing studies present evidence disputing the efficacy of milieu teaching than that these studies present limited evidence that is further constrained by the characteristics of the methods employed. Because specific types of generalization were not addressed in

---

[2] "Bootstrapping" operations are child strategies for using the linguistic input available in the natural environment to learn new language skills. Shatz (1985) has identified several possible strategies, including elicitation of needed information from conversational partners, practice or rehearsal procedures, and entry of information into memory, as conceptual units. Empirical evidence of children's use of these strategies is limited, although Shatz argues for their existence on the basis of her own analyses and related studies of normal development.

many studies, no conclusion about the efficacy of milieu teaching for a particular type of generalization can be reached. The absence of evidence regarding specific types of generalization does not indicate a limitation of the milieu procedures themselves, but does indicate the limit of the empirical analyses of the procedures. Nonetheless, the studies have sufficient internal validity to justify the conclusion that milieu teaching dependably produces primary, within–treatment setting changes in children's use of targets and general language performance. The extent to which these changes can be assumed to represent context-independent or generalized changes in children's behavior is less clear. There is evidence of across-setting and across-trainer generalization, but the strength of these effects appears to be tied closely to the similarity between training and generalization settings. Few tests of generalization in naturalistic settings with untrained adults using nontraining materials have been performed, and the results of these tests vary across studies and across participants within studies. Similarly, the parameters of generalized changes in children's knowledge resulting from milieu interventions are not well documented outside the setting in which the primary intervention occurred. This is particularly true for response class and recombinative generalization, for which there is abundant evidence based on within–treatment setting measures but few examinations of these types of generalization outside the treatment setting. Systematic examination of the changes in conceptual knowledge resulting from stimulus class formation or expansion is notably limited in this literature. Finally, no study to date has sought explicitly to document the impact of milieu teaching on language development using standardized measures to index developmental changes. Although the studies that have been done offer some evidence of developmental facilitation for some types of children, our conclusions must be tentative in view of the lack of direct evidence based on studies with appropriate controls. Although we have taken a purposely conservative approach in judging the efficacy of milieu teaching, the results of this review should be considered carefully in the context of contemporary research on the efficacy of all forms of language intervention.

The research on milieu teaching, although far from conclusive in its findings or complete in its analyses of generalization, is at least as rigorous and as comprehensive as the research on any other language intervention strategy. Systematic examination of the generalized outcomes of any experimental treatment reported in the literature is likely to lead to reservations about the strength of reported effects, criticism of the methods and research designs used in investigating these effects, and a call for more rigorously controlled studies. Furthermore, it seems unlikely that the research describing the generalized outcomes of didactic teaching would be judged acceptable using the standards applied in this review. Other intervention techniques, such as Responsive-Interaction, language stimulation, and modeling in context might fare even less well because there are relatively few empirical studies with sufficient internal validity to be used in a data-based evaluation of efficacy.

EDUCATIONAL AND CLINICAL IMPLICATIONS

Although milieu teaching has been recommended as an alternative to traditional individualized therapy outside the classroom, the evidence suggesting that it is generally more effective than other teaching methods is limited. The generalized effects of milieu teaching vary across children and targets and may depend on the duration and intensity of the intervention. While it appears possible that milieu teaching can positively affect children's global language development, the evidence is limited. Nevertheless, there is much to recommend milieu teaching as a language intervention technique. In addition to the empirical support provided by the studies of milieu teaching examined here, two general conclusions support the use of milieu teaching. First, we believe because of its specific approach to teaching productive language in its functional contexts, milieu teaching should be an effective intervention. Milieu teaching incorporates all of the instructional procedures (i.e., shaping, functional reinforcement, modeling) that have been shown to be effective in teaching new verbal behavior in the direct instruction format. Milieu teaching also programs for generalization by using multiple exemplars and multiple conversational contexts for teaching. By including both systematic instruction and natural variation, durable responding should result. Second, research on other naturalistic and direct instruction procedures for teaching new language skills has not produced unequivocal evidence of the effectiveness of these techniques in remediating language deficits. While our analysis of the outcomes resulting from milieu teaching leads us to a set of relatively conservative conclusions, analysis of the research available on other intervention strategies would not lead to stronger conclusions about the efficacy of those strategies. There is no unequivocal evidence of the success of any language intervention strategy in promoting global language development in children with severe language and cognitive deficits. Rationales and recommendations for the use of milieu teaching in everyday practice follow.

Milieu teaching consistently produces positive changes in children's use of language in conversational settings in which the procedures are being implemented. Milieu teaching appears to be a useful intervention for increasing the frequency of child utterances, the complexity and diversity of those utterances, and the use of specific targets within the training setting. These types of changes may be prerequisite to more generalized changes in child language skills and may have an important impact on the child's participation in social communicative interactions. Thus, while the dependable effects of milieu teaching may not be sufficient to remediate global language deficits, they represent clear, functional changes in children's use of language in training contexts. Milieu teaching is recommended as a functional intervention in naturalistic settings in which children engage in social communicative interactions.

Milieu teaching produces some generalized effects. Those effects may be variable, and additional supportive intervention may be needed to maximize them. Milieu teaching does appear to result in some generalization of newly learned skills. The extent and type of generalization do not appear to be consistent across children with varying needs, specific communication targets, and generalization contexts. Additional training to promote generalization may be needed. The practitioner using milieu techniques should not assume that generalization will occur, but should monitor the desired changes and intervene to facilitate these changes when they do not occur spontaneously.

Milieu teaching appears to be ideally suited to teaching children who are in the early stages of language learning, particularly children who do not verbalize frequently and who are learning vocabulary or early semantic relationships. The limited analyses of effects of milieu teaching across populations of children are not sufficient to prescribe specific interventions for children of varying characteristics. These studies—and the milieu teaching literature in general—do suggest that children in the early stages of language learning are likely to benefit consistently from milieu interventions. It is not clear whether the positive effects for children at this stage of development are the result of the children's specific characteristics or the type of language skills they are learning. There is no evidence to suggest that milieu teaching is ineffective with children at other stages of language learning. However, direct instruction or modeling in context may be more efficient for children in the later stages of development who are learning relatively complex syntactic skills. In addition, milieu teaching may be a useful secondary intervention to promote the use of already learned skills for children across the range of development. The positive effects of milieu teaching on frequency of verbalization, diversity and complexity of language in settings where milieu techniques are implemented, and the limited specific evidence that milieu teaching can facilitate generalization of previously learned targets suggest that the use of these techniques as an adjunct to other types of intervention may be appropriate for many children.

Fidelity, intensity, and duration of the application of milieu teaching are important to effective intervention. The research studies evaluated in this review consistently provided high levels of treatment fidelity, described specific treatments designed for target children, and continued application of the intervention for considerable lengths of time. The results reported for milieu interventions must be considered within the framework of these application parameters. Although specific criterion levels for fidelity, intensity, and duration of treatment to achieve consistent positive outcomes have not been investigated, the importance of these aspects of the intervention must be considered carefully in practical applications of the procedures. In classroom applications across several children simultaneously, the interventionist must ensure that each child receives sufficient milieu teaching, that the teaching is targeted to the child's level, and that child progress is monitored as a basis for changing goals. The mechanics of implementing milieu teaching require skill not only in using the techniques, but also in selecting targets and monitoring each child's progress and the application of the procedures.

DIRECTIONS FOR FUTURE RESEARCH

Research on five aspects of applications of milieu teaching is important to furthering our understanding of the effects of milieu teaching on children's language performance, generalized knowledge, and global development. These include:

1. Research directly addressing the effects of milieu teaching on changes in global language development
2. Research examining the changes in generalized linguistic knowledge resulting from milieu teaching, including research that focuses on the effects of milieu teaching on language use in nontraining conversational interactions, with a careful analysis of concept, response class, and recombinative generalization
3. Research directed toward the analysis of differential effects related to child developmental language level and skills targeted in intervention. Preliminary results suggest milieu teaching may be particularly efficient in facilitating generalized vocabulary development.
4. Research investigating the effects of the intensity and duration of intervention on child acquisition and generalization of new language skills as well as longer term changes in child language development
5. Analyses of changes in child strategies for interaction and for language learning resulting from applications of milieu teaching.

In investigating each of these areas, researchers will continue to need to consider carefully the methodology used. For the most part, the methods used to date have been appropriate and useful in establishing the primary effects of milieu teaching. With these studies as a base, it is both timely and appropriate to expand both the conceptual analysis of milieu teaching and the methodology used in this analysis. The critical relationship between the methods used and the strength of empirical evidence of efficacy is readily apparent in the preceding review. It is important that research in this area continues to meet the standards of the field as these standards shift toward more complex and better controlled, conceptually grounded examinations of the effects of interventions.

CONCLUSION

Milieu teaching may be a viable and important intervention for facilitating the functional use of language in communicative contexts. The extent to which milieu teaching produces generalized effects on children's knowledge and use of the language system must be assessed for individual children. Milieu teaching appears to be ideally suited for children who are learning vocabulary and who are in the earlier stages of language development. It may also be a useful intervention for a range of other children. As is the case in any educational intervention, the fidelity of the treatment itself must be monitored in order to achieve the level of outcomes that are the possible results of the treatment.

In this review, we have focused on the systematic evaluation of empirical analyses of milieu teaching. The review is intended to raise new research questions and to challenge researchers toward the use of more rigorous methods in future investigations as well as to provide a set of caveats to the practitioner. The studies on milieu teaching represent an important contribution to the examination of the effects of intervention on children's language use and global language development. Criticism, synthesis, and continued review of this data base is important both to our understanding of the effects of milieu teaching and to the development of a viable technology for language intervention.

REFERENCES

Alpert, C.L., & Kaiser, A.P. (in press). Training parents as milieu language teachers. *Journal of Early Intervention.*

Campbell, D., & Stanley, J. (1966). *Experimental and quasi-experimental designs for research.* Chicago: Rand-McNally.

Carr, E.G., & Kologinsky, E. (1983). Acquisition of sign language by autistic children: Spontaneity and generalization effects. *Journal of Applied Behavior Analysis, 16,* 297–314.

Cavallaro, C.C., & Bambara, L.M. (1982). Two strategies for teaching language during free play. *Journal of The Association for the Severely Handicapped, 7,* 80–92.

Charlop, M.H., Schreibman, L., & Thibodeau, M.G. (1985). Increasing spontaneous verbal responding in autistic children using a time delay procedure. *Journal of Applied Behavior Analysis, 18,* 155–166.

Charlop, M.H., & Walsh, M.E. (1986). Increasing autistic children's spontaneous verbalizations of affection: An assessment of time delay and peer modeling procedures. *Journal of Applied Behavior Analysis, 19,* 307–314.

Ezell, H.K., & Goldstein, H. (1989). Effects of imitation on language comprehension and transfer to production in children with mental retardation. *Journal of Speech and Hearing Disorders, 54,* 49–56.

Giumento, A.S. (1990). *The effectiveness of two intervention procedures on the acquisition and generalization of object labels by young children who are at-risk or who have developmental delays.* Unpublished doctoral dissertation, University of Oregon, Eugene.

Guess, D., & Baer, D.M. (1973). An analysis of individual differences in generalization between receptive and productive language in retarded children. *Journal of Applied Behavior Analysis, 6,* 311–329.

Halle, J.W., Marshall, A.M., & Spradlin, J.E. (1979). Time delay: A technique to increase language use and facilitate generalization in retarded children. *Journal of Applied Behavior Analysis, 12,* 431–439.

Hart, B.M., & Risley, T.R. (1968). Establishing the use of descriptive adjectives in the spontaneous speech of disadvantaged preschool children. *Journal of Applied Behavior Analysis, 1,* 109–120.

Hart, B.M., & Risley, T.R. (1974). Using preschool materials to modify the language of disadvantaged children. *Journal of Applied Behavior Analysis, 7,* 243–256.

Hart, B.M., & Risley, T.R. (1975). Incidental teaching of language in the preschool. *Journal of Applied Behavior Analysis, 8,* 411–420.

Hart, B.M., & Risley, T.R. (1980). In vivo language intervention: Unanticipated general effects. *Journal of Applied Behavior Analysis, 7,* 243–256.

Hart, B.M., & Rogers-Warren, A.K. (1978). Milieu language training. In R.L. Schiefelbusch (Ed.), *Language intervention strategies* (Vol. 2, pp. 193–235). Baltimore: University Park Press.

Johnston, J.R. (1988). Generalization: The nature of change. *Language, Speech and Hearing Service in Schools,* 19(3), 314–329.

Kaiser, A.P., & Warren, S.F. (1987). Pragmatics and generalization. In R.L. Schiefelbusch & L.L. Lloyd (Eds.), *Language perspectives: Acquisition, retardation, and intervention* (2nd ed.). Austin, TX: PRO-ED.

McGee, G.G., Krantz, P.J., & McClannahan, L.E. (1985). The facilitative effects of incidental teaching on preposition use by autistic children. *Journal of Applied Behavior Analysis, 18,* 17–31.

Miller, J.F., & Chapman, R.S. (1981). The relationship between age and mean length of utterance in morphemes. *Journal of Speech and Hearing Research, 24,* 154–161.

Mirenda, P.L., & Donnellan, A.M. (1986). Effects of adult interactive style on conversational behavior in students with severe communication problems. *Language, Speech and Hearing Services in the Schools, 17,* 126–141.

Oliver, C.B., & Halle, J.W. (1982). Language training in the everyday environment: Teaching functional sign use to a retarded child. *Journal of The Association for the Severely Handicapped, 8,* 50–62.

Rogers-Warren, A., & Warren, S.F. (1980). Mands for verbalization: Facilitating the display of newly trained language in children. *Behavior Modification, 4*(3), 361–382.

Shatz, M. (1985). An evolutionary perspective on plasticity in language development: A commentary. *Merrill-Palmer Quarterly, 31,* 211–222.

Spradlin, J.E., & Dixon, M.H. (1976). Establishing conditional discriminations without direct training: Stimulus classes and labels. *American Journal of Mental Deficiency, 80,* 555–561.

Warren, S.F., & Bambara, L.M. (1989). An experimental analysis of milieu language intervention: Teaching and action-object form. *Journal of Speech and Hearing Disorders, 54,* 448–461.

Warren, S.F., & Gazdag, G. (1990). Facilitating early language development with milieu intervention procedures. *Journal of Early Intervention, 14*(1), 62–86.

Warren, S.F., & Kaiser, A.P. (1986). Incidental language teaching: A critical review. *Journal of Speech and Hearing Disorders, 51,* 291–299.

Warren, S.F., McQuarter, R.J., & Rogers-Warren, A.K. (1984). The effects of teacher mands and models on the speech of unresponsive language-delayed children. *Journal of Speech and Hearing Research, 49,* 43–52.

Waryas, C.L., & Stremel-Campbell, K. (1983). *Communication training program.* New York: Teaching Resources.

Weiss, R.S. (1981). INREAL intervention for language handicapped and bilingual children. *Journal of the Division of Early Childhood, 4,* 40–52.

Yoder, P.J., & Davies, B. (1990). Do parental questions and topic continuations elicit developmentally delayed children's replies? A sequential analysis. *Journal of Speech and Hearing Research, 33,* 563–573.

Yoder, P.J., Kaiser, A.P., & Alpert, C.L. (1991). An exploratory study of the interaction between language teaching methods and child characteristics. *Journal of Speech and Hearing Research, 34,* 155–167.

Yoder, P.J., Kaiser, A.P., Goldstein, H., Mousetis, L., Alpert, C.L., & Fischer, R. (1990, October). *An analysis of the effects of milieu and responsive-interaction teaching used across the day to facilitate handicapped preschoolers' language.* Paper presented at the Division of Early Childhood Conference, Albuquerque.

3

Reassessing Parent-Focused Language Intervention Programs

Rosemary Tannock and Luigi Girolametto

O NE APPROACH TO PROVIDING LANGUAGE intervention to preschool children who have or are at risk for having communication or language delays is to train their parents to assume the role of primary intervention agents. This approach represents a radical shift in the role of the clinician from direct provision of service as a child therapist/educator to a parent consultant (Mahoney & Weller, 1980). The involvement of parents in the process of intervention is motivated by theoretical, empirical, and practical considerations. Numerous language intervention programs have been developed for parents of infants (e.g., Klein & Briggs, 1987), toddlers (e.g., Mahoney & Powell, 1986) and preschool children (e.g., Manolson, 1985). Although these programs differ in their objectives, theoretical perspectives, and modes of service delivery, they all share the goals of training parents to implement effective intervention, enhancing parents' sense of competence in facilitating their children's development, and encouraging parents to assume responsibility for making decisions concerning their children.

Empowerment of parents is entirely consistent with the philosophy underlying the Education of the Handicapped Act Amendments of 1986 (P.L. 99-457, Part H), but validation of this approach to intervention cannot be based solely on comparisons of ideology. It is essential to obtain sound empirical evidence of the efficacy of these parent-training programs. Only if these programs are truly effective in enhancing the linguistic and communicative abilities of children with developmental delays without making excessive or inappropriate demands on the parents can they be considered to be viable and cost-efficient alternatives to conventional clinic-based ap-

Development of this manuscript was partially supported by the Ministry of Community and Social Services, Ontario, in cooperation with the Ontario Mental Health Foundation funded by the Interprovincial Lottery Research Program, and by an Ontario Mental Health Foundation Post-Doctoral Fellowship awarded to Rosemary Tannock.

proaches in which a clinician works directly with each child (Manolson, 1979; McConkey, Jeffree, & Hewson, 1979).

The Interactive Model is one of several parent-training models that incorporate naturalistic intervention approaches and techniques. It is a widely accepted model of language intervention for infants and young children who are medically or biologically at risk for language delay, or who exhibit delays in the acquisition of communication and language skills. Despite its extensive use throughout Canada and the United States,[1] its effectiveness is uncertain (Fey, 1986). In part, this is attributable to its recent development. The purpose of this chapter is to provide a critical review of parent-focused language intervention programs based on this model. The chapter is divided into four sections. In the first section, we present the rationale for training parents to become primary language-intervention agents, discuss issues and problems associated with parent training, and summarize the general characteristics of naturalistic approaches to language intervention. The second section identifies the underlying theoretical assumptions and principal intervention techniques of the Interactive Model. This section also identifies important differences between the Interactive Model and other naturalistic parent-training models, and describes its diverse applications. A critical review of studies evaluating the effectiveness of this model is presented in the third section. Finally, the implications of these research findings for clinical practice and future research are discussed.

The underlying premise of this chapter, developed from our clinical and research experience and through our critique of the literature, is that this model of intervention may enable parents to motivate and enhance children's use of existing communicative and linguistic abilities. It is unclear, however, whether this model enhances the child's acquisition of new linguistic structures, particularly when the child has a cognitive impairment. It has yet to be demonstrated unequivocally that increased frequency of participation in mutually satisfying interactions will enhance the development of language.

INVOLVING PARENTS IN THE INTERVENTION PROCESS

The process by which children acquire language is not known, but various theories have been forwarded to explain its emergence and development. These theories differ in the relative emphasis placed on endogenous (i.e., cognitive) and exogenous (i.e., environmental) factors. Although all theories of language acquisition concede some role to parents, the nature of that role remains a source of controversy (Hoff-Ginsberg, 1986, 1990; Shatz, 1982).

---

[1]The number of parent-training programs based on the Interactive Model is not known, but data from one program—the Hanen Early Language Parent Program (Manolson, 1985)—suggest the model is used widely. The Hanen program has 175 registered users in Canada and 25 in the United States.

Irrespective of the theoretical underpinnings of the parent-focused language intervention programs, from a practical perspective, parents are in a pivotal position to assume the role of primary intervention agent with infants and preschool children. Parents have much more frequent and extensive contact with children than do clinicians, and are generally motivated to persist. Thus, parents can provide intervention at frequent intervals throughout the day, and can continue intervention over a longer time frame than can clinicians. Moreover, parents can provide intervention under conditions in which the child may be highly motivated to communicate. These conditions, which may be the most conducive to learning, are not easily replicated in a clinical setting. Furthermore, if language skills are facilitated in the home by parents and other family members, problems of generalization, which have bedevilled language interventionists, may be circumvented. Finally, training parents to become intervention agents may be a time- and cost-efficient alternative to direct provision of service to the child by the clinician.

Issues and Problems Associated with Parent Training

Despite the obvious advantages of training parents to assume major responsibility for language intervention, this approach may give rise to a number of problems. For example, most parent-training programs are based on the premise that at least one of the child's primary caregivers is at home and has ample time to use enhanced interaction strategies at frequent intervals throughout the day, thereby having a significant impact on the direction of child language. This may well be an erroneous assumption for many households, including those of two-career families, large families, families with low socioeconomic status, or single-parent families with a child in full-time daycare. The number of opportunities for optimal dyadic interaction between parent and child may be so few that their potential impact on language development is questionable. Given parents' available resources in terms of time and energy, the demands of these programs may be too great and thus inadvertently lead to increased stress or feelings of guilt (Dunst, Leet, & Trivette, 1988). Many of these programs are based on the implicit assumption that something is askew in the parent–child relationship, when in fact parents may be adapting appropriately to the abilities and limitations of their child (e.g., Marfo, 1990; Tannock, 1988). Training parents to adopt an interaction style that differs markedly from that elicited by the child or that is at odds with their own natural style may also cause unintended side effects (e.g., increased stress or guilt resulting from inability to maintain recommended style).

In light of the aforementioned issues, it could be argued that parent-training may be best applied to highly motivated, middle-class or upper–middle class families with sufficient resources to accommodate program demands. However, as discussed later in this chapter, many of these families may not require intervention because they are already interacting in an optimal manner for promoting language development. An interactive approach to language intervention may be most effective with parents and children who exhibit or who are at high risk for problematic interactions. In this case, interventionists will need to develop sensitive screening methods, and ensure that program demands do not overburden these parents, who may already be facing multiple demands on their resources.

The intent in this chapter is not to focus on the varied issues surrounding parent training, but rather to concentrate upon one issue—the extent to which the intended effects of parent-training are achieved using a parent-focused interactive model of language intervention. Before describing the theoretical basis and principal intervention techniques of this model, the main characteristics of naturalistic approaches to language intervention are defined.

Naturalistic Models of Parent Training

Early models of parent-focused language intervention programs taught parents to use formal training activities and instructional techniques based on operant principles (e.g., modeling, shaping, prompting, reinforcing, fading) to teach discrete linguistic forms and structures (e.g., Kemper, 1980; Mac-Donald, Blott, Gordon, Spiegel, & Hartman, 1974). In contrast, many current models incorporate naturalistic approaches to language intervention. Naturalistic approaches are characterized by a primary focus on the process of interaction between parent and child, and an orientation toward communication rather than language teaching per se. Intervention depends primarily upon spontaneously occurring events and communicative situations or fortuitously occurring behavior of the child that arises in the context of play and daily routines. One major goal of these models is to increase the frequency of the child's social interaction by enhancing the quality of interaction between the caregiver and child. Interaction tends to be initiated or controlled by the child in that parents are trained to: 1) follow the child's lead, 2) respond contingently to the child's behavior in a manner that is congruent with the child's immediate interests and developmental abilities, and 3) provide natural consequences that are directly and semantically related to the child's communication or immediate interest. Because these techniques can be and should be implemented during the routine daily activities of the child and family, naturalistic approaches to intervention have the clear advantage that they can be implemented frequently throughout the day.

Included under the rubric of naturalistic models of parent-training programs for language intervention are child-oriented approaches (Fey, 1986), transactional teaching (McLean & Snyder-McLean, 1978), milieu teaching (Alpert, Kaiser, Hancock, Hemmeter, & Ostrosky, 1988; Howlin & Rutter, 1989; Warren & Rogers-Warren, 1985), as well as the Interactive Model (MacDonald, 1989; Mahoney & Powell, 1986; Manolson, 1985). These models differ somewhat in their theoretical perspectives, primary goals, and intervention techniques, and in the extent to which organization and structure is imposed upon the naturalistic interactions. An in-depth discussion of all the variations of parent-training programs incorporating naturalistic techniques is beyond the scope of this chapter. We present the theoretical framework of the Interactive Model, describe its intervention techniques, review the characteristics that differentiate it from other naturalistic models of parent training, and examine various applications of the model. Readers are referred to more detailed discussions of other naturalistic models in Fey (1986), MacDonald (1989), McLean and Snyder-McLean (1978), Norris and Hoffman (1990), Warren and Kaiser (1988), Warren and Rogers-Warren (1985), and Yoder (1990).

THEORETICAL ASSUMPTIONS AND PRINCIPAL INTERVENTION TECHNIQUES OF THE INTERACTIVE MODEL

Theoretical Framework

Socio-interactionist theories propose that the child's active engagement in frequent reciprocal social interactions is critical for language acquisition (Bloom & Lahey, 1978; Bruner, 1975; McLean & Snyder-McLean, 1978). Contingent interactions, which are those controlled by or dependent on the child's behavior, are believed to be particularly facilitative for development (Dunst, 1981; Goldberg, 1977). Typically, interactions that are optimal for language acquisition are provided by caregivers who are willing to interact with the child in a style that is congruent with and responsive to the child's current focus of attention, interests, and developmental abilities.

The precise mechanisms by which these early social interactions facilitate language development are not known. It is believed that recurrent episodes of joint involvement, in which caregiver and child pay joint attention to and jointly act upon some specific object or topic, play a significant role in language development (Bruner, 1983; Schaffer, 1989). Various interactive techniques and the simplified register (i.e., Motherese) used by caregivers during these episodes are believed to provide motivational and informational functions that help the child make comparisons between the nonlinguistic and linguistic contexts, and induce the relationships among language content, form, and use (Cross, 1977; Hoff-Ginsberg, 1986; Moerk, 1976). For example, contingent parental speech in the form of repetitions, expansions, and recasts may provide ideal opportunities for the child to contrast his or her own productions with those of the parents (Hoff-Ginsberg, 1986; Nelson, 1981; Snow & Ferguson, 1978).

It is of concern, therefore, that parents and young children with developmental or language delays appear to experience problems in these early social interactions. Comparative studies have shown that children with developmental or language delays are less actively engaged in interactions and exert less control over the interactional activity than do children without delays matched for developmental level (Cunningham, Reuler, Blackwell, & Deck, 1981; Eheart, 1982; Jones, 1980; Tannock, 1988). Mothers of such children also tend to be less contingently responsive and more controlling of the interactional activity or topic (Cunningham et al., 1981; Hanzlik & Stevenson, 1986; Mahoney, 1988; Tannock, 1988). Thus, these parent–child dyads tend to exhibit difficulties with the two factors that are apparently crucial to language acquisition—active engagement by the child and contingent responsiveness by the caregiver.

Although the direction of influence cannot be ascertained from these studies, it had been suggested at one time that inadequate parental input may have a direct causal association with language delay (Buium, Rynders, & Turnure, 1974; Wulbert, Inglis, Kriegsman, & Mills, 1975). Major methodological flaws in these studies, including use of inadequate control groups in that children were matched for chronological age and not developmental level, invalidate such claims. Currently, it is believed that although group differences do exist, they arise through a continual system of inadequate feedback loops between the child and caregiver (Cross, 1984; Siegel & Cunningham, 1984). The difficulties that these children experience in structuring and organizing their environment due to intrinsic factors, such as attentional, memory, or other processing deficits, lead them to provide inadequate feedback to their caregivers. In turn, these inadequate and ambiguous cues prompt the adult to use a pattern of interactive techniques that may compound the child's difficulties and be less than optimal for language acquisition.

Language acquisition is probably a robust process that depends ultimately on the child's ability to organize and assimilate the information available in interaction (Barnes, Gutfreund, Satterly, & Wells, 1983; Gleitman, Newport, & Gleitman, 1984; Nelson, 1981; Pinker, 1984). However, the structure, content, and process of interaction may play a more important role in language acquisition for children who are unable to organize the information in a normal manner. These are the fundamental assumptions motivating the intervention approach used in the Interactive Model.

Intervention Techniques

Within this model, three clusters of intervention techniques are identified: child-oriented techniques, interaction-promoting techniques, and language-modeling techniques. Table 1 presents key intervention techniques, organized by type of the cluster. The precise impact of each technique is not known, but collectively they are believed to foster the child's development of early communicative, socio-interactional, and linguistic skills.

Child-Oriented Techniques

Child-oriented techniques are designed to establish frequent episodes of joint involvement around the child's immediate focus of attention, interest, or

Table 1.   Intervention techniques encompassed by three basic principles of the Interactive Model

Child-oriented	Interaction-promoting	Language-modeling
Respond to child's focus of attention.	Take one turn at a time.	Comment on activities of child and self.
Follow child's lead.	Wait with anticipation.	Use contingent labeling.
Match child's style and abilities.	Signal for turns.	Use short, simple utterances.
Organize environment.	Decrease directiveness.	Use repetition.
Enter child's world by situating self at same physical level, maintaining face-to-face interaction, establishing eye contact, playing, animating.		Expand or extend child's turn.

Adapted from Klein, Briggs, and Huffman (1988); MacDonald (1989); Mahoney and Powell (1986); Manolson (1985).

conversational topic. They enable parents to bring about change in the child by organizing and increasing the saliency of information in the child's physical and social environment; tuning its complexity to the child's current level of functioning; and providing the kind of input that the child can attend to, process, and assimilate without too much difficulty. One key factor appears to lie in the parent's sensitivity and responsiveness to the child's cues and signals.

Interaction-Promoting Techniques

The primary objectives of interaction-promoting techniques are to place the child in the role of communicator within the context of the ongoing activity, and to establish balanced turn-taking between parent and child so that each assumes the role of initiator as well as responder. Interaction-promoting techniques enable parents to provide frequent opportunities for the child to engage actively in, initiate, and maintain control in interaction, and to attempt new skills and practice recently acquired ones. Successful interactions depend upon the child's intrinsic motivation to communicate, as well as the parent's willingness to consider the child as a conversational partner, to interpret the child's behavior as communicative, and to expect and wait for a response.

Language-Modeling Techniques

Language-modeling techniques are designed to assist the child in inducing the relationships among language content, form, and use. They enable parents to communicate effectively with the child by providing simple linguistic stimuli that are meaningfully related to the child's actions, interests, focus of attention, and developmental competencies. One key factor appears to be the adult's ability to time his or her verbal input so that it corresponds precisely with the child's attentional focus at that moment, and to adapt the nature of that input to match the child's ability to process and assimilate it.

Distinguishing Characteristics of the Model

The Interactive Model of parent training differs from other naturalistic models in several important ways:

1. No specific communication or language targets (e.g., nouns, verbs, two-word utterances, requests) are preselected for teaching. Therefore, the child is not required to produce any specific linguistic forms or functions during interaction (cf. incidental teaching [Warren & Kaiser, 1986, 1988]).
2. No didactic teaching techniques are used. In contrast to other naturalistic models (Howlin & Rutter, 1989; Rogers-Warren & Warren, 1980; Warren & Kaiser, 1986), the Interactive Model does not incorporate any operant techniques (e.g., shaping, prompting, fading, differential reinforcement) that are evident in other naturalistic approaches (e.g., incidental teaching, time-delay, mand-model techniques).
3. Intervention techniques are not restricted to specific play or training activities (cf. McConkey et al., 1979). Parents are taught how to use techniques in all daily activities and routines.

Applications of the Model

Several parent-training programs have been developed that endorse the fundamental assumptions of the Interactive Model. Although all of these programs propose to foster a style of parent–child interaction that is believed to be optimal for language acquisition, they reveal considerable diversity. The ensuing discussion incorporates descriptions of published reports of several clinical or experimental treatment programs based on this model (Brown-Gorton & Wolery, 1988; Clark & Seifer, 1983; Fischer, 1988a, 1988b; Seitz, 1975) and five fully developed program packages: Mother–Infant Communication Project (MICP) (Klein, Briggs, & Huffman, 1988), Ecological Communication Organization (ECO) (MacDonald, 1989), Transactional Intervention Program (TRIP) (Mahoney & Powell, 1986), Hanen Early Language Parent Program (HELPP) (Manolson, 1985), and the Language Interaction Intervention Project (LIIP) (Weistuch & Lewis, 1986). These programs are described briefly in the appendix to this chapter.

Characteristics of parent-training programs based on the Interactive Model are summarized in Table 2. Most programs are offered to parents of children with developmental delay or with high risk for later language delay. Only one program (Clark & Seifer, 1983) reports the use of screening to determine which parent–child dyads would benefit from treatment. Presumably, the other programs assume (albeit erroneously) that all parents with infants or children with disabilities experience difficulties in their interactions, and would benefit from instruction in interactional techniques. Most programs attract primarily well-educated and highly motivated middle-class families, which may in part result from the criteria for enrollment and mode of service delivery. Many of these programs are center based, and several require an extensive time commitment on the part of the parent (e.g., LIIP requires parents to commit themselves for 2 hours twice a week for 20 weeks). Some of these programs even require parents to refer themselves (Girolametto, Greenberg, & Manolson, 1986). The MICP is unique in this regard in that it was designed explicitly to meet the needs of parents from lower educational and socioeconomic backgrounds (i.e., high-risk parents) whose infants had been placed in neonatal intensive care units at birth. Such intervention may be preventive as well as ameliorative because it starts in the first few weeks of the infant's life. The provision of several service delivery components from which parents may choose one or several in which to participate, and the affiliation with a developmental follow-up service to assist parents with the medical, nutritional, and basic caregiving needs of their infant illustrates the commendable "systems" approach of this program (Sameroff, 1983).

Intervention techniques used by the various programs, classified according to one of the three clusters described previously (i.e., child oriented, interaction promoting, and language modeling) are also summarized in Table 2. Techniques receiving major emphasis are indicated by a plus symbol, techniques receiving little emphasis are indicated by a plus symbol in parentheses, and techniques not used are indicated by a minus symbol. Table 2 shows that the TRIP program emphasizes child-orientation and interaction-promoting techniques, but does not incorporate any language-modeling techniques. One pattern emerging from Table 2 is that programs designed for preschool children who have already acquired a few words emphasize language modeling skills even to the exclusion of other techniques (Seitz, 1975; Weistuch & Lewis, 1986), whereas programs designed for infants or children with a wide range of developmental levels focus upon child-oriented and interaction-promoting strategies (Klein et al., 1988; Mahoney & Powell, 1986). Most programs, however, including those employing group training methods, attempt to individualize the program for each family. Program leaders typically use ongoing assessments of the quality of interaction to determine which techniques should be emphasized for which families.

These programs also reveal diversity in their formats of service delivery (i.e., group training, one-to-one training, or some combination of the two). These formats influence the range of specific training methods used to teach parents. For example, programs using one-to-one formats in which both child and parent are present enable staff to model techniques while interacting with the child, and to attempt to modify parental behavior at the moment it is exhibited by providing coaching and immediate feedback while the parent is interacting with the child (Klein et al., 1988; MacDonald, 1989; Mahoney & Powell, 1986; Seitz, 1975). Those that include group-training formats designed exclusively for parents incorporate direct instructional methods and

Table 2.   Parent-focused language intervention programs based on the Interactive Model

Program	Client population	Service delivery components	Instruction
Mother-Infant Communication Project (Klein, Briggs, & Huffman, 1988)	NICU infants Low SES mothers of high-risk children 0–2 yrs.	NICU Home visits Center based Community based	Individual Individual Group Group
Transactional Intervention Program (Mahoney & Powell, 1986)	Primarily middle-class mothers of children 0–3 yrs. with developmental disabilities	Home visits	Individual
Ecological Communication Organization (MacDonald, 1989)	Mixed SES children 0–5 yrs. with developmental disabilities	Center based	Individual
Hanen Early Language Parent Program (Manolson, 1985)	Highly motivated, primarily middle-class parents of preschool children with language delay or developmental disabilities	Center based Home visits	Group Individual
Language Interaction Intervention Project (Weistuch & Lewis, 1986)	Highly motivated mothers of children 2–5 yrs. with language delay or developmental disabilities	Center based Child component included	Group
Clark & Seifer (1983)	Mothers of children 0–3 yrs. with or at high risk for developmental disabilities	Center based	Individual
Seitz (1975)	Mothers of children with language delay or developmental disabilities	Center based	Individual

Note: + = major emphasis; (+) = little emphasis; − = not used.

more formal, informational resources, such as lectures, commercially prepared videotapes, parent manuals, or other written material (Manolson, 1985; Weistuch & Lewis, 1986). One method common to most programs is the use of private playback of individual videotapes to provide parents with feedback. Segments of these tapes may also be selected and used for group viewing to illustrate intervention techniques in use (Manolson, 1985). None of these programs, however, has relied on video training to the extent of some pro-

Table 2. (continued)

Leaders	Frequency of intervention	Duration of program	Nature of intervention		
			Child oriented	Interaction promoting	Language modeling
Nurse	Not reported	Not reported	+	+	(+)
Nurse	Not reported		+	+	(+)
Infant specialist	Bimonthly		+	+	(+)
Infant specialist, parent aide	Bimonthly		+	+	(+)
Teacher	Not reported	Variable (5–24 mos.)	+	+	−
Speech-language pathologist, teacher	Biweekly	Variable (average = 6 mos.)	+	+	+
Speech-language pathologist Parent aide	Once a week	11–15 wks.	+	+	+
Teacher Speech-language pathologist	Twice a week	20 wks.	(+)	(+)	+
Speech-language pathologist	Not reported	6 wks.	+	+	−
Not reported	Three days a week	8 wks.	(+)	−	(+)

grams based on the Focused-Stimulation Model (McConkey & O'Connor, 1982).

Finally, Table 2 reveals that program leaders come from a wide range of disciplines, not all of which provide in-depth training in the development of communication and language or in adult education. The interdisciplinary nature of this model of language intervention may account in part for the "readability" and avoidance of technical jargon in many of the instructional manuals designed for the interventionists and program leaders.

EVALUATION OF THE MODEL

Table 3 summarizes evaluation studies of the Interactive Model that were designed to evaluate the complete intervention package as it is typically implemented in the clinical setting. Reports that did not include outcome data for parent and child, or evaluated only individual components of the model (e.g., Brown-Gorton & Wolery, 1988; Clark & Seifer, 1983; Klein & Briggs, 1987) are not included. General terms have been used to summarize the major findings. The reader should refer to the original sources for precise definitions of measures used in each study. Increases in parents' use of any of the three clusters of intervention techniques (i.e., child oriented, interaction promoting, language modeling) are indicated in parentheses under the findings for parents in Table 3.

Given the widespread use of the Interactive Model throughout Canada and the United States, surprisingly few studies have evaluated its effectiveness. Moreover, most of these studies that have been done reflect methodological shortcomings, which are the nemesis of program evaluation and threaten the integrity of the research findings. In the following section, we note three methodological weaknesses—restricted sampling, pretest–posttest designs, and measurement problems—that complicate the interpretation and integration of findings reported by these evaluation studies.

Methodological Weaknesses

Restricted Sampling

As shown in Table 3, most of the studies rely on small samples and focus on families with children with developmental delay. The children show marked heterogeneity with respect to etiology, chronological age, and developmental level, as well as variability in communicative competencies. In virtually all cases, "parents" refers to mothers. The mothers are relatively homogeneous in terms of their demographic characteristics (i.e., primarily well educated and highly motivated middle-class mothers), but show variability in interactional style prior to participation in intervention (Mahoney & Powell, 1988; Tannock, Girolametto, & Siegel, 1990a, 1990b).

Treatment effects on mothers represent first-order, or direct, changes. The magnitude of these effects is likely to be larger than that of second-order, or indirect, effects on child behavior. Greater statistical power is required to detect small effect sizes (Ottenbacher, 1989). Thus, whereas the sample sizes appear to have been adequate for the detection of parent outcome and maturation effects on children's communication and language abilities (Tannock et al., 1990a, 1990b), they may be inadequate to reveal smaller treatment effects on children's abilities. Inadequate statistical power resulting from small samples and subject variability may account, in part, for the disappointing findings for child outcome in some studies.

Pretest–Posttest Designs

Numerous studies have demonstrated that mothers adjust their interactional style and language input in response to the child's changing competencies, even when the child is developmentally delayed. Mothers of such children become more responsive and less directive (Brooks-Gunn & Lewis, 1984; Hanzlik & Stevenson, 1986; Rondal, 1978). Although maturational changes in the children might be expected to be minimal in these evaluation studies given the relatively brief duration of some of the intervention programs (8–12 weeks), we found significant growth in these children's communicative abilities (Tannock et al., 1990a, 1990b). Maturation, one of the classic threats to the internal validity of the data (Campbell & Stanley, 1963), could account for postprogram changes in both parent and child behavior. Only four of the seven studies listed in Table 3 employed random assignment to a treatment or no-treatment control group in order to control for maturation (Girolametto, 1988; Tannock et al., 1990a; Weistuch & Lewis, 1985, 1986). However, it should be noted that these four controlled studies provide evaluation data for only two of the six programs under review here (LIIP and HELPP). The remaining three studies (MacDonald, 1989; Mahoney & Powell, 1988; Seitz, 1975) employed pretest–posttest designs only, and therefore cannot separate treatment and maturation effects.

Measurement Problems

A wide range of criteria may be used for program evaluation: Baker (1988) lists 11 possible criteria for evaluating parent-training programs. However, most of these studies restrict their evaluation to two criteria: the effects on parents' proficiency in implementing the recommended techniques and child gains. Moreover, most of the evaluation studies exhibit a disproportionate focus on parent change rather than child gains. One study even omitted any assessment of the child's interactive, communicative, or linguistic abilities (Mahoney & Powell, 1988). The narrow orientation of most of these studies provides an incomplete evaluation of the Interactive Model.

A second measurement problem stems from the reliance on a single brief sample of parent–child interaction before and after intervention as the sole source of data for estimating treatment effects (see Table 3). Only one study was designed to collect multiple samples of parent–child interaction before and after intervention (MacDonald, 1989). Ironically, in that study, statistical analyses were based upon data derived from a single sample of interaction at each assessment point. The reliance on a single observation before and after treatment is unlikely to be sufficient to provide a reliable sampling of behavior over time.

Another, related problem concerns the possible effect of the assessment or measurement situation on parents' behavior. Most of the studies use video technology in a laboratory situation to record the single, brief sample of

Table 3. Summary of design variables and major findings of evaluation studies of the Interactive Model

Study	Seitz (1985)	Mahoney and Powell (1988)	MacDonald (1989)	Weistuch and Lewis (1985)
Experimental design	Pretest–posttest design	Pretest–posttest design	Pretest–posttest design	Randomized control group design
Sample size	3	41	25	E1: 5 E2: 5 C1: 5 C2: 5
Average age of child	35 months	18 months	38 months	E1: 42 months E2: 22 months C1: 42 months C2: 22 months
Diagnostic group	LD (N = 2) DD (N = 1)	DD	DD	E1: DD E2: NC C1: DD C2: NC
Number of sessions	24	Variable (20–96)	12	8
Length of sessions	1 hour	2 hours	1½ hours	2 hours
Source and type of data	15-minute video, behavior counts	5-minute video, behavior counts, rating scales	4-minute video, rating scales, 1-minute video, social validation	30-minute videos, behavior counts
Findings Parent	More responsive, less directive (IP) More semantically related (LM)	Fewer turns, more responsive, less directive (IP). Better match with child's developmental level (CO)	More balanced turn-taking (IP), more responsive, less directive (IP), better match with child (CO)	Experimental group increased references to context and use of expansions and extensions (LM)
Child	MLU increased Frequency of utterance increased	MLU increased	Greater gains on ratings of turn-taking and communication than on language or conversation.	No change in MLU
Comments	Very small sample	No systematic assessment No impact on parent affect. Parent change correlated with child's overall developmental gains.	Parents show greater change than children. Changes in pre–post samples perceived by independent judges.	Mothers of children with DD more directive. MLU changes observed only for NC in experimental group.

Study	Weistuch and Lewis (1986)	Girolametto (1988)	Tannock, Girolametto, and Siegel (1990b)
Experimental design	Randomized control group design	Randomized control group design	Randomized control group design
Sample size	E: 16 C: 12	E: 9 C: 11	E1: 8 E2: 8 C1: 8 C2: 8
Average age of child	E: 2–5 years C: 2–5 years	E: 39 months C: 36 months	E1: 25 months E2: 40 months C1: 20 months C2: 35 months
Diagnostic group	E: LD, DD C: LD, DD	E: CD C: DD	E1: DD; MA < 16 months E2: MA > 16 months C1: MA < 16 months C2: MA > 16 months
Number of sessions	40	11	12
Length of sessions	2 hours	3 hours	3 hours
Source and type of data	15-minute video, behavior counts	10-minute video, behavior counts, norm-referenced language test	10-minute video, behavior counts, structured eliciting tasks, norm-referenced language test, parent record of child vocabulary, attendance records, consumer satisfaction rating, parent stress rating
Findings			
Parent	Experimental group used more contextual speech (LM), fewer commands (IP). No change in expansions.	Experimental group showed more balanced turn-taking, more responsiveness (IP), and less controlling of topic (CO).	Experimental group more responsive, less directive (IP). More comments and contextual, speech contingent on child's focus (LM, CO)
Child	Experimental group showed greater increase in MLU and frequency of multiword utterances. Controls showed greater increase in one-word utterances.	Experimental group initiated more topics, was more responsive, used more verbal turns, and used more diverse vocabulary. No change in language measure.	Experimental group used more vocal turns. No change in eliciting performance on tasks or norm-referenced test.
Comments	Intervention included clinician-directed group for children. Proficiency criterion of 25% change used to determine improvement.	Marked within-group variability. Little consistency between mothers who changed and children who changed.	Wide range of evaluation criteria, but pretreatment group differences in maternal style made some data difficult to interpret.

Note: E = experimental age; C = control group; LD = language delay without cognitive impairment; DD = development delay; NC = normal controls; MA = mental age; CO = child oriented; IP = interaction promoting; LM = language modeling; MLU = mean length of utterance.

parent–child interaction. Parents may be highly motivated to use the recommended techniques in front of the camera, but actually use them infrequently at home. Likewise, questioning may also result in overestimations of parents' use of the techniques, given their reasonable desire to appear like the "ideal parent-interventionist" portrayed in the program by the expert who may also be evaluating them (S. Warren, personal communication, July 9, 1990). Parental reactivity may account, in part, for the findings of increases in parents' use of the techniques, but minimal or no changes in the children's communicative or language abilities.

To summarize, most of the evaluation studies under review here, including our own recent study (Tannock et al., 1990a, 1990b), reveal methodological weaknesses that threaten the validity of the research findings. For these reasons, it is useful to review these studies systematically and critically. Inconsistencies between studies may indicate where statistically significant findings in a small sample may be chance occurrences, or where treatment effects may be obscured by considerable individual variability, whereas consistency in findings across studies may indicate better reliability than can be inferred from the individual studies. What, then, can we conclude about the effectiveness of the Interactive Model?

Immediate Effects of Intervention

Parent Outcome

As shown in Table 3, all seven studies report consistent positive effects in that participating mothers increased the frequency with which they used the recommended intervention techniques at posttest. Mothers take fewer turns or exhibit more balanced turn-taking (Girolametto, 1988; MacDonald, 1989; Mahoney & Powell, 1988). They are more likely to use the child's focus of attention or to follow the child's lead in order to establish and develop a topic (Girolametto, 1988; MacDonald, 1989; Mahoney & Powell, 1988; Tannock et al., 1990b). Additionally, mothers use fewer commands (Mahoney & Powell, 1988; Seitz, 1975; Weistuch & Lewis, 1986), more comments (Seitz, 1975; Tannock et al., 1990b) and refer more frequently and precisely to the child's current actions and focus of attention (Tannock et al., 1990b; Weistuch & Lewis, 1986). Finally, mothers match the child's behavior and developmental level more closely in terms of the mode, complexity, and semantic content of their contribution (MacDonald, 1989; Mahoney & Powell, 1988). Thus, given the consistency of findings across both controlled and uncontrolled studies, and across a wide variety of measures, we conclude that immediately following training (at least in the measurement situation), mothers tend to be: 1) more "in tune" with the child's abilities, 2) more responsive to the child's focus and communicative attempts, and 3) less controlling of the child's behavior and focus of the interactional activities or conversational topic.

It is important to note that not all mothers improved following training (Girolametto, 1988; Weistuch & Lewis, 1986). Considerable variability has been observed in mothers' style of interaction prior to training, as well as in their implementation of the recommended strategies after training (Girolametto, 1988; Mahoney & Powell, 1989). For example, Weistuch and Lewis (1986) found that only 56% of the mothers in the treatment group (compared to 17% of the control group) improved. These data were based upon an arbitrary criterion (established post hoc) of a minimum change of 25% in the expected direction on each of four specified variables (i.e., decreased commands; increased reference to context, child acts, own acts). When less stringent criteria were applied, the results appear more promising. For example, 88% of experimental mothers improved in the number of references they made to the children's acts. However, almost 60% of the control families showed comparable improvements without committing themselves to 80 hours of training in the 20-week program. Similarly, if we apply the same criteria to the data reported by Girolametto (1988), only 44% of the experimental mothers improved in terms of becoming less controlling of the topic (control group data were not reported).

These data cast a shadow over the positive findings based on group data, because they suggest that some parents adopt only one or two of the recommended strategies, and that many parents undergo appropriate changes in their interaction style without undertaking intensive training. However, it is important to note the difficulties associated with using change criteria. First, in spite of the common but erroneous assumption that the general style of interaction is less than optimal in most parents of children with disabilities, many parents may exhibit "desired" levels of responsiveness or directiveness before intervention (Crawley & Spiker, 1983; Tannock, 1988). Second, we do not know what constitutes "appropriate" levels of specific parental behaviors. Thus, the findings that many parents fail to meet criteria for improvement does not necessarily imply program ineffectiveness.

Child Outcome

At first glance, the findings summarized in Table 3 suggest that training parents to adopt a responsive and child-oriented style has numerous beneficial effects on the children's acquisition of sociocommunicative and language abilities. However, in contrast to the findings for parents, results pertaining to child outcome show marked inconsistencies across both controlled and uncontrolled studies. For example, although increased child initiations were reported by Girolametto (1988), we were unable to replicate this finding in a larger study using comparable observational measures as well as elicited tasks (Tannock et al., 1990b). Many of the studies that have found positive child outcomes have been flawed by the small number and limited range of the dependent variables for child outcome. For example, mean length of utterance (MLU) was used as the sole measure of child outcome in three of the six studies that assessed treatment effects on children's communication and language abilities (Seitz, 1975; Weistuch & Lewis, 1985, 1986). Given these methodological weaknesses, many of the purported treatment effects reported in these studies are unreliable. Consequently, changes observed may be attributable primarily to factors other than the parent-training program. For example, given the small sample size, the absence of any control for maturation, and the unreliability of MLU measures derived from a single brief sample of parent–child interaction pre- and postintervention, the increases in children's MLU reported by Seitz (1975) may simply represent spurious variability rather than reliable treatment effects. Furthermore, it is possible that the significant increase in MLU reported in the controlled study by Weistuch and Lewis (1986) is attributable to the combined treatment approach (i.e., parent training plus child-centered group) and not solely to parent training. Moreover, this positive treatment effect may have been carried primarily by the children who had language impairment without concomitant cognitive impairments (L. Weistuch, personal communication, April, 1985). The outcome of any intervention program may be more limited for children with cognitive impairments.

Based upon data from the controlled studies, the second-order treatment effects for child outcome are minimal and are restricted to increased use of existing competencies. For example, three of the controlled studies (Girolametto, 1988; Tannock et al., 1990b; Weistuch & Lewis, 1986) report greater increases in the frequency or proportion of children's vocal or verbal turns, or multiword utterances for children in the experimental group compared to the control group. We interpret these increases in use of existing communicative behavior as reflecting improvements in children's participation (i.e., performance). In contrast, we find no convincing evidence that this intervention approach facilitates acquisition of new competencies: three of the controlled studies (Girolametto, 1988; Tannock et al., 1990b; Weistuch & Lewis, 1985) failed to find treatment effects on various measures of child language and sociocommunicative abilities.

Long-Term Impact

What happens to the parents' style of interaction and children's communicative abilities after the training program has ended? Only two studies (MacDonald, 1989; Tannock et al., 1990b) included a follow-up component. MacDonald (1989) noted that although the ratings of all adult strategies diminished somewhat 1 month after the end of the 6-month program, they were still above pretreatment levels. Similarly, Tannock et al. (1990b) reported that parents' use of interaction-promoting and language-modeling techniques, but not child-oriented techniques, decreased somewhat during the 4-month period following the 12-week intervention program, but still exceeded pretreatment levels. Moreover, in a questionnaire administered at the follow-up assessment, parents reported continued use of the techniques on a daily basis. Moreover, 75% of the parents reported teaching the techniques to other caregivers, and 33% reported using them with their other children without disabilities. These data are suggestive of maintenance of change by parents, but a conclusion based upon such limited evidence would be premature.

There is a general clinical assumption that treatment effects on child outcome are likely to be greater after the program has ended, when parents have had more opportunity to implement the recommended strategies. According to the underlying theory of the Interactive Model, increased child participation is expected to occur immediately as a result of the increased opportunities proffered by the parents, whereas growth in children's language abilities may occur as delayed treatment effects. However, the follow-up data in our study did not reveal any increases in rate of development or any delayed treatment effects for children (Tannock et al., 1990b). Likewise, MacDonald (1989) found no changes in the ratings of children's communicative behavior 1 month after intervention, suggesting that any improvements in child outcome are likely to occur immediately after the parent-training program.

Significance of the Findings

Demonstrations of treatment outcome were based on reliable and consistent findings of statistically significant changes in the interactive behavior of mothers and children. What do these changes really mean from the perspective of parents or clinicians? Empirical findings have been criticized for limiting their evaluations to a single, brief sample of interaction before and after training (often videotaped in a laboratory setting). In contrast, parents have the experience of evaluating their interactions with their children in many different contexts. Their judgments of clinical outcome in terms of treatment effects and acceptability of the intervention provide a useful adjunct to the evidence from empirical studies. Using this approach in our recent study (Tannock et al., 1990b), we found that all parents reported improvements in their interactions with their children but, consistent with the data, they were equivocal about improvements in their childrens' communicative and linguistic abilities. Nonetheless, the absence of any increases in parents' stress and the high attendance figures and positive ratings given to the various components of the program suggested that the intervention program did not make excessive or inappropriate demands on these families (Girolametto, Tannock, & Siegel, 1990; Tannock et al., 1990b). However, parents who enrolled in this program referred themselves, and thus may be more likely to feel more positively about the intervention program and its outcome than parents who did not enroll or who dropped out.

A more objective approach to program validation is to assess the social significance of the treatment effects by determining whether individuals not involved with the program are able to see differences between parent–child interactions before and after training. The only study to use this approach reported that 18 judges of varied background (e.g., mothers of children with disabilities, speech-language pathologists, graduate students and adults not involved with children with disabilities or special education) perceived consistent differences in the quality of parent–child interaction before and after intervention (MacDonald, 1989). Analyses were based on judges' ratings of 1-minute samples of interaction from six dyads before and after the program. While these data appear promising, this study employed a pretest–posttest design and did not include an untreated control group. It is possible that the judges were perceiving changes due to maturation as well as intervention.

EDUCATIONAL AND CLINICAL IMPLICATIONS

The widespread use of this intervention approach attests to its clinical appeal and to clinician's belief that it is possible to facilitate communication and language development by promoting a more positive and responsive interaction style in the parents. This review substantiates the effectiveness of these programs for modifying the interactional style of mothers. (Their impact on fathers is not known.) However, we have found little evidence to support the clinical and theoretical beliefs that increasing parental responsiveness enhances children's acquisition of new communication and language abilities. Rather, it appears that the second-order treatment effects for child outcome may be restricted to increases in the use of existing behaviors. We do not wish to undermine the clinical importance of this positive outcome for the child, but rather to identify the apparent limitations of this intervention approach.

Screening Procedures

It is possible that these intervention programs are targeting or attracting a subset of families who may not require intervention, or at least do not require such intensive intervention. We noted previously that many of the parents participating in these programs were already interacting in a nonconstraining and highly responsive manner prior to receiving training (Mahoney & Powell, 1988; Tannock et al., 1990b). That is, prior to intervention, some children may be experiencing contingent responses and "ideal" language models, and may be progressing at an optimal rate (Tannock et al., 1990b). Although even "minimally directive and highly responsive" parents can be trained to become even more responsive (Mahoney & Powell, 1988; Tannock et al., 1990b), it is difficult to see how the extra "boost" afforded by the changes induced in these parents will add significantly to the children's existing experience and facilitate development (Fey, 1986).

We propose that this model of intervention might have a greater impact on child outcome if it were applied to parents with infants or children who exhibit problematic interaction patterns. Effective screening procedures, perhaps akin to those used by Clark and Seifer (1983), are necessary to identify such dyads. Several of the instruments used by the programs referenced in this review, including the ECO Scales (MacDonald, 1989) and the Observation of Communicative Interaction (Klein et al., 1988), together with recent profiling work by Fey (1986) and Wetherby, Yonclas, and Bryan (1989) may provide useful starting points for identifying interaction styles and learning styles of parents and children.

Adapting Intervention Techniques to Child Characteristics

It is possible that these programs may inadvertently train parents to become overly responsive, and in some cases to withdraw essential support from the child. Although contingent responsiveness appears to facilitate child development (Goldberg, 1977; Schaffer, 1989), it may be the "negotiation of failed messages" (Golinkoff, 1983) that is one of the critical underlying mechanisms. That is, the parents' failure to understand or respond may motivate children to revise and improve their original, inadequate communicative attempts in order to re-establish shared meaning. Many parents in these intervention programs appear to be overly responsive compared to parents of children without disabilities. For example, many parents were responding to over 80% of the child's communicative attempts (Girolametto, 1988; Mahoney, 1988; Tannock et al., 1990b), whereas parents of children without disabilities appear to respond to approximately 50%–60% of their children's communicative attempts (Fischer, 1988a). There may have been little need, therefore, for these children to revise their communicative attempts and negotiate the meaning. Training parents to discriminate between the child's adequate and inadequate signals, to respond selectively, and to withhold responses from inadequate signals might prompt the child to use more advanced forms. Preliminary support for this proposition comes from two single-subject design studies by Fischer (1988a, 1988b) that demonstrated that as maternal responsiveness was decreased experimentally to approximately 50%, children's spontaneous revisions increased. This modification (i.e., selective responsiveness) may be particularly beneficial for children who are active conversationalists (Fey, 1986).

Conversely, children who are passive and inactive may not benefit from a highly responsive albeit selectively responsive environment (Fey, 1986). Recent studies affording more precise investigations of parental directiveness have challenged the prevailing assumption that directiveness is detrimental to language development (Crawley & Spiker, 1983; Maurer & Sherrod, 1987; Tannock, 1988). Collectively, these studies suggest that directiveness and responsiveness are not necessarily incompatible. Moreover, they suggest that in some circumstances, higher levels of directiveness may be required to increase the participation of an unresponsive and passive child, whereas lower levels may be desirable for the child who readily initiates interaction but continues to use immature and inadequate ways of communicating (Fey, 1986; Tannock, 1988; Wetherby et al., 1989). Thus, the general clinical practice of counseling all parents to reduce their directiveness may be counterproductive to the intervention goal of increasing the child's active participation in interaction.

Modifying the Duration and Intensity of Intervention

Not all families require such prolonged and intensive intervention. Studies evaluating the effectiveness of the Focused Stimulation Model have indicated that some parents are able to adopt a more facilitative and responsive style of interaction after a few brief sessions with a clinician (Cheseldine & McConkey, 1979). Short programs, such as the full-day course offered by the Hanen Early Language Parent Program (Manolson, 1985) as an interim service to parents on a waiting list for the 12-week intervention program, may be all that is required to hone the interactions of parent–child dyads that do not exhibit any major problems. Less intensive parent-training programs may also provide a useful adjunct to other intervention approaches. For example, this approach could be used to train parents to maximize opportunities for the child to practice newly acquired behaviors trained by the clinician using structured tasks and eliciting procedures (Fey, 1986; Hubbell, 1981). Furthermore, the observation that many parents implement only one or two of the multiple techniques that are recommended suggests that parents either select those strategies that they find to be most effective or that they simply cannot learn to implement multiple techniques at any one time (Girolametto, 1988; Weistuch & Lewis, 1986). Some programs, particularly those using group-training formats, may be overloading parents with information. The precise impact of each technique is not known, but it is possible that one technique may produce other concurrent and desirable changes in parental behavior. For example, Brown-Gorton and Wolery (1988) found that teaching parents to imitate their children had the effect of decreasing parental directiveness. Thus, better individualization of parent training might result in greater second-order changes for the child.

DIRECTIONS FOR FUTURE RESEARCH

The limited research on the effectiveness of the Interactive Model has yielded discouraging results for child outcome in terms of facilitating language development. However, methodological weaknesses including small samples; reliance on single, brief samples of parent–child interaction for the data base; the paucity of dependent measures, particularly for child outcome; and the use of nonexperimental designs underscore the need for more rigorous evaluation studies to examine the full impact of this model. First, we require studies that adopt longitudinal prospective designs with random assignment to appropriate control or contrasting treatment groups. Second, we need greater specificity in the research designs in order to investigate the relationships among child and family characteristics (e.g., type or severity of disability, interactional styles, family resources, related demographics), program features (e.g., intensity, duration, methods of training), and treatment outcome. Although evaluations of the complete program package are advantageous in that the findings are generalizable to clinical practice, this approach does not allow us to estimate the particular effects of any single intervention technique or to compare the effectiveness of techniques for a given parent–child dyad (e.g., the use of observing and waiting versus observing and manding appropriately to child's immediate focus). We need to combine both evaluation approaches: to determine the effects of a treatment package as a whole and to investigate the particular effects of specific variables on parental and child behavior. Finally, we need studies to elucidate the relationships between parental and infant/child behavior.

CONCLUSION

From a theoretical viewpoint, this review indicates the need to re-examine the basic assumptions of the Interactive Model and the weak empirical base upon which they rest. One problem that continues to plague social interaction research is how to determine cause–effect sequences between caregiver variables and child outcome. Correlational studies, upon which most of the empirical support rests, cannot determine the direction of effect nor disentangle the role of shared genetic variance (Bates, Bretherton, Breegly-Smith, & McNew, 1982; Schaffer, 1989). Furthermore, many of the patterns of adult–child interaction believed to be essential for language development may be an artefact of the research methodology. For example, most studies have been conducted in intimate one-to-one situations (often in a laboratory setting) that were designed explicitly to foster dyadic interaction. In these situations, freed from the normal distractions of a busy household, the caregiver is able to devote undivided attention to the child, and thus appear optimally responsive and sensitive to the child's needs and abilities. In reality, these dyadic encounters appear to be rare. Children spend proportionately more time in nondyadic situations, such as day care, or polyadic interactions with siblings and parents (Ochs, 1988; Schieffelin & Ochs, 1983; Woollett, 1986). In nondyadic situations, the adult's attention must be divided among all participants, and is often required to engage the child in adult-directed activities (Schaffer & Liddell, 1984). Thus, the early reciprocal dyadic interactions between parent and child may not be the major determinants of language development (Schaffer, 1989;

Shatz, 1982). The precise significance of the interactive techniques of care-givers observed in dyadic encounters with infants and young children without disabilities is not known. Finally, we must consider the possibility that the extent of the child's disability may constrain what can be achieved by this model of intervention: children who are unable to organize information in a normal manner may benefit from more direct instructional approaches. As we suggested, programs based upon the Interactive Model may be a useful ad-junct to provide children with opportunities to practice newly acquired com-munication and language skills.

At the beginning of the chapter, we stated that the Interactive Model of intervention could be considered a viable and cost-effective alternative to conventional clinic-based intervention only if there was sound empirical evi-dence of its effectiveness in enhancing children's communicative and lin-guistic abilities without placing undue demands on parents. In response to the question asked by most of these evaluation studies—"Does this model of parent training work?"—we conclude with Baker's (1988) comments:

> It is reasonable that a programme will "work" quite well according to some . . . criteria but not others; it seems important for service providers to decide what benefits are important, and then to assess these and honestly adver-tise what the programme does and does not offer. The evaluation question, then, becomes multivariate: which programmes work for which families and according to what criteria? At present, we are far from being able to answer that question. (p. 326)

This review should not be interpreted as evidence that the Interactive Model cannot be effective. This approach may provide a useful adjunct to other intervention approaches in terms of enhancing children's use of newly acquired abilities. Its wholesale adoption by clinicians, however, as a primary means of facilitating communication and language development in children who have or who are at risk for having developmental delay, is premature and unwarranted at this time.

REFERENCES

Alpert, C., Kaiser, A., Hancock, T., Hemmeter, M., & Ostrosky, M. (1988, March). *Experimental analysis of milieu language teaching with parents and siblings.* Paper presented at the 21st annual Gatlinburg Conference on Research and Theory in Mental Retardation and Developmental Disabilities, Gatlinburg, TN.

Baker, B. (1988). Evaluating parent training. *Irish Journal of Psychology, 9*(2), 324–345.

Barnes, S., Gutfreund, M., Satterly, D., & Well, G. (1983). Characteristics of adult speech which predict children's language development. *Journal of Child Language, 10,* 65–84.

Bates, E., Bretherton, I., Breegly-Smith, M., & McNew, S. (1982). Social bases of language development: A reassessment. In H.W. Reese & L.P. Lipsitt (Eds.), *Advances in child development and behavior* (Vol. 16, pp. 8–75). New York: Academic Press.

Bloom, L., & Lahey, M. (1978). *Language development and language disorders.* New York: John Wiley & Sons.

Brooks-Gunn, J., & Lewis, M. (1984). Maternal responsivity in interactions with handicapped infants. *Child Development, 55,* 782–793.

Brown-Gorton, R., & Wolery, M. (1988). Teaching mothers to imitate their handicapped children: Effects on maternal mands. *Journal of Special Education, 22*(1), 97–107.

Bruner, J. (1975). From communication to language: A psychological perspective. *Cognition, 3,* 255–287.

Bruner, J. (1983). *Child's talk: Learning to use language.* Oxford: Oxford University Press.

Buium, N., Rynders, J., & Turnure, J. (1974). Early maternal linguistic environment of normal and Down's syndrome language learning children. *American Journal of Mental Deficiency, 79,* 52–58.

Campbell, D., & Stanley, J. (1963). *Experimental and quasi-experimental designs for research.* Chicago: Rand-McNally.

Cheseldine, S., & McConkey, R. (1979). Parental speech to young Down's Syndrome children: An intervention study. *American Journal of Mental Deficiency, 83,* 612–620.

Clark, G., & Seifer, R. (1983). Facilitating mother–infant communication: A treatment model for high-risk and developmentally delayed infants. *Infant Mental Health Journal, 4*(2), 67–82.

Crawley, S., & Spiker, D. (1983). Mother–child interaction involving two-year olds with Down syndrome: a look at individual differences. *Child Development, 54,* 1312–1323.

Cross, T. (1977). Mothers' speech adjustments: The contributions of selected child-listener variables. In C. Snow & C. Ferguson (Eds.), *Talking to children: Language input and acquisition* (pp. 157–188). Cambridge: Cambridge University Press.

Cross, T. (1984). Habilitating the language-impaired child: Ideas from studies of parent-child interaction. *Topics in Language Disorders, 4,* 15–23.

Cunningham, C., Reuler, E., Blackwell, J., & Deck, J. (1981). Behavioral and linguistic developments in the interactions of normal and retarded children. *Child Development, 52*(1), 62–70.

Dunst, C.J. (1981). *Infant learning: A cognitive-linguistic intervention strategy.* Hingham, MA: Teaching Resources Corp.

Dunst, C.J., Leet, H.E., & Trivette, C.M. (1988). Family resources, personal well-being, and early intervention. *Journal of Special Education, 22,* 108–116.

Eheart, B. (1982). Mother–child interactions with nonretarded and mentally retarded preschoolers. *American Journal of Mental Deficiency, 87,* 20–25.

Fey, M. (1986). *Language intervention with young children.* San Diego: College-Hill Press.

Fischer, M. (1988a). The relationship between child initiations and maternal responses in preschool-aged children with Down syndrome. In K. Marfo (Ed.), *Parent–child interaction and developmental disabilities: Theory, research, and prevention* (pp. 126–144). New York: Praeger.

Fischer, M. (1988b). Social communicative revision behaviors in children with Down syndrome. *Journal of Childhood Communication Disorders, 12,* 1–10.

Girolametto, L. (1988). Improving the social-conversational skills of developmentally delayed children: An intervention study. *Journal of Speech and Hearing Disorders, 53,* 156–167.

Girolametto, L., Greenberg, J., & Manolson, H.A. (1986). Developing dialogue skills: The Hanen Early Language Parent Program. *Seminars in Speech and Language, 7,* 367–382.

Girolametto, L., Tannock, R., & Siegel, L. (1990). *Evaluating consumer satisfaction of parent-focused language intervention programs.* Unpublished manuscript.

Gleitman, L., Newport, E., & Gleitman, H. (1984). The current status of the motherese hypothesis. *Journal of Child Language, 11,* 43–80.

Goldberg, S. (1977). Social competence in infancy: A model of parent-infant interaction. *Merrill-Palmer Quarterly, 23,* 163–177.

Golinkoff, R. (1983). The preverbal negotiation of failed messages: Insight into the transition period. In R. Golinkoff (Ed.), *The transition from prelinguistic to linguistic communication.* Hillsdale, NJ: Lawrence Erlbaum Associates.

Hanzlik, J.R., & Stevenson, M.B. (1986). Interaction of mothers with their infants who are mentally handicapped, handicapped with cerebral palsy, or nonhandicapped. *American Journal of Mental Deficiency, 90,* 513–520.

Hoff-Ginsberg, E. (1986). Function and structure in maternal speech: Their relation to the child's development of syntax. *Developmental Psychology, 22,* 155–163.

Hoff-Ginsberg, E. (1990). Maternal speech and the child's development of syntax: A further look. *Journal of Child Language, 17,* 85–99.

Howlin, P., & Rutter, M. (1989). Mothers' speech to autistic children: A preliminary causal analysis. *Journal of Child Psychology and Psychiatry, 30*(6), 819–843.

Hubbell, R. (1981). *Children's language disorders: An integrated approach.* Englewood Cliffs, NJ: Prentice Hall.

Jones, O. (1980). Prelinguistic communication skills in Down's syndrome and normal children. In T. Field, S. Goldberg, D. Stern, & A. Sostek (Eds.), *High-risk infants and children: Adult and peer interactions* (pp. 205–225). New York: Academic Press.

Kemper, R. (1980). A parent-assisted early childhood environmental language intervention program. *Language, Speech and Hearing Services in the Schools, 11*(4), 229–235.

Klein, D., & Briggs, M. (1987). Facilitating mother-infant communicative interaction in mothers of high-risk infants. *Journal of Childhood Communication Disorders, 10,* 95–106.

Klein, D., Briggs, M., & Huffman, P. (1988). *Mother–Infant Communication Project: Facilitating caregiver infant interaction.* Los Angeles: California State University, Division of Special Education.

MacDonald, J. (1989). *Becoming partners with children.* San Antonio, TX: Special Press.

MacDonald, J., Blott, J., Gordon, K., Spiegel, B., & Hartmann, M. (1974). An experimental parent-assisted treatment program for preschool language delayed children. *Journal of Speech and Hearing Disorders, 39*(4), 395–415.

Mahoney, G. (1988). Enhancing the developmental competence of handicapped infants. In K. Marfo (Ed.), *Parent–child interaction and developmental disabilities* (pp. 203–219). New York: Praeger.

Mahoney, G., & Powell, A. (1986). *Transactional intervention program: Teacher's guide.* Farmington, CT: Pediatric Research and Training Center, University of Connecticut Health Center.

Mahoney, G., & Powell, A. (1988). Modifying parent–child interaction: Enhancing the development of handicapped children. *Journal of Special Education, 22*(1), 82–96.

Mahoney, G., & Weller, E. (1980). An ecological approach to language intervention. In D. Bricker (Ed.), *New directions for exceptional children: Language intervention* (pp. 17–32). San Francisco: Jossey-Bass.

Manolson, H.A. (1979). Parent training: A means of implementing pragmatics in early language remediation. *Human Communication, 4,* 275–281.

Manolson, H.A. (1985). *It takes two to talk: A Hanen early language parent guidebook.* Available from the Hanen Early Language Resource Centre, 4-126, 252 Bloor St., West, Toronto, Ontario.

Marfo, K. (1990). Maternal directiveness in interactions with mentally handicapped children: An analytic summary. *Journal of Child Psychology and Psychiatry, 31,* 531–549.

Maurer, H., & Sherrod, K.B. (1987). Context of directives given to young children with Down syndrome and nonretarded children: Development over two years. *American Journal of Mental Deficiency, 91,* 579–590.

McConkey, R., Jeffree, D., & Hewson, S. (1979). Involving parents in extending the language development of their young mentally handicapped children. *British Journal of Disorders of Communication, 14*(3), 203–217.

McConkey, R., & O'Connor, M. (1982). A new approach to parental involvement in language intervention programmes. *Child: Care, health, and development, 8,* 163–176.

McLean, J., & Snyder-McLean, L. (1978). *A transactional approach to early language training.* Columbus, OH: Charles E. Merrill.

Moerk, E. (1976). Process of language teaching and training in the interactions of mother–child dyads. *Child Development, 47,* 1064–1078.

Nelson, K. (1981). Individual differences in language development: Implications for development and language. *Developmental Psychology, 17,* 170–187.

Norris, J.A., & Hoffman, P.R. (1990). Language intervention within naturalistic environments. *Language, Speech, and Hearing Services in Schools, 21,* 72–84.

Ochs, E. (1988). *Culture and language development: Language acquisition and language socialization in a Samoan village.* Cambridge: Cambridge University Press.

Ottenbacher, K. (1989). Statistical conclusion validity of early intervention research with handicapped children. *Exceptional Children, 55*(6), 534–540.

Pinker, S. (1984). *Language learnability and language development.* Cambridge: Harvard University Press.

Rogers-Warren, A., & Warren, S. (1980). Mands for verbalization: Facilitating the display of newly-trained language in children. *Behavior Modification, 4,* 361–382.

Rondal, J. (1978). Maternal speech to normal and Down's syndrome children matched for mean length of utterance. In C. Meyers (Ed.), *Quality of life in severely and profoundly mentally retarded people: Reasearch foundations for improvement* (pp. 193–265). Washington, DC: American Association on Mental Deficienty.

Sameroff, A.J. (1983). Developmental systems: Contexts and evolution. In W. Kessen (Ed.), *History theories and methods: Vol. 1. Handbook of child psychology* (pp. 237–294). New York: John Wiley & Sons.

Schaffer, H.R. (1989). Language development in context. In S. von Tetzchner, L.S. Siegel, & L. Smith (Eds.). *The social and cognitive aspects of normal and atypical language development* (pp. 1–22). New York: Springer-Verlag.

Schaffer, H.R., & Liddell, C. (1984). Adult–child interaction under dyadic and polyadic conditions. *British Journal of Developmental Psychology, 2,* 33–42.

Schieffelin, B.B., & Ochs, E. (1983). A cultural perspective on the transition from prelinguistic to linguistic communication. In R.M. Golinkoff (Ed.), *The transition from prelinguistic to linguistic communication.* Hillsdale, NJ: Lawrence Erlbaum Associates.

Seitz, S. (1975). Language intervention: Changing the language environment of the retarded child. In R. Koch & F. de la Cruz (Eds.), *Down's syndrome (Mongolism): Research, prevention and management* (pp. 157–179). New York: Brunner/Mazel.

Shatz, M. (1982). On mechanisms of language acquisition: Can features of the communicative environment account for development? In L. Gleitman & E. Wanner

(Eds.), *Language acquisition: The state of the art* (pp. 102–127). New York: Cambridge University Press.

Siegel, L., & Cunningham, C. (1984). Social interactions: A transactional approach with illustrations from children with developmental problems. In A. Doyle, D. Gold, & D. Moskowitz (Eds.), *Children in families under stress: New directions for child development* (pp. 85–98). San Francisco: Jossey-Bass.

Snow, C., & Ferguson, C. (1978). *Talking to children.* London: Cambridge University Press.

Tannock, R. (1988). Mothers' directiveness in their interactions with their children with and without Down syndrome. *American Journal of Mental Retardation, 93,* 154–165.

Tannock, R., Girolametto, L., & Siegel, L. (1990a). Are the social-communicative and linguistic skills of developmentally delayed children enhanced by a conversational model of language intervention? In L.B. Olswang, C.K. Thompson, S.F. Warren, & N.J. Minghetti (Eds.), *Treatment efficacy research in communication disorders. Proceedings of the American Speech-Language-Hearing Foundation National Conference on Treatment Efficacy.* (pp. 115–123). Rockville, MD: American Speech-Language-Hearing Association.

Tannock, R., Girolametto, L., & Siegel, L. (1990b). *The Interactive Model of language intervention with developmentally delayed children: An evaluation study.* Unpublished manuscript.

Warren, S.F., & Kaiser, A.P. (1986). Incidental language teaching: A critical review. *Journal of Speech and Hearing Disorders, 51,* 291–299.

Warren, S.F., & Kaiser, A.P. (1988). Research in early language intervention. In S.L. Odom & M.B. Karnes (Eds.), *Early intervention for infants and children with handicaps: An empirical base* (pp. 89–108). Baltimore: Paul H. Brookes Publishing Co.

Warren, S.F., & Rogers-Warren, A.K. (Eds.). (1985). *Teaching functional language.* Austin, TX: PRO-ED.

Weistuch, L., & Lewis, M. (1985). The language interaction intervention project. *Analysis and Intervention in Developmental Disabilities, 5,* 97–106.

Weistuch, L., & Lewis, M. (1986, April). *Effect of maternal language intervention strategies on the language of delayed two to four year olds.* Paper presented at the Eastern Psychological Association Conference, New York.

Wetherby, A., Yonclas, D., & Bryan, A. (1989). Communicative profiles of preschool children with handicaps: Implications for early identification. *Journal of Speech and Hearing Disorders, 54,* 148–158.

Woollett, A. (1986). The influence of older siblings on the language environment of young children. *British Journal of Developmental Psychology, 4,* 235–245.

Wulbert, M., Inglis, S., Kriegsman, E., & Mills, B. (1975). Language delay and associated mother–child interactions. *Developmental Psychology, 11,* 61–70.

Yoder, P.J. (1990). The theoretical and empirical basis of early amelioration of developmental disabilities: Implications for future research. *Journal of Early Intervention, 14,* 27–42.

Appendix

Descriptions and Rationale
for Language Intervention
Programs Based on the Interactive Model

Mother–Infant Communication Project
(MICP) (Klein, Briggs, & Huffman, 1988)

This program was developed for use with multirisk families and their medically/biologically high-risk infants living in urban environments. Parents of high-risk infants generally have much less concern about their children's development of communication skills than about other areas of health and development. Moreover, many of these parents are often at risk themselves for the use of positive and effective parenting strategies. This program attempts to address risk factors inherent in both the infants and the parents. The major focus is on communicative interaction strategies, especially parent responsivity to the infant's cues. Service delivery components include a newborn phase, conducted in the hospital neonatal intensive care unit, and a follow-up phase, conducted through home visits, a center-based program, and small local groups.

Mother–Infant Communication Project
California State University, Los Angeles
Division of Special Education
5151 State University Drive
Los Angeles, CA 90032

Ecological Communication Organization (ECO) (MacDonald, 1989)

This program was developed for individuals of any age and etiology with severe communication delays and their parents, and teachers or other professionals involved with these families. The program is particularly appropriate for individuals who are preverbal, noninteractive, or minimally communicative. Existing approaches to language intervention assume that the individuals have well-developed interactive skills and pragmatic knowledge, and pay little attention to primitive interaction skills and the role of preverbal communication in educational and social development. However, noninteractive and nonverbal behavior is common among individuals with severe disabilities. The primary goals of the program are to develop assessment and treatment tools for professionals to use with this population, and to assist parents of these individuals in helping them learn to interact and communicate. The major emphasis is on establishing a balanced, responsive, and matched social and communicative relationship between these individuals and their parents and teachers. ECO is implemented through a center-based program with home activities.

James D. MacDonald, Ph.D.
Parent–Child Communication Project
Nisonger Center for Developmental Disabilities
Ohio State University
1581 Dodd Drive
Columbus, OH 43210

Transactional Intervention Program (TRIP) (Mahoney & Powell, 1986)

This program was developed for children from birth to 3 with developmental delays and their parents. Parents of children with developmental delays tend to adopt a directive and nonresponsive style of interaction when attempting to teach specific developmental skills. TRIP was designed on the assumption that promoting a responsive style of interaction would influence parent's general behavioral style when playing with, communicating with, teaching, managing, and caring for their children with developmental delays. The major emphasis of the program is on establishing balanced interactions that focus on children's current interests and developmental level. TRIP is implemented in a home-based public school program.

Gerald Mahoney, Ph.D.
Pediatric Research Training Center
University of Connecticut Health Center
Farmington, CT 06032

Hanen Early Language Parent Program (HELPP) (Manolson, 1985)

This program was designed for families of children whose language development is delayed or at risk. Children with communicative delays have less well developed dialogue skills and are less able to benefit from their linguistic environment than are children without delays. Families are taught how to promote the development of dialogue skills by responding contingently to their children's actions and utterances. Families are taught how to increase opportunities for communication and learning by planning play activities with a communication goal in mind. The program focuses on initial and emerging language acquisition, particularly those communication and language skills normally acquired in the first 2 years of life. It is implemented through a center-based program, with several home visits to individualize information conveyed in the group sessions for each family.

Hanen Early Language Resource Centre
The Ontario Institute for Studies in Education
252 Bloor Street West
Toronto, Ontario M5S 1V6

Language Interaction Intervention
Project (LIIP) (Weistuch & Lewis, 1986)

This program is designed for highly motivated mothers of young children with expressive language delays. Children with cognitive delays are eligible, but children with severe hearing loss or severe emotional disturbance are not. Discourse features of maternal speech are assumed to facilitate children's acquisition of language skills, but mothers of children with language delays are at risk for difficulty in using facilitative strategies because of the children's poor turn-taking skills and the ambiguity of their communicative signals. Mothers are taught the principles of language development and how to engineer the environment to facilitate speech by mapping language onto the observable context using techniques to elicit children's requests, labels, and comments, and responding contingently to children's communications. Children participate in group activities devised and supervised by a speech-language pathologist while mothers participate in a series of center-based workshops.

Lucille Weistuch, Ph.D.
Institute for the Study of Child Development
Department of Pediatrics
UMDNJ-Robert Wood Johnson Medical School
One Robert Wood Johnson Place, CN-19
New Brunswick, NJ 08903-0019

4

Promoting Communicative Interaction Among Children in Integrated Intervention Settings

Howard Goldstein and Louise Kaczmarek

As we approach the beginning of full implementation of the Education of the Handicapped Act Amendments of 1986 (P.L. 99-457), increasing emphasis has been placed on identifying placement options for educating preschool children with disabilities. Providing suitable integrated settings has been a particular challenge (McLean & Hanline, 1990; Odom & Warren, 1988). The growing need for early childhood services for children with and children without disabilities are being addressed more often within community-based day care and preschool programs (Fewell, 1986; Odom & Warren, 1988). These programs provide greater opportunities for normalization and integration (Bailey & McWilliam, 1990; Salisbury & Vincent, 1990) and offer more promising results than those demonstrated in partially integrated or reverse mainstreamed programs (Guralnick, 1990). Hence, such programs have been identified as the service system of choice for the majority of children with disabilities despite the barriers that exist (Bailey & McWilliam, 1990; Guralnick, 1990; McLean & Hanline, 1990; Odom & McEvoy, 1990). As more and more emphasis is placed on integrating people with disabilities in our communities in terms of housing, employment, and recreation, integration at the preschool level is increasingly recognized as the first of many experiences that people with and people without disabilities may have to interact with each other.

Central to the preschool experience of all children is learning to interact with a variety of other children. Peer interaction is vitally important to the quality of children's current and future adaptations to their social environment

Preparation of this chapter was supported by Grant No. HD23705 from the National Institute of Child Health and Human Development and Grant No. G00-87-30526 from the U.S. Department of Education awarded to the University of Pittsburgh.

(Hartup, 1976, 1983, 1989). The differences between children with disabilities and children without disabilities are likely to be less pronounced at the preschool level than they will be later (Vincent, Brown, & Getz-Sheftel, 1981). The greater disparity in abilities at older ages often makes interaction between children with disabilities and children without disabilities less satisfactory, especially for children without disabilities. More effective interactions at the preschool level may help diminish this problem by developing a better foundation for acceptance of human differences at an earlier age.

For children with developmental disabilities, communication skills are among the most crucial social skills. Communication skills provide the primary means of controlling the social environment, be it friends, siblings, classmates, parents, caregivers, relatives, or teachers. Surprisingly, remediating deficits in social skills and remediating deficits in communicative behavior have been studied separately. This chapter highlights some of the research findings that are common to both bodies of literature. In particular, we describe how children without disabilities interact with one another, and examine the interactions that take place among children with and children without disabilities in integrated settings. This discussion provides the basis for examining the application of ecobehavioral analyses to the development of intervention strategies to increase and improve interactions among children with and children without disabilities. Current methods used to promote communicative interaction among peers are also explored. This discussion includes a review of peer-mediated intervention strategies, suggestions for improving such interventions, and a discussion of teaching interaction skills directly to children with disabilities. The chapter concludes with an analysis of the clinical/educational and research implications of the findings presented in the chapter.

This chapter provides an overview of the issues involved in programming communication in children with and children without disabilities. To readers who are practitioners, we offer a set of ecobehavioral guidelines for planning, implementing, and evaluating communicative interaction among peers. To readers who are researchers, we propose ways in which our empirical ecobehavioral base can be enriched.

Researchers have repeatedly shown that simply placing preschool children with disabilities in the same educational environment as preschool children without disabilities does not automatically facilitate high-quality social interactions (Devoney, Guralnick, & Rubin, 1974; Kohl & Beckman, 1984; Porter, Ramsey, Tremblay, Iaceobo, & Crawley, 1978). Hence, careful investigation of various aspects of social interaction among preschool children with and preschool children without disabilities is necessary in the development of a technology for achieving high-quality social integration in educational settings for this age group. This chapter examines the communicative aspect of these social interactions.

Divorcing communicative interaction from social interaction is a difficult, if not impossible, task. Communicative behavior is usually considered a subset of social behavior. But because communication refers to the process of exchanging information using both symbolic means (e.g., speaking, writing) and nonsymbolic means (e.g., facial expressions, gestures, movements, postures), almost any attempt to facilitate social interaction results in improved communication (Siegel-Causey & Guess, 1989). The distinction between the two becomes fuzzier still when we consider the myriad of ways to segment and describe social interchanges.

In early intervention settings, investigators typically observe children's interactions during play. Such observations differ considerably in the level of specificity used in describing social interactions. A general level of analysis determines whether children play cooperatively or associatively, engage in parallel play activity, watch other children play, engage in solitary independent play, or engage in no play activity (Parten, 1932). The proportion of time engaged in cooperative or associative play then provides a global measure of social interaction.

A somewhat more specific level of analysis quantifies whether children engage in social (positive or negative) or nonsocial behavior and whether the social behaviors represent initiations or responses. This level of analyses typifies most of the literature. It may be supplemented with more specific information on specific behaviors, such as sharing, rough-and-tumble play, and play organizers.

Investigators focusing on communicative interaction also differ in their scopes of inquiry. Data are usually analyzed at the level of utterances. Coding of utterances has relied heavily on the application of speech act theory, which tries to classify utterances according to their apparent function or their intention (Austin, 1962; Dore, 1974, 1975; Searle, 1969). At a more general level, investigators may seek to identify the rules for sequencing utterances within conversational discourse. Questions concerning how speakers construct and manage conversational discourse, what assumptions they make about the nature of conversation, how they deal with turn-taking, how they break into conversation, how they rectify misinformation and ambiguity, and how they resolve conflicts might be addressed. The form, content, timing, and sequencing of utterances also come into play. How speakers and listeners integrate linguistic and nonlinguistic information, presupposing and foregrounding information, in order to adapt to a variety of social contexts might also be examined.

Reflecting on the different levels of analysis possible allows some appreciation of the complexities of communicative interaction. Even in early intervention settings, we must acknowledge that a myriad of subtle discriminations is required to interact effectively within play situations. A review of studies of communicative interaction among children without disabilities highlights what progress has been made in addressing these issues.

COMMUNICATIVE INTERACTIONS
AMONG CHILDREN WITHOUT DISABILITIES

In order to understand the communicative aspects of interaction between young children with and young children without disabilities, it is useful to examine communicative and other social interactions among children without disabilities. Gaining a better understanding of communication among children without disabilities furthers the development of normative criteria for promoting communicative interactions between children with and children without disabilities. Basic questions that have been addressed include: 1) How frequently do children without disabilities talk to one another? 2) What types of communicative behaviors are displayed within the interactions? 3) What types of behaviors succeed in getting a response from another child?

Frequency of Verbal Interaction

Research has reported considerable variation in the frequency of verbal interaction among children without disabilities. This variation is due partly to the diversity of measurement codes, utterance segmentation procedures, and measurement conditions (e.g., freeplay versus triads versus dyads, types of materials available, number of adults present, listener characteristics). A review of eight studies published between 1932 and 1977 reveals the divergent results of such research (Paul, 1985). Collectively, these data suggest that children between the ages of 2 and 7 engage in verbal interaction between one third and two thirds of the time spent in freeplay. Based on 5-minute samples of child dyads, Garvey and BenDebba (1974) reported a mean rate of 6.9 utterances per minute per child. Mueller (1972) found that dyads of preschool children averaged 3.3 utterances per minute per child. Studies that have focused on combinations of verbal and nonverbal interactions have found similar variation. For example, Tremblay, Strain, Hendrickson, and Shores (1981) determined that children initiate interaction with other children at a rate of three times per minute.

A number of studies of dyadic interaction have described a tendency for both partners to contribute equal numbers of utterances (Garvey & BenDebba, 1974; Kramer, Bukowski, & Garvey, 1989; Schober-Peterson & Johnson, 1989). Garvey and BenDebba (1974) found that preschool children adapt the number of utterances to that of their partner, and that this ability increases with age. They proposed that the number of utterances is "not a stable characteristic of the individual, but rather a dynamic feature of the interaction process itself" (p. 1161). Although the total number of utterances may be approximately equal, there is evidence to suggest that often one child tends to initiate more than the other child while the other child responds more often (Schober-Peterson & Johnson, 1989). The tendency for preschool children to adapt the frequency of their contributions to that of their partners has been shown in social interactions as well (Kohn, 1966).

In summary, although the frequency of communicative interaction by preschool children varies significantly, several studies of dyadic interaction have shown that preschool children without disabilities tend to contribute equally in an interaction in terms of number of utterances. This tendency to balance their contributions is viewed as evidence that preschool children are able to adapt the frequency of communication to that of their partners.

Types of Communicative Behaviors

The studies that have examined the types of communicative behaviors engaged in by preschool children without disabilities have demonstrated the ability of such children to adapt their utterances to their peers. Much of the literature has focused on one aspect of listener adaptation, namely, conversational coherence (i.e., communicative behaviors that maintain the topic of conversation).

In sociodramatic play contexts, children focus their communication on creating the contexts for play (Goncu & Kessel, 1984; Schwartzman, 1978). In a study of 3- and 4½-year-olds, Goncu and Kessel (1984) found that 65% of the utterances communicated during dyadic interaction were devoted to conveying information about imagined identities, objects, and situations. Children offered few affirmations or negations of the statements made by their play partners, suggesting that there is a good deal of mutual acceptance of the imagined representations. Another 25% of the utterances in this study were statements about the possession of objects and plans for ensuing activities that further elaborated on the imaginative substance of the play activities. The children moved in and out of play episodes implicitly rather than explicitly, as evidenced by the small number of specific utterances marking the initiation and termination of interactive exchanges. This study also revealed that children were more likely to talk about their own activities rather than those of their partners, but that older children were more likely to refer to their partner's role than younger children. The conversations of the 4½-year-olds were found to link their utterances to those expressed previously by their partner, showing more conversational coherence. The 3-year-olds primarily communicated utterances that were unlinked to those of their playmates. The developmental progression of conversational coherence was further confirmed in an examination of 5-year-olds, 9-year-olds, and adults (Brinton & Fujiki, 1984), although there is some evidence that more coherence is demonstrated among younger children when nonverbal behaviors are also taken into account (Mueller, 1972).

The extent to which preschool children are able to maintain conversational coherence is controversial. The probability of cohesive exchanges between preschool children was reported in one study to be only .08 when the children were friends (George & Krantz, 1981). Although Brinton and Fujiki (1984) indicated that 5-year-olds made rapid and frequent topic changes in conversation (i.e., five utterances per topic), Schober-Peterson and Johnson (1989) found that approximately 25% of the topics discussed by the 4-year-old dyads in their study were maintained for between 13 and 91 utterances. Differences in the patterns displayed may be related to the specific characteristics of the play situations (Schober-Peterson & Johnson, 1989). Discrepancies in linguistic skills, which have not been examined directly in relation to conversational coherence, may also account for variations in these results.

In an analysis of turn-taking within the social play of 3-, 4-, and 5-year-olds, Garvey (1974) found that turns fell into two major categories—saying or doing the same thing and doing or saying a complementary thing. Older children displayed more complementary utterances and younger children tended to repeat their partner's utterances or actions. Thirty-month old children were found to make significantly more verbal responses and fewer "no" responses than 22-month old children (Mueller, Bleier, Krakow, Hegedus, & Cournoyer, 1977).

Other aspects of verbal interaction that are adapted to the listener include repairing communicative failures (Spilton & Lee, 1977), increasing the duration between speaker pauses (Welkowitz, Cariffe, & Feldstein, 1976), reducing linguistic complexity with younger partners (Shatz & Gelman, 1973), and maintaining linguistic and conversational consistency (Kramer et al., 1989). The study on consistency is of particular importance because of its conclusion that many linguistic and conversational behaviors appear to be a product of the dyadic interaction rather than a representative display of the abilities of individual children.

The context of the interaction also appears to affect the types (and frequency) of utterances and social behavior of preschool children. Types of materials and activities are among the most frequently mentioned factors that influence communicative and social interactions. Social toys (i.e., those played with most often by two to four children) were found to set the occasion for significantly more social behavior than isolated toys intended for the use of one child at a time (Quilitch & Risley, 1973). More social behavior was observed in the block area than in the housekeeping corner (Kinsman & Berk, 1979). Children used different types of topic initiators with different play materials (Wanksa, Bedrosian, & Pohlman, 1986) and displayed longer patterns of interaction when playing with toys that reflected knowledge of familiar and routine events in their daily lives (Schober-Peterson & Johnson, 1989).

Studies of spatial density in typical preschool settings have revealed conflicting findings (Brown, Bryson-Brockmann, & Fox, 1986). Fagot (1977) and Loo (1972) found that reducing the amount of space available for play was associated with an increase in disruptive and aggressive behaviors. McGrew (1970) showed that the amount of play space available had no effect on social responding. In another study, Brown, Fox, and Brady (1987) found that social-directed behavior increased when the amount of space available for play was reduced.

Adults also affect the social interaction of children in preschool environments. In settings in which there was a high ratio of adults to children, preschool children interacted significantly more with adults and less with peers (O'Connor, 1975). Adult prompting and reinforcement of social interaction among children has been shown to increase the social behaviors of preschool children (Allen, Hart, Buell, Harris, & Wolf, 1964; Goetz, Thomson, & Etzel, 1975; Shores, Hester, & Strain, 1976).

In summary, much of the literature on the communicative behaviors of preschool children without disabilities has focused on conversational coherence. These studies present conflicting evidence on the abilities of preschool children to sustain conversation by producing relevant utterances and nonverbal behaviors when taking their conversational turns. Although it is clear that preschool children are able to produce relevant utterances some of the time, the sophistication of their responses varies. Some of this variation appears to be related to age and perhaps the contextual circumstances surrounding the interaction. The literature also demonstrates that contextual variables, such as types of toys and activities, environmental density, and adult involvement, also affect the nature of the social and communicative interactions of preschool children.

Responses to Communicative Behavior

Interestingly, the most frequently appearing forms of communication are not necessarily the most effective in obtaining a response from a partner (Mueller, 1972; Tremblay et al., 1981). In an examination of social initiations by groups of 3-, 4-, and 5-year-olds in freeplay situations, Tremblay et al. (1981) found verbal initiations to be more frequent than motor/gestural initiations. The mean frequencies for statements, commands, and vocal attention-getters per 6-minute session were 6.4, 2.32, and 1.27, respectively. Play organizers (i.e., statements that specify or maintain an activity or role for the partner) and questions occurred at lower mean rates (0.77 and 1.18, respectively), but were more successful in getting a response from the partner than the other types of verbal initiations. Two forms of motor/gestural behavior—rough and tumble play and toy sharing—were more effective than play organizers in obtaining a response from the partner.

Mueller (1972) demonstrated that the probability of communicative success (i.e., a verbal or nonverbal response to the speaker that was related to what the speaker had said) for preschool speakers with same-sexed partners of similar age was predicted by the additive use of nine factors. These factors indexed properties of the speaker's utterances and the speaker's and listener's engagements at the time of the utterances. Success was found to be most likely when the speaker had the listener's attention at the start of the utterance and the utterance was a reply to something that the listener had just said. Success was least likely when utterances were technically poor (i.e., unclear or fragmentary). When both predictive power and frequency of occurrence were taken into account, the analysis revealed that commands or questions and listener attention were the most useful in producing resonses from listeners. Speaker attention to the listener and talking about the listener's activity were also found to be highly predictive of responses from the listener. Ninety-four percent of the utterances of the 3½- to 5½-year-old children in the Mueller study used one or more of the following three indicators of social intent: looking at the listener while speaking, talking about things of interest to the listener, and using attention-getting techniques. Similar results were obtained for 22-month- and 30-month-old children (Mueller et al., 1977).

In these descriptive studies, utterances that obligate a response from the listener (e.g., commands, questions, play organizers) occurred less frequently than other types of utterances but were more likely to elicit responses. Similarly, rough and tumble play and toy sharing, although nonverbal behaviors, could also be viewed as sufficiently intrusive so as to "oblige" the listener to respond. Attending behaviors of listeners as well as speakers and other forms of social intent (e.g., talking about things of interest to the listener, replying to a listener's response) also appear to increase the probabilities of obtaining a response. The literature reviewed has not explored the relationship between the demand characteristics of the initiation and the length of an interactive episode. It is possible that more responses are made to obligatory initiations, but that the length and quality of the ensuing interaction is shorter and less rich in content.

In short, the literature on communicative interactions among preschool children without disabilities reveals: 1) significant variation in the frequency of communicative interactions with a tendency toward a balance in communicative contributions, 2) an emerging ability to sustain conversation by producing relevant verbal and nonverbal responses, and 3) the use of attending behaviors and other forms of social intent to increase the probabilities of receiving communicative responses.

COMMUNICATIVE INTERACTIONS IN INTEGRATED SETTINGS

Integrated settings stimulate children with disabilities to become involved in more social interactions (Beckman & Kohl, 1984; Faught, Balleweg, Crow, & Van den Pol, 1983; Guralnick & Groom, 1988; Peterson & Haralick, 1977) and verbal interactions than do segregated situations (Devoney, Guralnick, & Rubin, 1974; Paul, 1985). This is so even though children without disabilities interact more frequently with other children without disabilities than they do with children with disabilities in such settings (Beckman, 1983; Devoney et al., 1974; Peterson & Haralick, 1977). Not surprisingly, the overall frequency of social interaction appears to be higher in settings comprised exclusively of children without disabilities (O'Connell, 1984; Van den Pol, Crow, Rider, & Offner, 1985).

Like they do with other children without disabilities, children without disabilities adapt their social and verbal behaviors when they interact with children with disabilities. Such children have been shown to reduce the level of their language (Guralnick & Paul-Brown, 1977, 1980, 1984, 1986) and the complexity of their play routines (Peterson & Haralick, 1977) in accordance with the developmental sophistication of their playmates with disabilities. Although these "natural" adaptations work to the advantage of children with disabilities, other "natural" tendencies are less desirable. For example, adapting the frequency of utterances to those produced by the partner implies that the less a child with disabilities talks, the less likely it will be that the child without disabilities will initiate (Ferrell, 1990). In addition, unclear and fragmented utterances, which are likely to be more common in children with disabilities, were the best predictors of a lack of response by preschool children without disabilities (Mueller, 1972). Similarly, listener attention at the start of an utterance, which is highly predictive of a response in children without disabilities, is likely to occur only infrequently in many children with disabilities. In short, many of the behaviors that help children without disabilities maintain interactions with each other are often those behaviors that children with disabilities have difficulty displaying.

There is some evidence to suggest that some peers without disabilities may be better than others at evoking responses from playmates with disabilities. Nietupski, Stainback, Gleissner, Stainback, and Hamre-Nietupski (1982) showed that children who were rated by their teachers as being socially outgoing were more successful in obtaining responses from children with developmental disabilities. In an intervention study, Goldstein and Ferrell (1987) noted that even among children without disabilities who completed training, some were more successful than others.

APPLYING ECOLOGICAL ANALYSES
TO INTERVENTION DEVELOPMENT

The preceding review of the literature underscores the ecological nature of communicative interaction among children. We have seen that young children are able to adapt their communication based on the sophistication of their listeners, improve this ability as they grow older, and modify their communication in accordance with other contextual elements. Some of these abilities bode well for the development of peer-mediated intervention for children with disabilities; others present challenges. The fact that children without disabilities interact less with children with disabilities than they do with other children without disabilities implies that there are limits to the "natural" adaptability of young children when their partners demonstrate lower levels of communicative functioning.

Our examination of the literature clearly demonstrates that a child's partners and the interative context affect a child's communicative performance qualitatively and quantitatively. Patterns of interaction are not easily predicted on the basis of the individual skills of the children present. Furthermore, studies have not attempted to quantify how much variation is normal. Thus, setting goals and evaluating interactions between children with and children without disabilities is difficult.

How much interaction should take place? How often should we expect a child without disabilities to initiate or respond to a peer with disabilities? How often should we expect a child with disabilities to initiate or respond to a peer without disabilities? Questions of this sort are not easily answered. At the very least, they need to be quantified as ranges rather than particular values to allow for normal variation in interaction.

The only normative standard of interaction that emerges from the literature is a tendency for children in dyads to make equal quantitative contributions to the dialogue. This notion of balanced contributions holds promise as a standard for goal setting and evaluation. One could contend that balance already exists in interaction between children with and children without disabilities, but that the contributions of each do not occur often enough or with sufficient success to produce a significant improvement in the quality of the interaction. Thus, the role of intervention is temporarily to upset the balance by increasing the frequency of interaction so that lasting improvements in frequency and quality occur. Training and prompting can be used to increase the contributions of children with and children without disabilities. From an ecobehavioral perspective, however, the turn imbalance accomplished by intervention must eventually result in restoration of balanced contributions at frequency levels that are consistently higher than baseline. Similarly, we would hope that the effects would occur in situations that were not part of the programmed intervention.

An ecobehavioral approach begins with observational studies of typical ecologies to reveal potentially important independent variables. For example, Greenwood, Delquadri, and Hall (1984) determined from descriptive research that achievement in spelling, reading, and math skills were correlated with opportunities to respond. Hence, they developed peer tutoring programs that resulted in large increases in opportunities to respond. Children who participated in the programs were found to have improved significantly (see Greenwood, Delquadri, & Hall, 1989).

Similarly, investigators have begun to apply an ecobehavioral approach to the development of intervention programs for enhancing interaction skills. Analyses of interactions in typical ecologies seek to reveal behaviors that are most effective in maximizing communicative functioning. This then allows us to improve intervention by capitalizing on existing or emerging behaviors. Because improving communicative interaction among children with and children without disabilities requires children without disabilities to move beyond what appears to be ecologically natural in some respects, it behooves us to capitalize on what is naturally most frequent and most successful when possible. An ecobehavioral approach can be applied to the study of communicative interaction patterns in preschool children without disabilities as well as in children with disabilities. In this way, we can select those behaviors that, if established or amplified, are most likely to have the greatest impact on the overall frequency and quality of interaction.

The study described below (Ferrell, 1990) demonstrates the application of an ecobehavioral approach to strategy selection for peer-mediated intervention. This descriptive study was conducted to gather information that could be applied to peer intervention efforts. Each of 10 preschool children without disabilities interacted with a partner with moderate disabilities, a partner with severe disabilities, and a partner without disabilities. The sequence of interactions between these dyads of preschool children and any interaction involving the adult monitor were coded. The communicative act (i.e., pragmatic function) for each utterance, the accompanying behavior or setting events (e.g., eye contact and attention getters), and the person to whom utterances were directed were coded. Data were collected during forty 15-minute sessions (comprised of three play activities).

These data were subjected to three types of analyses. First, the frequencies and proportions of general and specific observational categories were analyzed and compared across pairings. Second, sequential analyses were conducted to identify those behaviors that evoked responses more often than would be expected by mere chance. Third, qualitative analyses were done to determine whether selected variables distinguished between high- and low-quality interactions.

The results showed a high degree of concordance in the relative proportion of communicative acts across subjects and partners. As expected, the average frequency of communicative acts was highest with the partners without disabilities and lowest with the partners with severe disabilities. Sequential analyses revealed that many more communicative acts and accompanying behaviors evoked responses from the partner without disabilities than from the partner with severe disabilities. The partner with moderate disabilities was less responsive than the partner without disabilities but more responsive than the partner with severe disabilities. These analyses found that:

1. Mutual attention to an object or an activity accompanied social utterances that evoked responses more often than would be expected on the basis of mere chance.

2. Utterances that offered comments on current activities occurred frequently, and both comments and requests for information were likely to evoke responses.
3. Utterances that simply acknowledged the communication of the partner facilitated further partner interaction more often than other types of responses.

Two qualitative analyses were done based on the total number of prosocial utterances (responsiveness) and on the balance of prosocial utterances between subjects and partners (balance). For each of these metrics, the two best and two worst dyads for subject–partner pairings for each of the subject–partner pairs were selected for further analysis. For these six dyads, quality of interaction measures, derived from transcripts, were based on repetitiousness, mean number of turns per interchange, and percentage of responses to utterances. This analysis determined that the balance metric discriminated quality of interaction better than the responsiveness metric. It is worth noting that peer interventions have taught peers to initiate at high rates and sometimes to be responsive, but have disregarded the imbalance in utterances that may result.

In summary, this study illustrates the use of an ecobehavioral approach to identify those aspects of social behavior that are likely to characterize high-quality interactions among preschool children. Based on these findings, one might attempt to design ways to increase the frequency of potentially facilitative social behaviors and examine subsequent effects on peer interactions.

STRATEGIES FOR ENHANCING INTERACTION BETWEEN CLASSMATES WITH AND CLASSMATES WITHOUT DISABILITIES

The strategy for enhancing social interaction on the part of children with disabilities that has received the most attention has involved training their peers without disabilities as intervention agents. Targeted behaviors in peer intervention studies refer to social behaviors or strategies that peers without disabilities (sometimes called *peer confederates*) are asked to direct at their classmates with disabilities. Most interventions (e.g., Day, Powell, Dy-Lin, & Stowitschek, 1982; Odom, Hoyson, Jamieson, & Strain, 1985; Ragland, Kerr, & Strain, 1978; Strain, 1977; Strain, Kerr, & Ragland, 1979; Strain, Shores, & Timm, 1977; Tremblay et al., 1981) teach peers to initiate at high rates with peers with disabilities. Such social initiation strategies include asking a child to play, suggesting play ideas (i.e., "play organizers"), asking peers to share toys or offering to share toys, and offering assistance. Other peer interventions (e.g., Guralnick, 1976; McEvoy et al., 1988; Wahler, 1967; Young & Kerr, 1979) have focused more on peers as reinforcement agents by handing out requested materials, praising social behavior, providing social attention, and offering hugs.

We should note that these interventions were developed for children who are socially withdrawn, including children with behavior disorders, autism, and other developmental disabilities. These interventions may prove useful with a broad range of children with and children without disabilities who have difficulty forming and maintaining relationships with peers. Our intention, however, is to elucidate principles that can be applied to children with moderate and severe disabilities who are limited in their interactions within their social environments. It is our hope that by generating ideas for improving intervention efforts, increasing numbers of children deemed too low functioning to acquire meaningful communicative interaction skills can be incorporated into our treatment regimens.

In an attempt to focus on communicative interaction among preschool children, Goldstein and Wickstrom (1986) taught peers without disabilities to use a slightly different set of strategies. They selected these strategies based on studies of early language development and communicative interaction conducted by developmental psychologists (Bruner, 1974/75, 1975; Mueller et al., 1977), procedures speech-language pathologists had proposed for collecting spontaneous speech samples, and the peer-mediated approaches reported in the social interaction literature. These strategies included: 1) establishing eye contact, 2) establishing joint focus of attention, 3) initiating joint play, 4) prompting requests, 5) describing one's own or other children's play, and 6) responding by repeating or expanding children's utterances or by requesting clarification. These strategies were refined in a subsequent study (Goldstein & Ferrell, 1987), and an informal cost–benefit analysis led to the elimination of the second and fourth strategies.

The four remaining strategies taught to peers by Goldstein and Ferrell (1987) differ from some of the strategies described in the social interaction literature in notable ways. First, establishing eye contact or joint attention may be implicit in other intervention strategies, but was given more emphasis in the communicative interaction studies. This was justified based on the importance of these skills to early language acquisition (Bruner, 1974/75, 1975; Tomasello & Farrar, 1986).

Second, initiating joint play is similar to suggesting play ideas or play organizers, with one significant difference. Children were taught that they must suggest ideas that involved themselves and at least one other child, such as "Let's play doctor" or "You be the patient and I'll be the nurse." They were discouraged from (and given no credit for) simply telling another child what to do. A proliferation of statements such as "Check my temperature," "Get the Bandaids," and "You be the doctor now" risks creating the expectation that the peers take on more dominant roles and the children with disabilities take on more submissive roles.

Descriptive talking, which accounts for much of the talking in which children without disabilities engage during play, has not been included in social interaction research, primarily because it does not obligate a response. Nevertheless, subsequent verbal responses occurred frequently, averaging 30% in the Goldstein and Ferrell (1987) study.

Finally, the responding strategy differs from other social interaction studies in that peers are taught to respond to utterances that are often ignored. Trying to repeat, restate, or expand upon the comments of children with disabilities makes the acknowledgment of verbal attempts explicit. This acknowledgment can also be made explicit when a child is unable to understand a verbal attempt and consequently asks for clarification rather than ignoring the attempt.

Healthy doses of precedent, logic, and perhaps rationalization seemed sufficient to engender a set of strategies that has been surprisingly effective in promoting communicative interaction on the part of preschool children with moderate and severe disabilities (Goldstein & Ferrell, 1987; Goldstein & Wickstrom, 1986). Goldstein and his colleagues selected children with autistic characteristics whose expressive language ranged from single words to early syntactic levels. Goldstein and Wickstrom (1986) found that peer intervention resulted in increased interaction that persisted after teacher prompting was withdrawn for each of three preschool children with disabilities. Similar results were achieved with three additional preschool children with disabilities in a subsequent study (Goldstein & Ferrell, 1987) with gains comparable to freeplay observations shown by one subject in a generalization setting. Despite the success of these peer interventions, a need to improve on the selection of strategies and their training was still apparent. A major motivation for further study is the limited maintenance and generalization of treatment effects evidenced in the social skills literature.

The maintenance and generalization of intervention effects are likely to depend on the behavior of the peers when they are no longer prompted to use facilitative strategies and reinforced for doing so. One should expect that if peers continue to use these strategies, their classmates with disabilities will continue to exhibit higher rates of communicative interaction. However, the more pervasive these reciprocal relationships are, the more likely that natural contingencies will take hold and that widespread generalization as well as maintenance will take place. Reciprocity may involve the obvious give and take of play—from catching and throwing a ball or chasing and being chased in a game of tag to more sophisticated conversational interactions involving role enactment, such as taking turns talking on a phone or playing salesman and customer. Peers are not likely to continue using strategies if the effort to do so outweighs the rewards of doing so. When peers are no longer prompted to use facilitative strategies, some children with disabilities may begin to initiate interactions with peers at higher rates. That is, they may compensate for the peers' reduced effort in order to sustain the level of reciprocal interaction experienced previously. It is possible that increased initiations by children with disabilities will result in more balanced interaction patterns. In our previous studies (Goldstein & Ferrell, 1987; Goldstein & Wickstrom, 1986), this seemed most true of the children with disabilities who had made significant improvements in language development seemingly as a function of other language intervention going on in the classroom and in their homes. They may have been primed for an intervention that encouraged them to use language skills to control an important part of their social environment. For children with less verbal facility or for children for whom their social environment is less important, such as children with autism, a more systematic plan may be required. Clearly, the greatest testimony to the success of intervention programs would be the maintenance of long-term relationships between children with and children without disabilities after active intervention has been withdrawn.

CREATING IMPROVED PEER-MEDIATED INTERVENTIONS

Three tactics for improving peer-mediated interventions are worth exploring further. First, the appropriateness of the strategies selected for use in peer intervention studies should be questioned. Although successful, a practical approach to selecting strategies is less than satisfying conceptually. A more appealing approach is to explicate a set of criteria to guide the selection process and then to conduct an ecobehavioral analysis of child–child interaction to obtain a stronger empirical basis for the selection process. Second, the procedures used to teach strategies to peers may not adequately prepare them for the variety of challenging situations encountered in trying to facilitate interaction on the part of children with severe disabilities. In particular, the training of peers should enhance their appreciation of nonverbal communication to interactions. Finally, recent success with self-monitoring procedures can also enrich peers' training by getting them to take more responsibility for using strategies, and reducing the amount of teacher involvement during children's interactions.

Selecting Facilitative Strategies

The following criteria may be effective in guiding the identification of peer intervention strategies:

1. The strategies should include behaviors seen in high-quality interactions among children generally.
2. The strategies should include behaviors that have a high likelihood of inducing subsequent social behavior.
3. The strategies should not include behaviors that tend to place the child with disabilities in a subservient role.
4. The strategies should not include behaviors that take a great deal of time and effort to teach to peers.

5. The strategies should have the potential for natural reciprocal interactions that can be reflected in longer social interchanges.
6. The strategies should optimize rather than simply typify social interactions among children without disabilities.

In order to select strategies that meet these criteria (especially criteria 1, 2, and 5), Ferrell (1990) analyzed natural forms of communicative interaction and strategies used in dyads of preschool children without disabilities with their classmates with and classmates without disabilities. Following an eco-behavioral perspective, a careful evaluation of existing environments and behavior provided a basis for identifying naturally occurring strategies that could be incorporated into an intervention program. The natural occurrence of these strategies means that intervention can capitalize on existing and emerging behaviors. There are several possible benefits to this approach. First, training peers to use these behaviors will be less intensive because they exist in many children's behavioral repertoires although they may be used infrequently in desired contexts. Second, these naturally occurring behaviors appear to be reinforced in the everyday environment, thus lessening the need for service providers to manage additional or contrived reinforcement systems. Third, maintenance and generalization of these behaviors should involve less training, as these behaviors must be reinforced at some level to maintain their occurrence in the natural ecology.

Results of Ferrell's study (1990) have provided an ecobehavioral justification for experimental studies of the effects of increasing the rate of naturally occurring language facilitation strategies. Three strategies selected involve teaching peers: 1) to establish joint reference (i.e., eye contact on the same materials or activities) with their classmates with severe disabilities, 2) to comment on ongoing activities, and 3) to acknowledge and respond to partners' verbal and nonverbal communication. These strategies can be conceptualized as a chain of behaviors. Establishing joint reference alone may not be sufficient to solicit interaction very often (as indicated in the cost-effectiveness analysis of Goldstein and Wickstrom, 1986), but it may be a condition that greatly enhances the effectiveness of commenting or responding to partners (Mueller, 1972). An important difference between this intervention and peer interventions that have focused on social skills is the lack of reliance on initiation strategies with high-demand characteristics. Thus, this intervention in part responds to the problem of instituting a peer intervention program that emphasizes the training of compliance to peers' initiations.

Teaching Strategy Use to Peers

Investigators have taught facilitative strategies to peers without disabilities within the play situation with children with disabilities present (Shafer, Egel, & Neef, 1984; Strain, 1983) or, more typically, in segregated training sessions outside of the daily play situation. The former tactic avoids the potential problem of poor cross-setting generalization. If one need only prompt behaviors in the children's repertoires or provide minimal instruction, then training within the play setting may be an efficient training strategy.

The segregated training situation may be more appropriate when acquisition of behaviors or chains of behavior is required. The training is conducted outside of the play setting so that the children with disabilities are not exposed to the intervention during the acquisition process. Some of the training steps might include: presenting descriptions of strategies, teaching children to provide verbal responses to describe strategies, modeling the strategies, providing guided practice in role-play situations, providing opportunities for increasingly more independent practice of strategy use in role play situations, and perhaps providing practice with children with disabilities.

The training of strategies in a segregated setting has typically been conducted with role-play scenarios modeled after situations that are most likely to facilitate interaction. For example, the scenarios might involve one type of play activity, such as sociodramatic play, and one or two sets of materials. Training conducted with limited contexts places a great burden on peers when it comes to generalizing strategy use to a large variety of play situations in the classroom, gym, or elsewhere. Proponents of a general case programming approach advocate an in-depth preassessment in order to define the "instructional universe" (see Horner, Bellamy, & Colvin, 1984). Instruction must be related to the universe of situations in which trained skills should ultimately be displayed. A greater recognition of the complexities involved in adapting interaction patterns to different types of situations and different types of children is required to enhance training efforts. For example, instead of setting up the "generic" role-play situations for the child who is socially withdrawn, one might teach peers to recognize different interaction scenarios (e.g., cooperative play, isolated play, no play). The peers would need to learn to discriminate what variations in strategies are called for when encountering different antecedent conditions. What is called for is a more careful analysis of the exemplars of strategy use and corresponding situations that should be taught to maximize the likelihood of peers generalizing and adapting a set of rather sophisticated interaction skills as broadly as needed. Applying a general case programming scheme (Horner et al., 1984) to peer intervention training is one way in which generalized effects of this intervention strategy can be improved.

Asking peers to interact with classmates with severe disabilities may require them to subjugate their own play desires. Peers may resist such subjugation if they interpret their classmates' behavior as "not wanting to play with them anyway." One way to alleviate this problem is to sensitize peers to the contributions of nonverbal behavior to communication. Peers can be taught that a child with disabilities might interact by just smiling, by looking at what the peer is doing, by trying to touch the peer or his or her toy, by handing the peer something, by making sounds, or even by screaming. Acknowledging these nonverbal behaviors as communicative turns is important for peers to gain a sense of accomplishment when asked to interact with particularly challenging children. The peers must perceive some success if their persistence during play time is to be maintained.

Adult Prompting

Once peers have mastered the use of strategies in a role-play situation, they are expected to use them during play with their classmates with disabilities. Rarely is this accomplished without encouragement from the adult monitoring the play activity (Odom et al., 1985; Sainato, Goldstein, & Strain, in press). Often, the peers are prompted by an adult monitor, who suggests strategies for the peers to try. These verbal prompts can be provided quickly and easily, but can interrupt the play. Furthermore, the effects of strategy use are confounded because the child with disabilities is likely to hear the prompt. Goldstein and his colleagues (1986, 1987) were able to reduce these problems by teaching peers to recognize posters illustrating the strategies. Children were prompted during the play sessions by directing their attention to a poster depicting the suggested strategy. It is possible that gestural cues (e.g., pointing to one's eyes, ears, mouth) could be instituted in a similar manner to reduce the intrusiveness of prompting still further.

It is not uncommon to find that adult monitors direct a majority of their prompts to the children with disabilities before peer intervention is instituted (Goldstein & Ferrell, 1987; Sainato et al., in press). Prompting of children with disabilities can be reduced considerably once peer intervention is instituted. Peer intervention has usually been successful in increasing the rate of social responses with few prompts directed to the children with disabilities, even with children with autism and severe behavior problems (e.g., Odom et al., 1985; Odom, Strain, Karger, & Smith, 1986). Some investigators have mistaken a reduction in *teacher-initiated* initiations for a reduction in initiations by children with disabilities following peer intervention. Goldstein and Ferrell (1987) were able to recover initiating by reinforcing the child with disabilities for talking rather than having to reinstate teacher prompting.

In the communicative interaction peer intervention studies, consistent, albeit unprogrammed, declines in adult prompts were seen (Goldstein & Ferrell, 1987; Goldstein & Wickstrom, 1986). This natural reduction in adult prompts provides a positive prognosis for programming the maintenance of peer strategy use with minimal teacher involvement.

Promoting Independent Strategy Use in Play Interactions

Current techniques for promoting strategy use by peers may have inadvertently produced an abundance of prompt-dependent behavior. Peer dependence upon adult prompting may be one reason generalization of treatment effects to other play settings has been limited (Hendrickson, Strain, Tremblay, & Shores, 1982; Odom et al., 1985; Strain, 1983). Developing additional methods that rely less on teacher prompting seems an important step in the promotion of more widespread effects.

Sainato et al. (in press) found that peers who were taught facilitative strategies increased their use of strategies during play after a self-monitoring intervention was introduced. Self-monitoring involved several steps. First, the trainer asked peers to forecast how they would try to get their friends to play with them. They were allowed to flip through a self-monitoring book with illustrations depicting four strategies as they reviewed how they would use each strategy. After the session, the trainer met with the peers to help them evaluate their own performance. Children were reinforced if they met and reported the criteria for strategy use.

One advantage of this approach is that reductions in teacher prompting may result in patterns of social interaction that appear more normalized. Perhaps a more important advantage is that once children learn to monitor themselves, this skill is adaptable to generalization programming. That is, one could obtain a verbal commitment from a peer to use facilitative strategies in new settings or with new children with disabilities and depend upon a history of reinforcement for accurate self-monitoring to promote generalization. One would expect that an adult might need to monitor accuracy only intermittently to provide contingent reinforcement to maintain this correspondence between forecasting strategy use, actual strategy use, and reporting whether the promised obligations were met.

Assessment of Treatment Effects

Frequency or rate measures are the primary index used to assess treatment effectiveness. Frequency measures have proved to be sensitive measures of the changes that accompany peer intervention programs, but may obscure important information depending on the level of analysis. Most investigators use molar variables, such as initiation and response rates, to evaluate the effects of treatment on children's interaction patterns. Clearly, when one starts with interaction rates near zero, one can expect increased frequency to be associated with more acceptable social behavior. Many other cases are less clearcut, however. For example, children who are identified by their teachers as needing improved communicative interaction skills may exhibit a fair amount of positive interaction. Interaction rates may increase, but it may be the changes in the quality of interaction that are most relevant. As ecobehavioral analyses have indicated, not all communicative acts are equally effective in sustaining interaction (Gable, Hendrickson, & Strain, 1978; Tremblay et al., 1981). Lumping a variety of initiation categories together, for example, may ignore differential effects of communicative acts and how they are expressed. Initiations may vary in demand characteristics as determined by variables such as the status of speaker and listener, the politeness or directness of requests, or presuppositions about the desirability of different activities.

Increased rates alone may not always represent the most important improvements in interaction. Examples of other potentially important considerations abound. Decreases in negative social behavior, nonsocial utterances, or talking to adults may have profound influences on the sociability of children with disabilities. Increasingly long periods of interaction and greater variety in communicative acts may prove to be more significant clinically than increases in the number of communicative acts, which may capture merely an increase in the number of brief, stereotypic acts. A number of investigators (Garvey & BenDebba, 1974; Kramer, Bukowski, & Garvey, 1989; Schober-Peterson & Johnson, 1989) have pointed out how communicative partners contribute equally to communicative interaction. This may be an important measure of quality of interaction. Changes in nonverbal communication, which have not been examined comprehensively, may also be important for children with severe disabilities.

Given the early success in applying peer intervention approaches to the promotion of communicative interaction, better methods of assessing treatment effects should be developed. In selecting a measure of behavior change, researchers should keep in mind the difficulties in collecting observational data. These challenges include contending with quiet voices and speech that is not completely intelligible in noisy environments and observing simultaneous interactions. Goldstein and his colleagues (1986, 1987) have found it useful to supplement live recordings with a review of videotapes or audiotapes that were recorded using wireless microphones and multitrack tape recorders in order to obtain reliable communicative interaction data. In structured situations, it is possible, although expensive, to describe the behavior of peers and adults without disabilities as well as children with disabilities in detail. Because of the high cost of such tracking, practitioners may choose to restrict their assessments of treatment effects to the monitoring of initiations and responses by one child at a time.

The effects of peer intervention would be expected to be reflected in other measures of social behavior as well. For example, investigators have examined changes in sociometric ratings among peers. These methods have not been used often, mainly because of the unreliability of ratings by preschool children. Asher, Singleton, Tinsley, and Hymel (1979) have developed a set of procedures that yield a sociometric measure with good test–retest reliability when each child in a class rates all classmates according to a specified type of interaction. The assumption behind sociometric ratings is that as a consequence of peer intervention classmates would find children with disabilities more desirable to play with.

Finally, we would hope that the increased use of social validation measures in the behavior analysis literature will allow more examinations of the acceptability of outcomes of peer interventions. Parents, teachers, and even classmates might be asked to rate samples of communicative interaction taped before and after treatment. Ratings should assess the degree to which changes in interaction are perceptible to significant others. Raters might also indicate their perception of the potential for children with disabilities to succeed in normalized social environments before and after treatment.

TRAINING INTERACTION SKILLS
DIRECTLY TO CHILDREN WITH DISABILITIES

The focus on peer intervention in this chapter may seem to skirt an obvious question: why not teach children with disabilities communicative interaction skills directly? We would expect peer intervention to be more effective when direct teaching of communication and social skills is incorporated within early intervention programming. It may be unreasonable to expect general improvements in children's interactions and relationships unless children with disabilities are learning new skills. Peer intervention does provide a context for learning new social and communication skills. Peers model behaviors that children with disabilities can learn observationally. They may provide verbal instructions and prompts, and may differentially reinforce desired social behavior, contributing to a shaping of new behavior. But peer intervention is not as well suited to the learning of new skills as it is to setting the occasion for the generalization of existing skills. Therefore, peer intervention should be included within a more comprehensive program of communication training that includes adult-administered teaching components.

It is inappropriate to contemplate peer intervention approaches without considering other instructional domains addressed within early intervention settings. For example, other language skills, such as receptive and expressive vocabulary, semantic relations, morphology, and syntax, are taught. Greater emphasis may need to be placed on programming generalized use of those skills in interactions with other children. Although social skills (e.g., saying "please" and "thank you," learning how to share and how to resolve conflicts, respecting the rights or acknowledging the feelings of others) may be addressed episodically within the early intervention curriculum, this training approach may not be sufficient to produce significant improvements in interactive behavior and peer acceptance during play times. A peer intervention component is likely to produce better results than those attained through this type of adult-mediated teaching alone. The coupling of social skills training with peer intervention has proven profitable with older children (e.g., Ladd, 1981; Oden & Asher, 1977), but researchers have rarely employed this tactic with preschool children (Factor & Schilmoeller, 1983).

The paucity of studies that have attempted to teach children with disabilities critical skills for interacting with peers may be attributable to the difficulty in pinpointing which skills should be taught. Relatively little is known about the specific skills that are needed to converse effectively with other children. Clearly, more research is needed to identify initiation skills that can be taught effectively and that are successful in evoking positive responses from peers. The application of an ecobehavioral approach like the one used to identify facilitative strategies for peers may prove valuable in identifying strategies to teach to children with disabilities.

Nevertheless, it may not always be necessary to teach interaction skills directly, even with children with severe disabilities. One can argue that peer intervention is only effective to the extent that children with disabilities are provided sufficient opportunities to display communicative skills that exist (at least in some rudimentary way) in other children's behavioral repertoires (Strain, 1983). Clearly, providing a receptive context for interaction with peers allows children with disabilities the opportunity to practice previously acquired or trained behavior. It also provides an opportunity for peers to be exposed to improvements in social and communicative skills in children with disabilities that might otherwise go unnoticed and therefore unreinforced. This opportunity for peers to perceive their classmates with disabilities in new ways may enhance social acceptance.

EDUCATIONAL AND CLINICAL IMPLICATIONS

In this chapter, we have shown how focusing on communicative interaction provides an alternative way of examining social interaction among preschool children. This shift in emphasis leads to different types of analyses and, ultimately, to different strategies that can be taught to peers without disabilities so that the frequency and quality of their interaction with children with disabilities might be improved. We have also shown how ecobehavioral analysis strengthens the identification, implementation, and measurement of the facilitative strategies that are taught to children without disabilities. The clinical and educational implications of these complementary approaches can be explored by identifying some of the advantages and disadvantages.

Communication is defined as the exchange of information between people (Siegel-Causey & Guess, 1989). Such a focus implies that each of the individuals involved has a part to play in the interaction—each implicitly has a turn to take or a role to fill (initiator or responder) and such exchanges of information have no set limits. The interchange may go on for as long as the children involved are interested in participating in their changing reciprocal roles. Through communicative interaction training, peers without disabilities can begin to set positive expectations that their friends with disabilities have something to contribute even though their contribution may be different from theirs. Training involves helping peers without disabilities to identify and perhaps even to appreciate the ways in which their less developmentally sophisticated friends take their communicative turns. The peers need to learn that they play a role as a responder as well as an initiator, and that there is a balance to be struck between the two. This relieves the burden of always playing the role of initiator, and gives them an understanding that part of their communicative role is to be a watcher and listener.

Through systematic language training and other interactions with adults, many children with social and language impairments learn to exert control over adults in their social environment. If children without disabilities demonstrate interest and responsiveness, then children with disabilities may begin to realize that they also can exert control over other children in their environment. Within a play context, they can learn that they can affect other children by using language repertoires similar to those previously trained and displayed with adults. In this way, the opportunity to engage in social interaction with classmates provides additional opportunities for the generalization and maintenance of functional language skills that otherwise might be displayed only with adults.

Nonobligatory communication also deserves some consideration. One of the major differences in adult–child and child–child interaction patterns is the mutuality of interests and egalitarian relationships among children (Paul, 1985). The nature of adult–child interaction, especially with the adult acting as manager or teacher, usually places greater demands on child performance (e.g., expecting "accurate" and adequate responses to questions and requests) and heightens the contrast in interaction patterns. Furthermore, the research on children without disabilities cited earlier suggests that the type of child–child communication that places obligatory demands (e.g., commands, questions) is embedded in a context characterized by a higher frequency of nonobligatory communication (e.g., comments). This suggests the need to develop similar communicative patterns among children with and children without disabilities. This type of low-demand communicative interaction scheme may provide advantages to both groups of children. Children without disabilities need not subjugate their own play desires to the same extent (e.g., giving their toy to another child or just trying to interest another child in what they are doing). Pressure to get the children with disabilities to respond in very specific ways (e.g., answering questions, responding nonverbally to a command) is also reduced. Thus, a nonresponse or incorrect response on the part of the child with disabilities may seem like less of a failure to both children. This type of situation also gives children with disabilities an opportunity to use their skills in a less demanding environment.

Finally, our review of the literature on preschool children demonstrates that they adapt their communicative behaviors to those of their conversational partners. Children without disabilities who are enrolled in integrated preschools and participate in peer-mediated interventions have an opportunity to enhance these skills. The communicative interaction skills learned for purposes of interacting with their classmates with disabilities are the same types of skills that may improve their communicative effectiveness with other peers, siblings, and adults without disabilities. Through discussion of ways to converse more effectively, children without disabilities may learn additional metalinguistic skills that may enhance their social, cognitive, and language abilities. Such communication training could represent creative, developmentally appropriate aspects of the integrated preschool curriculum that go beyond what is traditionally offered in preschools for children without disabilities.

The disadvantages to the peer-mediated intervention approach lie in the lack of easily implemented, classroom-ready instructional procedures and the lack of a thorough research foundation. Teachers and clinicians who wish to implement peer-mediated communicative interventions will find little published curricular support available. Pending such support, the procedures outlined here should prove useful. Three general strategies seem to hold particular promise:

1. Peers without disabilities can be taught to adopt the interest of a child with disabilities or to redirect the attention of the child with disabilities so that a shared focus of attention is established.
2. Peers without disabilities can be encouraged to be observant of ongoing activities and to talk about them to children with disabilities.
3. Peers without disabilities need to be taught how to detect both obvious and subtle verbal and nonverbal communicative attempts by children with disabilities and to respond to those attempts to set the stage for sustained interaction.

Teaching these strategies and encouraging their use may not always be sufficient to develop long-term relationships between children with and children without disabilities. Peer intervention approaches do provide experiences in which all children can learn skills necessary for effective social functioning. Refinements in sensitivity to cues in social situations and in the expression of critical social skills or the avoidance of penalizing social behaviors take a long time for children without disabilities to master. Thus, peer-mediated intervention procedures represent only one tactic for reversing the deleterious effects of social isolation and social withdrawal among children with disabilities. Even when significant improvements are associated with peer intervention, attention still may need to be directed to the development of more sophisticated skills given the complexities inherent in communicative interaction.

DIRECTIONS FOR FUTURE RESEARCH

This chapter recommends the use of ecobehavioral analyses to develop a stronger empirical basis for peer intervention research. A relatively small sample of dyadic interactions constituted the data set analyzed in the descriptive study (Ferrell, 1990), and relationships among a taxonomy of communicative acts and setting events were examined. It may be useful to examine only certain aspects of communication in greater detail. Comments, for example, could be investigated to determine the variety of comment types and how their production influences conversation. Influences on conversations that go beyond relationships between adjacent acts could also be examined. Alternatively, it might be profitable to focus on particular situations (e.g., conversational breakdowns).

The need for descriptive research should not distract us from the second phase of ecobehavioral research. We must conduct experiments to examine the effects of variables suspected to influence interaction. A number of aspects of peer interventions that are currently under development have been outlined: the selection of facilitative strategies, procedures for training strategies, and procedures for promoting more independent and more pervasive strategy use. Adaptation to these intervention methods will be needed as they are applied to a variety of populations. For example, greater emphasis on nonverbal communication may be needed in adapting peer intervention procedures for children with less sophisticated linguistic skills. Peer intervention could also involve older children, siblings, or other children with mild disabilities, as well as preschool children without disabilities. Thus, an important line of research will attempt to produce more effective treatment packages and assess the bounds of effectiveness in different situations.

More information on the effects of peer intervention needs to be generated. Little research has addressed the effects of peers as intervention agents. Most investigators have reported favorable or neutral effects, but short- and long-term changes in social behavior and community adjustment have not been examined. Investigations of long-term effects of interventions designed to promote communicative interaction might examine sociometric status, friendship building, and other indices of interpersonal relationships for peers without disabilities as well as children with disabilities. It will be important to ensure that improved interaction patterns with peers generalize to interaction skills with other children and adults in other environments.

Preschool children without disabilities are likely to respond in different ways to variations in their classmates' behavior. In order to engage in optimal conversational interchanges, each child might be expected to take multiple turns. Unfortunately, our current technology does not necessarily optimize sustained conversation. A variety of strategies could be explored:

1. Following a peer intervention study, successful interactions could be examined to identify the behaviors of children with disabilities that contribute most reliably to sustained interaction. That is, once interaction patterns appear optimal, ecobehavioral analyses may reveal facilitative strategies that could be taught directly to children with disabilities. This research strategy should help investigators select behaviors typically

present in the repertoires of children with disabilities that can be prompted and reinforced in appropriate contexts.

2. Critical deficiencies in behavior that could be taught directly (e.g., learning to acknowledge verbalizations by peers) could be identified.
3. Behavioral excesses that impede the maintenance of interaction could be reduced.
4. Controlled observations could be conducted to generate hypotheses about the conditions responsible for maintenance of patterns of maladaptive behavior to determine whether these behaviors function communicatively. Carr and Durand (1985) demonstrated this strategy by systematically evaluating whether behavior problems were associated with high- or low-task difficulty or high or low teacher attention. These assessments distinguished between children whose misbehavior was escape motivated and children whose behavior was attention motivated. Following this functional analysis it was possible to select alternative behaviors more astutely. Subsequent experimental analyses confirmed that when appropriate communicative behaviors were taught, misbehavior virtually disappeared in those contexts.

CONCLUSION

As methods for enhancing the successful mainstreaming of children with developmental disabilities are developed, the likelihood that such children will be accepted by the society at large increases. Being able to initiate and respond appropriately in conversational contexts seems a critical skill for the development of meaningful social relationships and for taking advantage of opportunities to participate fully in community contexts or least restrictive environments. Indeed, the pervasiveness of communicative interaction skills points out the need for research with adults with disabilities, as well as longitudinal research with children receiving early intervention.

REFERENCES

Allen, K.E., Hart, B.M., Buell, J.S., Harris, F.R., & Wolf, M.M. (1971). Effects of social reinforcement on isolated behavior of a nursery school child. *Child Development, 35,* 511–518.

Asher, S.R., Singleton, L.C., Tinsley, B.R., & Hymel, S. (1979). A reliable sociometric measure for preschool children. *Developmental Psychology, 15,* 443–444.

Austin, J. (1962). *How to do things with words.* London: Oxford University Press.

Bailey, D.B., Jr., & McWilliam, R. A. (1990). Normalizing early intervention. *Topics in Early Childhood Special Education, 10*(2), 33–48.

Beckman, P. (1983). The relationship between behavioral characteristics of children and social interaction in an integrated setting. *Journal of the Division for Early Childhood, 7,* 69–77.

Beckman, P., & Kohl, F.L. (1984). The effects of social and isolate toys on the interactions and play of integrated and nonintegrated groups of preschoolers. *Education and Training of the Mentally Retarded, 19,* 169–175.

Brinton, B., & Fujiki, M. (1984). Development of topic manipulation skills in discourse. *Journal of Speech and Hearing Research, 27,* 350–358.

Brown, W., Bryson-Brockmann, W., & Fox, J. (1986). The usefulness of J.R. Kantor's setting event concept for research on children's social behavior. *Child and Family Behavior Therapy, 8*(2), 15–25.

Brown, W.H., Fox, J.J., & Brady, M.P. (1987). The effects of spatial density on socially directed behaviors of 3- and 4-year old children during freeplay: An investigation of a setting factor. *Education and Treatment of Children, 10,* 247–258.

Bruner, J.S. (1974/5). From communication to language—A psychological perspective. *Cognition, 3,* 225–287.

Bruner, J.S. (1975). The ontogenesis of speech acts. *Journal of Child Language, 2,* 1–19.

Carr, E.G., & Durand, V.M. (1985). Reducing behavior problems through functional communication training. *Journal of Applied Behavior Analysis, 18,* 111–126.

Day, R., Powell, T., Dy-Lin, E., & Stowitschek, J. (1982). An evaluation of the effects of a social interaction training package on mentally handicapped preschool children. *Education and Training of the Mentally Retarded, 17,* 125–130.

Devoney, C., Guralnick, M.J., & Rubin, H. (1974). Integrating handicapped and nonhandicapped preschool children: Effects on social play. *Childhood Education, 50,* 360–364.

Dore, J. (1974). A pragmatic description of early language development. *Journal of Psycholinguistic Research, 3,* 343–350.

Dore, J. (1975). Holophrases, speech acts and language universals. *Journal of Child Language, 2,* 21–40.

Factor, D.C., & Schilmoeller, G.L. (1983). Social skill training of preschool children. *Child Study Journal, 13,* 41 56.

Fagot, B.I. (1977). Variations in density: Effect on task and social behaviors of preschool children. *Developmental Psychology, 12,* 166–167.

Faught, K.K., Balleweg, B.J., Crow, R.E., & Van den Pol, R.A. (1983). An analysis of the social behaviors of handicapped and nonhandicapped preschool children. *Education and Training of the Mentally Retarded, 18,* 210–214.

Ferrell, D.R. (1990). *Communicative interaction between handicapped and nonhandicapped preschool children: Identifying facilitative strategies.* Unpublished doctoral dissertation, University of Pittsburgh.

Fewell, R. (1986). A handicapped child in the family. In R. Fewell & P. Vadasy (Eds.), *Families of handicapped children: Needs and supports across the life span* (pp. 3–34). Austin, TX: PRO-ED.

Gable, R., Hendrickson, J.M., & Strain, P.S. (1978). Assessment, modification, and generalization of social interaction among severely retarded, multihandicapped children. *Education and Training of the Mentally Retarded, 13,* 279–286.

Garvey, C. (1974). Some properties of social play. *Merrill-Palmer Quarterly, 20,* 163–180.

Garvey, C., & BenDebba, M. (1974). Effects of age, sex, and partner on children's dyadic speech. *Child Development, 45,* 1159–1161.

George, S.W., & Krantz, M. (1981). The effects of preferred partnerships on communication adequacy. *Journal of Psychology, 109,* 245–253.

Goetz, E.M., Thomson, C.L., & Etzel, B.C. (1975). An analysis of direct and indirect teacher attention and primes in the modification of child social behavior: A case study. *Merrill-Palmer Quarterly, 21,* 55–65.

Goldstein, H., & Ferrell, D.R. (1987). Augmenting communicative interaction between handicapped and nonhandicapped preschoolers. *Journal of Speech and Hearing Disorders, 19,* 200–211.

Goldstein, H., & Wickstrom, S. (1986). Peer intervention effects on communicative interaction among handicapped and nonhandicapped preschoolers. *Journal of Applied Behavior Analysis, 19,* 209–214.

Goncu, A., & Kessel, F. (1984). Children's play: A contextual-functional perspective. *New Directions for Child Development, 25,* 5–22.

Greenwood, C., Delquadri, J., & Hall, R.V. (1984). Opportunity to respond and student academic performance. In W. Heward, T. Heron, D. Hill, J. Trap-Porter (Eds.), *Focus on behavior analysis in education* (pp. 58–88). Columbus, OH: Bell & Howell.

Greenwood, C.R., Delquadri, J., & Hall, R.V. (1989). Longitudinal effects of classwide peer tutoring. *Journal of Educational Psychology, 81,* 371–383.

Guralnick, M.J. (1976). The value of integrating handicapped and nonhandicapped preschool children. *American Journal of Orthopsychiatry, 42,* 236–245.

Guralnick, M.J. (1990). Major accomplishments and future directions in early childhood mainstreaming, *Topics in Early Childhood Special Education, 10*(2), 1–18.

Guralnick, M.J., & Groom, J.M. (1988). Peer interactions in mainstreamed and specialized classrooms: A comparative analysis. *Exceptional Children, 5,* 415–425.

Guralnick, M.J., & Paul-Brown, D. (1977). The nature of verbal interactions among handicapped and nonhandicapped preschool children. *Child Development, 48,* 254–260.

Guralnick, M.J., & Paul-Brown, D. (1980). Functional and discourse analyses of nonhandicapped preschool children's speech to handicapped children. *American Journal of Mental Deficiency, 84,* 444–454.

Guralnick, M.J., & Paul-Brown, D. (1984). Communicative adjustments during behavior request episodes among children at different developmental levels. *Child Development, 55,* 911–919.

Guralnick, M.J., & Paul-Brown, D. (1986). Communicative interactions of mildly delayed and normally developing preschool children: Effects of listeners developmental level. *Journal of Speech and Hearing Research, 29,* 2–10.

Hartup, W.W. (1976). Peer interaction and the behavioral development of the individual child. In E. Shopler & R. Reichler (Eds.), *Psychopathology and child development* (pp. 203–218). New York: Plenum Press.

Hartup, W.W. (1983). Peer relations. In E.M. Hetherington (Ed.), *Handbook of child psychology: Vol. 4. Socialization, personality and social development* (pp. 103–196). New York: John Wiley & Sons.

Hartup, W.W. (1989). Social relationships and their developmental significance. *American Psychologist, 44,* 120–126.

Hendrickson, J.M., Strain, P.S., Tremblay, A., & Shores, R.E. (1982). Interactions of behaviorally handicapped children: Functional effects of peer social initiations. *Behavior Modification, 6,* 323–352.

Horner, R., Bellamy, G.T., & Colvin, G. (1984). Responding in the presence of nontrained stimuli: Implications of generalization error patterns. *Journal of The Association for Persons with Severe Handicaps, 9,* 287–295.

Kinsman, C.A., & Berk, L.E. (1979). Joining the block and housekeeping areas: Changes in play and social behavior. *Young Children, 39,* 66–75.

Kohl, F.L., & Beckman, P.J. (1984). A comparison of handicapped and nonhandicapped preschoolers' interactions across classroom activities. *Journal of the Division for Early Childhood, 8,* 49–56.

Kohn, M. (1966). The child as a determinant of his peers' approach to him. *Journal of Genetic Psychology, 109,* 91–100.

Kramer, T., Bukowski, W., & Garvey, C. (1989). The influence of the dyadic context on the conversational and linguistic behavior of its members. *Merrill-Palmer Quarterly, 35,* 327–341.

Ladd, G.W. (1981). Effectiveness of a social learning method for enhancing children's social interaction and peer acceptance. *Child Development, 52,* 171–178.

Loo, C.M. (1972). The effects of spatial density on the social behavior of children. *Journal of Applied Social Psychology, 2,* 372–381.

McEvoy, M.A., Nordquist, M.M., Twardosz, S., Heckaman, K.A., Wehby, J.H., & Kenton, D.R. (1988). Promoting autistic children's peer interaction in an integrated early childhood setting using affection activities. *Journal of Applied Behavior Analysis, 21,* 193–200.

McGrew, P.L. (1970). Social and spatial density effects on spacing behavior in preschool children. *Journal of Child Psychology and Psychiatry, 2,* 197–205.

McLean, M., & Hanline, M.F. (1990). Providing early intervention services in integrated environments: Challenges and opportunities for the future. *Topics in Early Childhood Special Education, 10*(2), 62–78.

Mueller, E. (1972). The maintenance of verbal exchanges between young children. *Child Development, 43,* 930–938.

Mueller, E., Bleier, M., Krakow, J., Hegedus, K., & Cournoyer, P. (1977). The development of peer verbal interaction among two-year-old boys. *Child Development, 48,* 284–287.

Nieptupski, J., Stainback, W., Gleissner, L., Stainback, S., & Hamre-Nietupski, S. (1982). Effects of socially outgoing versus withdrawn nonhandicapped peer partners on nonhandicapped/handicapped student interactions. *Behavior Modification, 6,* 244–250.

O'Connell, J.C. (1984). Preschool integration and its effects on the social interaction of handicapped and nonhandicapped children: A review. *Journal of the Division for Early Childhood, 8,* 38–49.

O'Connor, M. (1975). The nursery school environment. *Developmental Psychology, 11,* 556–561.

Oden, S., & Asher, S.R. (1977). Coaching children in social skills for friendship making. *Child Development, 48,* 495–506.

Odom, S.L., Hoyson, M., Jamieson, B., & Strain, P.S. (1985). Increasing handicapped preschoolers' peer social interactions: Cross-setting and component analysis. *Journal of Applied Behavior Analysis, 18,* 3–16.

Odom, S.L., & McEvoy, M.A. (1990). Barriers and tasks for the field. *Topics in Early Childhood Special Education, 10*(2), 48–62.

Odom, S.L., Strain, P.S., Karger, M.A., & Smith, J. (1986). Using single and multiple peers to promote social interaction of preschool children with handicaps. *Journal of the Division for Early Childhood, 10,* 53–64.

Odom, S.L., & Warren, S.F. (1988). Early childhood special education in the year 2000. *Journal of the Division for Early Childhood, 2*(2), 56–59.

Parten, M.B. (1932). Social participation among preschool children. *Journal of Abnormal and Social Psychology, 27,* 243–269.

Paul, L. (1985). Programming peer support for functional language. In S. Warren & A.K. Rogers-Warren (Eds.), *Teaching functional language* (pp. 289–307). Austin, TX: PRO-ED.

Peterson, N.L., & Haralick, J.G. (1977). Integration of handicapped and nonhandicapped preschoolers: An analysis of play behavior and social interaction. *Education and Training of the Mentally Retarded, 12,* 234–235.

Porter, R.H., Ramsey, B., Tremblay, A., Iaceobo, M., & Crawley, S. (1978). Social interaction in heterogeneous groups of retarded and normally developing children: An observational study. In G.P. Sackett (Ed.), *Observing behavior: Theory and application in mental retardation* (Vol. 1, pp. 311–328). Baltimore: University Park Press.

Quilitch, M.R., & Risley, T.R. (1973). The effects of play materials on social play. *Journal of Applied Behavior Analysis, 6,* 573–578.

Ragland, E.U., Kerr, M.M., & Strain, P.S. (1978). Behavior of withdrawn autistic children: Effects of peer social initiations. *Behavior Modification, 2,* 565–578.

Sainato, D.M., Goldstein, H., & Strain, P.S. (in press). Effects of self-monitoring on preschool children's use of social interaction strategies with their autistic peers. *Journal of Applied Behavior Analysis.*

Salisbury, C.L., & Vincent, L.J. (1990). Mainstreaming and integration 10 years later. *Topics in Early Childhood Special Education, 10*(2), 78–90.

Schober-Peterson, D., & Johnson, C. (1989). Conversational topics of 4-year-olds. *Journal of Speech and Hearing Research, 32,* 857–870.

Schwartzman, H.B. (1978). *Transformations: The anthropology of children's play.* New York: Plenum Press.

Searle, J. (1969). *Speech acts.* Cambridge: Cambridge University Press.

Shafer, M.S., Egel, A.L., & Neef, N.A. (1984). Training mildly handicapped peers to facilitate changes in the social interaction skills of autistic children. *Journal of Applied Behavior Analysis, 17,* 461–476.

Shatz, M., & Gelman, R. (1973). The development of communication skills: Modifications in the speech of young children as a function of listener. *Monographs of the Society for Research in Child Development, 38,* 1–37.

Shores, R.E., Hester, P., & Strain, P.S. (1976). The effects of amount and type of teacher-child interaction on child-child interaction. *Psychology in the Schools, 13,* 171–175.

Siegel-Causey, E., & Guess, D. (1989). *Enhancing nonsymbolic communication interactions among learners with severe disabilities.* Baltimore: Paul H. Brookes Publishing Co.

Spilton, D., & Lee, L.C. (1977). Some determinants of effective communication in four-year-olds. *Child Development, 48,* 968–977.

Strain, P.S. (1977). Effects of peer social initiations on withdrawn preschool children: Some training and generalization effects. *Journal of Abnormal Child Psychology, 5,* 445–455.

Strain, P.S. (1983). Generalization of autistic children's social behavior change: Effects of developmentally integrated and segregated settings. *Analysis and Intervention in Developmental Disabilities, 3,* 23–34.

Strain, P.S., Kerr, M.M., & Ragland, E.U. (1979). Effects of peer-mediated social initiations and prompting/reinforcement procedures on the social behavior of autistic children. *Journal of Autism and Developmental Disorders, 9,* 41–54.

Strain, P.S., Shores, R.E., & Timm, M.A. (1977). Effects of peer social initiations on the behavior of withdrawn preschool children. *Journal of Applied Behavior Analysis, 10,* 289–298.

Tomasello, M., & Farrar, M.J. (1986). Joint attention and early language. *Child Development, 57,* 1454–1463.

Tremblay, A., Strain, P., Hendrickson, J.M., & Shores, R.E. (1981). Social interactions of normal preschool children: Using normative data for subject and target behavior selection. *Behavior Modification, 5,* 237–253.

Van den Pol, R.A., Crow, R.E., Rider, D.P., & Offner, R.B. (1985). Social interaction in an integrated preschool: Implications and applications. *Topics in Early Childhood Special Education, 4*(4), 59–76.

Vincent, L.J., Brown, L., & Getz-Sheftel, M. (1981). Integrating handicapped and typical children during the preschool years: The definition of best educational practice. *Topics in Early Childhood Special Education, 1*(1), 17–25.

Wahler, R.G. (1967). Child-child interactions in free field settings: Some experimental analyses. *Journal of Experimental Child Psychology, 5*, 278–293.

Wanska, S., Bedrosian, J., & Pohlman, J. (1986). Effects of play materials on topic performance of preschool children. *Language, Speech, and Hearing Services in Schools, 17*, 152–159.

Welkowitz, J., Cariffe, G., & Feldstein, S. (1976). Socialization in children. *Child Development, 47*, 269–272.

Young, C.C., & Kerr, M.M. (1979). The effects of a retarded child's social initiations on the behavior of severely retarded school-aged peers. *Education and Training of the Mentally Retarded, 14*, 185–190.

5

Developing Augmented Language in Children with Severe Mental Retardation

Mary Ann Romski and Rose A. Sevcik

Aᴸᴹᴏˢᴛ ᴇꜰꜰᴏʀᴛᴸᴇˢˢᴸʏ, ᴀʀᴏᴜɴᴅ ᴛʜᴇ ʙᴇɢɪɴɴɪɴɢ of the second year of life, first words emerge in children without disabilities (Bates, 1979; Bruner, 1983). These words are framed within the child's earlier comprehension of speech in context (Benedict, 1979). By 20 months of age, children quickly expand their vocabularies to include more than 50 words (Nelson, 1973); they then begin to combine words and develop into competent multiword communicators (Brown, 1973).

In sharp contrast, children with severe mental retardation experience great difficulty acquiring their first words (Romski & Sevcik, 1988a, in press). Unlike many other learners with disabilities (e.g., children with vision or hearing impairments), the majority of children with severe retardation fail to develop functional spoken words even after considerable speech and language instruction. By way of contrast, most other learners with cognitive disabilities do gain functional expressive language skills following instruction (see Rosenberg, 1982, for a review of the literature on this topic). For the most part, traditional instructional approaches to teaching spoken language have not been successful with learners with severe mental retardation. Consequently, most teaching efforts have focused on augmenting spoken language (e.g., with manual signs, visual-graphic symbols) to facilitate language development. As a result of this pressing clinical/educational need, the course of

Preparation of this chapter and the research described within were funded by Grant No. 06016 from the National Institute of Child Health and Human Development, which sustains the Language Research Center cooperatively operated by Georgia State University and the Yerkes Regional Primate Research Center of Emory University. Additional support was provided by the College of Arts and Sciences, Georgia State University and by Grant No. RR-00165 to the Yerkes Center. The authors gratefully acknowledge the children who participated in this study, their families, and the Clayton County school personnel for their enthusiastic cooperation during the conduct of the study reported in this chapter.

augmented language development has largely been ignored. Specifying the developmental process will permit researchers and practitioners alike to study the substance and progression of language skills being learned as well as the mechanisms that might contribute to their acquisition. Even more importantly, by studying the developmental process, researchers will be able to identify principles that permit modification and/or advancement of current augmented language learning approaches.

Children with severe mental retardation who do not speak have long challenged researchers and practitioners alike (McLean, Yoder, & Schiefelbusch, 1970; Schiefelbusch, 1980; Schiefelbusch & Hollis, 1979). Early research suggested that the auditory-vocal modalities may be at the foundation of the language learning difficulty for learners with severe retardation (Romski, Lloyd, & Sevcik, 1988; Romski & Sevcik, 1988a; Schiefelbusch & Hollis, 1979). Researchers posited that if the modality in which the child hears and produces language was altered, the child would readily acquire language production skills (see Romski, Sevcik, & Joyner, 1984, for a discussion of this issue). Modifying the modalities from auditory-vocal (i.e., speech) to visual-manual (i.e., signs) offered promising results for some children with mental retardation. Even after changing the modality, however, a large number of children did not acquire language. These nonlearners, as they were judged, called attention to the complexity of the learning process as well as the influence that the child, the environment, and their interrelationships may exert on the outcomes of augmented language instruction.

While information about language acquisition in children without disabilities highlights the course of development, it is sometimes difficult to devise instructional strategies from phenomena that occur spontaneously. Nonhuman primate research can provide another framework based on instructional information, including environmental manipulations gained via the use of a communication device (Romski, 1989; Romski & Savage-Rumbaugh, 1986).

WHAT SKILLS DO NONSPEAKING CHILDREN BRING TO THE LANGUAGE LEARNING TASK?

Historically, research on augmented language has grouped together all children with severe retardation who do not speak. Over the years, however, the heterogeneity of this group has been recognized. Their profiles vary depending on their natural endowments, their environments, and their experiences. Learners with different characteristics interact differently with instructional strategies to influence communicative outcomes. Among the factors that affect communicative competence are related disabilities, communicative experience, speech comprehension skills, and vocal production skills.

Cognitive Development and Related Disabilities

In the past, children with severe mental retardation were frequently excluded from language instruction because their assessed levels of intelligence and their sensorimotor development were not commensurate with cognitive and sensorimotor skills that had been linked to early language development (Romski & Sevcik, 1988a; Sheehan, Martyn, & Kilburn, 1968). While one may argue that some basic cognitive skills are essential for language to develop, the precise relationship between the domains of cognition and language have not been specified (see Rice, 1983; Rice & Kemper, 1984, for reviews). Thus, more recently, investigators have argued against excluding children from language instruction based upon intellectual performance and/or prerequisite sensorimotor skills (Kangas & Lloyd, 1988; Reichle & Karlan, 1988; Romski & Sevcik, 1988a). Given the overall impact language exerts on cognitive development, a lack of productive language skills may put a child at a distinct developmental disadvantage (Rice & Kemper, 1984). Developing language skills becomes of critical importance if the child is to make functional cognitive gains.

A range of related disabilities may accompany severe mental retardation. These may include cerebral palsy, seizure disorders, sensory impairments, or maladaptive behaviors. Each of these disabilities may have additional influences on the child's communicative profile and on his or her ability to learn language skills (Guess & Horner, 1978; Snell, 1987).

Communicative Experience

Experience is often overlooked when characterizing the child factors that may affect instructional outcomes. Because children who are candidates for augmented language do not demonstrate productive language, it is often presumed that they are functioning below the 12- to 18-month-old developmental level. This presumption often leads to an inaccurate, or perhaps incomplete, description of the child's competencies. Children with severe mental retardation often communicate in a range of alternative ways, and thus sometimes function beyond the sensorimotor stage (Romski, Sevcik, Reumann, & Pate, 1989). These natural communicative repertoires may have been employed for prolonged periods of time, and may have included multiple conversational experiences, communicative partners, and settings that often do not resemble those of 12- to 18-month-old children without disabilities. Instead, such repertoires are used in more variable contexts and perhaps less flexibly than those of young children without disabilities.

Speech Comprehension Skills

The ability to process the speech signal also varies among children with severe retardation. Such children may reveal speech comprehension skills that range from little or no comprehension to comprehension comparable to that of a 3-

or 4-year-old child. Children who do comprehend speech come to the augmented language learning task with knowledge of spoken word referents (Romski & Sevcik, in press; Romski, Sevcik, & Pate, 1988). Learning augmentative language skills may be quite different for these children than it is for children who do not have such a foundation. Children who do not comprehend spoken words must establish conditional relationships between the visual symbols to be learned and their referents while relying almost exclusively on the visual modality (Romski et al., 1988).

Vocal Production Skills

Perhaps one of the most striking findings of the Romski et al. (1989) study was the extent to which the children vocalized naturally, albeit unintelligibly, prior to the introduction of an augmented language device. While vocal skills are not necessary for learning an augmented system, the ability to imitate vocally may play a role in the child's subsequent gains with speech as well as with the augmented language system (Clark, Remington, & Light, 1983; Romski, Sevcik, Robinson, & Wilkinson, 1990; Yoder & Layton, 1988).

WHAT INSTRUCTIONAL FACTORS INFLUENCE THE CHILD'S LANGUAGE LEARNING?

Augmented language approaches were originally considered feasible alternatives to speech for learners with mental retardation because of the visual stimuli such approaches used, which were thought to help focus the child's attention and control perceptual factors (Fristoe & Lloyd, 1979). The teaching approaches that were coupled with the signs or visual-graphic symbols were, at best, highly variable.

Early instructional strategies usually employed highly structured environments and massed discrete trial instruction to teach specific productive lexical or syntactic skills (e.g., Carrier's Non-SLIP program, Carrier, 1974). More recent studies have focused on teaching a single, early developing communicative function (e.g., requesting, labeling) with a small vocabulary under controlled conditions via augmented instructional routes and then probing transfer to another communicative function (e.g., Gobbi, Cipani, Hudson, & Lapenta-Neudeck, 1986; Keogh & Reichle, 1985; Romski et al., 1988). While findings from these more recent studies indicate that such approaches hold promise, a longitudinal and/or developmental perspective to learning has not, for the most part, been examined. One study (Romski et al., 1988) described the establishment of a 20-symbol vocabulary by three institutionalized nonspeaking young women with severe retardation using a communicative request paradigm adapted from research with nonhuman primates (Savage-Rumbaugh, 1986). While initial learning was slow, once the subjects learned how to learn, their rate increased, and transfer to labeling as well as to comprehension emerged. Spontaneous communicative symbol usage also emerged.

Most of the studies described here have emphasized teaching productive language skills using structured approaches. The overall effectiveness of augmented language approaches, however, will ultimately be measured in terms of the child's ability to participate in communicative exchanges with various partners in everyday settings. Thus, the child must be both a competent speaker and a competent listener in communicative exchanges. Two instructional topics that must also be considered, then, are comprehension skills and the instructional setting (Romski & Sevcik, 1988a).

Comprehension Considerations

Symbol production has been perceived as empowering children with the ability to have an immediate and visible effect upon their environment. While this focus may be functional, it may underestimate the other role of the child as a listener (Romski & Sevcik, 1988b). Like the process observed in children without disabilities in developing their first words, comprehension permits the child to observe and to absorb the communicative process prior to actually taking on the role of speaker (Huttenlocher, 1974). Augmented language approaches require a carefully balanced blend of receptive and productive experiences with symbols. Although an adequate accounting of the relative roles of comprehension and production in the long-term augmented language learning process is still needed, relationships between the instructional approaches employed and the subsequent outcomes must be considered if optimal learning environments are to be available for augmented language acquisition.

Setting Considerations

Another issue that demands attention is the setting in which instruction takes place. Since the 1970s the philosophical emphasis has been on integrating language instructional approaches into naturalistic teaching settings. This shift has reflected the impact of pragmatics—the use of language in context—from the child language acquisition literature (McLean & Snyder-McLean, 1988; Warren & Kaiser, 1986) and of generalization of learned language skills to natural environments from the behavioral literature (Warren & Kaiser, 1986; Warren & Rogers-Warren, 1985).

Instructional procedures such as milieu teaching (Hart & Rogers-Warren, 1978), incidental teaching (Warren & Kaiser, 1986), and the integrative model of natural environmental teaching (mand-model + time delay + incidental teaching, Halle, 1982) were developed to facilitate the transfer of spoken language learning from its instructional environment to the natural environment. As Halle (1982) has carefully noted, no single procedure alone can facilitate functional communication. Taken as an instructional package, however, these three procedures may promote spoken communication in natural settings.

Although contemporary theory recommends the use of augmented language devices in natural environments (Calculator, 1988), to date only one study has demonstrated the effectiveness of these procedures for augmented language learning (Oliver & Halle, 1982). The ability to integrate milieu instructional methods within natural settings offers great promise for teaching language to nonspeaking children with severe retardation (Robinson, Wilkinson, Sevcik, & Romski, 1990).

LONGITUDINAL INVESTIGATION
OF AUGMENTED LANGUAGE LEARNING

In order to understand the natural augmented language learning process, we conducted a longitudinal study of symbol acquisition and use (Romski & Sevcik, in press). In this chapter, we limit our discussion to the learning and use of single symbols during the first year of the 2-year investigation.

Thirteen primary and secondary school–age youngsters (mean chronological age = 12 years) with moderate or severe retardation and a severe spoken language impairment and their communicative partners (e.g., parents, teachers), participated in the study. Each learner resided at home and attended the special education program for students with moderate or severe cognitive disabilities of the Clayton County, Georgia, public school system. At the outset of the study, each child had an expressive language repertoire of no more than 10 spoken words intelligible to the classroom teacher. Receptive language skills were variable, ranging from an inability to obtain a basal score on the Peabody Picture Vocabulary Test-Revised (Dunn & Dunn, 1981) to an age equivalent score of 3 years, 5 months.

Naturalistic Communicative Experience

The essential components of the naturalistic augmented communicative experience are summarized in Table 1. Mealtime was chosen as the daily activity during which electronic speech output communication devices were initially used, with additional activities and settings added during the school year.

Children participating were provided with the Words+ Portable Voice II. (This study was initiated prior to the availability of the Speech Pac Eval Unit, AllTalk, Wolf, and IntroTalker. Words+ no longer produces the Personal Voice II and the subjects who participated in this study currently use the SuperWolf.) It was a specially modified portable rechargeable Epson HX-20 notebook computer coupled with an adapted Votrax Personal Speech System voice synthesizer. Since the children in this study could not use the Epson keyboard in the conventional manner due to their inability to read, spell, or write, a Unicorn touch-sensitive display panel was used to access the Words+

Table 1. Components of the augmented language learning approach

• Electronic computer-based speech-output communication devices are available for use in natural communicative environments.

• Appropriate, initially limited, symbol vocabularies with the printed English word above each symbol are placed on the devices.

• Children are encouraged, although not required, to use the device.

• Communicative partners are taught to use the device to augment their speech input to the child with symbol input.

• Ongoing resource and feedback mechanisms are provided to support the communication efforts of the children and their partners.

system via direct selection (i.e., pointing). After a lexigram (i.e., an arbitrary visual-graphic symbol, Rumbaugh, 1977) was activated on the Unicorn panel, the synthesized equivalent of the spoken word for that symbol was produced. The printed English word equivalent of the symbol also appeared in reduced size above the symbol to facilitate partner interpretation and convenience. Since the devices were available for use in natural communicative environments (i.e., home and school), both the children and their partners were able to use the device.

Prior to the introduction of the devices to the children, the partners attended a series of three 1-hour instructional sessions. During these sessions, the partners received instruction in the physical operation of the electronic communication device. Videotapes depicting interactions with the devices were also presented to offer samples of communicative use. Communicative partners were encouraged to integrate the use of the devices into their own spoken language communications by employing what we have described as augmented input. In the example, "Johnny, let's go OUTSIDE and PLAY.", "OUTSIDE" and "PLAY" are symbols on the board and are produced by the synthesizer as well as by the partner. This communicative model was suggested so as to permit each partner to feel comfortable with the device and to incorporate its use into his or her specific interactions. During the sessions, the partners also provided input to the investigators about the choice of specific vocabulary items to be placed on the subjects' Unicorn boards. Initially, vocabulary was selected from food-related words (e.g., Coke, fork, salad). Subsequently, at least 6 months after initial implementation, vocabulary items representing social-regulative words (e.g., more, please), leisure words (e.g., bike, outside) and work-related words (e.g., break time, time clock) were incorporated into the vocabulary.

Communicative use of the device was not taught in the traditional sense. Since instruction was broadly defined as an effort to assist or to shape growth patterns (Bruner, 1966), loosely structured naturalistic communicative experiences were provided to encourage, but not require, the children to use symbols when natural communicative opportunities arose. Research with pygmy chimpanzees (Savage-Rumbaugh, McDonald, Sevcik, Hopkins, & Rupert,

1986) provided the general guidelines on how to manipulate the community environment and which types of skills to teach to conversational partners so that communication could be facilitated. Table 2 provides a sample of a communicative experience.

Since this approach relied heavily on the partners' cooperation and use of the device, ensuring that their perceptions remained positive or interceding to remedy difficulties that arose was a critical component of the successful completion of the study. In order to support the partners' participation in the study, a resource and feedback mechanism was devised and implemented by the investigators. The Teacher/Parent Questionnaire (QUEST) consisted of a questionnaire that provided information about the pattern of communicative use each week, and the accomplishments and/or difficulties that might have been experienced. It was administered to the partners by the investigators on a regular basis in conjunction with the collection of the communicative use probes (CUPs), described in the next section.

Measurements of Symbolic Change

Communicative use in everyday settings necessitated a twofold data collection method that included information about both the child's pattern of use and his symbol learning. CUPs provided information about who the child communicated with, how the child communicated (i.e., which modes), what functions the child's communications served, and how successfully the child used communications and discourse skills (e.g., turn-taking, topic maintenance). Measures of symbol learning, called *vocabulary assessment measures* (VAMs), ascertained what the subjects had learned about the meanings of the symbols they used without the supporting contextual framework.

CUPs consisted of a verbal and a nonverbal communicative sample collected by a nonparticipant observer in the setting of use. The sample consisted of an event-based observational Communication Coding Scheme (CCS), shown in Table 3, and an audiotape of the interaction, that were compiled with

Table 2.   Sample of loosely structured naturalistic communication

M:	And I/'m go/ing to use a [L] {KNIFE} to spread it with.
M:	J, what would you like for a drink?
M:	Tell me what drink you would like.
J:	[3L3S] {JUICE}.
M:	You would?
	I kinda thought so.
	Look what I have at the table.
M:	Look here.
	M holds up the container of orange juice.
M:	I already had some [L] {JUICE}.
	I think I'll shake it.
J:	[1V4S] XX.

Note: All transcripts are presented in SALT format. Codes are from the Communication Coding Scheme (see Table 3).

Table 3. Communication Coding Scheme

Code	Meaning
1	
1.000	Initiation, adult
2.000	Initiation, peer
3.000	Response, adult
4.000	Response, peer
2	
0.W00	Spoken word, intelligible
0.L00	Symbol
0.G00	Gesture
0.V00	Vocalization
0.P00	Physical manipulation
0.A00	Symbol + gesture
0.B00	Word + gesture
0.C00	Vocalization + gesture
0.D00	Symbol + vocalization
0.E00	Symbol + vocalization + gesture
0.F00	Physical manipulation + vocalization
0.H00	Physical manipulation + word
3	
0.000	Imitating
0.010	Greeting
0.020	Naming
0.030	Requesting
0.040	Attention directing
0.050	Questioning
0.060	Answering
0.070	Affirming
0.080	Negating
4	
0.00S	Successful
0.00U	Unsuccessful

Adapted from Romski and Sevcik (1988b).

the SALT (Systematic Analysis of Language Transcripts) computer software program (Chapman & Miller, 1985). Audiotapes were employed to capture the spoken language input of the communicative partners directed to the learners during the CUPs. Since the communication devices produced synthetic speech output, each time a symbol(s) was used, the synthesized word was also heard on the audiotape. This feature permitted the investigators to merge the coded behaviors with the audiotape. As was illustrated in Table 2, the resulting language transcript incorporated both the subjects' and their partners' communications for subsequent analyses.

VAMs consisted of a series of 10 structured tasks administered by the investigators on a monthly basis outside of the settings of communicative use. These tasks, shown in Table 4, included measures of symbol comprehension and production using a nonidentity match-to-sample task format. In addition to providing a comprehensive profile of the child's vocabulary learning over

Table 4. Vocabulary assessment probes

Task	Stimuli	Response
Comprehension	Spoken word	Select photograph[a]
	Synthetic speech	Select photograph
	Symbol	Select photograph
	Printed word	Select photograph
Production	Photograph	Produce spoken word
	Symbol	Produce spoken word
	Photograph	Select symbol
	Spoken word	Select symbol
	Synthetic speech	Select symbol
	Printed word	Select symbol

Adapted from Romski and Sevcik (1988b).

[a]Selection is from a choice of three foils and one target that remain consistent across all tasks.

the course of the study, VAMs measured skills that have been reported to emerge during augmented instruction (e.g., recognition of printed English words, production of intelligible spoken words).

Augmented Language Learning Outcomes

Immersion and use of speech output communication devices within the child's natural communicative environment offered a viable learning opportunity for the participants. All of the subjects acquired and used symbols during communicative exchanges. Across the first school year, 13.9%–70% (mean = 36%) of the children's total sampled utterances included symbol usages.

The subjects incorporated use of the speech output device within their extant communicative repertoires rather than relying on the new device as their only form of communication. For example, one subject vocalized and simultaneously used a symbol to indicate the need for a spoon. Surprisingly, their reliance on natural, unintelligible vocalizations did not change after the introduction of the communication device. Even after intervention the vocal mode accounted for nearly 50% of their utterances, and was often used to gain the attention of their partners. Symbols were employed to encode a variety of messages (e.g., requesting objects or information) and to answer questions directed to them. There was, however, individual variability in the number of different symbols the subjects used and in the extent to which they comprehended and produced symbols outside of the context of use.

At the outset of the study, the subjects differed in their ability to comprehend spoken language. While all subjects understood, in a very general sense, that spoken words represented real items, four of the subjects had not established specific word-referent relationships. On a post hoc basis, the subjects were divided into two groups (low comprehenders, high comprehenders) based on comprehension skills. These two groups were defined by statistically different performance on the Peabody Picture Vocabulary

Test-Revised (Dunn & Dunn, 1981). Low comprehenders did not comprehend spoken words for the initial symbols to be placed on their boards whereas high comprehenders did.

Two distinct symbol learning patterns emerged based on this grouping (Figure 1). Low comprehenders learned to comprehend individual symbols before they produced them. Symbol production skills emerged later in the learning process after comprehension of the symbol was in place, suggesting that low comprehenders learned to comprehend a symbol before learning to produce it. In contrast, high comprehenders learned to comprehend and produce symbols concurrently, suggesting that they employed their extant speech comprehension of the word and transferred it to the symbol with which the word was paired, as in a stimulus equivalence paradigm (see Sidman, 1970; Sidman & Cresson, 1973, for examples). Over the course of the school year, high comprehenders also learned to recognize significantly more symbols than did low comprehenders.

For both groups, comprehension played a major role in the symbol learning process. Understanding some spoken words provided a foundation upon which children who did not speak could grasp relationships between symbols

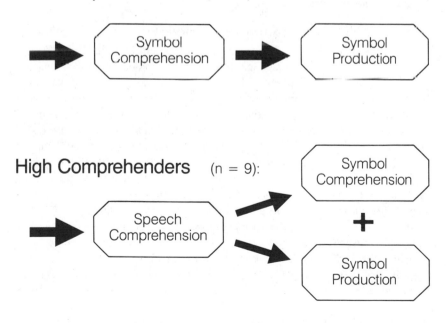

Figure 1. Symbol learning sequence.

and their referents. When a viable productive communicative route (e.g., an electronic device) was made available, they became relatively facile symbol users. For children who did not comprehend speech, learning to understand symbols provided the route by which symbol–referent relationships were established. For these low comprehenders, a production focus may have actually concealed, and, in fact, disregarded, a viable avenue for symbol learning.

Extant speech comprehension skills were also significantly correlated with the child's ability to transfer his or her symbol knowledge to the printed English word form. By the end of the first school year, all of the high comprehenders recognized at least 60% of the printed English words that appeared above the symbol when the printed words were presented without the symbol. The written words were those that corresponded to the symbols they had learned in the communicative use context, although they had not received any explicit instruction concerning the relationships between the symbols and their written word equivalents. This finding suggests that the high comprehenders employed an equivalence relationship to learn to recognize the printed English words.

Another finding associated with this augmented language experience was the emergence of intelligible speech in the vocal repertoires of seven of the learners (54%). Following intervention, each of these children improved in more closely approximating the conventional spoken word that corresponded to the symbol (Romski et al., 1990).

Accounting for Augmented Language Learning

Given previously unsuccessful language development histories, what factors might contribute to the language learning described in our longitudinal investigation? Immersing the augmented device within natural communicative opportunities and including communicative partners in the intervention may have facilitated the extraction of previously unobtainable, relevant language learning information from the environment. The way in which symbols were produced and paired with synthetic speech segmented the critical word/symbol from the natural stream of speech and may have facilitated the matching of the symbol with its referent. The high comprehenders readily extracted the critical visual information from the environment, paired it with their extant spoken language knowledge, processed it, and produced symbolic communications. The low comprehenders segmented the visual component of the signal, developed a set of visually based symbol experiences, processed the visual information, comprehended, and then produced symbol communications.

Snyder and McLean (1977) and Snyder-McLean and McLean (1978) proposed a framework in which they suggested that children with mental retardation who encountered difficulty learning spoken language had deficits in information processing strategies and/or in nonverbal (i.e., selective listening, establishment of joint reference, feedback mechanisms) and verbal (i.e., selective imitation and metalinguistic utterance production) information gathering strategies. Our findings suggest that the augmented language learning approach may facilitate the child's ability to gather language-relevant information. Once the stage is set by the unique configuration of technology and experience, the language learning process must be child driven. The overarching theme in the literature has been that children with severe mental retardation require continuous prompting and practice in order to learn language. Our findings lead us to argue for an alternative hypothesis similar to the explanation Savage-Rumbaugh (in press) presented for language learning by the rare pygmy chimpanzee. What children with severe retardation may need to learn language are relevant moments within the natural course of everyday augmented communicative interaction. Our hypothesis would then support Nelson's theory that language learning is a series of carefully timed rare events (Nelson, 1989, in press). It would also extend the milieu teaching literature by suggesting that initial lexical learning can occur directly in natural settings rather than requiring transfer from a structured teaching environment.

EDUCATIONAL AND CLINICAL IMPLICATIONS

Augmented language development in children with severe mental retardation has clinical and educational relevance. Facilitating the translation from research to practice is often difficult, however (Landesman & Ramey, 1989). One approach to interpreting the research findings is to delineate scientific principles that may then be incorporated into treatment philosophies and practices. The following principles emerge from our research findings:

1. Augmented language learning can occur during natural communicative interaction between children and their partners.
2. For at least some children, comprehension may play a critical role in the augmented language learning process.
3. Electronic speech output devices may provide an interface between the child and the auditory world.
4. Integration of the electronic speech output device within the child's natural, extant communication skills facilitates a multimodal system for communication.
5. Augmented language learning provides the child with an entry point to related symbolic skills.

As a cooperative outgrowth of the research effort described in this chapter, the Language Research Center of Georgia State University and the Clayton County Board of Education have developed Project FACTT (Facilitating Augmentative Communication Through Technology). FACTT provides augmented language services to school-age children with moderate, severe, or profound mental retardation within the Clayton County School program through the implementation of practices that are based on these principles.

DIRECTIONS FOR FUTURE RESEARCH

The study of augmented language development is in its infancy. While there are a broad range of topics that deserve scholarly attention, we consider here five broad research directions. First, all of the children we have studied to date have been at least of primary school age. What short-term as well as long-term outcomes would augmented language experience promote if it were initiated during infancy or the preschool years? While empirical data support the statement that augmented language approaches do not inhibit or prevent speech development for older children, clinical and parental concerns regarding augmentation and its effect on speech development remain. Still needed are sensitive criteria for differentiating young children who are at high risk for later language development from those who will develop functional speech, albeit at a delayed rate, so that early language learning can be augmented.

A second related issue to be pursued is an expansion of the study of mother–child interaction to include augmented symbol input. While our own descriptive findings suggest that partners are sensitive to the language skills of the child (Sevcik, Watkins, & Romski, 1990), the relationship between early augmented input and later child symbol use must be investigated. The effect of augmented input on social interaction skills also deserves investigation.

Third, technology can be an important tool for the augmented language learning process. The speech output available on electronic communication devices provides the child with a voice, albeit an electronic one. This voice permits the child to interface with the auditory world in social interactional contexts. As social policy encourages the integration of children with severe disabilities into society, studies are needed to examine the effects of voice on child social competence as well as on familiar and unfamiliar partner perception of communicative competence.

Fourth, the role of speech comprehension in the augmented language development process warrants study. Many nonspeaking children encounter difficulty demonstrating their receptive knowledge via traditional assessment methods. To delineate their receptive abilities more accurately, new and innovative methodologies must be developed and appraised.

Finally, a critical component of augmented language learning is that the environment must be configured so as to permit the child to extract relevant linguistic information. While for this group of children such a notion appears counterintuitive, it produces generalizable language learning outcomes that deserve serious study.

CONCLUSION

This chapter characterizes the augmented language development of children with severe mental retardation and severe oral language disabilities. Their development shares some commonalities with the process through which all children proceed as they learn to speak (Cicchetti & Pogge-Hesse, 1982; Lewis, 1987) and through which nonhuman primates proceed as they learn symbols (Savage-Rumbaugh et al., 1986). Children build upon comprehension and learn through carefully orchestrated experience. Our findings emphasize a child-driven learning process that couples extant skills and a unique configuration of technology and naturalistic augmented language learning opportunities and experiences to account for the child's ability to learn augmented language. The developmental outcome of augmented language learning is a rich multimodal system of functional communication that serves as a foundation upon which related symbolic skills may emerge in children with severe mental retardation. Precise examination of the augmented language learning process strengthens our understanding of some of the intricacies of very early language development, such as the critical roles early speech comprehension skills and natural experiential conditions play in the emergence of children's first productive words. These components of acquisition may be more subtle within the typical developmental process because the normally developing child is such an adept learner.

REFERENCES

Bates, E. (1979). *The emergence of symbols: Cognition and communication in infancy.* New York: Academic Press.
Benedict, H. (1979). Early lexical development: Comprehension and production. *Journal of Child Language, 6,* 183–200.
Brown, R. (1973). *A first language.* Cambridge: Harvard University Press.
Bruner, J. (1966). *Towards a theory of instruction.* Cambridge: Harvard University Press.
Bruner, J. (1983). *Child's talk.* New York: Norton.
Calculator, S. (1988) Evaluating the effectiveness of AAC programs for persons with severe handicaps. *Augmentative and Alternative Communication, 4,* 177–179.
Carrier, J. (1974). Nonspeech noun usage training with severely and profoundly retarded children. *Journal of Speech and Hearing Research, 17,* 510–517.
Chapman, R., & Miller, J. (1985). *Systematic analysis of language transcripts.* Madison: University of Wisconsin Press.
Cicchetti, D., & Pogge-Hesse, P. (1982). Possible contributions of the study of organically retarded persons to developmental theory. In E. Zigler & D. Balla (Eds.), *Mental retardation: The developmental-difference controversy* (pp. 277–318). Hillsdale, NJ: Lawrence Erlbaum Associates.
Clark, S., Remington, B., & Light, P. (1983). The role of referential speech in sign learning by mentally retarded children: A comparison of total communication and sign-alone training. *Journal of Applied Behavior Analysis, 21,* 419–426.
Dunn, L., & Dunn, L. (1981). *Peabody Picture Vocabulary Test-Revised.* Circle Pines, MN: American Guidance Service.
Fristoe, M., & Lloyd, L. (1979). Nonspeech communication. In N. R. Ellis (Ed.)., *Handbook of mental deficiency: Psychological theory and research* (pp. 401–430). Hillsdale, NJ: Lawrence Erlbaum Associates.
Gobbi, L., Cipani, E., Hudson, C., & Lapenta-Neudeck, R. (1986). Developing

spontaneous requesting among children with severe retardation. *Mental Retardation, 24,* 357–363.

Guess, D., & Horner, R. (1978). The severely and profoundly handicapped. In E.L. Meyen (Ed.), *Exceptional children and youth: An introduction* (pp. 218–268). Denver: Love Publishing Co.

Halle, J. (1982). Teaching functional language to the handicapped: An integrative model of natural environment teaching techniques. *Journal of The Association for the Severely Handicapped, 7,* 29–37.

Hart, B., & Rogers-Warren, A. (1978). A milieu approach to teaching language. In R.L. Schiefelbusch (Ed.), *Language intervention strategies* (pp. 193–235). Baltimore: University Park Press.

Huttenlocher, J. (1974). The origins of language comprehension. In R.L. Solso (Ed.), *Theories in cognitive psychology: The Loyola symposium.* Hillsdale, NJ: Lawrence Erlbaum Associates.

Kangas, K., & Lloyd, L. (1988). Early cognitive skill prerequisites to augmentative and alternative communication use: What are we waiting for? *Augmentative and Alternative Communication, 4,* 211–221.

Keogh, W., & Reichle, J. (1985). Communication intervention for the "difficult-to-teach" severely handicapped. In S. Warren & A.K. Rogers-Warren (1985). *Teaching functional language* (pp. 157–194). Baltimore: University Park Press.

Landesman, S., & Ramey, C. (1989). Developmental psychology and mental retardation: Integrating scientific principles with treatment practices. *American Psychologist, 44,* 409–415.

Lewis, V. (1987). *Development and handicap.* New York: Basil Blackwell.

McLean, J., & Snyder-McLean, L. (1988). Applications of pragmatics to severely mentally retarded children and youth. In R.L. Schiefelbusch & L.L. Lloyd (Eds.), *Language perspectives: Acquisition, retardation and intervention* (2nd ed., pp. 255–288). Austin, TX: PRO-ED.

McLean, J., Yoder, D., & Schiefelbusch, R. (1970). *Language intervention with the retarded.* Baltimore: University Park Press.

Nelson, K. (1973). Structure and strategy in learning to talk. *Monographs of the Society for Research in Child Development, 38,* (1–2, Serial No. 139).

Nelson, K.E. (1989). Strategies for first language teaching. In R.L. Schiefelbusch & M. Rice (Eds.), *The teachability of language* (pp. 263–310). Baltimore: Paul H. Brookes Publishing Co.

Nelson, K.E. (in press). On differentiated language learning models and differentiated interventions. In N. Krasnegor, D. Rumbaugh, R. Schiefelbusch, & M. Studdert-Kennedy (Eds.), *Biological and behavioral determinants.* Hillsdale, NJ: Lawrence Erlbaum Associates.

Oliver, C., & Halle, J. (1982). Language training in the everyday environment: Teaching functional signs to a retarded child. *Journal of The Association for the Severely Handicapped, 7,* 50–62.

Reichle, J., & Karlan, G. (1988). The selection of an augmentative system in communication intervention: A critique of decision rules. *Journal of The Association for the Severely Handicapped, 10,* 146–156.

Rice, M. (1983). Contemporary accounts of the cognition/language relationship: Implications for language clinicians. *Journal of Speech and Hearing Disorders, 48,* 347–359.

Rice, M., & Kemper, S. (1984). *Child language and cognition.* Baltimore: University Park Press.

Robinson, B., Wilkinson, K., Sevcik, R.A., & Romski, M.A. (1990, November).

Integrating AAC systems into the classroom: Strategies and applications. Poster presented at the annual meeting of the American Speech-Language-Hearing Association, Seattle.

Romski, M. A. (1989). Two decades of language research with great apes. *Asha, 31,* 81–82.

Romski, M.A., Lloyd, L.L., & Sevcik, R.A. (1988). Augmentative and alternative communication issues. In R.L. Schiefelbusch & L.L. Lloyd (Eds.), *Language perspectives: Acquisition, retardation and intervention* (2nd ed., pp. 343–366). Austin, TX: PRO-ED.

Romski, M. A., & Savage-Rumbaugh, E. S. (1986). A nonhuman primate model: Implications for language intervention research. In E. S. Savage-Rumbaugh (Ed.), *Ape language: From conditioned response to symbol* (pp. 355–374). New York: Columbia University Press.

Romski, M.A., & Sevcik, R.A. (1988a). Augmentative and alternative communication: Considerations for individuals with severe intellectual disabilities. *Augmentative and Alternative Communication, 4,* 83–93.

Romski, M.A., & Sevcik, R.A. (1988b). Augmentative communication system acquisition and use: A model for teaching and assessing progress. *NSSLHA Journal, 16,* 61–75.

Romski, M.A., & Sevcik, R.A. (in press). Patterns of language learning by instruction: Evidence from nonspeaking persons with mental retardation. In N. Krasnegor, D. Rumbaugh, R. Schiefelbusch, & M. Studdert-Kennedy (Eds.), *Biological and behavioral determinents of language development.* Hillsdale, NJ: Lawrence Erlbaum Associates.

Romski, M.A., Sevcik, R.A., & Joyner, S.E. (1984). Nonspeech communication systems: Implications for language intervention with mentally retarded children. *Topics in Language Disorders, 5,* 66–81.

Romski, M.A., Sevcik, R.A., & Pate, J.L. (1988). The establishment of symbolic communication in persons with mental retardation. *Journal of Speech and Hearing Disorders, 53,* 94–107.

Romski, M.A., Sevcik, R.A., Reumann, R., & Pate, J.L. (1989). Youngsters with moderate or severe retardation and severe spoken language impairments. I: Extant communicative patterns. *Journal of Speech and Hearing Disorders, 54,* 366–373.

Romski, M.A., Sevcik, R.A., Robinson, B., & Wilkinson, K. (1990). *Intelligibility and form changes in the vocalization of augmented communicators.* Paper presented at the annual meeting of the American Speech-Language-Hearing Association, Seattle, November.

Rumbaugh, D. M. (1977). *Language learning by a chimpanzee: The Lara project.* New York: Academic Press.

Rosenberg, S. (1982). The language of the mentally retarded: Development, processes, and intervention. In S. Rosenberg (Ed.), *Handbook of applied psycholinguistics* (pp. 329–392). Hillsdale, NJ: Lawrence Erlbaum Associates.

Savage-Rumbaugh, E. S. (1986). *Ape language research: From conditioned response to symbol.* New York: Columbia University Press.

Savage-Rumbaugh, E. S. (in press). Language learning in the Bonobo: How and why they learn. In N. Krasnegor, D. M. Rumbaugh, R. L. Schiefelbusch, & M. Studdert-Kennedy (Eds.), *Psychological and behavioral determinants of language development.* Hillsdale, NJ: Lawrence Erlbaum Associates.

Savage-Rumbaugh, E. S., McDonald, K. Sevcik, R. A., Hopkins, W. D., & Rupert, E. (1986). Spontaneous symbol acquisition and communicative use of pygmy chimpanzees (Pan paniscus). *Journal of Experimental Psychology: General, 115,* 211–235.

Schiefelbusch, R.L. (1980). *Nonspeech language and communication: Analysis and intervention.* Baltimore: University Park Press.

Schiefelbusch, R.L., & Hollis, J. (1979). *Language intervention from ape to child.* Baltimore: University Park Press.

Sevcik, R.A., Watkins, R., & Romski, M.A. (1990). *A descriptive analysis of augmented linguistic input to nonspeaking children.* Unpublished manuscript.

Sheehan, J., Martin, M., & Kilburn, K. (1968). Speech disorders in retardation. *American Journal of Mental Deficiency, 73,* 251–256.

Sidman, M. (1970). Reading and auditory-visual equivalences. *Journal of Speech and Hearing Research, 14,* 5–13.

Sidman, M., & Cresson, O. (1973). Reading and crossmodal transfer of stimulus equivalences in severe retardation. *American Journal of Mental Deficiency, 77,* 515–523.

Snell, M. (1987). *Systematic instruction of persons with severe handicaps.* Columbus, OH: Charles E. Merrill.

Snyder, L., & McLean, J. (1977). Deficient acquisition strategies: A proposed conceptual framework for analyzing severe language deficiency. *American Journal of Mental Deficiency, 81,* 338–349.

Snyder-McLean, L., & McLean, J. (1978). Verbal information gathering strategies: The child's use of language to acquire language. *Journal of Speech and Hearing Disorders, 43,* 306–325.

Warren, S., & Kaiser, A. (1986). Incidental language teaching: A critical review. *Journal of Speech and Hearing Disorders, 51,* 291–299.

Warren, S., & Rogers-Warren, A. (1985). *Teaching functional language.* Baltimore: University Park Press.

Yoder, P., & Layton, T. (1988). Speech following sign language training in autistic children with minimal verbal language. *Journal of Autism and Developmental Disabilities, 18,* 217–229.

6

Beginning Augmentative Communication Systems

Joe Reichle, Pat Mirenda,
Peggy Locke, Laura Piché, and Susan Johnston

To BE UNABLE TO PRODUCE communicative behavior that can be understood by others represents one of the most frustrating experiences imaginable. Communicating through a communication board or with gestures lessens this frustration but does not eliminate it. Since 1975, remarkable advances have been made in our ability to provide augmentative and alternative communication services to persons for whom speech is not a viable alternative. This chapter highlights that progress and identifies issues that require further empirical scrutiny.

IDENTIFYING COMMUNICATIVE
OBLIGATIONS AND OPPORTUNITIES

Franklin and Beukelman (1991) noted that most of the research on conversational interaction has focused on characteristics of interactions between users of augmentative systems and their speaking partners. Most of these investigations support the notion that augmented communicators primarily respond rather than initiate, produce a limited number of turns within a topic exchange, produce a limited number of communicative functions, and often fail to produce communicative repair strategies. According to Franklin and Beukelman, speaking partners dominate conversations and structure interactions to require minimal responses from users of augmentative communication systems.

Children who use augmentative and alternative communication systems act on as few as 50% of the available conversational opportunities during the course of an interaction (Light, Collier, & Parnes, 1985). An important aspect of communication intervention thus requires that the interventionist carefully identify the potential communicative opportunities and obligations that occur in a learner's environment. Subsequently, the interventionist must develop instructional objectives to assist the learner in taking advantage of these occasions. A learner's communicative opportunities depend on his or her environment. At work, communicative opportunities may include requesting more work materials, commenting on the food served in the cafeteria, offering a peer assistance in carrying a heavy box, and answering questions posed by a supervisor. In contrast, the communicative opportunities that arise while a learner is playing video games with friends may include commenting on a peer's play, requesting an opportunity to take a turn during the game, and requesting change. The differences in communicative opportunities between these two environments illustrate the importance of conducting environmental analyses in order to develop a comprehensive list of possible communicative situations for a given learner. Conducting this type of analysis will ensure that the communicative needs that are identified are relevant to the learner.

Scrutiny of the learner's environment will yield a continuum of opportunities (Reichle, York, & Sigafoos, 1991). At one end are utterances that require the learner to respond (e.g., "How are you today?"). At the other end are utterances that do not require responses (e.g., "Gee, it's cold."). Although the discussion that follows is couched in terms of obligatory and nonobligatory communicative events, we emphasize the importance of viewing the continuum between the two.

One type of obligatory communicative event that appears to be overused by speakers in talking to users of augmentative communication systems is questions that require a "yes" or "no" answer. Many users of augmentative communication systems appear to adopt the strategy of waiting for their speaking partners to arrange the interaction so that they can simply answer using "yes" or "no." Because a relatively high proportion of obligatory communicative opportunities directed to augmentative system users demand only a yes/no response, the burden for continuing an interaction falls largely on the speaking partner.

The reason for the overabundance of yes/no questions may relate in part to the speed with which such an exchange can occur. During conversations between speakers, utterances can be produced rapidly. Among even the most competent graphic mode users, messages are transmitted significantly more slowly. As a result, there is a tendency for the graphic mode communication system user to be unable to produce messages quickly enough to keep the conversation moving fluently. Other variables may also explain the tendency of participants to rely heavily on yes/no interactions. Some learners may find it physically demanding to use a communication board or gestures. As a result, they may tend to respond only to the most important utterances produced by their communicative partners. Other learners may comprehend far more vocabulary than they are able to produce. Their range of topics available for discussion may thus be significantly greater if the conversation can be structured to accommodate their production of "yes" and "no" responses to questions.

In some instances, a learner's reluctance to participate fully in a communicative exchange may be the result of learned helplessness (Guess, Benson & Siegel-Causey, 1985; Seligman, 1975). That is, if the desired outcome has historically occurred with minimal learner participation, the learner has been reinforced for minimal participation. There is evidence that, over time, learners placed in such situations tend to become increasingly dependent on those with whom they interact (Guess et al., 1985). To avoid the establishment of learned helplessness, it is crucial that early in a learner's communicative experiences, interventionists identify communicative obligations and opportunities in which the learner will be taught to engage. Accomplishing this task requires a careful match between communicative interactions, communicative intents to teach, and vocabulary.

SELECTING COMMUNICATIVE INTENTS TO TEACH

Cirrin and Rowland (1985) have provided compelling evidence that among persons with severe developmental disabilities with the least sophisticated communicative repertoires, the greatest proportion of their communicative behavior is directed at requesting objects. As learners become communicatively more sophisticated, their proportional use of other communicative intents increases dramatically. Cirrin and Rowland's observations lend credence to the contention by Guess, Sailor, and Baer (1974) that the easiest way to convince beginning communicators of the benefits of communication is to enable them to control access to reinforcers through use of an augmentative communicative system. Of course, if there are important communicative obligations that do not call for requesting, the interventionist should not automatically back away from selecting them as intervention targets.

We believe that an initial repertoire of communicative intents to teach must be carefully matched to the communicative obligations and opportunities each learner experiences. Some communicative intents have very different implications for use in an augmentative communication mode.

An important communicative function is requesting attention. When a speaker makes a request or comment, two communicative functions are performed simultaneously. First, the speaker obtains the listener's attention. Second, the speaker communicates information about a specific referent. Like a speaker, a learner using an electronic communication aid with voice output is able to perform these functions simultaneously. However, in the gestural mode or the graphic mode without voice output, the learner must produce one behavior to recruit attention and a second behavior to communicate a specific idea.

In selecting communicative intents to teach, the interventionst must examine the range of stimulus conditions that should elicit the targeted communicative intent. For example, a number of stimuli call for the production of the utterance "I don't want to do this." In one instance, an undesired item is offered to a learner. In another instance, an item that is normally desired is rejected because the learner has become satiated (e.g., rejecting a third refill of coffee). In a third instance, a learner may be engaged in a neutral event (i.e., one that is neither very boring nor particularly interesting). Over time, the drudgery of the task gradually increases until, at some point, the learner indicates that he or she wishes to discontinue the activity. Ideally, a learner will recognize that in all three of these instances, the same communicative behavior—"I don't want to do this"—could be produced. If this is the case, the learner who has a limited communicative repertoire would maximize the use of that repertoire across stimulus conditions. Unfortunately, for many learners with severe disabilities, establishing this level of generalization is likely to require intervention.

Reichle (1990) demonstrated that three learners who were taught to use a generalized rejecting gesture in the presence of undesired objects readily generalized the use of their rejecting gesture to undesired items that had not previously been the focus of intervention efforts. However, when offered repeated access to an object that served as a reinforcer (coffee), none of the learners used the rejecting gestures after becoming satiated. Two of the learners failed to engage in any communicative behavior upon becoming satiated, and allowed the interventionist to pour more coffee, which they left untouched. The third learner got up and walked away from the table as the interventionist approached.

Reichle (1990) also taught each of three learners to use a reject gesture to escape the delivery of undesired food items. The learners were taught that as the interventionist approached, producing a "no" headshake resulted in the interventionist turning away from them and returning the undesired item to a storage location. All three learners demonstrated generalization of the rejecting gesture to other undesired items that were not the original focus of intervention. However, these learners were unable to generalize the use of the reject gesture to instances in which satiation occurred. For example, one learner's job was assembling ballpoint pens. This learner preferred to assemble blue pens rather than white ones (presumably because white pens required one more assembly step). Traditionally, offering a box of white pens to assemble resulted in an unauthorized leave from work. This learner had a history of darting to escape work some time between 10 and 15 minutes into the task even when blue pens were the focus of the assembly task. Initially, the learner acquired his generalized rejecting response in the context of escaping the presentation of undesired food items at mealtime. Subsequently, the learner generalized his newly acquired rejecting response when an offer of white pens was made. However, when the staff approached him as his interest in blue pen assembly began to wane and asked, "Want to keep going?", the learner darted rather than produce his reject gesture. Equally poor generalization was observed in the other two learners.

We believe that for the learners whose performance has just been described, the stimulus classes that occasion a particular communicative utterance may be narrowly defined. Consequently, steps need to be taken to ensure that all of the antecedents that we wish to control a particular behavior are, in fact, represented during the acquisition phase of intervention. In the case of the second example presented, the learner's existing communicative behavior at the outset of intervention (i.e., darting) was so socially unacceptable that it had to be replaced. The learner's existing communicative repertoire may not always require actions as drastic as total replacement, however. Consequently, it is very important for the interventionist to consider what existing communicative repertoire the learner may have and what portion of that repertoire can remain part of the learner's long-term communicative system.

INCORPORATING EXISTING REPERTOIRES
INTO A COMPREHENSIVE COMMUNICATION SYSTEM

The initial communicative behavior of many learners often contains repertoires of idiosyncratic gestures that have an extensive history of use and are often very efficient means of communication for the learner. These idiosyncratic forms can be thought of as lying along a continuum of acceptability. At one end of the continuum are behaviors such as headshakes representing "yes" and "no" or a raised hand to indicate "stop your approach toward me." At the other end of the continuum are gestures such as crotch holding to indicate a need to use the bathroom. In this instance, the interventionist may be eager to replace the learner's idiosyncratic behavior with a more socially acceptable communicative behavior.

While the notion of social acceptability is a useful dimension on which to evaluate the functionality of idiosyncratic gestures, it is only one dimension. Several other criteria need to be considered when making a decision about whether to leave an idiosyncratic gesture in the learner's repertoire, shape it into a more recognizable form, or replace it with a new behavior. These criteria include: 1) the guessability of the learner's current gesture, 2) the use of an undesired reflex or movement pattern, and 3) the use of an existing repertoire of challenging behavior. Each of these criteria is discussed in the following sections.

Guessability of Gestures

From a listener's perspective, the guessability of a gesture is very important. Consider a learner who asks to go to the bathroom by running for the door of his classroom and vocalizing loudly. Unless his teacher understands the intent of this message, it is highly likely that she will respond by telling him to return to his seat or by approaching him before he leaves the room. Since neither of these responses is appropriate to his intent, a communication breakdown is almost certain to occur. This is in contrast to other gestures, such as crotch holding or "dancing around," that might be used to communicate the same message. While such gestures are problematic for other reasons (e.g., their social unacceptability), their meanings are clear. In general, gestures that are not highly guessable restrict the communication partner with whom and the settings in which a learner can communicate successfully. For this reason, they are high priority targets for intervention.

Reflex Patterns Used as Communicative Gestures

A learner's initial communicative repertoire may contain idiosyncratic gestures comprised of undesirable reflex or movement patterns. Consider, for example, a learner who produces a gesture using atypical muscle tone or an abnormal coordination pattern. If this gesture is functionally reinforced, over time its continued production could by physically harmful to the learner (Campbell, 1989). Campbell (1989) suggested that if the interventionist decides to leave such a gesture in a learner's repertoire, it should be "shaped into a more normally organized pattern once the pattern is functionally used in self-directed situations" (p. 178). Other alternatives also exist. For example, the interventionist might choose to select a new form of behavior to be taught while placing the existing reflexive gesture on extinction. Decisions regarding the incorporation of gestures that involve the production of undesirable reflex patterns constitute a challenging dilemma that has rarely been addressed.

Challenging Behavior Used as Communicative Gestures

Some learners communicate very efficiently, yet very inappropriately. For example, a child may communicate his refusal to eat green beans by crying and tantrumming. Although the intent of this behavior is clear, the behavior is socially unacceptable. Other, more extreme instances of socially unacceptable communicative behavior include self-injury, aggression, and property destruction. The communicative intents that may motivate these behaviors include requesting, rejecting/protesting, and leavetaking.

The overlap between challenging behavior and communicative behavior presents a host of issues to be addressed by the interventionist. The first of these involves communicative intentionality. Children cry at birth. Yet few would claim that an infant's crying is always intentionally communicative in nature. We do know that very early in life, highly contingent relationships develop between crying episodes and subsequent caregiver behaviors. For example, when an infant cries at feeding time, his or her parents are likely to provide immediate reinforcement in the form of food (milk). Contingent relationships may also develop between antecedent events and the learner's behavior. For example, an infant may cry or fuss when he or she loses the nipple and has difficulty finding it. In some instances, clear chains of predictable events occur in which an antecedent event (e.g., losing the nipple) is followed by a child's response (e.g., crying), which culminates with a consequence (e.g., providing more food). Although initially the child did not intend to communicate, at some point he or she begins to realize that crying can be used to obtain desired items. What started out as a nonintentional, reflexive behavior may become a deliberate behavior that poses social challenges.

A critical issue for the interventionist is determining whether the challenging behavior is intentional or not. If the behavior is not intentional, the primary thrust of the intervention may be to teach the listener to refrain from reinforcing the behavior, and to identify the antecedent events(s) that typically precede it. Subsequently, a more socially acceptable behavior can be established before the challenging behavior becomes associated with a particular communicative intent. If the challenging behavior is intentional, the primary thrust of intervention must focus on replacing the challenging behavior with a new, more socially acceptable form. In the former instance, the interventionist assumes a more preventive posture. In the latter instance, the interventionist faces a far greater challenge.

Unfortunately, in many instances, it is difficult to identify the precise relationship between a specific challenging behavior and its communicative function(s). However, it is vital to identify clearly the communicative function(s) of the behavior prior to instituting intervention procedures. This principle was demonstrated by Durand and Crimmins (1987), who investigated the influence that teaching a nonmatching communicative intent, such as obtaining attention, had on a challenging behavior that was motivated by a request for assistance. Their data suggested that teaching the communicative function that matched the social motivation of the challenging behavior served to replace the behavior. Teaching a nonmatching communicative function had little influence on the challenging behavior. Additional work to develop a continuum of assessment strategies aimed at matching social intents to challenging behaviors for the purpose of intervention efficiency is critically needed.

Another important factor that influences intervention is the timing of the challenging behavior. In some instances, learners may refrain from engaging in challenging behavior immediately after the precipitating stimulus occurs. For example, one learner may destroy the work materials of a peer. Because a teacher is present, the learner whose materials were destroyed may not retaliate immediately. Instead, he may wait until the peer is alone on the playground to retaliate. If care is not taken to identify the relationship between these two temporally distant events, interventions may fail because a narrow focus on immediate antecedent and consequent events prevent analysis of the bigger picture.

A third factor that may complicate intervention planning is the inconsistency with which some challenging behaviors may be produced in the presence of certain antecedents or consequences. This inconsistency may occur for a variety of reasons. Prior experience with an item or event may influence responding. For example, if a learner has just consumed a plate of beans, offering the learner more beans may provoke rejecting behavior. In other instances, a pre-existing stressor, such as a bad cold, a menstrual period, or having to wear a nonpreferred shirt, may provoke a behavior that would not ordinarily occur.

There is growing empirical support for the use of assessment strategies designed to analyze challenging behaviors in natural contexts through systematic manipulation of antecedents or consequences. A number of investigators (Carr & Durand, 1985; Carr & Newsom, 1985; Carr, Newsom, & Binkoff, 1980; Durand, 1986; Durand & Carr, 1987; Durand & Crimmins, 1987; Iwata, Dorsey, Slifer, Bauman, & Richman, 1982; and others) have implemented analog assessment tasks, in which conditions are organized to compare the influence of certain variables upon the production of challenging behavior. For example, in an effort to determine whether challenging behavior was motivated by a desire to request items, Durand (1986) compared a situation in which tangible reinforcers were freely available with a situation in which such reinforcers were visible but not readily available. Table 1 summarizes a number of reports of the use of analog assessment tasks to assess the influence of attention, tangible reinforcers, and task demands on the production of challenging behavior. Such analog assessment tasks must be used in natural contexts in order to preserve the social validity of the outcomes.

To date, few investigations have examined potential variables that may influence the selection of initial communicative targets. Few empirically validated strategies exist for deciding whether to: 1) shape an existing behavior into a communicative utterance, 2) conditionally reinforce an existing behavior used communicatively, or 3) replace an existing behavior with a new, more conventional communicative form. There is a critical need for empirically based investigations of these variables and their influence on the development of efficient intervention procedures. Once a learner's existing repertoire of communication has been identified, the interventionist's attention can begin to focus on selecting the communication mode(s) that might best be used to expand the learner's communicative repertoires.

CHOOSING AN AUGMENTATIVE MODE(S)

The needs of the learner have not always determined the selection of an augmentative and alternative communication mode. Many people with severe developmental disabilities who spent their youths in institutions were taught to use manual signs or gestures simply because few alternatives were available. As the literature on the successful application of graphic mode techniques has

Table 1.   Summary of empirical reports that have used analog assessment tasks to assess the influence that attention, tangible reinforcers, and task demands have on the production of challenging behavior

Motivation	Methodology	Study
Effect of attention	A condition in which the excess behavior resulted in obtaining attention was compared to one in which the absence of behavior resulted in attention.	Iwata, Dorsey, Slifer, Bauman, & Richman, 1982; Sturmey, Carlsen, Crisp, & Newton, 1988
	A condition in which relatively little adult attention was available was compared to one in which much attention was available.	Carr & Durand, 1985; Durand & Carr, 1987; Durand & Crimmins, 1988
Effect of tangibles or activities controlled by attending adult	A condition in which the excess behavior resulted in the opportunity to perform various activities controlled by the attending adult was compared to a condition in which no such contingency was in effect.	Lovaas, Freitag, Gold, & Kassorla, 1965
	A condition in which preferred tangibles were freely available was compared to a condition in which the tangibles were visible but not available.	Durand, 1986
Effect of task demands	A condition in which demands were delivered frequently was compared to one in which no demands were delivered.	Carr & Newsom, 1985; Carr, Newsom, & Binkoff, 1976; Carr, Newsom, & Binkoff, 1980; Durand, 1982; Weeks & Gaylord-Ross, 1981
	A condition in which the task was difficult to perform was compared to one in which the task was easier to perform.	Carr & Durand, 1985; Durand, 1982; Durand & Carr, 1987; Weeks & Gaylord-Ross, 1981
	A condition in which task demands and the contingent removal of the demands following the excess behavior were present was compared to one in which task demands were present but their contingent removal was not.	Durand & Carr, 1987; Durand & Crimmins, 1987
	A condition in which task demands and the contingent removal of the demands following the excess behavior were present was compared to one in which no task demands were present.	Iwata et al., 1982; Sturmey et al., 1988

From Doss, L. S., & Reichle, J. (1991). Replacing excess behavior with an initial communicative repertoire. In J. Reichle, J. York, & J. Sigafoos, *Implementing augmentative and alternative communication:* Strategies for learners with severe disabilities. Baltimore: Paul H. Brookes Publishing Co. Reprinted by permission.

grown, so, too, has the proportion of beginning communicators who have been taught to use this mode (Reichle et al., 1991). Some of the advantages and disadvantages of both graphic and gestural modes are displayed in Table 2.

One of the earliest reported attempts to select a primary communication mode systematically was reported by Alpert (1980). She described the implementation of a sequential sampling procedure in which the interventionist first implemented instruction in a single mode. Contingent on an arbitrarily imposed failure criterion being met, a second mode was implemented. Although this sequential sampling strategy was systematic, the learner faced the risk of expending substantial time and effort in attempting to learn to use one or more modes before encountering one that proved useful.

As an alternative, Reichle and Karlan (1985) suggested implementing a

Table 2. Advantages and disadvantages of graphic and gestural modes

Mode	Advantages	Disadvantages
Gestural	• Transporting the system is easy. • Guessing the meaning of some gestures is possible. • Producing gestures is quick. • Communicating with gestures does not require the use of additional materials. • Producing gestures provides a unique topography for each response.	• Communicating with partners who are not familiar with gestural systems may be difficult. • Providing a permanent display of the system is not possible. • Producing gestures requires fluent motor skills. • Requesting specific items (e.g., Milky Way versus candy bar) may be difficult.
Graphic	• System results in a permanent display of symbols. • Communicating with unfamiliar listeners is possible. • Adapting the system for learners with visual impairments is feasible.	• Transporting symbols may be difficult. • Accommodating a large vocabulary may be cumbersome.

concurrent sampling strategy in which both graphic mode and gestural mode intervention were taught concurrently. The advantage of concurrent implementation is that the learner is in a position to use his or her optimal communication mode from the outset of intervention. Assuming that the initial vocabulary items targeted for instruction in the two modes are of equal interest to the learner, over time, it is possible to determine which mode is more useful. Another attractive feature of concurrent sampling is the fact that it parallels the processes that occur in normal development: children without disabilities rely heavily on multiple modes to communicate their initial communicative intents.

Although concurrent modality sampling has received increasing support as a best practice, a number of questions regarding its use remain. Most currently used strategies focus on the introduction of simultaneous mode, mixed mode, and duplicated mode instruction. However, it is not yet clear which implementation strategy best leads to concurrent mode implementation.

Simultaneous Mode

A number of studies have addressed the utility of teaching communication in more than one mode simultaneously. Most of the work in this area has documented the successful implementation of gestural and vocal mode intervention programs (e.g., Barrera, Lobato-Barrera, & Sulzer-Azaroff, 1980; Brady & Smouse, 1978). Barrera et al. (1980) found a combined gestural and vocal mode intervention to be more effective in establishing production than either mode taught alone. Brady and Smouse (1978) showed multiple mode intervention to be superior to single mode intervention in establishing an initial repertoire of comprehension skills. However, other investigators have reported that, when vocal and gestural modes are combined, learners with childhood autism may be more apt to attend to the gestural component than the vocal component (Carr, Binkoff, Kologinsky, & Eddy, 1978). Some research has suggested that the usefulness of simultaneous mode instruction may depend on whether the learner has mastered generalized imitation at the point of intervention (Carr & Dores, 1981; Carr, Pridal, & Dores, 1984; Remington & Clarke, 1983).

Mixed Mode

Keogh and Reichle (1985) speculated that some learners may benefit from a communication system in which some vocabulary items are taught in one mode while other vocabulary items are taught in another. In a mixed mode strategy, vocabulary items are assigned to a particular mode after the interventionist scrutinizes the communicative demands of the learner's environment. Some vocabulary items may be able to be produced with highly guessable gestures. Other items, such as Diet Coke, may require a level of specificity that can be achieved only through the use of graphic mode product logos. Proponents of mixed mode systems suggest that use of a mixed mode allows both the learner and the interventionist to take advantage of the best features of two or more modes.

Duplicated Mode

Proponents of duplicated mode instruction believe that the learner should be able to represent the same vocabulary in both the graphic and the gestural mode. The rationale for a duplicated mode is that it is difficult and impractical to assign vocabulary to a specific mode, since communicative production depends on the situation in which vocabulary is used. For example, a learner with duplicated vocabulary in both the gestural and graphic modes who wishes to ask for a drink while at the playground would probably find it easier to gesture than to take out a communication wallet and locate a symbol. However, when interacting with a babysitter who is unfamiliar with his gestures, the learner might find it more effective to use a graphic symbol. There is some evidence that learners with developmental disabilities can learn to make decisions about the most appropriate modality to use in such situations (Reichle & Ward, 1985).

The introduction of duplicated mode vocabulary often occurs sequentially. For example, a learner may have acquired a significant repertoire of signs and gestures while residing in an institution. Upon moving into the community, the learner is no longer able to rely on signs and gestures, since few people in the community sign. As a result, some of the signs in the learner's repertoire must be duplicated.

Summary

There is a need to maximize the use of multiple modes among prospective users of augmentative and alternative communication systems. However, to date, little attention has been given to which implementation strategy (simultaneous, mixed, or duplicated) might be most efficient with any given learner. The exploration of each of the implementation strategies represents a critical area for empirical scrutiny.

CHOOSING A GRAPHIC MODE SELECTION TECHNIQUE

Once a communication mode(s) has been selected, the interventionist must determine how the learner will access that mode. In the graphic mode, some learners may have physical disabilities so significant that they cannot directly select symbols without the assistance of either the listener or an electronic menuing system. Most intervention studies describing the successful implementation of graphic mode communication systems have focused on the use of a direct selection technique, in which the learner touches, points to, or looks at the symbol or symbol combinations that he or she wishes to communicate. Some investigators have focused on the use of a scanning selection technique, in which the learner is presented with a sequence of symbols, and indicates his or her choice by producing a predetermined signal to inform the listener when the desired symbol has been presented. Traditionally, scanning selection techniques have been reserved for learners who exhibit severe upper extremity motor disabilities, poor head control, and/or poor eye pointing skills.

Few investigators have addressed the range of conditions in which it might be advantageous for a learner to use both direct selection and scanning. Young speakers typically use a combination of direct selection and scanning. At the dinner table, for example, it is common for an 18-month-old to request a specific food item by saying its name. This is a direct selection technique. In other instances, however, the learner may not yet have learned to produce the name of a desired item. In such a case, the learner is apt to point in the direction of a desired item and say "want that." If the desired item is clustered among the food items in the center of the table, it is likely that the communicative partner will then begin to scan through the options, one by one (e.g., "Do you want ketchup? Mustard?"). Although detailed intervention procedures to establish initial scanning skills have been identified (Piché & Reichle, 1991), there is a critical need for investigators to explore the conditions under which it might be advisable to teach both techniques.

There seems to be general agreement that it is more difficult to acquire the use of a scanning technique than a direct selection technique, and there is some research to support this (e.g., Ratcliff, 1988). This may be due, at least in part, to the conditional nature of the discrimination that must be taught to the user of a scanning technique. When scanning is used, the learner must wait until his or her communicative partner or the cursor on an electronic communication aid highlights a symbol (visually or verbally). Thus, the learner must recognize that a symbol can be selected only under a particular condition and not under any other condition.

Because scanning selection techniques are very slow, a number of variations on a simple scanning technique are available. For example, in row-column scanning, the cursor usually begins at the top-left corner of the learner's communication board and systematically moves down rows. The row containing the target symbol is selected by the learner producing a discrete voluntary signaling response (e.g., pushing a switch). Subsequently, each symbol in the row selected is menued. The learner must once again produce the signaling response to select the exact symbol. The primary advantage of row-column scanning is that it is significantly faster than a simple scanning technique. Typically, learners move from a simple scanning technique to a row-column technique as more symbols are added to their array. However, in order to participate in a row-column scanning technique, the learner must be able to produce a chain of two signaling responses to arrive at the desired symbol. Additionally, the learner must be able to anticipate which row contains the desired symbol by constantly visually monitoring the relative positions of the cursor and the desired target symbol. To date, there has been limited empirical research on reliable intervention procedures that can be implemented to teach learners with developmental disabilities the complex skills needed for row-column scanning. Once a selection technique has been identified and intervention procedures have been designed to enable the learner to become a more efficient user of the technique, attention may be refocused on selecting vocabulary to be represented in the communication models selected.

SELECTING VOCABULARY AND MATCHING
VOCABULARY TO COMMUNICATIVE INTENTS

Unfortunately, interventionists often select vocabulary to teach based on what they think might be useful without validating those beliefs. Reichle (1983) conducted a survey in which he asked interventionists to describe the procedures they used to select vocabulary for augmentative and alternative communication system users. The most prevalent strategies, in order of frequency, included: 1) selecting vocabulary that the interventionist and/or parent thought would be important, 2) selecting vocabulary from the first 50 word developmental data, 3) selecting vocabulary from word lists obtained from surveying service providers, and 4) selecting vocabulary from word lists derived from vocabulary actually used by learners with developmental disabilities. Perhaps the most dismaying aspect of the survey was that only 12%

of the respondents reported that they actually scrutinized learners' existing and future environments in an effort to anticipate the range of vocabulary that might be useful.

In a follow-up survey, Reichle (1985) examined the vocabulary items actually used in a 2-week period by 10 learners whose teachers and speech-language pathologists reported that they selected vocabulary in terms of its projected appropriateness. Each learner had mastered a mean of 4.5 symbols that were selected because of their presumed applicability in school. During daily observations across a 2-week period, a mean of 1.5 of these symbols were never used or needed by the learners. A mean of 0.75 symbols were used fewer than five times in the 2-week period. Reichle concluded that over 33% of the vocabulary items selected had minimal applicability to the learners' ongoing daily routines. Ecological inventories were then conducted for each of the 10 learners in order to identify situations that called for a communicative behavior and to which the learners consistently responded in a non-symbolic manner (e.g., fussing whenever a favorite toy was removed). A mean of 19.8 such instances per day were identified across the 10 learners observed. Clearly, these situations represented excellent opportunities for expanding the communicative repertoires of the learners through the introduction of vocabulary items that corresponded to their nonsymbolic behaviors. Such an approach would appear to be more fruitful than the approach previously used with these learners that made no effort to validate vocabulary selections socially through the use of an ecological inventory. (An extensive discussion of the protocol for conducting an environmental inventory is described in Sigafoos & York, 1991.)

Guessability of Symbols

A number of criteria may be applied to the selection of vocabulary. One of these is the guessability, or iconicity, of a sign or symbol. Iconicity is a term that refers to the notion of how readily a symbol's meaning can be guessed from the information provided. Mustonen, Locke, Reichle, Solbrack, and Lindgren (1991) have suggested that iconicity can be viewed as a continuum with transparent signs/symbols at one end, translucent signs/symbols in the middle, and opaque signs/symbols at the far end of the continuum. A transparent sign is one whose meaning is easy to guess from its topography (e.g., the ASL sign for *toothbrush* is the index finger rubbing back and forth across the teeth). A translucent sign is one whose meaning is not easily guessed without some additional information (e.g., the ASL sign for *milk* is not readily guessable unless one is familiar with the process of milking a cow). An opaque sign is one whose meaning is not readily guessable and whose relationship with its referent seems quite arbitrary (e.g., the sign for *play* is not easily guessable, and bears no apparent relationship to the act of playing). The guessability of a sign or gesture is often cited as an important variable when teaching the use of manual signs. In addition, from the perspective of a signer who is not familiar with signs, the more guessable the learner's signs, the more likely it is that the listener will be able to decipher them.

Another factor that affects a sign or gesture's guessability is concreteness, that is, how easily the referent is perceived through the senses, particularly sign or touch (Mustonen et al., 1991). For example, *drink* is a very concrete sign, because one can readily see, feel, and imagine holding a glass and drinking. Luftig (1983) reported that learners with moderate to severe disabilities acquire signs rated as transparent and concrete faster than those rated opaque and abstract.

There is also evidence that guessable graphic symbols are more easily acquired than those that are opaque. For example, Hurlbut, Iwata, and Green (1982) found that adolescents with multiple disabilities demonstrated better acquisition, generalization, maintenance, and spontaneous usage of symbols that were transparent than they did of Blissymbols, which are relatively opaque. Sevcik and Romski (1986) found that learners with severe retardation were able to match photographs to their referents more successfully than line drawings. Finally, in a comprehensive study involving 40 learners with mild to severe intellectual disabilities, Mirenda and Locke (1989) identified the following hierarchy of difficulty for nouns across 10 different symbol sets (from easiest to most difficult): real objects, color photographs, black and white photographs, miniature objects, black and white line symbols (including Picsyms [Carlson, 1985], Picture Communication Symbols [Mayer-Johnson Co., 1986], Rebuses [Clark, Davies, & Woodcock, 1974], and Self-Talk symbols [Johnson, 1986]), Blissymbols (Hehner, 1980), and written words. However, only the results for objects, Blissymbols, and written words were found to be significantly different from those of other symbol sets. Much additional information is needed, especially regarding the iconicity and learnability of symbols representing categories other than nouns, to guide practitioners in making decisions about the optimum types of symbols to use for specific learners.

Opportunities for Using Symbols

Karlan and Lloyd (1983) suggested that the number of opportunities to practice the vocabulary chosen may affect the success with which the vocabulary is acquired. That is, the more opportunities the learner has to use the vocabulary, the quicker the learner might acquire it and the greater the likelihood that it will be maintained. Keogh and Reichle (1985), echoing Guess et al. (1974), suggested that vocabulary representing items and events of great interest to the learner represent highly desirable initial intervention targets.

Specificity of Symbols

In addition to the consideration of which vocabulary items would be most useful for the learner to acquire, the interventionist must consider carefully the level of specificity with which to represent vocabulary. For example, in selecting a graphic symbol to represent Diet Pepsi, the interventionist could choose between a Diet Pepsi container label or, alternatively, a more generic symbol representing all carbonated beverages. How is this decision best made? We know that in normal development learners tend to select symbols of intermediate specificity (Anglin, 1977). That is, given the continuum of *animal, dog,* and *collie,* children are likely to acquire the word *dog* first. Subsequently, the learner will acquire discriminative use of the more general form (i.e., *animal*) and, finally, of the more specific form (i.e., *collie*). Thus, selection of a generic symbol seems natural. In addition, there are a number of other benefits of generic symbols. First, the more generic the symbol, the greater the range of opportunities there are for intervention applications. For example, a symbol for "Oreo" can be used to obtain Oreo cookies only, whereas a more generic "treat" symbol can be used not only to request cookies but to ask for a host of other desirable items as well. Second, generic symbols are less susceptible to satiation and shifting preferences. Third, satiation indirectly influences the frequency of requesting opportunities. If satiation occurs before sufficient instructional opportunities are made available to establish a new vocabulary item, both the learner and the interventionist will experience considerable frustration. The use of shifting preferences is relevant to learners who initially exhibit strong preferences but, over time, lose interest in one or more items as they discover others. For example, a learner may like Diet Pepsi until he discovers Orange Slice; however, if a generic symbol is being used to represent "soft drink" this shift in preference can be accommodated easily.

Accompanying the advantages of more generic symbols are certain disadvantages. The more generic the vocabulary, the greater the demands on the communicative partner to interpret the message accurately. For example, if a learner orders a "soft drink," the listener must make certain inferences to determine what kind of soft drink the learner would like. Currently, there exists no empirical base to assist the interventionist in deciding how specifically initial vocabulary should be represented. Research on symbol specificity must address both the ease of acquisition for the user and the demands for interpretation placed on the communicative partner.

Similarity of Symbols

In both the graphic and gestural modes, the interventionist must consider how the symbols selected are similar or different in appearance. We know that dissimilar response forms are generally more discriminable to the learner. In some cases, response form similarity may actually interfere with establishing initial repertoires. For example, the ASL signs representing *eat* and *drink* are both produced in the same location of the body, using approximately the same handshapes and movement patterns. Additionally, they are often produced in the same setting and in the presence of the similar objects (food and beverages). Best practice literature in the area of discrimination learning suggests choosing initial responses that are as different as possible. Thus, it would not be wise to teach the symbols both for *eat* and *drink* at the same time and in the same place. Once initial learning has occurred, steps can be taken to introduce new vocabulary items that share increasingly more characteristics with previously established items.

Motoric Complexity of Symbols

In the gestural mode, there is growing evidence that the motor characteristics of some signs may make them easier to acquire. The shape or shapes assumed by the hands, the orientation of the hands and arms to the learner's body, and the location from which the sign or gesture is produced all appear to influence acquisition (Doherty, 1985). Signs and gestures that require contact between both hands or between hand and body (contact signs) have been reported to be easier to acquire than those that do not (Stremel-Campbell, Cantrell, & Halle, 1977). Signs and gestures that require symmetrical movements of both hands (particularly if the movements occur at the anatomical midline) may also be easier to learn (Doherty, 1985).

DELINEATING THE ROLE OF COMPREHENSION IN AUGMENTATIVE COMMUNICATION PRODUCTION

Romski and Sevcik note that "children who do comprehend speech come to the augmented language learning task with knowledge of spoken word referents" (Chapter 5, p. 116). They reported procedures used in a longitudinal investigation that focused on naturalistic intervention techniques to establish electronic communication aid use. After the completion of their investigation, they implemented a retrospective analysis in which learners were divided into two groups. Low comprehenders consisted of those learners who did not understand the spoken words for the initial symbols placed on their communication aids. High comprehenders were learners who did understand the spoken representations for the vocabulary items placed on their communication aids. Romski and Sevcik reported that the high comprehending students learned to recognize and use a larger number of symbols than did their low comprehending counterparts. Additionally, the high comprehenders moved more quickly from line drawn graphic symbols to printed words. The authors suggest that comprehension was the route by which their subjects learned to produce language.

This logic seems compelling, especially since the subjects were taught to use electronic communication aids with synthetic speech output. Thus, each time the learners produced a message by touching a symbol, they heard the corresponding spoken word modeled. Assuming that the spoken output of the electronic communication aid was sufficiently intelligible for the learners to understand it, those learners who were able to comprehend spoken utterances were in a better position to learn from this spoken input.

Although it seems logical that there would be a correspondence between the ability to produce and comprehend vocabulary within a given communication mode, relatively few data demonstrate such a relationship. For example, in the vocal mode, there is a good deal of corroborative evidence to suggest that children's initial expressive and receptive repertoires are often different (Guess, 1969; Guess & Baer, 1973; Siegel & Vogt, 1984).

In the graphic mode, the distinction between receptive and expressive communicative repertoires is less clear, highlighting the fact that these two repertoires are perhaps best viewed as different points along a continuum rather than as separate entities. For example, in the graphic mode, when the samples are real objects or events, the learner's responsibility is to select the matching graphic representation from an array. This task meets the conditions for an expressive discrimination. In contrast, when the samples are line drawings and the choices are real objects, the task is similar to a receptive discrimination.

It may be easier to generalize across reception and expression in the graphic mode since the learner engages in the same form of response regardless of whether the task is receptive or expressive—in both instances, the learner points to either a graphic representation or a real item. Nevertheless, some individuals with severe disabilities have difficulty generalizing when what have been choices in a nonidentity graphic mode matching array become samples and what have been samples become choices (Brady & Saunders, in press).

In summary, few data directly address the relationship between reception and expression among users of augmentative and alternative communication systems. We have not yet satisfactorily resolved whether comprehension is facilitative of production, as Romski and Sevcik suggest (Chapter 5), or whether the response classes of reception and expression are somewhat independent. Also unclear is the extent to which stimulus overselectivity may influence the benefit to language understanding derived from pairing speech synthesized/digitized output with symbol selections. The relationship between reception and expression in augmentative and alternative communication system users is ripe for applied research.

TAILORING INTERVENTION TECHNIQUES TO LEARNING STYLES

Since 1980 a significant and growing array of intervention strategies that can be used to implement an initial repertoire of augmentative and alternative communication skills has been developed. Unfortunately, few investigators have addressed decision strategies to use in selecting an intervention strategy from those available that might best suit the learner's style of acquiring new skills.

Of particular importance is comparing the conditions under which each of two acceptable intervention procedures might be used. For example, several significantly different intervention procedures aimed at establishing an initial repertoire of leavetaking communicative behavior can be identified. In one procedure, the interventionist teaches the learner that producing a leave-take gesture or graphic symbol will virtually always result in release from task. Once the learner is using this communicative form, the interventionist begins to introduce a delay prior to consequating the learner's production. In effect, the learner is told "just a second" and is then released. Over time, this delay prior to release is increased. Eventually, the interventionist may request the learner to continue to engage in the task at hand for a brief time prior to release. Gradually, this length of engagement may be increased.

An alternative procedure involves teaching the learner to engage in an activity for a brief period and then be released to a break. Early in the program, the interventionist introduces a "safety signal." Its function is to signal the learner that if he or she refrains from unacceptable behavior for a brief period of time, he or she will be released from the activity. Once the safety signal has been conditioned and the learner is participating during greater intervals of time, the interventionist begins to introduce a symbol for leavetaking. The symbol is made available just prior to the safety signal. As soon as the learner comes in contact with the symbol, after the delivery of the safety signal, he/she is released to a break. Inadvertent selections prior to the safety signal are not reinforced with release from the task.

In the latter procedure, the use of a leavetaking symbol is conditionally reinforced from the beginning, thereby avoiding the necessity of placing the learner's use of a symbol on extinction. In the former procedure, conditional uses of the leavetaking gesture were gradually shaped.

EDUCATIONAL AND CLINICAL IMPLICATIONS

A number of implications for best practice can be derived from recent empirical advances. Some of these best practices focus on the selection of initial communicative intents to teach, vocabulary to best represent those intents, and communication modes that will be implemented to enable the learner to produce communicative utterances. Traditionally, interventionists have focused on establishing a single communication intent during the early phases of communication intervention. Evidence described in this chapter suggests that such a practice may make it more difficult to establish a fully generalized repertoire of communicative intents.

Additionally, we know that for some communicative intents, nonelectronic augmentative communication system users must engage in significantly more effort to derive the same outcome as their vocal mode counterparts. For a learner using a nonelectronic communication device, requesting attention and requesting object intents must be two separate chained acts. A verbal mode user consolidates these two communicative intents when he or she yells a request for a desired object.

There are indications that traditional communicative intents designed to describe pragmatic intents may actually describe response classes that are too broad for persons with severe disabilities. For example, a learner may request assistance either to access a positive reinforcer (e.g., ask for assistance in getting a candy unwrapped) or to avoid or escape a negative reinforcer (e.g., ask for assistance with a highly nonpreferred task in hopes that the interventionist will model performance while the learner watches). Recent evidence suggests that learners may not readily generalize across these two instances. Once a range of objects and activities has been identified as the focus of initial teaching procedures, we believe that a very important consideration focuses on characteristics that include the specificity, the motoric difficulty, and the similarity of graphic symbols and gestures that might be taught.

Sometimes communication interventionists are so intent on identifying new behaviors to teach that they tend to ignore existing repertoires. Interventionists must take greater care in determining learners' existing repertoires. Greater effort is required to determine what portions of the existing repertoire should be left as is, shaped into more appropriate forms, used conditionally, or completely replaced.

As mentioned earlier in this chapter, some learners may have acquired communication systems that will not be efficient in all environments. For example, an individual who has learned to sign will have a difficult time ordering fast food at McDonald's. Instances such as these require a duplicated mode application in which a graphic symbol would be used in the community while sign would continue to be used at home. We believe that interventionists must more thoughtfully consider when to consider implementing duplicated communication modes where indicated without creating an overly cumbersome communication system. We believe that with learners who do not already have a single well-established alternative communication system, concurrent modality sampling described earlier in this chapter represents a viable technique for helping determine the relative contribution of available augmentative modes.

In the area of instructional technology, there is a significant need to disseminate best practice information. Only recently have preservice programs begun to offer courses in augmentative and alternative communication. Among interventionists who received their preservice training before 1980, few studied augmentative and alternative communication systems. This suggests that there is a critical need to develop a continuum of inservice training and technical assistance for professionals and paraprofessionals serving clients in schools, residences, and day care.

DIRECTIONS FOR FUTURE RESEARCH

The study of augmentative and alternative communication is in its infancy. Consequently, much important research remains to be done. Particularly timely is research on: 1) the relationship between comprehension and production for the augmentative system user, 2) the interactional use of augmentative and alternative communication systems, 3) the replacement of challenging behavior with augmentative and alternative systems, and 4) the design of selection techniques to accommodate the learner's level of progress or deteriorating medical status.

To date, the bulk of the intervention research regarding augmentative and alternative communication has focused on the establishment of instrumental communicative intents. With the growing body of empirical demonstrations in this area, the attention of researchers has begun to focus on interactional uses of those instrumental intents. Research suggests that the slowness with which users of augmentative and alternative communication systems produce utterances causes communicative partners to alter their interactive style to "speed up" the interaction. There is a critical need for empirical scrutiny of selection techniques aimed at speeding up interactive exchanges without correspondingly increasing the number of listener queries for message clarification.

Few studies have examined the degree to which learned helplessness affects the establishment of initial communicative repertoires. There is a tremendous need for intervention research that delineates effective strategies to overcome passivity that represents the outcome of extensive histories of learned helplessness.

Interventionists are just beginning to understand fully the relationship between challenging behavior and the lack of a socially acceptable communicative repertoire. We know that the most efficient procedures are those that result in approximation of communicative alternatives in the presence of provoking stimuli. There is a critical need for assessment and intervention research that creatively embraces the technology offered by general case instructional technology.

Finally, the area of prevention has become a significant priority in the delineation of communication intervention programs in early childhood education. However, very little work has been done in the area of prevention of challenging behavior. At present, it is unclear whether it is possible to establish criteria that identify young learners as being at risk for the development of challenging behaviors. We are beginning to learn that the interactional patterns of individuals who engage in challenging behavior may affect the interactional behavior of their communicative partners. This evidence suggests possible avenues for intervention efforts aimed at preventing communicative partners from lapsing into less efficient interactional patterns with those who engage in challenging behavior.

The bulk of assessment and intervention studies have focused on the immediate establishment of systems, and rarely consider longitudinal planning for the use of an augmentative or alternative communication application across the individual client's life span. Intervention protocols for learners whose physical condition may be deteriorating, thus necessitating the use of a different selection technique, need to be developed.

CONCLUSION

Although the field of augmentative and alternative communication is in its infancy, significant advances have been made. Interventionists and researchers appear to be increasingly sensitive to the effect that selecting particular communicative intents, symbols, and vocabulary may have on the learner's propensity to acquire a generalized and functional communicative repertoire. There seems to be general agreement that most learners can benefit from gestural, graphic, and vocal modes as components of their overall communication system. What is not yet clear, however, is how best to go about determining the relative contributions of each of these modes.

Increasingly, there is a need for instructional procedures that can be used to serve younger learners. These procedures must be sufficiently practical so that they can be taught to all interventionists, including teachers, paraprofessionals, and parents. This represents a particularly challenging task when one considers that procedures must address the acquisition of vocal, gestural, and graphic communication modes.

Adults who may be at risk of losing or failing to be placed in a community residence because of communicatively motivated challenging behavior (e.g., aggression, tantrumming) require intervention procedures that fully address the range of antecedents and consequences that have come to strengthen unacceptable behavior. As with younger learners, there is a need to develop instructional procedures that are practical yet relatively easy to implement. Particularly acute is the need to develop sound inservice and technical assistance models for those who serve adults, among whom turnover is extremely high.

Longitudinal planning must be done in implementing augmentative and alternative communication systems. In some cases, learners using augmentative communication systems can be expected to acquire speech-motor control that may lessen the need for a communication aid. Other learners may become more severely impaired and require augmentative selection techniques that differ from those originally selected. To date, most interventionists' efforts have focused on demonstrating that individual augmentative communication applications can be successful without attempting to plan for the future.

The 1980s witnessed remarkable advances in the area of augmentative and alternative communication. Rapid advances in instructional technology have resulted in the acquisition of substantial communicative repertoires among learners who, in the past, would not have been considered as candidates for communication intervention. We look forward to the next 10 years with confidence that many of the issues raised in this chapter will have been resolved.

REFERENCES

Alpert, C. (1980). Procedures for determining the optimal nonspeech mode for the autistic child. In R. Schiefelbusch (Ed.), *Nonspeech language and communication: Analysis and intervention* (pp. 389–420). Baltimore: University Park Press.

Anglin, J.M. (1977). *Word, object, and conceptual development.* New York: Norton.

Barrera, R., Lobato-Barrera, D., & Sulzer-Azaroff, B. (1980). A simultaneous treatment comparison of three expressive language training programs with a mute autistic child. *Journal of Autism and Developmental Disorders, 10,* 21–38.

Brady, D.O., & Smouse, A.D. (1978). A simultaneous comparison of three methods for language training with an autistic child: An experimental single case analysis. *Journal of Autism and Childhood Schizophrenia, 8,* 271–279.

Brady, N., & Saunders, K. (in press). Some considerations in the effective teaching of object-to-symbol matching. *Augmentative and Alternative Communication.*

Campbell, P. (1989). Dysfunction in posture and movement in individuals with profound disabilities. In F. Brown & D. Lehr (Eds.), *Persons with profound disabilities: Issues and practices* (pp. 163–189). Baltimore: Paul H. Brookes Publishing Co.

Carlson, F. (1985). *Picsyms categorical dictionary.* Lawrence, KS: Baggeboda Press.

Carr, E.G., Binkoff, J.A., Kologinsky, E., & Eddy, M. (1978). Acquisition of sign language by autistic children I: Expressive labeling. *Journal of Applied Behavior Analysis, 11*(4), 459–501.

Carr, E., & Dores, P. (1981). Patterns of language acquisition following simultaneous communication with autistic children. *Analysis and Intervention in Developmental Disabilities, 1,* 347–361.

Carr, E.G., & Durand, V.M. (1985). Reducing behavior problems through functional communication training. *Journal of Applied Behavior Analysis, 18,* 111–126.

Carr, E., & Newsom, C. (1985). Demand related tantrums: Conceptualization and treatment. *Behavior Modification, 9,* 403–426.

Carr, E.G., Newsom, C.D., & Binkoff, J.A. (1976). Stimulus control of self-destructive behavior in a psychotic child. *Journal of Abnormal Child Psychology, 4*(2), 139–153.

Carr, E., Newsom, C., & Binkoff, J. (1980). Escape as a factor in the aggressive behavior of two retarded children. *Journal of Applied Behavior Analysis, 13,* 101–117.

Carr, E., Pridal, C., & Dores, P. (1984). Speech vs. sign comprehension in autistic children. Analysis and prediction. *Journal of Experimental Child Psychology, 37,* 587–597.

Cirrin, F., & Rowland, C. (1985). Communicative assessment of nonverbal youths with severe/profound mental retardation. *Mental Retardation, 23,* 52–62.

Clark, C.R., Davies, C.O., & Woodcock, R.W. (1974). *Standard Rebus glossary.* Circle Pines, MN: American Guidance Service.

Doherty, J.E. (1985). The effects of sign characteristics on sign acquisition and retention: An integrative review of the literature. *Augmentative and Alternative Communication, 1*(3), 108–121.

Doss, L.S., & Reichle, J. (1991). Replacing excess behavior with an initial communicative repertoire. In J. Reichle, J. York, & J. Sigafoos, *Implementing augmentative and alternative communication: Strategies for learners with severe disabilities.* Baltimore: Paul H. Brookes Publishing Co.

Durand, V.M. (1982). Analysis and intervention of self-injurious behavior. *Journal of The Association for the Severely Handicapped, 7*(1), 44–53.

Durand, V.M. (1986). Self-injurious behavior as intentional communication. In K.D. Gadow (Ed.), *Advances in learning and behavioral disabilities* (Vol. 5, pp. 141– 155). Greenwich, CT: JAI Press.

Durand, V.M., & Carr, E.G. (1987). Social influence on "self-stimulatory" behavior: Analysis and treatment application. *Journal of Applied Behavior Analysis, 20,* 119– 132.

Durand, V.M., & Crimmins, D.B. (1987). Assessment and treatment of psychotic speech in an autistic child. *Journal of Autism and Developmental Disorders, 17*(1), 17–28.

Durand, V.M., & Crimmins, D.B. (1988). Identifying the variables maintaining self-injurious behavior. *Journal of Autism and Developmental Disorders, 18*(1), 99– 117.

Franklin, K., & Beukelman, D. (1990). Augmentative communications: Directions for future research. In J. Miller (Ed.), *New directions in research on child language disorders* (pp. 321–338). Austin, TX: PRO-ED.

Franklin, K., & Beukelman, D. (1991). Augmentative communication: Directions for future research. In J. Miller (Ed.), *Research on child language disorders* (pp. 321– 338). Austin, TX: PRO-ED.

Guess, D. (1969). A functional analysis of receptive language and receptive speech: Acquisition of the plural morpheme. *Journal of Applied Behavior Analysis, 2,* 55– 64.

Guess, D., & Baer, D. (1973). An analysis of individual differences in generalization between receptive and productive language in retarded children. *Journal of Applied Behavior Analysis, 6,* 311–329.

Guess, D., Benson, H., & Siegel-Causey, E. (1985). Concepts and issues related to choice making and autonomy among persons with severe disabilities. *Journal of The Association for Persons with Severe Handicaps, 10*(2), 79–86.

Guess, D., Sailor, W., & Baer, D. (1974). To teach language to retarded children. In R.L. Schiefelbusch & L. Lloyd (Ed.), *Language perspectives: Acquisition, retardation and intervention.* Baltimore: University Park Press.

Hehner, B. (1980). *Blissymbols for use.* Toronto: Blissymbolics Communication Institute.

Hurlbut, B., Iwata, B., & Green, J. (1982). Nonvocal language acquisition in adolescents with severe physical disabilities: Blissymbol versus iconic stimulus formats. *Journal of Applied Behavior Analysis, 15,* 241–258.

Iwata, B.A., Dorsey, M.F., Slifer, K.J., Bauman, K.E., & Richman, G.S. (1982). Toward a functional analysis of self-injury. *Analysis and Intervention in Developmental Disabilities, 2,* 3–20.

Johnson, J. (1986). *Self-Talk: Communication boards for children and adults.* Tucson: Communication Skill Builders.

Karlan, G.R., & Lloyd, L.L. (1983, June). *Examination of recall comprehension learning by moderately retarded individuals responding to oral and manual cues.* Paper presented at the 107th Annual Meeting of the American Association on Mental Deficiency, Dallas.

Keogh, B., & Reichle, J. (1985). Communication intervention for the "difficult-to-teach" severely handicapped. In S. Warren & A. Rogers-Warren (Eds.), *Teaching functional language* (pp. 157–196). Baltimore: University Park Press.

Light, J., Collier, B., & Parnes, P. (1985). Communicative interaction between young nonspeaking physically disabled children and their primary caregivers: Part I, Discourse patterns. *Augmentative and Alternative Communication, 1,* 74–83.

Lovaas, O.I., Freitag, G., Gold, V.J., & Kassorla, I.C. (1965). Experimental studies in childhood schizophrenia: Analysis of self-destructive behavior. *Journal of Experimental Child Psychology, 2*, 67–84.

Luftig, R.L. (1983). Translucency of sign and concreteness of gloss in the manual sign learning of moderately-severely mentally retarded students. *American Journal of Mental Deficiency, 88*(3), 279–286.

Mayer-Johnson Co. (1986). *The Picture Communication Symbols, Books 1 and 2.* Solana Bech, CA: P.O. Box AD, 92075.

Mirenda, P., & Locke, P. (1989). A comparison of symbol transparency in nonspeaking persons with intellectual disabilities. *Journal of Speech and Hearing Disorders, 54*, 131–140.

Mustonen, T., Locke, P., Reichle, J., Solbrack, M., & Lindgren, A. (1991). An overview of augmentative and alternative communication systems. In J. Reichle, J. York, & J. Sigafoos, *Implementing augmentative and alternative communication: Strategies for learners with severe disabilities.* Baltimore: Paul H. Brookes Publishing Co.

Piché, L., & Reichle, J. 1991). Teaching scanning selection techniques. In J. Reichle, J. York, & J. Sigafoos, *Implementing augmentative and alternative communication: Strategies for learners with severe disabilities.* Baltimore: Paul H. Brookes Publishing Co.

Ratcliff, A. (1988). Can user cognitive style predict augmentative and alternative communication aid use? *Augmentative and Alternative Communication, 4*, 157–158.

Reichle, J. (1983). *A survey of professionals serving persons with severe handicaps.* Unpublished manuscript, University of Minnesota, Minneapolis.

Reichle, J. (1985). *A survey of vocabulary selection and use strategies for learners using augmentative and alternative communication systems.* Unpublished manuscript, University of Minnesota, Minneapolis.

Reichle, J. (1990). *Examining subtle generalization patterns within a pragmatic intent.* Unpublished manuscript, University of Minnesota, Minneapolis.

Reichle, J., & Karlan, G. (1985). The selection of an augmentative system in communication intervention: A critique of decision rules. *Journal of The Association for Persons with Severe Handicaps, 10*, 146–156.

Reichle, J., & Ward, M. (1985). Teaching discriminative use of an encoding electronic communication device and Signing Exact English to a moderately handicapped child. *Language, Speech, and Hearing Services in Schools, 16*, 58–63.

Reichle, J., York, J., & Sigafoos, J. (1991). *Implementing augmentative and alternative communication: Strategies for learners with severe disabilities.* Baltimore: Paul H. Brookes Publishing Co.

Remington, B., & Clarke, S. (1983). Acquisition of expressive signing by autistic children: An evaluation of the relative effects of simultaneous communication and sign alone training. *Journal of Applied Behavior Analysis, 16*, 315–328.

Seligman, M. (1975). *Helplessness: On depression, development and death.* San Francisco: W.H. Freeman.

Sevcik, R., & Romski, M. (1986). Representational matching skills for persons with severe retardation. *Augmentative and Alternative Communication, 2*, 160–164.

Siegel, G., & Vogt, M. (1984). Pluralization instruction in comprehension and production. *Journal of Speech and Hearing Disorders, 49*, 128–135.

Sigafoos, J., & York, J. (1991). Using ecological inventories to promote functional communication. In J. Reichle, J. York, & J. Sigafoos, *Implementing augmentative and alternative communication: Strategies for learners with severe disabilities* (pp. 61–70). Baltimore: Paul H. Brookes Publishing Co.

Stremel-Campbell, K., Cantrell, D., & Halle, J. (1977). Manual signing as a language system and as a speech initiator for the nonverbal severely handicapped student. In E. Sontag (Ed.), *Educational programming for the severely and profoundly handicapped* (pp. 335–347). Reston, VA: Council for Exceptional Children.

Sturmey, P., Carlsen, A., Crisp, A.G., & Newton, J.T. (1988). A functional analysis of multiple aberrant responses: A refinement and extension of Iwata et al.'s (1982) methodology. *Journal of Mental Deficiency Research, 32,* 31–46.

Weeks, M., & Gaylord-Ross, R. (1981). Task difficulty and aberrant behavior in severely handicapped students. *Journal of Applied Behavior Analysis, 14,* 449–463.

7

Facilitating Early Social
and Communicative Development
in Children with Autism

Laura Grofer Klinger
and Geraldine Dawson

CHILDREN WITH AUTISM HAVE SIGNIFICANT impairments in reciprocal social interaction including verbal and nonverbal communication (Rutter, 1983).[1] Those children who develop language often use it inappropriately, communicating through rote phrases or lengthy monologues. Kanner (1943), who originally described the fundamental deficit in autism as "the children's inability to relate themselves in the ordinary way to people and situations" (p. 242), proposed that their communication difficulties lie within the area of social communication rather than speech production. He wrote that "from the start, language—which the children did not use for the purpose of communication—was deflected in considerable measure to self-sufficient, semantically and conversationally valueless, or grossly distorted memory exercises" (p. 243). Despite Kanner's emphasis on the social deficit of autism, until the 1980s investigators viewed autism as a basic disorder of cognitive and linguistic processes, and virtually ignored examination of the social and affective contributions to the syndrome. The emphasis recently has shifted back to the social-emotional domain, as investigators have focused on the early development of children with autism.

The authors wish to thank the Washington Association for Retarded Citizens for funds provided to Geraldine Dawson to study early intervention methods with children with autism, and the parents and children who participated in these studies, who have much to teach us about intervention.
[1]Since most of the available research has been conducted with children with specific diagnoses of autism, we have chosen to focus our discussion on autism, rather than on the broader category of pervasive developmental disorder. However, most of the ideas discussed here, including those pertaining to intervention, are generally applicable to children with pervasive developmental disorder.

Indeed, several researchers now consider the language dysfunction in autism to be a direct reflection of underlying impairments in early social-emotional development (Prizant & Wetherby, 1989), or at least a function of combined interrelated deficits in social-emotional and linguistic-communicative functioning (Tager-Flusberg, 1989). Children with autism display either delayed or aberrant development of attention to social stimuli (Dawson & Lewy, 1989a; Ferrara & Hill, 1980), social gaze (Dawson, Hill, Spencer, Galpert, & Watson, 1990; Mundy, Sigman, Ungerer, & Sherman, 1986), motor imitation (Curcio, 1978; Dawson & Adams, 1984; DeMyer et al., 1972; Hammes & Langdell, 1981), joint attention (Mundy et al., 1986; Wetherby & Prutting, 1984), and affective communication (Dawson et al., 1990; Kasari, Sigman, Mundy, & Yirmiya, 1990). In contrast, children with autism display relative strengths in nonsocial precursors to language, including object permanence skills (Dawson & Adams, 1984) and early categorization abilities (Tager-Flusberg, 1985; Ungerer & Sigman, 1987).

In this chapter, we review current research on the development of early social-emotional precursors to language in children without disabilities and in children with autism. We then propose a psychobiological framework for understanding the impairments observed in children with autism. Finally, we use this framework to explore methods for facilitating social-emotional development and communication.

SOCIOEMOTIONAL PRECURSORS TO LANGUAGE

Through social interaction during the first year of life, infants learn to engage in nonverbal reciprocal exchanges with their caregivers (Stern, 1985; Tronick, Als, & Adamson, 1979) that provide a necessary foundation for the intentional use of language (Bates, 1979; Bruner, 1975, 1977). These reciprocal caregiver–infant interactions may be precursors to the development of reciprocal interactions involving language. Children with autism do not readily engage in social reciprocal interaction, and thus often lack many prelinguistic skills that are normally achieved during the first year of life. In the following sections, the normal development of these precursors to language is briefly discussed and current knowledge of the development of children with autism is reviewed.

Attention to Social Stimuli and the Development of Contingency

The development of reciprocal social and communicative interaction may depend upon the ability to understand contingency, that is, the fact that actions of others affect oneself, and that one's own actions affect others. Through contingent, predictable, and repetitive interactions with caregivers, infants develop a sense of control over their environments (Lamb, 1981), and begin to perceive themselves as effective social agents (Schaffer, 1977). By 2 months of age, infants have developed an understanding of the contingent relationships between their own actions and environmental events. For example, Watson (Watson, 1978; Watson & Ramey, 1972) provided 2-month-old infants with an opportunity to control a mobile above their cribs by kicking their legs. Not only did these infants display an understanding of the contingent relationships between their actions and the mobile, as demonstrated by increased kicking, they also responded emotionally to the mobile, as evidenced by smiling and cooing in its direction.

It has been theorized that children who do not develop a sense of contingency may develop a sense of learned helplessness (Seligman, 1975). That is, if their ability to recognize relationships between their own behavior and external consequences, including responses from others, is impaired, they may not develop a sense of social effectiveness. Seligman suggested that individuals who have a perceived lack of control over environmental stimuli may develop cognitive, motivational, and affective deficits.

Interestingly, social interaction is not always contingent. When a young infant vocalizes, it is likely but not certain that the mother will vocalize in return (Strain & Vietze, 1975). Similarly, an infant's crying may often, but not always, elicit attention from caregivers. Given the fact that early social interaction is often noncontingent, how do normally developing children avoid learned helplessness and develop a sense of social effectiveness? Suomi (1981) proposed that infants have "perceptual systems that are 'tuned' to be especially sensitive to particular social stimuli" (p. 189). Studies have shown that infants quickly develop attentional preferences for social stimuli (Carpenter, 1974; Field, 1979; Sherrod, 1979). Indeed, it appears that the human infant's attention is inherently drawn to any stimulus that is novel and slightly discrepant from expectation (Kagan, Kearsley, & Zelazo, 1978). This is of great adaptive significance since social stimulation is, by nature, novel and not fully predictable. This inherent feature of the mind to attend to novelty while at the same time seeking to detect invariant features in the everchanging flow of social stimulation provides an essential foundation for the infant's interest in and comprehension of the social world (Bruner, 1977; Stern, 1985).

We have proposed that children with autism have difficulty attending to and processing unpredictable information (Dawson, in press; Dawson & Lewy, 1989a, 1989b). This difficulty is hypothesized to interfere with their ability to develop an understanding of the social world. This hypothesis is supported by Ferrara and Hill's (1980) finding that in a nonpredictable, noncontingent situation, children with autism displayed disorganized behavior, and were less likely to respond to their environment. However, children with autism were able to form expectations from highly predictable environmental events. Similarly, in two studies of young children with autism, Dawson and her colleagues (Dawson & Adams, 1984; Dawson & Galpert, 1990) found that the children's attention to a social partner increased significantly when the partner's responses were highly contingent and predictable.

Unlike children without disabilities, children with autism do not appear to adapt to the noncontingent nature of social interactions. It is possible that they lack an innate predisposition to attend to social stimuli, and thus do not easily develop a sense of social effectiveness. This perceived lack of control over social stimuli may lead to cognitive, motivational, and affective deficits characteristic of learned helplessness. Indeed, Koegel and Mentis (1985) have suggested that the low motivation and apathy displayed by some children with autism may be indicative of learned helplessness.

Gaze

Infant–caregiver eye-to-eye gaze is an early form of reciprocal interaction that mimics the temporal patterns of adult conversations (Jaffe, Stern, & Peery, 1973). Infants engage their caregivers in alternating patterns of eye contact and gaze withdrawal. This pattern is similar to an adult conversation in which one person speaks to another, stops, and then resumes speaking. Researchers (e.g., Brazelton, 1982; Stern, 1971, 1985) have suggested that eye-to-eye gaze also provides a means by which infants regulate the amount of social stimulation they receive.

Children with autism often fail to engage in the normal patterns of eye-to-eye gaze. Although they do not typically avoid looking at others (Hermelin & O'Connor, 1970), they do not appear to use eye-to-eye contact as a means of social communication. In a recent study, Dawson, Hill, Spencer, Galpert and Watson (1990) reported that children with autism differed from children without disabilities not in the amount of time they spent gazing at others, but rather in the quality of their eye contact. Dawson et al. (1990) found that young children with autism observed during freeplay gazed at their mothers just as often as did children without disabilities matched on receptive language ability. However, the children with autism were less likely to combine gaze with affective expression toward their mothers in a way that conveys communicative intent. Thus, it appeared that they did not use eye-to-eye gaze as a means of communicating emotion with others.

Dawson et al. (1990) also found that, compared with mothers of children without disabilities, mothers of children with autism displayed significantly fewer smiles during interaction with their children, and were less likely to smile in response to their children's smiles. Given the fact that the children failed to express affect in a communicative way, it is not surprising that their mothers did not smile as often in return.

Imitation

During the first 6 months of life, caregivers frequently communicate with their infants by directly imitating their infants' body movements, facial expressions, and vocalizations (Kaye, 1982; Malatesta & Izard, 1984; Uzgiris,

1981). This early imitative play is a social exchange, which is evident in the infant's tendency to respond to his or her parent's imitations with visual interest and smiles. Young infants are also capable of imitating their caregivers' actions. Studies have shown that infants can imitate facial expressions and finger movements shortly after birth (Abravanel & Sigafoos, 1984; Field, Woodson, Greenberg, & Cohen, 1982; Meltzoff & Moore, 1977). Heimann (1989) examined the relationship between early infant imitation and infant eye contact. Infant imitative behavior at 2–3 days, at 3 weeks, and at 3 months of age was found to be related to the frequency of gaze aversion at 3 months of age. That is, infants who engaged in more imitation at an early age displayed fewer episodes of gaze aversion, suggesting that even neonatal imitation has a role in early social interaction.

As a communicative act, imitation serves to facilitate an early reciprocal interaction involving mutual mimicking of actions and vocalizations. These early experiences are likely to play an important role in the infant's growing awareness that he or she has participated in a social exchange and that others have mental states that are knowable (Stern, 1985). Uzgiris (1981) suggested that "an instance of imitation can epitomize the presence of mutuality; to do something that has just been done by the other is to know something not only about the act but also about the similarity between oneself and the other" (p. 151).

Given their lack of participation in early social exchanges, it is likely that children with autism often fail to engage in early interactions in which their parents imitate their actions. Furthermore, children with autism display significant delays in their own use of motor imitation (Curcio, 1978; Dawson & Adams, 1984; DeMyer et al., 1972; Hammes & Langdell, 1981). Dawson and Adams (1984) assessed imitation in a group of preschool children with autism. Although the majority demonstrated well-developed object permanence skills, half of the children were functioning at the 1–4 month level in their ability to imitate actions produced by others. Children's ability to imitate was positively correlated with their social responsiveness, free-play, and language. The question of whether the impairment in motor imitation is a primary perceptual-motor deficit in crossmodal processing (Ozonoff, Pennington, & Rogers, 1990), or is secondary to a lack of experience in early imitative interactions (e.g., parental imitation) has not been answered. Whatever the cause, without participation in early imitative interactions, children with autism are likely to display delayed or aberrant development of more advanced reciprocal interactions that provide a foundation for communication, and may lack an understanding of self as related to others.

Joint Attention

During the middle of the first year, social interactions evolve from face-to-face dyadic exchanges between caregivers and their infants to triadic exchanges involving objects (Bakeman & Adamson, 1984; Bruner, 1975; Sugarman, 1984). In these triadic exchanges, caregivers and infants coordinate their attention around objects of mutual interest. Joint attention is observed through the use of referential looking between the object and caregiver and gestural communication, such as pointing. Referential looking develops between 6 and 9 months of age (Walden & Ogan, 1988). Pointing as a nonverbal social gesture develops between 9 and 12 months of age (Hannan, 1987). The ability to share a focus of attention is considered an important prerequisite to the development of verbal communication (Bruner, 1975; Sugarman, 1984), as infants gradually learn to use language rather than gaze and gesture to direct another's attention.

Although children with autism look at others as frequently as do children without disabilities, they tend to appear not to use gaze as a means of sharing their attention with others. Wetherby and Prutting (1984) reported that children with autism consistently used gestural communication to request objects or actions, but rarely attempted to direct adult attention through gestures. Mundy et al. (1986) compared the joint attention skills of children with autism, developmentally matched children with mental retardation, and children without disabilities. Although children with autism showed some ability to use gestures to request objects, they displayed consistent delays in their use of indicating behaviors, such as referential looking and pointing. On the basis of their referential looking abilities, 94.4% of the children with autism could be correctly classified as autistic. The deficit in joint attention abilities thus does not appear to be a function of mental retardation.

Mundy and Sigman (1989a) have suggested that the difficulties with joint attention shown by children with autism may be a result of disturbances in affective expression that "significantly attenuate the opportunities of the young autistic child to experience contingent caregiver affective responses" (p. 216). They proposed that this disturbance, in combination with delayed representational development, may lead to additional difficulties in metarepresentational development. In particular, they suggest that the difficulty children with autism have in understanding that others have mental states different from their own (i.e., "theory of mind" deficits, Baron-Cohen, 1989; Baron-Cohen, Leslie, & Frith 1985, 1986) may be related to early disturbances in affective expression.

Affective Sharing

Affective sharing involves the interpersonal coordination of affective expression between an infant and his or her caregiver. In normal development, the infant and caregiver experience mutual interest and pleasure in each other's smiling and vocalizations, ensuring that they will often experience shared feeling states. Hobson (1989, 1990) and Stern (1985) have proposed that the interpersonal coordination of affective expression is intimately related to the infant's realization that inner subjective experiences are potentially sharable with another person. Stern has described a particular form of affective sharing, "affective attunement," in which feeling states are coordinated not through an exact imitation of the affective expression of another, but rather through an elaboration of the affect of another. That is, between 9 and 15 months of age, infants learn that the same emotional states can be expressed through different modalities (Stern, 1985). For example, excitement can be expressed through activities such as banging of toys, waving of hands, and babbling. Thus, during interactions involving affective attunement, infants and their caregivers express similar feeling states using different modalities. Stern hypothesizes that this form of interaction involves a representation of subjective states, and is a precursor to symbolic development.

Two recent studies have demonstrated that, compared to developmentally matched children, children with autism exhibit less positive affect during playful interactions with others (Snow, Hertzig, & Shapiro, 1986; Yirmiya, Kasari, Sigman, & Mundy, 1989). Moreover, Dawson et al. (1990) found that, compared with children without disabilities matched on language ability, children with autism were less likely to smile in response to their mothers' smiles. Indeed, in this study, only 3 of the 15 children with autism ever smiled in response to their mothers' smiles. These results led Dawson (Dawson, in press; Dawson & Lewy, 1989a) to suggest that children with autism may not readily experience the mutual sharing of positive emotion. Without such experiences, the subsequent emergence of affective attunement would be expected to be lacking.

Summary

In summary, children with autism often display significant impairments in the socioemotional precursors to language. Impairments in the basic understanding of the reciprocal nature of social interactions as well as difficulties in conceptualizing that others have different attentional foci and feeling states are suggested by commonly seen delays in social gaze, imitation, joint attention, and affective sharing.

A PSYCHOBIOLOGICAL FRAMEWORK FOR UNDERSTANDING EARLY SOCIOEMOTIONAL DEFICITS IN AUTISM

The development of socioemotional precursors to language depends fundamentally upon the capacity to direct and sustain attention to social stimuli, and to extract meaning from this information. For infants without disabilities, an attentional preference for social stimuli appears to be innate, as is evident in infants' preferences for animate rather than inanimate objects (Carpenter, 1974; Field, 1979; Sherrod, 1979) and for the human face and voice. In response to the infant's attention, caregivers provide additional social stimulation that tends to be exaggerated and repetitive, with slight variations during each presentation. For example, caregivers engage in "baby talk," characterized by raised pitch, simplified syntax, reduced rate, and exaggerated pitch contours (Snow, 1972); "baby faces," consisting of facial expressions of longer duration and slower composition and decomposition (Malatesta & Haviland, 1982; Stern, 1977); and exaggerated eye contact. During these interactions, caregivers follow a "theme-and-variation" format, in which they vary some aspects of their behavior while keeping other features constant (Stern, 1985). This interaction involves a degree of predictability and repetitiveness, but also introduces a certain amount of unpredictability and novelty. It has been suggested that this type of social interaction maintains the infant's attention by providing optimal levels of novelty while at the same time, teaching the "invariant features" of interpersonal behavior (Stern, 1985).

The natural tendency to attend to information that is novel and not fully predictable is seen in its most basic form in the orienting response that is evoked by stimuli that are of mild intensity, novel, and slightly discrepant from expectations (Graham & Clifton, 1966; Graham & Jackson, 1970; Sokolov, 1963). The orienting response is characterized by predictable physiological changes, such as pupil dilation, electroencephalogram (EEG) desynchronization, increased electrodermal activity, suppression of respiratory frequency, decreased peripheral blood flow, and an initial slowing of heart rate. Gradually, as the novel stimulus is repeated, habituation occurs during which the infant's physiological responses return to prestimulus baseline levels. Stimuli that are maximally effective for eliciting an orienting response shift from simple to more complex during development (Graham, Anthony, & Zeigler, 1983).

Several studies have demonstrated that children with autism display abnormal orienting responses to novel, unpredictable stimuli. They have been found to display accelerations in heart rate (Palkowitz & Wiesenfeld, 1980) as well as a reduced electrodermal response to initial stimulation (Bernal & Miller, 1971; Van Engeland, 1984). Reductions in rate of habituation for heart rate (Palkowitz & Wiesenfeld, 1980) and respiratory responses (James & Barry, 1980) have also been reported. Cortical event-related brain potential studies have demonstrated a reduced P3 component, normally associated with the processing of unexpected novel stimuli, in individuals with autism (Courchesne, Lincoln, Kilman, & Galambos, 1985; Dawson, Finley, Phillips, Galpert, & Lewy, 1988; Novick, Vaughn, Kurtzberg, & Simson, 1980). Taken together, these findings suggest that children with autism fail to attend adaptively to and process unpredictable, novel stimuli.

We have proposed that autistic children's abnormal orienting response may be related to difficulties in arousal regulation (Dawson, in press; Dawson & Lewy, 1989a, 1989b). Physiological studies suggest that children with autism are easily overaroused. Hutt, Forrest, and Richer (1975) found significantly higher levels of spontaneous heart rate variability in children with autism compared with children without disabilities. This variability decreased when the children engaged in a simple, repetitive task. Several other studies of spontaneous heart rate, measured in a variety of environmental conditions, have demonstrated that children with autism exhibit both greater heart rate variability and significantly elevated heart rates, as compared with children without disabilities (Cohen & Johnson, 1977; Kootz & Cohen, 1981; Kootz, Marinelli, & Cohen, 1982). Furthermore, Kootz et al. (1982) found that more severely impaired children with autism were more likely than less severely impaired children to exhibit increased heart rate in response to changes in the environment.

The notion that there are individual differences in biologically determined optimal levels of stimulation has been discussed by Hebb (1955), Schneirla (1959), and Berlyne (1960). Field (1982) discussed the role of optimal levels of stimulation in mother–infant social interaction. She suggested that attention and positive affect during social interaction may occur within a range of activation that has as its lower limit an attention-orienting threshold and as its upper limit an attention-aversion threshold. Following this "activation band model," she theorized that the frequent negative affect, gaze aversion, and elevated heart rates displayed by preterm infants reflect a lower aversion threshold and a narrow range of optimal stimulation. We hypothesize that children with autism have an unusually narrow range of optimal stimulation, so that their ability to make sense of and relate to their environments depends, in a large part, on the amount of regularity and familiarity (Dawson, in press; Dawson & Lewy, 1989a, 1989b). We further hypothesize that the difficulty displayed by persons with autism in processing social information, including facial expressions, vocalizations, and gestures, is a function of the basic differences in the nature of information provided by animate versus inanimate objects. Social, emotional, and linguistic stimuli are, by nature, relatively unpredictable and indeterminate, whereas object-related stimuli, such as pattern, space, and the mechanical aspects of an object, tend to be more predictable, repeatable, and determinate. Thus, object-related information, over which the child may have control and which may be repeated, may be more easily assimilated, and is less likely to elicit overarousal and inattention. The child with autism may lack the biologically innate ability to detect invariants in stimuli that are unpredictable and probabilistic. As a result, as Mundy and Sigman (1989a, 1989b) have suggested, the child with autism may have difficulty detecting the contingent relationships between his or her own actions and the responses of others. However, social contingency is but one example of the many aspects of interpersonal knowledge that depend upon the ability to detect the invariant features from the complex, unpredictable information inherent in social interaction. Without the ability to impose meaning upon the everchanging flow of social information, the person with autism may be overwhelmed and overaroused by such information, and respond by failing to attend or even withdrawing from such stimuli.

A DEVELOPMENTAL PSYCHOBIOLOGICAL APPROACH TO INTERVENTION

Social Responsiveness Through Imitative Play

In normal development, parental imitation of an infant's behavior is one of the earliest forms of communication between a caregiver and an infant, and is commonly observed during the first 6 months of life. Several social functions of parental imitation have been proposed, including increased attentiveness toward social interaction (Piaget, 1962); facilitation of early turn-taking behavior (Stern, 1985); the development of a sense of self as related to others (Baldwin, 1973; Uzgiris, 1981); enhancement of infant imitation of others (Francis, Self, & Noble, 1981); and the shaping of emotional expression and awareness (Malatesta & Haviland, 1982). Imitating an infant also serves to reduce the amount of stimulation experienced by the infant by placing the infant in the role of initiator. Field (1977, 1979) found that preterm infants became more attentive when their mothers systematically imitated their infants' behavior instead of interacting freely. Corresponding decreases were noted in infant tonic heart rate.

It has been found that children with autism also display increased amounts of social attention and responsiveness when they are imitated (Dawson & Adams, 1984; Dawson & Galpert, 1990; Tiegerman & Primavera, 1981, 1984). Specifically, Dawson and Adams (1984) found that imitation increased children's use of gaze and social responsiveness (e.g., touching, vocalizations, gestures). Encouraged by these effects of imitation, Dawson and Galpert (1990) examined the cumulative effects of parental imitation over a 2-week intervention period. Fifteen preschool children with autism, ranging from 2 to 6 years of age, and their mothers participated in this study. At the beginning of the study, mothers and their children were observed during a free-play period. Next, each mother was given two sets of identical toys and asked to imitate her child's actions with the toys daily for 20 minutes for the next 2 weeks. At the end of the 2-week period, the mothers and their children were videotaped during another freeplay session and during imitation sessions with both novel toys and toys that had been used at home. Compared with freeplay sessions, children showed significant increases in the average duration of gaze toward mother's face during the imitation sessions (Figure 1). Corresponding decreases in the amount of time spent looking at mothers' actions with the toys were noted, suggesting that parental imitation had an

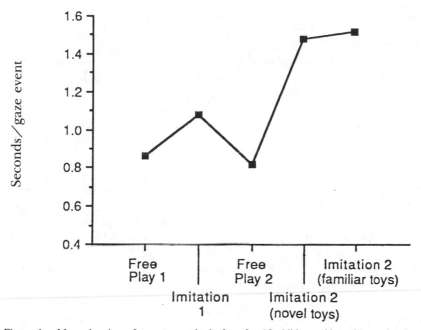

Figure 1.   Mean duration of gaze at mother's face for 15 children with autism under five different conditions: 1) freeplay with mother, before the 2-week intervention (Free Play 1); 2) mother imitates child's play, before the 2-week intervention (Imitation 1); 3) freeplay with mother, after the 2-week intervention (Free Play 2); 4) mother imitates child's play with unfamiliar toys, after the 2-week intervention (Imitation 2—Novel Toys); and 5) mother imitates child's play with familiar toys, after the 2 week intervention (Imitation 2—Familiar Toys). (From Dawson, G., & Galpert, L. [1990]. Mother's use of imitative play for facilitating social responsiveness and toy play in young autistic children, *Development and Psychopathology, 2,* 151–162. Reprinted by permission of Cambridge University Press.)

effect on the children's social attention. That is, the children did not simply find their mothers' contingent interactions with toys more interesting, but rather found social interaction more interesting.

The use of imitation by parents has been a component of other intervention programs. Mahoney and colleagues (Mahoney, 1990; Mahoney & Powell, 1988) developed a parenting program for birth to 3-year-old children with disabilities. The focus of their Transactional Intervention Program (TRIP) was to increase parental use of turn-taking skills by imitating the child's behavior and following the child's lead. Children of parents who effectively used TRIP techniques made relative mental development gains that were 48% greater than those of children of parents who used the techniques less frequently. These gains were mediated by affective characteristics of the parents, with children of high-affect parents displaying the most improvement. Taken together, these findings suggest that parental imitation of children with developmental delays is an effective intervention technique.

Strategies for Facilitating Social Interaction

General Principles

During the past several years, a series of early social interactive strategies has been designed to promote early social responsiveness, including verbal and nonverbal communication, contingency, social gaze, turn-taking, imitation, and joint attention, in children with autism. These strategies are based on five general principles. First, they are modeled from naturally occurring patterns of early social interaction. Thus, as in normal development, social skills are facilitated naturally through play rather than taught explicitly.

Second, the strategies are based on knowledge of normal developmental sequences, progressing from very simple interactions to increasingly complex social interactive skills.

Third, "scaffolding" is used. Scaffolding occurs naturally during caregiver–infant interaction, and refers to the process by which parents provide stimulation that is close to or slightly above the child's current developmental level (Bruner, 1982). For children with autism, it is very likely that their impairments prevent them from benefiting from their caregivers' natural attempts to guide them through developmental sequences. Therefore, these intervention strategies seek to build an "augmented scaffold" in which social experiences are not only geared toward the child's developmental level, but are also exaggerated and simplified so that the relevant aspects of social interaction are distilled and become highly salient and more easily assimilable.

A fourth principle is that all interventions need to be sensitive to the possibility that a child with autism may have a narrow range of optimal stimulation. Therapy sessions are designed to reduce the amount of novelty and unpredictability in social interactions and to allow the child to regulate the amount of social stimulation received. In this way, the strategies minimize the possibility that the child will become overstimulated.

Finally, interventions seek to place the child in the role of initiator while maintaining a predictable environment. While children with autism appear to learn better in highly structured situations, they often accept a passive role, placing the caregiver in the role of initiator. Through a series of child-directed strategies in which the adult predictably follows the child's lead, the child is placed in the role of initiator, and thus experiences a sense of control and effectiveness in the social environment. These strategies can be implemented by the child's teacher, communication disorders specialist, psychologist, and parents. These social interactive strategies are examined in the following sections. A detailed description of these strategies appears in the appendix.[2]

---

[2]These strategies are in the process of undergoing further refinement, particularly in Level Two. Thus, the reader interested in using this approach may want to contact the second author for updated information.

Level One Strategies:
Facilitating Attention to People, Social Contingency, and Turn-Taking

The first set of interactive strategies focuses on the goals of increasing eye contact and enjoyment of play, teaching an understanding of social contingency, and promoting early turn-taking behavior. Facilitation of these skills is broken down into four sequential phases. Phase One focuses on increasing attention to others and promoting the child's feeling of comfort in interactions and understanding of simple contingent interactions with objects. The strategy involves simultaneous and exact imitation of the child's actions, body movements, and vocalizations. In order to facilitate the child's recognition that he or she is being imitated, the adult's imitations are exaggerated. The goal of this phase is for the child to begin to attend to the adult's actions rather than to his or her own toys, thus providing a basis for the child to notice the connection between his or her own actions, and the actions of the adult.

Phase Two is included to promote eye contact in those children who do not readily begin to attend to the adult's face in Phase One. The adult attempts to make the face more salient by placing his or her face within the child's line of vision and exaggerating facial expressions while imitating the child.

In Phase Three, the adult incorporates turn-taking and anticipatory behavior in the imitative play. To facilitate this kind of interaction, the adult pauses before imitating the child rather than imitating the child simultaneously. This naturally leads the child to anticipate the adult's actions and creates a back-and-forth, or turn-taking, type of interaction. When the child realizes that he or she is being imitated (Phase One and Phase Two) a game frequently will develop in which the child will hastily switch the type or speed of activities in order to see if the adult will follow. This is often accompanied by an affective response in which the child laughs and looks at the adult's face.

Finally, in Phase Four, the child learns that contingent interactions need not involve exact imitations. In this phase, the adult imitates the child's actions with a similar, but not identical, object, focusing more on intensity and rhythm than on direct imitation, or the adult modifies the actions using the same toy as the child. The goal of this stage is for the child to continue to display anticipation and turn-taking despite the indirect nature of the imitation.

As the child progresses through each of these phases, it is important for the adult to retain components of earlier phases. It is especially important to return to an earlier phase when the child becomes inattentive. Although these phases have been designed in a developmental fashion, some children may not follow this particular pattern of development. Thus, we suggest an occasional advance to a developmentally higher phase in order to gauge the child's response to strategies at higher levels.

Level Two Strategies:
Imitation, Early Communication, and Joint Attention Skills

After the child has achieved the goals targeted in Level One, two sets of skills—imitation of others and early communicational joint attention—can be facilitated in tandem. The two sets of skills can be incorporated simultaneously during the therapy sessions. These strategies are inserted throughout the session—during which the adult primarily continues to imitate and follow the child's lead—at moments when the child is engaged and attentive.

Imitation

The strategies for increasing the child's imitation of others are based on Piaget's (1962) sequence of imitation development. According to Piaget, the development of imitation begins with "pseudo-imitation," in which the infant simply attends to other people's imitation of his or her own actions and responds by repeating the actions. This is equivalent to the Level One phases, in which the adult does the bulk of the imitating. In the next stage, the infant first becomes capable of imitating actions that are in the infant's own behavioral repertoire. Only later does the infant become capable of imitating novel actions modeled by others. Thus, in Phase One of Level Two, the goal is for the child to imitate familiar schemes introduced by the adult. The strategy involves occasionally introducing a familiar action for the child to imitate rather than solely imitating the child. Ideally, the familiar action is introduced at times when the child is optimally engaged and paying attention to the adult. Next, in Phase Two, the adult begins to introduce novel schemes for the child to imitate. If the child does not begin to imitate the adult, after several trials, the adult simply returns to imitating the child's actions, and tries these strategies again at a later time in the session.

Early Communication and Joint Attention

We have used several strategies to facilitate communication and joint attention skills. Again, these strategies are interspersed throughout a session involving imitative play. In Phase One, the goal is to have the child spontaneously communicate with the adult in order to achieve a desired goal. This is accomplished by structuring the environment in such a way that the child is highly motivated to communicate in order to meet his or her needs. To do this, we have incorporated Koegel and Johnson's (1989) strategies for motivating language use in children with autism by "salting the environment" (e.g., by putting interesting objects inside a jar that is difficult to open or out of reach). In this way, a child will be motivated to use gesture, gaze, or language spontaneously in order to obtain a desired object. In Phase Two, the goal is to have the child spontaneously communicate with the adult about a goal that necessitates shared participation and attention. To achieve this, we introduce interesting activities that require another person's help (e.g., bubbles, balloons, a see-saw that takes two people to operate, a pinwheel that the child is not able to make spin). Alternatively, the shared attention can occur around a social routine. Often, children will initiate ritualized interactions with objects or body movements. The adult can facilitate the development of these routines by interpreting a child's action as if it represented a request for a shared activity. For example, the adult can hang a string of beads in the room and then twirl the child around the room every time that the child touches the beads.

Once the child has begun to engage in and communicate about shared activities systematically, the adult can then alter his or her behavior to facilitate the child's use of eye contact during communication about the shared activities (Phase Three). Again, the environment is structured so that the child must incorporate the adult in a shared activity to achieve a goal. To begin with, the adult simply pauses before following through with these activities. Frequently, the child will look at the adult's face spontaneously in order to prompt the beginning of the activity. When this gaze occurs, the adult immediately carries out the desired activity. Thus, the adult starts to require that the child combine his or her own verbal and nonverbal requests with gaze at the adult's face. Another strategy, which is appropriate only for higher-functioning children, involves feigning confusion about the child's request. For example, if the child asks the adult to draw a letter on the blackboard without turning around to face the adult, the adult acts confused about whether he or she is being asked to draw a "B" or a "G." Only when the child turns to look at the adult and says, "B," does the adult immediately comply with the request. In this way, the child begins to understand that his or her own nonverbal cues are vital to successful communication.

Once the child begins to look at the adult's face systematically when requesting, the adult can then alter his or her behavior in such a way that the child must attend to and take into account the adult's verbal and nonverbal cues (including facial expressions and attentional focus) in order to achieve a goal (Phase Four). To begin with, the adult can provide exaggerated nonverbal cues that indicate whether or not he or she is likely to carry out the activity. For example, the adult may pause and then display an exaggerated smile or head nod only before performing the activity. Certain objects naturally draw the child's attention to the adult's face. For instance, when blowing a pinwheel for a child, an adult can exaggerate and hold an indrawn breath waiting for the child to prompt the exhalation. In this way, the child learns that the nonverbal cues of others are important components of successful communication. Eventually, the adult can pretend that he or she is not paying attention to the child in order to motivate the child to try to direct the adult's attention to the desired activity.

It is important for the adult to vary the strategies (i.e., objects and nonverbal cues used) so that the child generalizes the skills rather than simply learns isolated responses. It is also important to respond positively when the child uses the most advanced forms of communication in his or her existing repertoire rather than holding out for a skill the child has not yet developed.

EDUCATIONAL AND CLINICAL IMPLICATIONS

Since the 1970s, treatment for autism has consisted primarily of either phar-macological or behavioral interventions. Pharmacological interventions have been effective only with a relatively small subgroup of individuals, and the benefits for even this subgroup have been circumscribed (Holm & Varley, 1989). Behavioral interventions have focused on direct training of appropriate behavior via operant conditioning and modeling, and have been more suc-cessful for increasing specific cognitive and language skills, and reducing maladaptive behaviors, such as self-abuse, particularly when initiated at a young age and applied intensively (Lovaas, 1987; Strain, 1983). However, even the most successful behavioral interventions have not yet been able to address adequately certain core features of autism, namely, the impairments in reciprocal social interaction and pragmatic language abilities. The most suc-cessful social skill programs have focused mainly on increasing peer interac-tion (Strain, 1983). Few intervention programs have been specifically de-signed to promote the early social abilities that normally emerge in the first 2 years of life and provide the foundation for developing reciprocal social interaction and relationships with others, including peers.

Indeed, several authors (Duchan, 1983; Hubbell, 1977; Seibert & Oller, 1981; Wetherby, 1986) have argued that the distinct communicative profile observed in children with autism may actually be exacerbated by traditional behavioral approaches to intervention, suggesting that these interventions may unintentionally inhibit the development of certain social and communication skills. For example, traditional interventions have adopted an adult-directed approach in which the child learns to follow the adult's external cues and prompts during social interaction without learning to initiate spontaneous interaction. Wetherby (1986) has noted that traditional therapies have used "pragmatically irrelevant reinforcers" (p. 308), such as food, which do not teach the child that social interaction itself can be reinforcing. Problems with generalization and validity occur when isolated behaviors are taught outside the rich social context in which they normally emerge.

The child-directed strategies presented in this chapter were developed to increase the spontaneous use of skills that are necessary for early social interaction and communication. This approach places the child in the role of initiator, and capitalizes on naturally occurring patterns of social interaction. The approach can be used with children of all levels of functioning, requiring virtually no prerequisite skills. In fact, a long-term goal is the use of this approach with infants with autism. It has become increasingly recognized that early intervention can have a profound impact on the development of children with autism (Simeonsson, Olley, & Rosenthal, 1987). It is anticipated that intervention strategies focused on early social abilities will have positive benefits for parents' emotional well-being as they become more capable of forming successful social relationships with their young children with autism.

DIRECTIONS FOR FUTURE RESEARCH

We must emphasize that the expanded series of interactive strategies described in this chapter, while theoretically appealing and relatively easy to implement, needs to be subjected to more rigorous study before we can confidently claim its usefulness for children with autism. We currently have only tentative empirical support for the effectiveness of the expanded series of strategies. We have recently completed a single-subject, multiple baseline intervention study with two 5-year-old boys with autism attending the Experimental Education Unit at the University of Washington. Each child received a diagnosis of autism based on the *Diagnostic and Statistical Manual of Mental Disorders-Revised* (American Psychiatric Association, 1987), and the Childhood Autism Rating Scale (Schopler, Reichler, & Renner, 1986). Communication and joint attention skills were targeted for the first child, who demonstrated mild impairments in expressive language and was capable of imitating familiar and novel actions with objects and body movements. He participated in 1 month of baseline (consisting of freeplay with the examiner), followed by 14 months of intervention using Level Two strategies. Early social contingency, eye contact, and imitation skills were targeted for the second child, who was nonverbal and whose imitation abilities were low. This child participated in 2 months of baseline, followed by 4 months of intervention using Level One strategies. Therapy was conducted in 15-minute sessions, three times per week by a graduate student therapist. The sessions took place in a small room located at the Experimental Education Unit. Additionally, parents conducted 15-minute therapy sessions at home approximately five times a week. Parents met with the graduate student therapist once each week to learn additional strategies and to discuss any difficulties that were occurring at home. In addition, once a month, the second author evaluated target skills in a structured assessment session. The child's responses were rated by the second author and a naive observer.

Results from the monthly assessment sessions indicate that the higher-functioning, verbal child developed more spontaneous eye contact during communication tasks following intervention (Figure 2). These tasks were designed to motivate instrumental communication (e.g., giving the child a difficult to open jar with a cookie inside and waiting for the child to initiate a request for help) and declarative communication (e.g., asking the child to put a block on the string while the child is stringing beads, and waiting for the child to comment about the fact that the block will not work). This child also developed more advanced joint attention skills during therapy. At the beginning of the baseline period, he was able to show an object to the examiner consistently only upon request. By the 12th week of therapy, he consistently demonstrated several other joint attention skills, including following the examiner's point and looking toward the examiner when a novel toy was introduced (referential looking).

Percentage of tasks passed

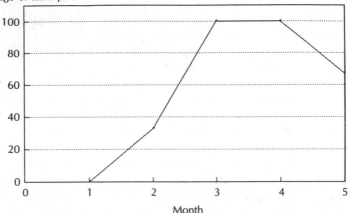

Figure 2.   Percentage of communication tasks during which subject 1 engaged in spontaneous eye contact during baseline (month 1) and treatment (months 2–5) assessments.

The nonverbal child (Figure 3) developed more advanced imitation abilities. At the beginning of the baseline, he was able to imitate only familiar body movements. By the completion of therapy, he was able to imitate familiar and unfamiliar actions with toys and body movements consistently passing all items on the Uzgiris-Hunt Imitation Scale (Uzgiris & Hunt, 1975). We are encouraged by these preliminary results, and are in the process of coding each videotaped therapy session for instances of eye contact, turn-taking, imitation, and spontaneous initiations of verbal and nonverbal communication.

Future research should investigate to what extent the benefits from these strategies generalize to other environments and how best to facilitate generalization. A reasonable approach to generalization would be to have teachers and other adults working with the child adopt the strategies used in the therapy sessions intermittently throughout the day in a variety of contexts. For example, Level One imitative play strategies could be used in the classroom during a freeplay period; Level Two communication strategies could be used during snacktime. Another possible variation would be to use peers as therapists instead of adults. Strain (1983) and Lord and Hopkins (1986) reported positive effects of using same-age peers without disabilities as tutors in an intervention study. Children with autism showed gains in proximity, orientation, and social responsiveness. Ideally, peer tutors could be taught to adopt at least some of the strategies for facilitating social interaction described in this chapter.

CONCLUSION

It should be stressed that this intervention approach is viewed as but one component of an overall treatment program for young children with autism

Percentage of tasks passed

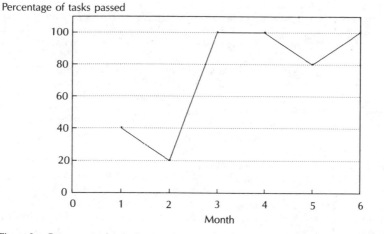

Month

Figure 3.   Percentage of tasks imitated by subject 2 during baseline (months 1–2) and treatment (months 3–6) assessments.

that would be expected to include other treatment strategies, including ones based on traditional behavioral principles. This component is designed to promote early reciprocal social interaction and communication, and does not address several other important needs of children with autism (e.g., building self-help skills, decreasing maladaptive behaviors), which can, perhaps, be more effectively addressed using other intervention methods. If the approach described here is found to be effective, the goal would be to incorporate these strategies into the child's larger educational curriculum. The potential benefits of adding a child-directed component to an intervention program are increasing the child's involvement and enjoyment of social interactions, and promoting early social and communicative skills that typically evolve in the context of such interactions.

REFERENCES

Abravanel, E., & Sigafoos, A. (1984). Exploring the presence of imitation during infancy. *Child Development, 55*, 381–392.

American Psychiatric Association.(1987). *Diagnostic and statistical manual of mental disorders* (3rd ed., rev.). Washington, DC: Author.

Bakeman, R., & Adamson, L. (1984). Coordinating attention to people and objects in mother–infant and peer–infant interaction. *Child Development, 55*, 1278–1289.

Baldwin, J. (1973). *Social and ethical interpretations in mental development.* New York: Arno Press. (Original work published 1899).

Baron-Cohen, S. (1989). The autistic child's theory of mind: A case of specific developmental delay. *Journal of Child Psychology and Psychiatry, 30*, 285–297.

Baron-Cohen, S., Leslie, A., & Frith, U. (1985). Does the autistic child have a "theory of mind"? *Cognition, 21*, 37–46.

Baron-Cohen, S., Leslie, A., & Frith, U. (1986). Mechanical, behavioural and intentional understanding of picture stories in autistic children. *British Journal of Developmental Psychology, 4,* 113–125.

Bates, E. (1979). *The emergence of symbols: Cognition and communication in infancy.* New York: Academic Press.

Berlyne, D. (1960). *Conflict, arousal and curiosity.* New York: McGraw-Hill.

Bernal, M., & Miller, W. (1971). Electrodermal and cardiac responses of schizophrenic children to sensory stimuli. *Psychophysiology, 7,* 155–168.

Brazelton, T. (1982). Joint regulation of neonate-parent behavior. In E. Tronick (Ed.), *Social interchange in infancy* (pp. 7–22). Baltimore: University Park Press.

Bruner, J. (1975). From communication to language—A psychological perspective. *Cognition, 3,* 255–287.

Bruner, J. (1977). Early social interaction and language acquisition. In H. Schaffer (Ed.), *Studies in mother–infant interaction* (pp. 271–289). London: Academic Press.

Bruner, J. (1982). The organization of action and the nature of adult–infant transaction. In E. Tronick (Ed.), *Social interchange in infancy* (pp. 23–35). Baltimore: University Park Press.

Carpenter, G. (1974). Visual regard of moving and stationary faces in early infancy. *Merrill-Palmer Quarterly, 20,* 181–194.

Cohen, D., & Johnson, W. (1977). Cardiovascular correlates of attention in normal and psychiatrically disturbed children. *Archives of General Psychiatry, 34,* 561–567.

Courchesne, E., Lincoln, A., Kilman, B., & Galambos, R. (1985). Event-related brain potential correlates of the processing of novel visual and auditory information in autism. *Journal of Autism and Developmental Disorders, 15,* 55–75.

Curcio, F. (1978). Sensorimotor functioning and communication in mute autistic children. *Journal of Autism and Childhood Schizophrenia, 8,* 281–292.

Dawson, G. (in press). A psychobiological perspective on the early socioemotional development of children with autism. In D. Cicchetti & S. Toth (Eds.), *Rochester symposium on developmental psychopathology* (Vol. 3). Hillsdale, NJ: Lawrence Erlbaum Associates.

Dawson, G., & Adams, A. (1984). Imitation and social responsiveness in autistic children. *Journal of Abnormal Child Psychology, 12,* 209–226.

Dawson, G., Finley, C., Phillips, S., Galpert, L., & Lewy, A. (1988). Reduced P3 amplitude of the event-related brain potential: Its relationship to language ability in autism. *Journal of Autism and Developmental Disorders, 18,* 493–504.

Dawson, G., & Galpert, L. (1986). A developmental model for facilitating the social behavior of autistic children. In E. Schopler & G. Mesibov (Eds.), *Social behavior in autism* (pp. 237–261) New York: Plenum.

Dawson, G., & Galpert, L. (1990). Mothers' use of imitative play for facilitating social responsiveness and toy play in young autistic children. *Development and Psychopathology, 2,* 151–162.

Dawson, G., Hill, D., Spencer, A., Galpert, L., & Watson, L. (1990). Affective exchanges between young autistic children and their mothers. *Journal of Abnormal Child Psychology, 18,* 335–345.

Dawson, G., & Lewy, A. (1989a). Arousal, attention, and the socioemotional impairments of individuals with autism. In G. Dawson (Ed.), *Autism: Nature, diagnosis, and treatment* (pp. 49–74). New York: Guilford Press.

Dawson, G., & Lewy, A. (1989b). Reciprocal subcortical-cortical influences in autism: The role of attentional mechanisms. In G. Dawson (Ed.), *Autism: Nature, diagnosis, and treatment.* (pp. 49–74). New York: Guilford Press.

DeMyer, M., Alpern, G., Barton, S., DeMyer, W., Churchill, D., Hingtgen, H., Bryson, C., Pontius, W., & Kimberlin, C. (1972). Imitation in autistic, early schizophrenic, and nonpsychotic subnormal children. *Journal of Autism and Childhood Schizophrenia, 2,* 264–287.

Duchan, J. (1983). Autistic children are noninteractive: Or so we say. *Seminar in Speech, Hearing and Language, 4,* 53–62.

Ferrara, C., & Hill, S. (1980). The responsiveness of autistic children to the predictability of social and nonsocial toys. *Journal of Autism and Developmental Disorders, 10,* 51–57.

Field, T. (1977). Effect of early separation, interactive deficits and experimental manipulations on infant–mother face-to-face interaction. *Child Development, 48,* 731–771.

Field, T. (1979). Visual and cardiac responses to animate and inanimate faces by young and preterm infants. *Child Development, 50,* 188–194.

Field, T. (1982). Affective displays of high-risk infants during early interactions. In T. Field & A. Fogel (Eds.), *Emotion and early interaction* (pp. 101–125). Hillsdale, NJ: Lawrence Erlbaum Associates.

Field, T., Woodson, R., Greenberg, R., & Cohen, D. (1982). Discrimination and imitation of facial expression by neonates. *Science, 218,* 179–181.

Francis, P., Self, P., & Noble, C. (1981, March). *Imitation within the context of mother-newborn interaction.* Paper presented at the annual Eastern Psychological Association, New York.

Graham, F., Anthony, B., & Zeigler, B. (1983). The orienting response and developmental processes. In D. Siddle (Ed.), *Orienting and habituation: Perspectives in human research* (pp. 371–430). New York: John Wiley & Sons.

Graham, F., & Clifton, R. (1966). Heart rate changes as a component of the orienting response. *Psychological Bulletin, 65,* 305–320.

Graham, F., & Jackson, J. (1970). Arousal systems and infant heart rate responses. In H. Reese & L. Lipsitt (Eds.), *Advances in child development and behavior* (Vol. 5, pp. 79–117). New York: Academic Press.

Hammes, J., & Langdell, T. (1981). Precursors of symbol formation and childhood autism. *Journal of Autism and Developmental Disabilities, 11,* 331–346.

Hannan, T. (1987). A cross-sequential assessment of the occurrences of pointing in 3- to 12-month-old human infants. *Infant Behavior and Development, 10,* 11–22.

Hebb, D. (1955). Drives and the CNS. *Psychological Review, 9,* 243–252.

Heimann, M. (1989). Neonatal imitation, gaze aversion, and mother–infant interaction. *Infant Behavior and Development, 12,* 495–506.

Hermelin, B., & O'Connor, N. (1970). *Psychological experiments with autistic children.* Elmsford, NY: Pergamon.

Hobson, R. (1989). Beyond cognition: A theory of autism. In G. Dawson (Ed.), *Autism: Nature, diagnosis, and treatment.* New York: Guilford Press.

Hobson, R. (1990). On acquiring knowledge about people and the capacity to pretend: A response to Leslie (1987). *Psychological Review, 97,* 114–121.

Holm, V., & Varley, C. (1989). Pharmacological treatment of autistic children. In G. Dawson (Ed.), *Autism: Nature, diagnosis, and treatment.* New York: Guilford Press.

Hubbell, R. (1977). On facilitating spontaneous talking to young children. *Journal of Speech and Hearing Disorders, 42,* 216–231.

Hutt, S., Forrest, S., & Richer, J. (1975). Cardiac arrhythmia and behavior in autistic children. *Acta Psychiatrica Scandinavica, 51,* 361–372.

Jaffe, J., Stern, D., & Peery, J. (1973). "Conversational" coupling of gaze behavior in prelinguistic human development. *Journal of Psycholinguistic Research, 2,* 321–329.

James, A., & Barry, R. (1980). Respiratory and vascular responses to simple visual stimuli in autistics, retardates and normals. *Psychophysiology, 17,* 541–547.

Kagan, J., Kearsley, R., & Zelazo, P. (1978). *Infancy: Its place in human development.* Cambridge: Harvard University Press.

Kanner, L. (1943). Autistic disturbance of affective contact. *Nervous Child, 2,* 217–250.

Kasari, C., Sigman, M., Mundy, P., & Yirmiya, N. (1990). Affective sharing in the context of joint attention interactions of normal, autistic, and mentally retarded children. *Journal of Autism and Developmental Disorders, 20,* 87–100.

Kaye, K. (1982). *The mental and social life of babies.* Chicago: University of Chicago Press.

Koegel, R., & Johnson, J. (1989). Motivating language use in autistic children. In G. Dawson (Ed.), *Autism: Nature, diagnosis, and treatment* (pp. 310–325). New York: Guilford Press.

Koegel, R., & Mentis, M. (1985). Motivation in childhood autism: Can they or won't they? *Journal of Child Psychology and Psychiatry, 26,* 185–191.

Kootz, J., & Cohen, D. (1981). Modulation of sensory intake in autistic children: Cardiovascular and behavioral indices. *Journal of the American Academy of Child Psychiatry, 20,* 692–701.

Kootz, J., Marinelli, B., & Cohen, D. (1982). Modulation of response to environmental stimulation in autistic children. *Journal of Autism and Developmental Disorders, 12,* 185–193.

Lamb, M. (1981). The development of social expectations in the first year of life. In M. Lamb & L. Sherrod (Eds.), *Infant social cognition: Empirical and theoretical considerations* (pp. 155–176). Hillsdale, NJ: Lawrence Erlbaum Associates.

Lord, C., & Hopkins, J. (1986). The social behavior of autistic children with younger and same-age nonhandicapped peers. *Journal of Autism and Developmental Disorders, 16,* 249–262.

Lovaas, O. (1987). Behavioral treatment of normal educational and intellectual functioning in young autistic children. *Journal of Consulting and Clinical Psychology, 55,* 3–9.

Mahoney, G. (1990). *Responsive parenting: A practical guide for fostering the development of young children with developmental complications.* Ypsilanti, MI: High Scope Press.

Mahoney, G., & Powell, A. (1988). Modifying parent–child interaction: Enhancing the development of handicapped children. *Journal of Special Education, 22,* 82–96.

Malatesta, C., & Haviland, J. (1982). Learning display rules: The socialization of emotion expression in infancy. *Child Development, 53,* 991–1003.

Malatesta, C., & Izard, C. (1984). The ontogenesis of human social signals: From the biological imperative to symbol utilization. In N. Fox & R. Davidson (Eds.), *The psychobiology of affective development* (pp. 161–206). Hillsdale, NJ: Lawrence Erlbaum Associates.

Meltzoff, A., & Moore, M. (1977). Imitation of facial and manual gestures by human neonates. *Sciences, 198,* 75–78.

Mundy, P., & Sigman, M. (1989a). Second thoughts on the nature of autism. *Development and Psychopathology, 1,* 213–217.

Mundy, P., & Sigman, M. (1989b). The theoretical implications of joint-attention deficits in autism. *Development and Psychopathology, 1,* 173–183.

Mundy, P., Sigman, M., Ungerer, J., & Sherman, T. (1986). Defining the social deficits of autism: The contribution of non-verbal communication measures. *Journal of Child Psychology and Psychiatry, 27,* 657–669.

Novick, B., Vaughn, H., Jr., Kurtzberg, D., & Simson, R. (1980). An electrophysiological indication of auditory processing defects in autism. *Psychiatry Research, 3,* 107–114.

Ozonoff, S., Pennington, B., & Rogers, S. (1990). Are there emotion perception deficits in young autistic children? *Journal of Child Psychology and Psychiatry, 31,* 343–361.

Palkowitz, R., & Wiesenfeld, A. (1980). Differential autonomic responses of autistic and normal children. *Journal of Autism and Developmental Disorders, 10,* 347–360.

Piaget, J. (1962). *Play, dreams, and imitation.* New York: Norton.

Prizant, B., & Wetherby, A. (1989). Enhancing language and communication in autism: From theory to practice. In G. Dawson (Ed.), *Autism: Nature, diagnosis, and treatment* (pp. 282–309). New York: Guilford Press.

Rutter, M. (1983). Cognitive deficits in the pathogenesis of autism. *Journal of Child Psychology and Psychiatry, 24,* 513–531.

Schaffer, R. (1977). *Mothering.* Cambridge: Harvard University Press.

Schneirla, T. (1959). An evolutionary and developmental theory of biphasic processes underlying approach and withdrawal. In M. Jones (Ed.), *Nebraska symposium on motivation* (Vol. 7, pp. 1–42). Lincoln: University of Nebraska Press.

Schopler, E., Reichler, R., & Renner, B. (1986). *The Childhood Autism Rating Scale (CARS).* New York: Irvington.

Seibert, J., & Oller, D. (1981). Linguistic pragmatics and language intervention strategies. *Journal of Autism and Developmental Disorders, 11,* 75–88

Seligman, M. (1975). *Helplessness: On depression, death, and development.* San Francisco: W.H. Freeman.

Sherrod, L. (1979). Social cognition in infancy: Attention to the human face. *Infant Behavior and Development, 2,* 279–294.

Simeonsson, R., Olley, J., & Rosenthal, S. (1987). Early intervention for children with autism. In M. Guralnick & F. Bennet (Eds.), *The effectiveness of early intervention for at-risk and handicapped children* (pp. 275–296). New York: Academic Press.

Snow, C. (1972). Mother's speech to children learning language. *Child Development, 43,* 549–565.

Snow, M., Hertzig, M., & Shapiro, T. (1986). *Affective expression in young autistic children.* Paper presented at the annual meeting of the American Academy of Child Psychiatry, Los Angeles.

Sokolov, E. (1963). *Perception and the conditioned reflex.* New York: Macmillan.

Stern, D. (1971). A micro-analysis of mother–infant interaction: Behavior regulating social conduct between a mother and her 3½ month old twins. *Journal of the American Academy of Child Psychiatry, 10,* 501–517.

Stern, D. (1977). *The first relationship: Infant and mother.* Cambridge: Harvard University Press.

Stern, D. (1985). *The interpersonal world of the infant.* New York: Basic Books.

Strain, P. (1983). Generalization of autistic children's social behavior change: Effects of developmentally integrated and segregated settings. *Analysis and Intervention in Developmental Disabilities, 3,* 23–34.

Strain, B., & Vietze, P. (1975, March). *Early dialogues: The structure of reciprocal infant-mother vocalizations.* Paper presented at the meeting of the Society for Research in Child Development, Denver.

Sugarman, S. (1984). The development of preverbal communication. In R. Schiefelbusch & J. Pickar (Eds.), *The acquisition of communicative competence* (pp. 23–67). Baltimore: University Park Press.

Suomi, S. (1981). The perception of contingency and social development. In M. Lamb & L. Sherrod (Eds.), *Infant social cognition* (pp. 177–201). Hillsdale, NJ: Lawrence Erlbaum Associates.

Tager-Flusberg, H. (1985). Basic level and superordinate level categorization in autistic, mentally retarded and normal children. *Journal of Experimental Child Psychology, 40,* 450–469.

Tager-Flusberg, H. (1989). A psycholinguistic perspective on language development in the autistic child. In G. Dawson (Ed.), *Autism: Nature, diagnosis, and treatment* (pp. 92–115). New York: Guilford Press.

Tiegerman, E., & Primavera, L. (1981). Object manipulation: An interactional strategy with autistic children. *Journal of Autism and Developmental Disorders, 11,* 427–438.

Tiegerman, E., & Primavera, L. (1984). Imitating the autistic child: Facilitating communicative gaze behavior. *Journal of Autism and Developmental Disorders, 14,* 27–38.

Tronick, D., Als, H., & Adamson, L. (1979). Structure of early face-to-face communicative interaction. In M. Bullowa (Ed.), *Beyond speech* (pp. 349–372). Cambridge: Cambridge University Press.

Ungerer, J., & Sigman, M. (1987). Categorization skills and receptive language development in autistic children. *Journal of Autism and Developmental Disorders, 17,* 3–16.

Uzgiris, I. (1981). Experience in the social context: Imitation and play. In R. Schiefelbusch & D. Bricker (Eds.), *Early language: Acquisition and intervention* (pp. 139–168). Baltimore: University Park Press.

Uzgiris, I., & Hunt, J. (1975). *Assessment in infancy.* Urbana, IL: University of Illinois Press.

Van Engeland, H. (1984). The electrodermal orienting response to auditive stimuli in autistic children, normal children, mentally retarded children, and child psychiatric patients. *Journal of Autism and Developmental Disorders, 14,* 261–279.

Walden, T., & Ogan, T. (1988). The development of social referencing. *Child Development, 59,* 1230–1240.

Watson, J. (1978). Perception of contingency as a determinant of social responsiveness. In E.B. Thoman (Ed.), *The origins of the infant's social responsiveness* (pp. 33–64). Hillsdale, NJ: Lawrence Erlbaum Associates.

Watson, J., & Ramey, C. (1972). Reactions to response-contingent stimulation in early infancy. *Merrill-Palmer Quarterly, 18,* 219–227.

Wetherby, A. (1986). Ontogeny of communicative functions in autism. *Journal of Autism and Developmental Disorders, 16,* 295–316.

Wetherby, A., & Prutting, C. (1984). Profiles of communicative and cognitive-social abilities in autistic children. *Journal of Speech and Hearing Research, 27,* 364–377.

Yirmiya, N., Kasari, C., Sigman, M., & Mundy, P. (1989). Facial expressions of affect in autistic, mentally retarded, and normal children. *Journal of Child Psychology and Psychiatry, 30,* 725–735.

Appendix

Strategies for Facilitating Social Interaction

LEVEL ONE: FACILITATING ATTENTION TO PEOPLE, SOCIAL CONTINGENCY, AND TURN-TAKING

Phase One: Noticing Contingent Relationships Between the Actions of Self and Other

Method:

The purpose of this phase is to help the child notice the similarity and contingent relationship between his or her actions and the adult's actions. The adult performs exact imitations of the child's actions with toys, body movements, and vocalizations that are carried out simultaneously or as soon as possible after the child's actions. Imitations should be as similar as possible to the child's behavior, but exaggerated. Care should be taken to catch the child's attention by placing the toys within the child's field of vision.

Goals:

1. Child begins to attend to the adult's actions.
2. Child begins to realize that the adult is following his or her actions.

Phase Two: Facilitating Eye Contact

Method:

A minority of children focuses its attention on the adult's actions with toys rather than the adult's face. The purpose of this phase is to shift the child's attention away from the adult's toys and toward the adult. The strategy is essentially the same as in the previous phase except that eye contact is facilitated by the adult strategically placing his or her face within the child's field of vision. As the adult imitates the child's actions, his or her face should be directly behind the toys. Thus, if the child looks at the toys, he or she will also see the adult's face. The adult can smile and express enjoyment and exaggerate his or her own facial expressions when the child looks in his or her direction.

Goals:

1. Child begins to look at the adult's face.
2. Child continues to realize that the adult is following his or her actions.

Phase Three: Facilitating Turn-Taking

Method:

The purpose of this phase is to help the child learn the back-and-forth nature of interactions. Occasionally, the adult waits a few seconds before imitating the child to see if the child waits for the adult to imitate him or her. This type of alternating imitation creates a sense of turn-taking in which the child takes a turn, and then the adult takes a turn. Often, the child will enjoy this activity and make a game out of speeding up or slowing down his or her actions to see if the adult will follow.

Goals:

1. Child waits for the adult to imitate.
2. Child begins to change his or her own behavior and watches to see how the adult's behavior changes.
3. Child shows signs of participating in a game.

Phase Four: Teaching Contingency versus Mimicry

Method:

The purpose of this phase is to help the child learn that back-and-forth interaction can occur even when the adult is not exactly imitating his or her behavior. Instead of exactly imitating the child's actions, the adult makes slight modifications. For example, the adult may imitate the child's actions, but use a different toy, or may use the same toy but slightly modify his or her imitations. For example, the adult may alter the speed of his or her imitation (e.g., faster, slower). The adult may also feed back slightly more complex vocalizations. For example, if the child is using consonant-vowel sounds (e.g., "ma-ma-ma"), the adult adds a sound to make it a word (e.g., "mom," "mom," "mom").

Goals:

1. Child continues to anticipate the adult's imitations even though they are not exact imitations.
2. Child continues to enjoy the turn-taking interactions.

LEVEL TWO: IMITATION AND EARLY
COMMUNICATION JOINT ATTENTION SKILLS

Imitation Skills

Phase One: Imitating Familiar Schemes

Method:

The purpose of this phase is to facilitate the child's imitation of the adult. Some children can imitate if given the proper command or cues. The focus here is on spontaneity. The strategy is occasionally to introduce a familiar scheme and/or sound that is already within the child's behavioral repertoire. When the child is optimally engaged and attending to the adult, the adult introduces a simple familiar action with a toy. To begin with, this action is one the child has recently performed. The adult may need to introduce it several times, and the child's imitation may be delayed. The adult returns to imitating the child after several attempts at facilitating the child's spontaneous imitation.

Goals:

1. Child spontaneously imitates familiar simple schemes with toys.
2. Child spontaneously imitates familiar vocalizations.
3. Child spontaneously imitates complex schemes with toys and/or vocalizations.

Phase Two: Imitating Novel Schemes

Method:

The purpose of this phase is to facilitate the child's spontaneous imitation of novel actions. This strategy is the same as in the previous phase, except that unfamiliar schemes are introduced. The adult begins with schemes that are slight modifications of the child's familiar schemes and progresses slowly to more novel actions and sounds.

Goals:

1. Child spontaneously imitates slight modifications of familiar schemes with toys and/or vocalizations.
2. Child spontaneously imitates more novel schemes with toys and/or vocalizations.

Early Communication and Joint Attention

Phase One: Communicating to Achieve a Desired Goal

Method:

The purpose of this phase is to motivate the child to communicate spontaneously with the adult in order to achieve a desired goal. This is accomplished by placing interesting objects inside a jar that is difficult to open or out of reach. The adult waits for the child to use gesture, gaze, or language to indicate that he or she wants the desired object, and then immediately complies with the child's request.

Goal:

1. Child engages in spontaneous communication (gesture, gaze, or language) to request a desired object.

Phase Two: Sharing Activities

Method:

The purpose of this phase is to facilitate the child's participation in and communication about shared activities. Objects used in the session are designed to require another person's help (e.g., balloons, bubbles, a wind-up toy that is difficult to wind, a train on tracks). The child is then motivated to share a desired object with another person. Objects that naturally draw attention to the adult's face (e.g., bubbles, balloons) are useful. Additionally, the shared attention can occur around a social routine. Often, children will initiate ritualized interactions with objects or body movements. The adult can facilitate the development of these routines by interpreting a child's actions as if they were requests for a shared activity. For example, the adult can hang a string of beads in the room and then twirl the child around the room every time that the child touches the beads.

Goals:

1. Child continues to engage in spontaneous communication to request help.
2. Child requests that the adult participate in a shared activity.
3. Child requests that the adult engage in shared social routines.

Phase Three: Using Eye Contact in the Context of Communication

Method:

The purpose of this phase is to teach the child that his or her own nonverbal cues (namely, eye contact) are important in communicating with another person. This is facilitated by the adult pausing before complying with the child's requests. Often, the child will then spontaneously look at the adult's face to prompt the beginning of the activity. For higher-functioning children, another strategy involves feigning confusion or lack of understanding to the child when a request is made. For example, the adult can act confused about whether he or she is being asked to draw a "B" or a "G" until the child turns and looks at the adult while making a request.

Goal:

1. Child begins to request activities while looking at the adult's face, combining eye contact with requests.

Phase Four: Attending to the Nonverbal
Cues of Others and Directing Another's Attention

Method:

The purpose of this phase is to have the child begin to take into account more complex nonverbal cues from the adult when communicating. Once the child begins consistently to follow his or her request with looking at the adult's face, the adult then produces an exaggerated nonverbal cue (e.g., exaggerated smile or head nod) to indicate whether or not he or she will perform the activity. In this way, the child learns that other people's nonverbal cues are important in determining their compliance with a request. Eventually, the adult can pretend not to be paying attention to the child and, in this way, motivate the child to direct the adult's attention to a desired object or activity.

Goals:

1. Child begins to attend to nonverbal cues provided by the adult.
2. Child directs the adult's attention to an object or activity.

CHOOSING THE THERAPIST AND THE THERAPY ENVIRONMENT

In our clinical use of these strategies, we have experimented with different therapists. We believe that the therapy can be successfully implemented by the child's teacher, communication disorders specialist, and parents. If the profes-. sionals and parents in the child's life are working in unison, the intervention can occur at school and at home. Generally, the therapy is conducted at least three times per week for approximately 15–20 minutes per session. This figure is based on our previous finding that 15–20 minutes of imitation five times per week increased eye contact and creative toy play. However, we have no data supporting an optimum frequency or length of session. We stress that these sessions should be fun, for both the adult and the child.

The therapy environment should be relatively small and distraction-free, containing only objects that are being used for the therapy. A mirror can be useful for some children who prefer to watch themselves being imitated in the mirror rather than directly watching the adult. At school these sessions can occur in either a partitioned section of the classroom or in a separate room. If other children are present during therapy sessions, they may want to play with the child's toys or may want attention from the adult. If the room contains objects that are off limits to the child, the adult may be placed in the role of initiator by constantly having to restrict the child's activities.

If the child loses interest and wants to end the session, he or she can usually be redirected back to the session by introducing a new toy. If the child continues to protest, it is best to terminate the session and, in the future, shorten the session and alter the methods used. Some children require more or less intense or dramatic responses by the adult, others respond better to gross motor rather than fine motor activities, and so on. Aggressive and other problem behaviors should be handled as they normally would outside the therapy session. These and other problem behaviors, such as self-abuse, obviously should not be imitated.

TOYS THAT FACILITATE SOCIAL INTERACTION

It is important to select toys that facilitate social interaction. Toys to which the child is readily drawn should be used. Often, the child will become bored with the toys. When this happens, one new toy set is introduced and one of the original sets is removed. Some children with autism do not engage in toy play, but rather engage in feeling surfaces, turning pages of books, and so forth. These types of activities can be used in the Level One phases of therapy. By using "special toys" only during the therapy sessions, the child begins to use toys as a cue that the session is about to begin.

Below is a list of toys that we have found successful in facilitating social interaction.

Toys that Draw Attention to the Adult's Actions

- Push toys that make noise and represent animate objects (e.g., dogs, bees)
- Musical instruments (e.g., drums, tambourine, xylophone, maracas)
- Pom-poms
- Mechanical toys
- Rattles
- Squeaky toys

Toys that Draw Attention to the Adult's Face

- Bubbles
- Pinwheels
- Balloons
- A plastic transparent drawing board that allows the child and adult to draw on either side of the board, thus facilitating eye contact while drawing

Toys that Facilitate Reciprocal Interaction

- Balls
- Blocks in a form box
- A train on a track between the adult and child
- Puppets

Toys that Facilitate Requests for Help

- A jar of candy with a lid that is difficult to open
- A favorite object that is placed out of reach
- Wind-up toys that are difficult to wind
- Pinwheels that are difficult to blow

8

Using Dynamic Assessment with Children with Language Disorders

Lesley B. Olswang,
Barbara A. Bain, and Glenn A. Johnson

An ISSUE OF GREAT CONCERN to speech-language pathologists is how best to serve children with language impairments, and in particular, when to provide intervention. Intervention is defined as focused, intensive stimulation designed to enhance performance in language. This is in contrast to monitoring, in which intervention is not provided, but natural development is allowed to occur and is observed periodically. Intervention may come in the form of direct or indirect treatment (Guidelines, 1984). *Direct treatment* is treatment that the speech-language pathologist plans and implements directly. Such treatment may be delivered intermittently through an itinerant program or more intensively through a resource room program or self-contained classroom program. It may occur individually or in small groups. *Indirect treatment* is treatment that is planned and evaluated by the speech-language pathologist but implemented by others. Indirect treatment comes in the form of consultation or collaboration with teachers, parents, or others, who perform the intervention and act as the agent for change. Both kinds of intervention may focus on general language stimulation or the teaching of specific language behaviors or sets of behaviors. The focus of this chapter is on the teaching of specific language behaviors.

Determining when a child will best benefit from intervention is complex, and requires examination of relevant child and environmental variables. To narrow the scope of this chapter, we discuss only child variables, and specifically address only issues related to the child's readiness for learning new behaviors or sets of behaviors.

This chapter was supported in part by Grant No. R29DC00431 from the National Institute of Deafness and Other Communication Disorders.

Deciding that a child is ready to learn a new behavior, skill, or rule under the speech-language pathologist's guidance requires knowledge about the child's current performance and his or her potential for change through instruction. For years, traditional assessment procedures (including standardized tests, questionnaires, and behavioral observation) have guided us in determining which children have impairments. They have allowed us to compare particular children to their peers and gain important information about their levels of functioning. Where assessment procedures have fallen short is in providing information about children's responsiveness to instruction and potential for immediate growth, and thus for helping us determine when to provide intervention for specific behaviors or skills. Procedures designed to examine learning potential provide a more dynamic view of performance and ability. They expand the information obtained from norm- or criterion-referenced instruments in which adult input is held to a minimum. Dynamic assessment procedures systematically introduce adult guidance to determine if a child's performance can be enhanced through instruction. Such procedures are essential for making informed decisions about when children with language impairments might best benefit from direct treatment.

VYGOTSKY AND THE THEORY BEHIND DYNAMIC ASSESSMENT

The use of dynamic assessment procedures for assessing the potential for improving language functioning is based on the work of the Russian psychologist Lev Semenovich Vygotsky (1896–1934). Vygotsky was a brilliant thinker who was interested in the development, modification, and social transmission of symbol systems (speech and language foremost among them) within cultural contexts (Bruner, 1987; Kozulin, 1985; Wertsch, 1981). For our purposes in explicating the value of dynamic assessment of linguistic performance, only the most directly relevant of Vygotsky's many contributions are reviewed. Because his ideas grew out of a unique concatenation of his own intellectual development and that of the times in which he lived (Wertsch, 1985), we briefly review the intellectual and historical framework within which Vygotsky worked.

Initially trained as a lawyer, Vygotsky maintained broad interests in the arts and philosophy, which led him to study psychology, a field he believed was in a profound crisis (Cole & Scribner, 1978). The behaviorists' reductionism denied the possibility of studying what Vygotsky saw as the fundamental difference between human and animal behavior—man's conscious mind (Vygotsky, 1978; 1934/1986). Gestaltists and other phenomenologists ignored the possibility that lower level psychological functions influenced higher-order behavior, and seemed merely to describe mental life. They too denied that "mind" could be subject to scientific study, since mental phenomena were held to be indivisible. Vygotsky was also dissatisfied with the lack of attention psychology paid to solving the problems of people with impaired learning potential (Yaroshevsky, 1989).

Vygotsky had no instant answers to these crises. Between the time of his appointment to the Moscow Institute of Psychology in 1924 and his death in 1934, he embarked on an expansive program of thinking and research with two major goals: to develop a new, Marxist vision of a scientific psychology to replace the fragmented approaches then current and to develop practical means for helping people whose learning problems kept them from participating in the ordinary routines of daily life (Vygotsky, 1934/1986). Toward this end, Vygotsky and his colleagues (A. R. Luria among them) wrote over 180 papers, monographs, and books before Vygotsky's death at 37 (Wertsch, 1985). Vygotsky correctly identified his first problem as methodological. How was he to use psychology as a tool for studying human consciousness? He saw no value in using the methodologies of behaviorism or phenomenalism. Instead, he applied Marxist sociohistorical method to the study of individual development (1934/1986). This ontogenetic method has two major ingredients.

The first, and central, tenet of this view is that all phenomena are to be studied as "processes in motion and in change" (Cole & Scribner, 1978, p. 7). This activity-oriented, or praxic, view suggested to Vygotsky that human behavior could be understood only by examining the ontogeny of behavior, and by tracing developmental change over time (1960/1981). Accordingly, Vygotsky thought that the higher mental functions (such as language, voluntary attention, mnemonic strategies, and logical reasoning) could be decomposed into their lower, developmentally primary, components (e.g., attention, perception, eidetic memory, arousal, and temperament). While the component parts of the higher functions might be identified, this decomposition did not fully explain or predict the development of the higher forms. For example, while one could identify the plaster, pigments, and progression of activities that went into creating the ceiling of the Sistine Chapel, one could not look at the tubes of paint, buckets of plaster, and scaffolding and "know" a priori that they would become transformed into a magnificent work of art. Only through the purposeful coordination of activities are those components transformed into a unique symbolic product. We can only deduce from the raw materials what some of the parameters of the completed project might be, not exactly what it will be. Similarly, with a higher-level system such as language, we may identify component skills, but we can know the product only by observing it in action. This action transforms the components into something qualitatively different from the mere sum of the parts (Vygotsky, 1934/1986).

A second aspect of the sociohistorical approach followed from the arguments by Marx and Engels that historical and material changes in society both lead to changes in human nature (Cole & Scribner, 1978) and reflect the accumulated history of a culture. For example, the shape and design of a saw reflect both the accumulation of the culture's discoveries about how to organize labor to produce the saw and the way in which the saw is used. The use of the saw also changes its user: man now operates within a manmade universe of right angles, rather than a natural universe of caves and bent branches. As a corollary, man also masters nature through the use of tools (Engels, 1940). Vygotsky extended this concept of human–tool interactions to include the use of signs and other psychological tools (1960/1981). Sign systems behave like tools; they are both created and changed by human societies, and their use alters the nature of those societies over the course of history. The development of mathematical symbols and logic is a classic example.

Use of the sociohistorical method led Vygotsky to conclude that "the mechanism of individual developmental change is rooted in society and culture" (Cole & Scribner, 1978, p. 7). In opposition to Piaget, Vygotsky argued that the child's conscious understanding and knowledge of the world develops first through social interactions. Consciousness is not individual but social and shared between the child and caregivers (Vygotsky, 1960/1981). Only later is knowledge internalized within an individual. This internalization is a dynamic process (Kozulin, 1985). Voluntary mental functions (i.e., higher function) are learned through active interchanges between the child and adult or more capable peer; the structure of these higher functions is shaped by these social interactive contexts. These contexts are both culturally conditioned and unique to each individual. Every child should, therefore, demonstrate both culturally conditioned commonalities and significant individual variation. Unlike Piaget, who viewed the child as struggling to reason individually with the universe, Vygotsky cast the development of higher cognitive processes as essentially a social activity.

Bruner (1986) has expanded on this theme of individual development arising from shared social exchanges. Through a "loan of consciousness" (Bruner, 1986, p. 76), an adult helps the child to focus on the elements of an interaction that are important, both to the culture's view of the world and the specific context within which the child–adult interaction is occurring. The adult can help by directing the child's basic attention, acting as an external memory resource, providing structure to the interaction, and suggesting alternatives. These events are often not explicitly pedagogical. Vygotsky used as an example the development of the indicatory gesture. Initially, the child's pointing response is nothing but a failed motor scheme. The child is interested in an object and tries to attain it directly. Observing the child's reach, an adult may interpret it as a point ("Oh, Kate, you want the ring. Let me get it for you."). When the child later addresses the gesture to the adult, the gesture comes to act as a request for action. Only after the adult has supplied meaning (verbally and/or by getting the object) can the child come to awareness of the gesture's symbolic value. At this point the child has cognitively mastered his or her visually directed reach, and through the effect of adult mediation has substituted and internalized a symbolic action in its place. Both the child and the adult participate jointly in the creation of meaning, within a specific context. Context allows the adult to develop a plausible interpretation of the child's behavior (Bruner, 1985). The adult guides the child to higher ground, but the child prompts the adult's guidance.

Vygotsky saw psychology as an applied science, one that would help remediate individual learning deficits. The constructs he developed were applied to and modified in light of his work with people with mental retardation, learning disabilities, and deafness (Luria, in Yaroshensky, 1989). In 1925, Vygotsky founded the Laboratory of Psychology for Abnormal Childhood, where he developed means for assessing and remediating various learning deficits. Unlike many other psychologists of his era (e.g., Terman, Binet), Vygotsky opposed the use of static, standardized tests as the sole means of categorizing an individual's learning potential and determining his or her educational placement. Vygotsky (1978) argued that standardized tests (in which the tester cannot actively intervene to enhance the test taker's performance) provided data only on the individual's past history and present functioning, not on his or her future potential. He sought to find out where (and how) education could optimize each individual's performance across a variety of skills. Vygotsky thought that in principle a child could demonstrate greater readiness for learning in some areas than in others, due to the interaction of natural endowment and varied exposure to appropriate mediation.

This orientation created a practical problem: How does one go about determining an individual's learning potential? Vygotsky's rejection of IQ measures did not imply abandoning an empirical approach to determining learning potential. One of his major goals was to develop a scientific basis for both theoretical and applied psychology. This meant that assessment of learning potential must follow logically from a developmental framework in which higher mental functions are acquired through the active collaboration of an adult (or more capable peer) and a child on tasks of joint interest. The role of the adult or more experienced peer is to guide the child's attention and understanding. The conceptual structure Vygotsky introduced to guide his work on assessing learning potential is called the *zone of proximal development* (1934/1986; 1978).Vygotsky defined the zone of proximal development (zpd) as "the distance between the actual developmental level as determined by independent problem solving and the level of potential development as determined through problem solving under either adult guidance or in collaboration with more capable peers" (1978, p. 86). The zpd is thus bounded by both the child's independent functioning level and by the level of potential development when working collaboratively. This is where teaching–learning interactions are developed and the potential for change is determined through a dynamic assessment.

As Wertsch (1984) notes, three major tenets of the zpd can be identified. First, teaching-learning activity within the zone involves the active conscious collaboration of two or more individuals. However, by definition, the two participants do not identify the task to be solved in the same way. Rather, it is through their mediated interaction that the child's conception is brought closer in some respects to the adult's view. Second, activity within the zpd is jointly regulated. The child brings interests, attitudes, motivations, and a set of developing knowledge structures to a given task. The child's capability is one regulator of the direction and pacing of activities. However, the adult is simultaneously responsible for attaining and maintaining the child's interest, and for structuring activities in ways that lead the child forward just enough to expand his or her learning while staying within the zone. This also implies that different outcomes are possible in dynamic assessment when clinicians' competencies cause them to be better or worse mediators. Third, interactions in the zpd are "oriented toward the child's future skills and knowledge" (Rogoff & Wertsch, 1984, p. 4). That is, adults do not usually focus exclusively on what a child already knows well, but rather on the edge of the child's interest and skills.

The notions of dynamic assessment within a zpd are not unfamiliar to speech-language pathologists. Use of stimulability testing in articulation (Milisen, 1954) acknowledges that some prompts and cues can facilitate correct sound production and that some misarticulations may be more "ready to move" than others. Selecting a period of diagnostic therapy for a child after initial assessment and before the writing of explicit therapeutic goals is essentially an admission that we often need to supplement standardized test results with a hands-on feel for what a child is or is not capable of doing. However, this activity is too often done on an ad hoc basis, which limits its reliability and generalizability.

In summary, the zpd is a socially constructed cognitive "region" in which the raw material of a child's emerging mastery is shaped by the joint activity between a child and a knowledgeable adult into a more advanced level of independent functioning. The "floor" of the zpd is what the child can do on his or her own; the ceiling is what he or she can do given a "reasonable" amount of restructuring by an adult, or collaboratively with more capable peers. However, because development is progressive (until the child reaches a developmental plateau), the zpd necessarily shifts, since it seeks to be at the cutting edge of competency. In a simple analogy, the zpd acts like a Slinky going down a set of stairs. The bottom step represents the highest level of functioning. When set in motion, the base of the Slinky initially remains on the top step while the leading edge pulls the body of the spring after it. The leading edge then becomes the base as the spring moves to another step. The nature of the spring (analogous to the child's endowment), the width and drop of each step (analogous to the environment), and one's skill in setting the spring in motion (analogous to the skill of the adult or collaborative peer) all influence how far the Slinky goes before it needs another push.

Regrettably, the issues surrounding language learning are rather more complex than Slinkys. For example, what do we mean by independent functioning in early emerging language? Is our goal to teach the child to attain a system of generative rules, or to teach the child to attain limited combinatorial ability for a closed set of items? Clearly, we must define what we mean by language acquisition. This issue, among others, makes the task of dynamically assessing language complex. Before turning to this challenge, we first review the application of Vygotsky's approach in related disciplines.

TYPES OF CLINICAL APPLICATION OF DYNAMIC ASSESSMENT

For more than 30 years, Vygotsky's conceptualization of the zpd has motivated research and clinical practice in psychology (Budoff & Friedman, 1964; Mearig, 1987; Minick, 1987), neuropsychology (Luria, 1961), and education (Brown, Bransford, Ferrara, & Campione, 1983; Feuerstein, Rand, & Hoffman, 1979; Tzuriel & Klein, 1987). The concept of the zpd has been used to investigate learning potential throughout the lifespan, from preschool (Lidz, 1983) through school-age and adolescence (Ferrara, Brown, & Campione, 1986; Feuerstein et al., 1979) to adulthood (Barr & Samuels, 1988; Brown & Campione, 1986; Molenaar, 1987). The zpd has been investigated in children without disabilities (Bethge, Carlson, & Wiedl, 1982; Brown & Ferrara, 1985; Ferrara et al., 1986); in children with developmental disabilities, such as mental retardation (Budoff & Friedman, 1964; Budoff & Hamilton, 1976; Campione & Brown, 1984; Feuerstein et al., 1979); and in children with learning and reading disabilities (Braun, Rennie, & Gordon, 1987; Cioffi & Carney, 1983). It has also been investigated in children from different cultural and socioeconomic backgrounds (Carlson, 1983; Lidz, 1982). The following sections examine knowledge about the zpd that has been obtained from related disciplines, with a particular focus on those findings most relevant to the assessment and intervention of children with language disorders.

Static Versus Dynamic Assessment

Application of the concept of the zpd to assessment requires the differentiation between static and dynamic assessment. Both types of assessment are critical in defining an individual's performance and potential for change. *Static assessment* is the type of evaluation that is traditionally employed in determining a child's current abilities. The focus in a static assessment is on determining a child's independent performance at a particular point in time (Brown et al.

1983). In general, the examiner remains neutral, does not consequate the child's response or help the child perform at a more advanced level in any way (Brown & Ferrara, 1985). The purpose of the static assessment is to measure the child's ability in a particular domain (e.g., cognition, language, motor abilities) or in a variety of domains. Although static assessment is often used by professionals to infer or predict what a child can learn, it is more appropriately used to determine which children might have disorders or delays.

Dynamic assessment provides a professional with at least three types of information: 1) information about the child's potential for learning, 2) information about the factors that may influence the child's success or failure on particular tasks, and 3) information about what might be done to facilitate the child's development or functioning (Minick, 1987). Dynamic assessment allows the professional to hypothesize why a child might encounter difficulty on a task. The professional then identifies how the child independently attempts to achieve mastery on a task, how the child's performance can best be facilitated, and how modifiable the child is (Lidz, 1983). These issues are addressed by the examiner through an interactive relationship with the child in which the examiner provides cues, instructions, prompts, and feedback to aid the child in successfully completing previously failed tasks.

Feuerstein, Miller, Rand, and Jensen (1981) suggest that dynamic assessment requires professionals to make several changes in their traditional (i.e., static assessment) procedures. (Although these changes are discussed separately, they actually overlap.) First, the professional must focus on a process orientation rather than a product orientation. During dynamic assessment, an attempt is made to help a child function at a more advanced level by changing or modifying his or her performance. The focus of assessment is on identifying those processes that enable the child to move toward higher or more advanced functioning. In contrast, the focus of a static assessment is on what is known by the child at a particular point in time. Furthermore, both the structure and the context of testing differ significantly in the two forms of assessment. In a static assessment, the professional is neutral in delivering instruction, recording responses, and so forth. In dynamic assessment, the professional assumes an active role by providing detailed and accurate feedback regarding the child's performance. Once a child encounters difficulty on a specific task, the professional manipulates aspects of the task to aid the child in mastery of that task. If an initial task has been mastered, the child is given a more advanced task to attempt. In essence, the assessment paradigm changes from "only test" to one of "test-teach-test," in which the teaching involves active manipulation of the task at hand. The professional's goal is to interact with the child to determine if and how his or her performance might be improved. The success of this process assumes a constructive rapport between the child and the examiner as they jointly work on difficult tasks.

Finally, the professional must change the manner in which results are interpreted. In static assessment, emphasis is placed on responses that best represent the child's current functioning in a particular, controlled context. In dynamic assessment, the professional gives considerable weight to the response that indicates the child is capable of performing at a higher, more conventional, more abstract, adultlike level. This response may occur only once and be made with support or help from the professional, but this more advanced response is viewed as an indication of the child's potential for future learning.

Much of the success of dynamic assessment procedures depends on the training of the professional who conducts the evaluation. Many professionals who are adept at static assessment have not been exposed to the principles of dynamic assessment. The different philosophy and purposes of dynamic versus static assessment require the professional to employ an active process of generating and testing hypotheses within the "test-teach-test" framework (Meyers, 1987). Through this process, the professional obtains information about the teachability of specific skills. Changing emphasis from static to dynamic assessment procedures requires that professionals broaden their approach to assessment, and gain an understanding of theories and techniques different from those to which they were exposed during their training. Meyers and his colleagues (Meyers, 1987; Meyers, Pfeffer, & Erlbaum, 1985) have developed some techniques that may help professionals gain the necessary skills to conduct dynamic assessment affectively. The success of dynamic assessments ultimately depends upon the skills and abilities of the professional performing the assessment.

A variety of dynamic assessment tools and procedures have been developed by educators and psychologists. Perhaps the first was the Learning Potential Assessment Device (LPAD) (Feuerstein et al., 1979), devised for school-age children. This was followed by the development of several instruments or procedures to be used with preschool children, such as Preschool Learning Assessment Device (PLAD) (Lidz & Thomas, 1987), Children's Analogical Thinking Modifiability (CATM) (Tzuriel & Klein, 1985, 1987), and a modification of the LPAD for kindergarten children (Mearig, 1987). Two different perspectives of the zpd—quantitative and qualitative analyses—have emerged from administration of these and other procedures.

Quantitative Analysis of the Zone of Proximal Development

Two means have been used in an attempt to quantify the zpd. The first involves determining the amount of change or growth demonstrated by a child on a given task or set of tasks using the "test-teach-test" paradigm. The results from static assessment provide an estimate of the child's independent performance. The professional and the child then interact during the teaching phase, and the amount of change demonstrated then is an indication of the child's zpd. This approach has been used by Budoff and his colleagues (Budoff & Friedman, 1964; Budoff & Hamilton, 1976) and to a lesser extent by Feuerstein and his colleagues (Feuerstein et al., 1981; Feuerstein et al., 1979). As expected, the results of these studies indicated that following instruction, which included cues, verbal and nonverbal prompting techniques, and feedback, children were able to perform at more advanced levels than during the pretest periods. However, Budoff and Friedman (1964) noted considerable individual variation in performance, with some children profiting more from instruction than others. This form of quantifying the zpd is based on the difference in an individual's performance before and after instruction, and is assumed to be an indication of the child's teachability. If performance is greatly improved following instruction, a child is assumed to have more potential than a child whose performance improves only slightly. The emphasis in this quantitative approach is the amount of change, as indicated by the difference between pretest and posttest measures.

The second means of quantifying the zpd has been employed by Brown, Campione, and their colleagues (Brown & Ferrara, 1985; Campione, Brown, Ferrara, & Bryant, 1984; Campione, Brown, Ferrara, Jones, & Steinberg, 1985; Ferrara et al., 1986). Figure 1 shows an example of a task used by Campione et al. (1984) to quantify the zpd. This figure illustrates a problem in which a child fills the blanks with letters that "continue the pattern determined by a certain periodicity and by certain alphabetic relations" (Campione et al., 1984, p. 81). The child then applies the strategies to solve other similar but different patterns by completing the sequences. Quantifying the zpd involves several steps. First, Brown, Campione, and their colleagues determine the amount of instruction needed to bring the subjects to some specified level of competence. They then identify the degree of maintenance and transfer of the problem-solving ability that occurs following the initial task performance and with additional instruction. Using the terminology of Brown and her colleagues, *maintenance* refers to the assessment of the individual performing tasks that are identical in form to the training task but contain different exemplars to which the same problem-solving strategy can be applied. *Transfer* refers to the assessment of the individual performing tasks that not only contain different exemplars, but require different problem-solving strategies. While the terms *maintenance* and *transfer* cannot be translated neatly into a stimulus/response generalization paradigm, on the surface they represent different types or degrees of response generalization. Response generalization is defined here as changes in behavior that are similar to, but not the same as, the target behavior (Kazdin, 1980), or as "different although related response" (Warren, Rogers-Warren, Baer, & Guess, 1980). Using Brown's terminology, transfer tasks can be viewed on a continuum from *near transfer* items (in which the task is very similar to the training task), to *far transfer* and *very far transfer* items (in which the task is very different from the training task). Thus, a continuum of

Problem type	Pattern	Sample problem		Correct answer
Original learning	NN	NGOHPIQJ	____	(RKSL)
	NINI	PZUFQZVF	____	(RZWF)

Maintenance (Learned pattern types; new instantiations)

Near transfer (Learned relations and periodicities, but in new combinations)

	NI	DVEVFVGV	____	(HVIV)
	NNNN	VHDPWIEQ	____	(XJFR)

Far transfer (New relation, backward-next, or new periodicity, three letters)

	BN	UCTDSERF	____	(QGPH)
	NBNI	JPBXKOCX	____	(LNDX)
	NIN	PADQAERA	____	(FSAG)

Very far transfer (Backward-next as well as next relations and "period" of two letters, but relations must be sought between strings of letters rather than within a string)

Instructions: Pretend that you are a spy. You want to send the message on top in a secret code that only your friends will understand. Someone has begun coding the message for you on the second line. Try to figure out the secret code and finish coding the message by filling in the blanks with the letters that follow the code.

SIX SHIPS GONE

THY RIHQR ____ (I INOD)

Figure 1. Examples of learning, maintenance, and transfer items. The letters in the pattern notations refer to the alphabetic relations: N = next, I = identity, B = backward-next. In the *next* relation, the letters appear in alphabetical sequence; in the *identity* relation, the letters repeat; and in the *backward-next* relation, the letters appear in reverse alphabetical sequence. The number of letters in each pattern notation equals the period. (From Campione, J., Brown, A., Ferrara, R., & Bryant, N. [1984]. The zone of proximal development: Implications for individual differences and learning. In B. Rogoff & J. Wertsch [Eds.], *Children's learning in the "zone of proximal development"* [pp. 77–91]. San Francisco: Jossey-Bass. Reprinted with permission.)

transfer ability is assessed in identifying the zpd. Accordingly, children who demonstrate wide zpds require few prompts to learn a task and demonstrate far transfer ability; children who demonstrate narrow zpds require many prompts to learn a task and demonstrate limited transfer ability.

Brown and her colleagues have investigated the width of zpds as a function of age and IQ through tasks requiring analyzing, decoding, and completing letter or design sequencing patterns (Brown & Ferrara, 1985; Campione et al., 1984; Campione et al., 1985; Ferrara et al., 1986). In general, the results of this research indicate that younger children require more prompts than older children to learn a task but that after training, no significant differences are found between the younger children (3rd graders) and the older children (5th graders) in the maintenance and near transfer tasks (Ferrara et al., 1986). Older children required fewer prompts than younger children to perform the far transfer tasks (Ferrara et al., 1986). Similar results were also obtained with children with average intelligence and children with above average intelligence (Brown & Ferrara, 1985; Campione & Brown, 1984; Campione et al., 1984). Studies conducted with children with mental retardation indicated that these children needed more prompts to learn the task, but more importantly, needed more prompts to perform the maintenance and near transfer tasks than did children with normal intelligence (Campione et al., 1984, 1985).

Qualitative Analysis of the Zone of Proximal Development

Much of the work of Feuerstein and his colleagues (Feuerstein, Miller, Rand, et al., 1981; Feuerstein, Miller, Hoffman, et al., 1981; Feuerstein, Rand, Hoffman, & Miller, 1980; Feuerstein et al., 1979) has focused on qualitative aspects of the zpd. The purpose of Feuerstein's LPAD is to provide qualitative information about children's performance. The examiner is interested in identifying processes or factors that interfere with the child's successful completion of the task. These might include attention to the task, amount of effort expended, and types of errors made by the child being assessed. The examiner is also interested in identifying processes or means that enable the child to learn to complete the task successfully. This approach depends upon a positive interaction between the child and examiner and the examiner's competency with dynamic assessment procedures and interpretation (Feuerstein et al., 1979; Feuerstein, Miller, Rand, et al., 1981; Wertsch, 1984).

Implications for Intervention

The concept of dynamic assessment bridges the continuum from assessment to intervention. Instructional prescription is often derived from assessment (Campione, 1989; Feuerstein, 1979; Missiuna & Samuels, 1989; Palincsar, Brown, & Campione, 1989; Vye, Burns, Delclos, & Bransford, 1987). The quantitative perspective provides information as to whether or not someone is "ready" to learn a specific skill. A qualitative perspective in dynamic assessment provides different information. Such an approach allows a professional to identify how a child goes about solving a task or problem and to identify specific instructions that allow the child to complete tasks that he or she had been unable to complete. Thus, qualitative information can be used to bridge the assessment–intervention gap by providing specific recommendations as to how someone should be treated.

Professionals from education and psychology seem to agree that static assessment in and of itself is inadequate for determining the potential for immediate learning. Dynamic assessment enriches the information provided by traditional assessment procedures by revealing a picture of a child's zpd and suggesting his or her immediate potential for change. Dynamic assessment has been studied from quantitative and qualitative perspectives, each providing useful information for planning intervention. The concepts put forth by Vygotsky and applied to psychology and education have been successful in improving services to children. These strides have provided a solid foundation from which other disciplines can learn.

APPLICATION OF DYNAMIC
ASSESSMENT TO LANGUAGE ACQUISITION

We turn our attention now to language acquisition, and the application of the concept of the zpd to this phenomenon in children with and children without language impairments. In the remainder of this chapter, we explore some ways in which dynamic assessment can be applied to the language acquisition process.

Language Acquisition in Children without Disabilities

Rice (1989) has suggested three major components of language acquisition: "One is the language to be acquired or . . . the task to be mastered; another is the child and the abilities and predispositions that he or she brings to language acquisition; and the third is the environmental setting, that is the language that the child hears and the speaking context" (p. 149). Vygotsky's view requires consideration of the interaction between the components, focusing particularly upon the relationship between the child and his or her language environment.

This view holds that while language learning is ultimately internalized by the child, it takes place within an influential and responsive social context. The social context provides structure to the child's experiences that "not only constrains attention, reduces possible interpretations of actions, and sets up expectations within which the communicative value of specific expressions can be learned, but also places the child's actions and vocalizations in a context within which they are interpretable and pragmatically effective" (Snow, 1989, p. 85).

Bruner (1982) has discussed parents' use of scaffolding techniques to describe how children without disabilities are guided in their language learning by adult–child interactions. During joint attentional formats (Bruner, 1983a, 1983b) or routines (Snow, Perlmann, & Nathan, 1987), the caregiver provides models and cues to evoke communicative behaviors by the child. The caregiver imposes regularity on the task, reduces distraction, and guides the child's behaviors toward success. He or she also pushes the child to more advanced levels of performance by challenging the child to use new behaviors or by expanding the complexity of the familiar routine.

Scaffolding techniques may be effective in facilitating language development because the parent, when interacting directly with the child, typically operates within the child's zpd, providing the necessary amount of contextual support to move the child's performance to a more advanced level. Potential for learning may be observed when behaviors appear modifiable with the right combination of contextual support. Thus, normal language learning may be seen as a process of interaction between a changing biological organism and a supportive, nurturing environment, where the environment is structured gently but consistently to encourage the child to perform at the limits of his or her zpd. These principles of interaction can be applied to the assessment and treatment of children with language disorders. The discussion that follows focuses on assessment, illustrating how environmental manipulation can allow a child to perform at the limits of his or her zpd.

Language Acquisition in Children with Disabilities

The concept of the zpd provides valuable construct for assessing children who exhibit any kind of language disorder. The dynamic assessment principles should apply to children from differing populations, exhibiting different levels of language performance. The zpd is useful for determining a child's range of performance, and providing critical information for planning intervention.

A dynamic assessment language protocol based on Feuerstein's (1979) LPAD is presented here and examined as a tool for predicting children's immediate potential for language learning. To prepare for our discussion of that protocol, four of the major components of Feuerstein's LPAD are presented. They are: 1) the initial learning task, 2) related tasks (i.e., modifications of the initial task), 3) the teaching needed to perform these tasks, and 4) the modality of task presentation.

Initial Learning Task

In the initial task the child is provided with a problem that demands a behavior or skill he or she needs to learn. These behaviors include the entire gamut of possible language behaviors a child may need to acquire. In terms of a developmental model, they may be behaviors that are next in the developmental hierarchy of behaviors to be learned (e.g., two-word utterances for a child at the single-word utterance stage). In terms of a social-communicative model, they may be behaviors that enhance the functional communication of a child (e.g., verbal initiations). Behavior selection is based upon the speech-language pathologist's view of the child's language competence and areas of ecological deficiency. Simply stated, these are important behaviors that the speech-language pathologist believes are missing from or occurring infrequently in a child's repertoire. The initial learning task is one that is designed to exemplify and evoke the target behavior. The child is presented with the task and asked to perform in a particular manner.

Related Tasks

After being presented with the initial task, the child is presented with related novel tasks so that the examiner can investigate learning and transfer ability. As we discuss transfer ability here, we are not limiting our discussion to the terminology used by Brown and her colleagues. Rather, the related tasks, performance on which measures transfer ability, can differ from the initial learning task in a multitude of ways, reflecting the differing demands of stimulus and response generalization. Related tasks are designed to examine the child's ability to generalize what he or she has learned. As such, they are different, untrained exemplars of the initial task. "To a great extent, this array of interrelated tasks of varying novelty, difficulty, and complexity simulate the adaptational requirements that often confront the growing individual in real life" (Feuerstein, 1979, p. 92).

Teaching of Tasks

As each task is presented, the adult provides guidance to help evoke the desired behavior. Initially, few cues are provided and the child is asked to perform based upon his or her existing skills. This performance reflects the child's ability with minimal guidance (similar to the performance measured by static assessment). If the child is successful, the examiner is quick to provide reinforcement that identifies the skills and motivates the child to continue in the activity. If the child fails, the examiner provides feedback to help facilitate successful performance on the next attempt. Since the goal is mastery of the task, continued failures are greeted with supportive feedback to encourage successful performance. Feedback, in the form of prompts and cues, reflects different teaching strategies that the adult deems appropriate for the child. For example, a child might need an additional model prior to responding, or a visual prompt to help identify a salient feature of the task. Feedback consists of any cues or prompts that are designed to enhance the child's performance. The emphasis is on providing teaching strategies (i.e., cues or prompts) when necessary to enable a child to perform successfully on the tasks.

Modality of Task Presentation

The final component of the model addresses the modality, or avenue of presentation, of the initial task and subsequent related tasks. The modality of the task refers to the type of stimuli (e.g., manipulatives, pictorial-concrete representations, figural-abstract representations) provided by the adult in the initial task and the related tasks. The modality of presentation need not remain the same, but may change as the assessment proceeds.

According to Feuerstein (1979), this model can yield important information about a child's immediate potential for change. Specifically, the following types of information should be obtained through these dynamic assessment procedures:

1. The capability of the child to grasp the new behavior (or solve a problem)
2. The amount and nature of investment required in order to teach the child the new behavior (i.e., the type and number of cues or prompts that must be provided in order to achieve success)
3. The extent to which the newly acquired behavior is successfully applied in producing progressively more difficult (or more novel) behaviors

4. The effects of various teaching strategies (i.e., cues, prompts) used to help the child function at a higher level
5. The child's preference for a particular modality of presentation for a given behavior

An example of dynamic assessment, which illustrates how this information can be obtained when assessing language in young children, is presented in the next section.

Dynamic Assessment of Two-Term Utterances

Protocol

Applying Vygotsky's principles and Feuerstein's learning potential assessment model, we have designed a dynamic assessment protocol to explore the language learning potential of preschool children with language impairments. Specifically, this protocol examines the immediate potential for children performing at the one-word stage of language development, as determined through static assessment, to produce two-term utterances. The following semantic relations are investigated: entity + attribute, entity + locative, possessor + possession, agent + action, action + object, and action + locative. These structures were selected because they reflect major relations studied in other research, and they seem to be the more frequently occurring types of two-word utterances (Bloom, 1973; Bloom, Lightbown, & Hood, 1975; Leonard, 1976). (Although comprehension was also examined, only production is described in this chapter.) The modality of the initial task and related tasks includes manipulatives and verbal cuing by the examiner. Object manipulation refers to the presentation of toys designed to represent the most salient semantic features of the two-term utterances. For example, to test production of the entity + attribute relation, two cups, one of which is dirty and one of which is clean, are used. To test production of the agent + action relation, a dog puppet that can be manipulated to walk is used. The verbal cueing proceeds in a hierarchy from minimum prompting (a general statement calling the child's attention to the task) to maximum verbal prompting (shaping the child's production of a two-term utterance by having the child imitate each single word and then the two words together). The cue types, from least supportive to most supportive, include: general statement, elicitation question, cloze or sentence completion, indirect model, direct model, direct model plus an elicitation question, and shaping. (Table 1 includes definitions and examples of these terms.) The different cue types allow for variety in communicative intentions. For example, the general statement (e.g., "Oh look") may elicit a comment or a request; the elicitation question (e.g., "Whose is this?") evokes an answer that may also be a request (e.g., "What do you need"). The initial task consists of four associated two-term utterances, designed to illustrate the semantic relation being elicited. The related tasks consist of two

Table 1. Dynamic assessment protocol for two-term utterances

Prompt	Definition	Example
General statement	Adult provides a general statement directing the child's attention to the relevant object or activity in the situational context. The statement is designed to focus the child's attention, but allow for a spontaneous production of the relational term.	"Oh, look at this."
Elicitation question	Adult asks a *wh*-question in reference to the objects or ongoing activity.	"What's happening?" "What's he doing?"
Cloze or sentence completion	Adult presents the objects in the relevant situational context in such a way as to provide a contrast in the event, highlighting the relational term. The verbal cue partially models the target relation by presenting the contrastive item in a sentence. This is followed by a "wh" question, or elicitation statement—open ended remark.	"Look here, the dog is sitting" (manipulating the dog so he sits) and "Here he is ___" (manipulating the dog so he walks). "This is a dirty spoon (presenting dirty spoon) and this is a ___ (presenting a clean spoon)."
Indirect model	Adult provides an embedded or delayed model of the relational term presenting the exact lexical items: the model is followed by an elicitation question or comment.	"Look at that dog; he's walking." "See the dog walking on the table." "What's happening?" "Look at that."
Direct model and direct model + elicitation question	Adult provides a direct model of the relational term and pauses for possible spontaneous imitation (DM). If there is no response, the adult directly requests a direct imitation of the relational utterance (DM + E).	"Dog walk." (pause) "Tell me dog walk." or "Dog walk, tell me."
Shaping	If the child produces a related single word in response to the direct model + elicitation cue, the adult repeats that word, then provides a direct model of the other component of the relational term, requesting an imitation of it and then modeling the entire utterance.	"Yes, dog, tell me dog (pause); tell me walk (pause); tell me dog walk."

Table 2. Two-term semantic relations expressed in early production

Words include those that appear on Bloom's (1970) or Nelson's (1973) lists of commonly produced first words. Efforts were made to have the phonemic structure of the words contain at least two early developing consonants.

Entity + attribute	Agent + action
dirty spoon	dog walk
clean spoon	pig walk
dirty cup	dog kick
clean cup	pig kick
broken dish	monkey jump
big truck	frog hop

Entity + locative	Agent + object
cow in barn	open box
cow in bowl	open can
horse in barn	push car
horse in bowl	push train
man under blanket	kiss bunny
mouse in sock	bounce ball

Possessor + possession	Action + locative
clown's hair	fly over tree
doll's hair	fly over house
clown's eye	climb tree
doll's eye	climb house
baby's bottle	drive under bridge
bear's dress	sit chair

novel two-term utterances to examine near transfer ability. Thus, for each semantic relation, the child is presented with six items, four associated items and two novel items. (See Table 2 for a listing of specific items.)

Presentation of an item begins with object manipulation by the examiner plus a general statement. Failure of the child to respond correctly results in the administration of a more explicit verbal cue by the examiner. The provision of additional verbal cues is continued until the child is successful on an item or until the last cue (shaping) has been administered. In essence, each cue serves to provide accuracy feedback for an incorrect response and additional support in the form of a prompt or cue for the child's next attempt.

Interpretation

Data from two children are presented here in order to illustrate the application and interpretation of this protocol. These children (age 32 and 35 months) were identified as being at the single-word level of language development. Static assessment results indicated that these preschool boys were developing normally in the cognitive, social-emotional, and motor domains, but were delayed in language, specifically expressive language (see Table 3). Both children were producing more than 50 single-word utterances, but no two-word utterances. Their productions included a variety of consonants and vowels, with age-appropriate phonological errors. Both children used their

Table 3. Results of static assessment

Measure	Subject 1	Subject 2
Peabody Picture Vocabulary Test		
(Mean = 100; standard deviation = 15)		
Standard score	106	89
Percentile rank	66	24
Sequenced Inventory of		
Communication Development		
Receptive Communication Age	36 months	28 months
(scattered success through)	(48)	(40)
Expressive Communication Age	20 months	20 months
(scattered success through)	(36)	(36)
Stanford-Binet Intelligence Scale		
(Mean = 100; standard deviation = 15)		
Test composite standard score	105	117
Boyd Development Scale		
Motor and Self-Sufficiency	Age appropriate	Age appropriate

single words, plus gestures and vocalizations, to communicate a variety of intentions. Their receptive language skills were at age level, and they demonstrated comprehension of semantic relations by acting out unpredictable two-word utterance instructions (e.g., "Show me 'shoe fly.' ").

Although the children performed similarly on the static assessment, their performances on dynamic assessment were quite different (see Table 4). The

Table 4. Results of dynamic assessment

Semantic relations	Number correct — First four associated items	Last two novel items	Cue types resulting in correct production	Number of productions
Subject 1				
Entity + attribute	0	0	—	—
Entity + locative	0	0	—	—
Possessor + possession	0	0	—	—
Agent + action	0	0	—	—
Action + object	1	0	DM + E	1
Action + locative	0	0	—	—
Subject 2				
Entity + attribute	3	2	DM + E	5
Entity + locative	0	0	—	—
Possessor + possession	0	0	—	—
Agent + action	4	1	DM + E	2
			SH	3
Action + object	4	2	IM	2
			DM;	1
			DM + E	3
Action + locative	4	0	DM + E	4

Note: DM + E = direct model plus elicitation question; SH = shaping; IM = indirect model; DM = direct model.

dynamic assessment results reflect the children's correct production of two-word semantic relations. The first column in Table 4 shows the number of correct productions on the first four associated items per relation. The second column details the number of correct productions on the final two novel items (i.e., transfer) per relation. Column 3 indicates the cue types that evoked correct productions (i.e., how much cueing was necessary to support a correct response per semantic relation). Column 4 indicates the number of correct productions by cue type.

Table 4 reveals the performance of the two subjects on the dynamic assessment protocol. Subject 1 produced only one two-word semantic relation when presented with numerous opportunities and over 200 cues. His one correct production occurred on the first four items; no correct productions occurred on the last two (transfer) items. Correct production occurred following a direct model plus an elicitation question. In contrast, Subject 2 produced 20 types of two-word semantic relations. These productions were observed on all but two of the six relational categories. Correct productions occurred on the first four associated items, as well as on the last two (transfer) items. Subject 2 was able to produce two-word utterances with an indirect model, direct model with no elicitation question, direct model with an elicitation question, and shaping.

Using a quantitative analysis of these data, one can see clear differences in performance. The data indicate that the two children, who appeared similar on their static assessment results, differed markedly in the degree to which they were ready to move ahead in their language learning. During dynamic assessment, Subject 2 demonstrated greater potential for immediate change: he produced more two-word relations with cues and he demonstrated success on both the teaching and the transfer items. Qualitative analysis of the results leads to an examination of the different cues that elicited correct productions. Subject 1's correct production required a direct model plus an elicitation question. While Subject 2 also frequently required a direct model plus an elicitation question, or even shaping, he was also able to respond correctly with only an indirect or direct model, considered less supportive cue types. According to Vygotsky, dynamic assessment is the process by which the zpd is defined; the better the child's performance (i.e., the greater the child's success with examiner support), the greater the inferred learning potential. In this example, the success of the children in producing two-word utterances with calibrated support by the examiner determined the boys' zpd, which in turn can be viewed as a guide to predicting the immediate benefits of direct instruction. (Dynamic assessment and identification of a child's zpd provide short-term predictions; that is, they reveal the benefits of direct instruction provided at a particular time for the purpose of teaching a specific behavior. Long-term predictions about language acquisition require the examination of numerous other child and environmental variables, a discussion of which is beyond the scope of this chapter.)

After assessment, both children received 3 weeks of direct treatment designed to teach particular categories of two-word utterances through a script (Nelson, 1986) or joint action routine (Snyder-McLean, Solomonson, McLean, & Sack, 1984) therapy approach. Treatment sessions occurred three times a week, each session lasting approximately an hour. The children's productions of semantic relations were monitored during a separate session held each week. During this 30-minute freeplay session, a second clinician interacted with the children by playing with materials not used during treatment. These sessions were designed to provide opportunities for the productions of the semantic relations without modeling or instruction. The data from these sessions were used to examine the hypothesis that the boys would make differential progress in their language learning. Summary data are presented in Figures 2 and 3. These data reflect the subjects' productions of target and control two- and three-word utterances during the baseline, treatment, and withdrawal phases of the study. Target semantic relations are defined as those three semantic categories that are conceptually related to the treatment target. Control semantic relations are defined as those three semantic categories that are not conceptually related to the treatment target. The target semantic relations for Subject 1 included agent + action (the identified treatment target), action + object, and action + locative. These were considered in the same response class because of their common action component and noun + verb or verb + noun construction. Subject 1's control relations included possessor + possession, entity + attribute, and entity + locative. The target semantic relations for Subject 2 included possessor + possession (the identified treatment target), entity + attribute, and entity + locative. These were considered in the same response class because of their common static component and modifier + noun construction. Control semantic relations for Subject 2 included agent + action, action + object, and action + locative.

The data for Subject 1 (Figure 2) reflect changes in the target language following direct treatment, with more productions of the target semantic relations than the controls. The effects of treatment appear to be delayed. The data for Subject 2 (Figure 3) reflect changes occurring prior to the beginning of treatment. However, treatment does seem to result in rapid change in the target relations and a slower change in the control relations. Recall that during dynamic assessment, Subject 1 demonstrated a smaller zpd than Subject 2, suggesting that perhaps Subject 2 was "more ready" for change than Subject 1. The data in Figures 2 and 3 clearly reflect this outcome. Whether or not the changes in the boys' productions of two-word semantic relations was due entirely to treatment is debatable. The disparity between the target data and the control data support the benefits of treatment, but the effects of maturation or other variables cannot be conclusively ruled out.

These data support the predictive value of dynamic assessment, albeit on a very small sample. The results indicated that Subject 2 was most responsive to adult cueing. Indeed, he first demonstrated changes in his language follow-

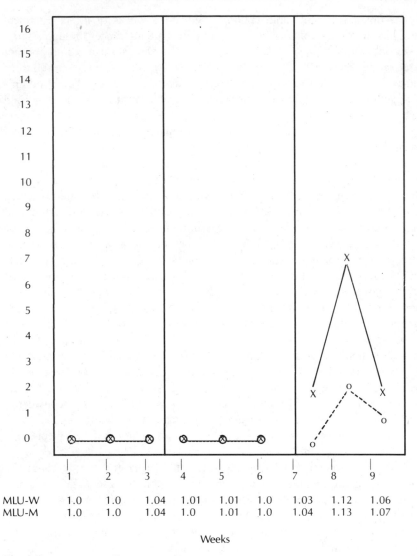

MLU-W	1.0	1.0	1.04	1.01	1.01	1.0	1.03	1.12	1.06
MLU-M	1.0	1.0	1.04	1.0	1.01	1.0	1.04	1.13	1.07

Weeks

Target X ——————— X
Control O ------------- O

Figure 2. Productions of target and control semantic relations by Subject 1 during weekly freeplay sessions, expressed in mean length of utterances in words (MLU-W) and mean length of utterances in morphemes (MLU-M).

ing adult cueing. The dynamic assessment process may also be helpful in suggesting which teaching strategies might be most beneficial in treatment. In this example, both boys demonstrated their dependence upon some type of verbal model. Accordingly, the script treatment employed ample modeling with and without requests for production. The effectiveness of treatment

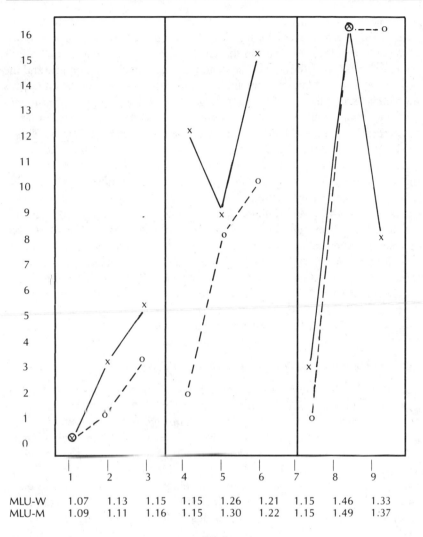

	1	2	3	4	5	6	7	8	9
MLU-W	1.07	1.13	1.15	1.15	1.26	1.21	1.15	1.46	1.33
MLU-M	1.09	1.11	1.16	1.15	1.30	1.22	1.15	1.49	1.37

Weeks

Target X ——————— X
Control O ------------- O

Figure 3. Productions of target and control semantic relations by Subject 2 during weekly freeplay sessions, expressed in mean length of utterances in words (MLU-W) and mean length of utterances in morphemes (MLU-M).

strategies suggested from dynamic assessment procedures has not been systematically addressed in this research, and is in need of investigation.

To view learning potential based only on performance during dynamic assessment would be improper. The knowledge gained through static assessment and dynamic assessment come together with other variables, including the home environment, to reveal a child's immediate potential for change on a given skill. Performance during assessment procedures contributes to the clinician's hypotheses regarding the child's level of functioning, the child's responsiveness to differing amounts and types of contextual support, and the possible etiology of the impairment. These in turn contribute to the clinician's predictions about the benefits of language intervention. By predicting immediate potential for change, dynamic assessment lets the clinician know when targeted, intensive stimulation designed to teach specific behaviors or skills is likely to be effective. Three different predictions are hypothesized. First, successful performance on teaching and transfer tasks with minimal cueing by the adults suggests immediate potential for change, and possibly change that is imminent without instruction (Belmont, 1989; Olswang, Bain, Rosendahl, Oblak, & Smith, 1986). Subject 2 may have been such a child. Second, performance in the mid- to upper-zone region (i.e., responsiveness to but dependence upon adult cues) reflects immediate learning potential with instruction (Belmont, 1989; Olswang et al., 1986). Third, no success in response to adult cueing may be demonstrating a lack of potential for immediate change, suggesting that a child may not be able to benefit from instruction on the target skill at a particular point in time. Given the questionable benefits of treatment for Subject 1, his performance may place him in the latter category.

EDUCATIONAL AND CLINICAL IMPLICATIONS

Current research strongly argues for some kind of biological basis for language development. Equally strong is the premise that biology and the environment interact to facilitate or inhibit language at certain developmental levels throughout the life span. As Vygotsky recognized, language is unique in that it is both a higher mental function and a psychological tool by which lower functions are transformed into higher functions (1934/1986). Therefore, when we assess language, we are examining both a process and a product. This fact creates an interesting and challenging state. Examining a process dynamically without simultaneously changing the product is a difficult task. It requires that we proceed carefully in structuring the content and sequence of assessment activities. We hope that the protocol outlined here is useful in guiding clinicians in determining the extent to which environmental context might facilitate language learning at a particular time.

In Vygotskian thinking, "learning is interpersonal" (Belmont, 1989). Children bring to a task their capabilities, but these capabilities are realized through adult guidance and contextual support. "Human learning occurs as a transfer of responsibility" (Belmont, 1989, p. 145) from the instructor to the student, with the skill of the instructor shaping the performance of the student. The blending of the two is the critical component of the learning process. A socio-instructional approach to assessing children with language impairment requires that clinicians share the burden of performance. A child's skills are evaluated, but his or her capabilities can be seen only through careful manipulation of the context to reveal the zpd. As such "the child does not have a zpd, but rather, shares one with an instructor" (Belmont, 1989, p. 145).

DIRECTIONS FOR FUTURE RESEARCH

Future research addressing the issues raised in this chapter should focus on three primary areas:

1. Research needs to examine the precursors to the acquisition of particular language milestones. As in the case of the research presented in this chapter, behaviors heralding the onset of two-word utterances need to be examined. These include gestural and verbal, semantic, syntactic, pragmatic, and phonologic precursor behaviors.
2. Dynamic assessment procedures need to be examined in terms of their role in the elicitation of these precursor behaviors. This avenue of research should examine the ways in which context can be manipulated (i.e., adult guidance) as a tool for evoking particular child behaviors. Given the multidimensional aspects of context, the complexities of this task cannot be minimized.
3. The relationship between dynamic assessment outcomes and actual language learning should be investigated. This line of research might directly address Vygotsky's concept of the zone of proximal development. The research will need to examine systematically the relationship between behaviors that can and cannot be elicited through adult guidance (i.e., dynamic assessment outcomes) and their subsequent rate of acquisition with and without intervention.

CONCLUSION

Knowing how a child performs with adult guidance provides the interventionist with a measure of the child's potential and suggests whether immediate intervention is likely to be useful. Management options for children with language impairments include monitoring natural language learning and providing intervention in an attempt to enhance the acquisition process. The issue raised in this chapter regarding the delivery of service is one of timing—when is a child ready to benefit from intervention on a specific skill? We have suggested that static and dynamic assessment procedures will yield information to help speech-language pathologists make more informed decisions regarding the management of language impaired children. Our thinking has been guided by Vygotsky's notions regarding the zone of proximal development and dynamic assessment. Application of these concepts holds exciting promises for the discipline of communication science and its disorders.

REFERENCES

Barr, P., & Samuels, M. (1988). Dynamic assessment of cognitive and affective factors contributing to learning difficulties in adults: A case study approach. *Professional Psychology Research and Practice, 19*, 6–13.

Belmont, J. (1989). Cognitive strategies and strategic learning: The socio-instructional approach. *American Psychologist, 44*, 142–148.

Bethge, H., Carlson, J., & Wiedl, K. (1982). The effects of dynamic assessment procedures on Raven Matrices performance. *Intelligence, 6*, 89–97.

Bloom, L. (1970). *Language development: Form and function in emerging grammars.* Cambridge: MIT Press.

Bloom, L. (1973). *One word at a time.* The Hague: Mouton.

Bloom, L., Lightbown, P., & Hood, L. (1975). Structure and variation in child language. *Monograph of the Society for Research in Child Development, 40.*

Braun, C., Rennie, B., & Gordon, C. (1987). An examination of contexts for reading assessment. *Journal of Educational Research, 80*, 283–289.

Brown, A., Bransford, J., Ferrara, R., & Campione, J. (1983). Learning, remembering and understanding. In P. Musse (Ed.), *Handbook of child psychology. Vol. 3. Cognitive development* (4th ed., pp. 77–166). New York: John Wiley & Sons.

Brown, A., & Campione, J. (1986). Cognitive science principles and work force education. *Advances in Reading, and Language Research, 4*, 217–229.

Brown, A., & Ferrara, R. (1985). Diagnosing zones of proximal development. In J. Wertsch (Ed.), *Culture, communication, and cognition: Vygotskian perspective* (pp. 273–305). New York: Cambridge University Press.

Bruner, J. (1982). The organization of action and the nature of the adult–infant transaction. In E. Tronick (Ed.), *Social interchange in infancy: Affect, cognition and communication* (pp. 23–35). Baltimore: University Park Press.

Bruner, J. (1983a). The acquisition of pragmatic commitments. In R. Golinkoff (Ed.), *The transition from prelinguistic to linguistic communication* (pp. 27–42). Hillsdale, NJ: Lawrence Erlbaum Associates.

Bruner, J. (1983b). *Child's talk: Learning to use language.* New York: Norton.

Bruner, J. (1985). Vygotsky: A historical and conceptual perspective. In J.V. Wertsch (Ed.), *Culture, communication and cognition: Vygotskian perspective* (pp. 21–34). Cambridge: Cambridge University Press.

Bruner, J. (1986). *Actual minds, possible worlds.* Cambridge: Harvard University Press.

Bruner, J. (1987). Prologue. In R.W. Rieber & A.S. Carton (Eds.), *The collected works of Vygotsky* (Vol. 1, pp. 1–16). New York: Plenum.

Budoff, M., & Friedman, M. (1964). "Learning potential" as an assessment approach to the adolescent mentally retarded. *Journal of Consulting Psychology, 28*, 434–439.

Budoff, M., & Hamilton, J. (1976). Optimizing test performance of moderately and severely retarded adolescents and adults. *American Journal of Mental Deficiency, 81*, 49–57.

Campione, J. (1989). Assisted assessment: A taxonomy of approaches and an outline of strengths and weaknesses. *Journal of Learning Disabilities, 22*, 151–165.

Campione, J., & Brown, A. (1984). Learning ability and transfer propensity as sources of individual differences in intelligence. In P. Brooks, R. Sperber, & C. McCauley (Eds.), *Learning and cognition in the mentally retarded* (pp. 265–309). Hillsdale, NJ: Lawrence Erlbaum Associates.

Campione, J., Brown, A., Ferrara, R., & Bryant, N. (1984). The zone of proximal development: Implications for individual differences and learning. In B. Rogoff & J. Wertsch (Eds.), *Children's learning in the "zone of proximal development"* (pp. 77–91). San Francisco: Jossey-Bass.

Campione, J., Brown, A., Ferrara, R., Jones, R., & Steinberg, E. (1985). Breakdowns in flexible use of information: Intelligence-related differences in transfer following equivalent learning performance. *Intelligence, 9,* 297–315.

Carlson, J. (1983). *Applications of dynamic assessment to cognitive and perceptual functioning of three ethnic groups.* Riverside: University of California (ERIC Document Reproduction Service No. ED 233 040).

Cioffi, B., & Carney, J. (1983). Dynamic assessment of reading disabilities. *Reading Teacher, 36,* 764–768.

Cole, M., & Scribner, S. (1978). Introduction. In M. Cole, V. John-Steiner, S. Scribner, & E. Souberman (Eds.), L.S. Vygotsky, *Mind in society* (pp. 1–14). Cambridge: Harvard University Press.

Engels, F. (1940). *Dialectics of nature.* New York: International Publishers.

Ferrara, R., Brown, A., & Campione, J. (1986). Children's learning and transfer of inductive reasoning rules: Studies of proximal development. *Child Development, 57,* 1087–1099.

Feuerstein, R. (1979). *The dynamic assessment of retarded performers.* Baltimore: University Park Press.

Feuerstein, R., Miller, R., Hoffman, M., Rand, Y., Mintzker, Y., & Jensen, M. (1981). Cognitive modifiability in adolescence: Cognitive structure and the effects of intervention. *Journal of Special Education, 15,* 269–287.

Feuerstein, R., Miller, R., Rand, Y., & Jensen, M. (1981). Can evolving techniques better measure cognitive change? *Journal of Special Education, 15,* 201–219.

Feuerstein, R., Rand, Y., & Hoffman, M. (1979). *The dynamic assessment of retarded performers.* Baltimore: University Park Press.

Feuerstein, R., Rand, Y., Hoffman, M., & Miller, R. (1980). *Instrumental enrichment.* Baltimore: University Park Press.

Guidelines for caseload size for speech-language services in the schools. (1984). *Asha, 26*(4), 53–58.

Kazdin, A. (1980). *Behavioral modification in applied settings* (2nd ed.). Homewood, IL: Dorsey Press.

Kozulin, A. (1985). *Psychology in Utopia: Toward a social history of Soviet psychology.* Cambridge: MIT Press.

Leonard, L. (1976). *Meaning in child language.* New York: Grune & Stratton.

Lidz, C. (1982). *Psychological assessment of the preschool disadvantaged child.* Paper presented at the annual International Convention of the Council for Exceptional Children, Houston.

Lidz, C. (1983). Dynamic assessment and the preschool child. *Journal of Psychoeducational Assessment, 1,* 59–72.

Lidz, C., & Thomas, C. (1987). The preschool learning assessment device: Extension of a static approach. In C. Lidz (Ed.), *Dynamic assessment: An interaction approach to evaluating learning potential* (pp. 288–326). New York: Guilford Press.

Luria, A. (1961). Study of the abnormal child. *American Journal of Orthopsychiatry, 31,* 1–14.

Mearig, J. (1987). Assessing the learning potential of kindergarten and primary-age children. In C. Lidz (Ed.), *Dynamic assessment: An interaction approach to evaluating learning potential* (pp. 237–267). New York: Guilford Press.

Meyers, J. (1987). The training of dynamic assessors. In C. Lidz (Ed.), *Dynamic assessment: An interactional approach to evaluating learning potential* (pp. 403–425). New York: Guilford Press.

Meyers, J., Pfeffer, J., & Erlbaum, V. (1985). Process assessment: A model for broadening assessment. *Journal of Special Education, 19*, 73–89.

Milisen, R. (1954). A rationale for articulation disorders. *Journal of Speech and Hearing Disorders, Monograph Supplement, 4*, 6–17.

Minick, N. (1987). Implications of Vygotsky's theories for dynamic assessment. In C. Lidz (Ed.), *Dynamic assessment: An interactional approach to evaluating learning potential* (pp. 116–140). New York: Guilford Press.

Missiuna, C., & Samuels, M. (1989). Dynamic assessment of preschool children with special needs: Comparison of mediation and instruction. *Remedial and Special Education, 10*, 53–62.

Molenaar, P. (1987). Dynamic assessment and adaptive optimization of the psycho-therapeutic process. *Behavioral Assessment, 9*, 389–416.

Nelson, K. (1973). Structure and strategy in learning to talk. *Monographs of the Society for Research in Child Development, 38*, 1–135.

Nelson, K. (1986). *Event knowledge: Structure and function in development.* Hillsdale, NJ: Lawrence Erlbaum Associates.

Olswang, L., Bain, B., Rosendahl, P., Oblak, S., & Smith, A. (1986). Language learning: Moving performance from context dependent to independent state. *Child Language Teaching and Therapy, 2*, 180–210.

Palincsar, A., Brown, A., & Campione, J. (1989, March). *Structure dialogues among communities of first grade learners.* Paper presented at the AERA symposium Extending Vygotskian theory: Discourse and interaction in the classroom, San Francisco.

Rice, M. (1989). Children's language acquisition. *American Psychologist, 44*, 129–156.

Rogoff, B., & Wertsch, J. (Eds.). (1984). *Children's learning in the zone of proximal development.* San Francisco: Jossey-Bass.

Snow, C. (1989). Understanding social interaction and language acquisition: Sentences are not enough. In M. Bornstein & J. Bruner (Eds.), *Interaction in human development.* Hillsdale, NJ: Lawrence Erlbaum Associates.

Snow, C., Perlmann, R., & Nathan, D. (1987). Why routines are different: Toward a multiple-factors model of the relation between input and language acquisition. In K. Nelson & A. Van Kleeck (Eds.), *Children's language* (Vol. 6, pp. 65–97). Hillsdale, NJ: Lawrence Erlbaum Associates.

Snyder-McLean, L., Solomonson, B., McLean, J., & Sack, S. (1984). Structuring joint action routines: A strategy for facilitating communication and language development in the classroom. *Seminars in Speech and Language, 5*(3), 213–228.

Tzuriel, D., & Klein, P. (1985). The assessment of analogical thinking modifiability among regular, special education, disadvantaged and mentally retarded children. *Journal of Abnormal Child Psychology, 13*, 539–552.

Tzuriel, D., & Klein, P. (1987). Assessing the young child: Children's analogical thinking modifiability. In C. Lidz (Ed.), *Dynamic assessment: An interaction approach to evaluating learning potential* (pp. 268–287). New York: Guilford Press.

Vye, N., Burns, M., Delclos, V., & Bransford, J. (1987). In C. Lidz (Ed.), *Dynamic assessment: An interaction approach to evaluating learning potential* (pp. 327–359). New York: Guilford Press.

Vygotsky, L. (1978). *Mind in society: The development of higher psychological processes.* Cambridge: Harvard University Press.

Vygotsky, L. (1981). The genesis of higher mental functions. In J.V. Wertsch (Ed. and Trans.), *The concept of activity in Soviet psychology* (pp. 144–188). Armonk, NY: M.E. Sharpe, Inc. (Original work published in 1960.)

Vygotsky, L. (1986). *Thought and language.* (A. Kozulin, Ed. and Trans.) Cambridge: MIT Press. (Original work published 1934.)

Warren, S., Rogers-Warren, A., Baer, D., & Guess, D. (1980). Assessment and facilitation of language generalization. In W. Sailor, B. Wilcox, & L. Brown (Eds.), *Methods of instruction for severely handicapped students* (pp. 227–258). Baltimore: Paul H. Brookes Publishing Co.

Wertsch, J. (Ed. and Trans.). (1981). *The concept of activity in Soviet psychology* (pp. 1–36). Armonk, NY: M.E. Sharpe, Inc.

Wertsch, J. (1984). The zone of proximal development: Some conceptual issues. In B. Rogoff & J. Wertsch (Eds.), *Children's learning in the "zone of proximal development"* (pp. 7–18). San Francisco: Jossey-Bass.

Wertsch, J. (Ed.). (1985). *Culture, communication, and cognition.* Cambridge: Cambridge University Press.

Yaroshevsky, M. (1989). *Lev Vygotsky.* Moscow: Progress Publishers.

9

Profiling Young Children's Communicative Competence

Amy M. Wetherby and Barry M. Prizant

COMMUNICATION DISORDERS ARE AMONG THE most prevalent disabilities in early childhood. As many as 11% of kindergarten children have communication disorders (Beitchman, Nair, Clegg, & Patel, 1986). Of all 3- to 5-year-old children identified as having disabilities, 70% have speech and language impairments (U.S. Department of Education, 1987). This chapter examines clinical issues pertaining to the assessment and early identification of communication disorders; reviews the literature exploring the emerging communication and language patterns of children with communication impairments; and presents a model for communication assessment that profiles communicative, social-affective, and symbolic abilities of young children. Clinical profiles from case examples are presented, and clinical implications discussed.

IMPORTANCE OF EARLY DETECTION

The national priority of early identification and intervention is reflected in the passage of the Education of the Handicapped Act Amendments of 1986 (P.L. 99-457). This legislation establishes the provision of new funds to states choosing to develop and implement early identification and intervention services for at risk or disabled infants and preschool children from birth to 3, including children with delays in speech and language development. The funds are targeted to be allocated by the 1991–1992 school year. The early identification of children with communication or language disorders traditionally has posed a dilemma. The first symptom attended to by parents and professionals may be a delay in or failure to acquire language in the absence of other significant disabilities (e.g., sensory impairments, physical disabilities, severe to profound cognitive impairments). Since the normal range of first-word acquisition is between 12 and 20 months of age, a child is not likely to be referred for a language delay until at best 20–24 months, but more typically, after 36 months. A delay in referral is particularly significant because assessment of early language abilities may lead to identification of language disorders associated with primary conditions, such as mild to moderate hearing impairment or mental retardation, and thus may lead to appropriate early intervention (Miller, 1983).

Prior to the passage of P.L. 99-457, there was not a strong impetus to identify children before the age of 3. Education and treatment programs for children with special needs with less severe developmental disabilities have not been readily available. The program established by P.L. 99-457 encourages states to develop systems for early identification and intervention for a broad range of infants and preschool children who have or are at risk of developing disabilities. There is thus an urgent need to develop assessment frameworks that contribute to the early identification of children with language and communication disorders, since they affect 70% of all preschool children with disabilities.

Early identification leading to appropriate intervention is crucial, because of the far-reaching effects of early communication disorders. The detrimental impact of early language and communication impairments on later educational achievement, emotional and behavioral development, development of peer relations, and family well-being have been clearly documented (Aram & Hall, 1989; Aram & Nation, 1980; Baker & Cantwell, 1987; Hall & Tomblin, 1978; Howlin & Rutter, 1987; Prizant et al., 1990). Increasing awareness of the effect of early language and communication impairments on preschool and school-age children and their families underscores the need for earlier identification and the development of family- and child-oriented interventions based upon profiles of abilities and disabilities.

Research has documented the positive effects of early intervention in fostering the development of young children (Guralnick & Bennett, 1987; Shonkoff & Hauser-Cram, 1987; Warren & Kaiser, 1988). Providing families with an earlier and clearer understanding of their child's disability has been identified as an important factor in mitigating family stress (Bristol & Schopler, 1984). Early communication intervention may also be an important preventive measure to preclude or mitigate the development of emotional or behavioral disorders and later academic problems. Therefore, priority should be placed on early identification and treatment of communication disorders, since the positive effects of appropriate treatment may be far-reaching.

CHARACTERISTICS OF COMMONLY USED
ASSESSMENT PROCEDURES FOR INFANTS AND TODDLERS

Crais and Leonard (1990) surveyed 67 U.S. graduate school programs in communication disorders or speech-language pathology in order to determine which assessment instruments were most frequently taught and used in graduate programs and university clinics for children from birth to 3. Instruments cited include developmental scales for the birth to 3 population that are designed to be cursory measures of early communication skills, and more broadly based assessment instruments that do not assess or comprehensively profile communication and symbolic behavior (Rossetti, 1990). These instruments have the following characteristics and limitations (Prizant & Wetherby, 1988; Wetherby & Prizant, 1989):

1. A focus of assessment is on forms of communication (e.g., presence of words, gestures) rather than the functions served by the forms or intentions expressed.
2. Analysis of preverbal communication (i.e., gestural, vocal) is limited or absent.
3. Social-affective signaling is generally not assessed as part of communicative interactions.
4. Specific profiles of strengths and weaknesses across crucial domains of speech, language, and communicative functioning and related abilities are not generally provided.
5. Some instruments rely solely on parent report, without direct assessment of the young child.
6. Instruments using direct assessment are primarily clinician directed, putting the child in a respondent role and thus limiting observations of initiated and spontaneous communication.
7. Caregivers are not involved as informants as well as active participants during the assessment.

Thus, although a child's communicative, symbolic, and social-affective profile has important implications for the early identification of speech, language, and communication impairments, there are currently no formal measures of communication that assess these early abilities in a systematic and comprehensive manner. Furthermore, available instruments do not provide direct implications based on assessment findings for planning contexts and contents for early intervention.

The ten instruments most frequently used, according to the survey of Crais and Leonard, are listed in Figure 1 and rated as to whether they address these limitations.

NEED FOR NEW EMPHASIS IN EARLY ASSESSMENT

The development of language involves a complex interplay of emerging abilities in social-affective, communicative, cognitive, and linguistic domains (Bates, 1979). Pragmatic-social interactive theories of the 1970s and 1980s have placed great emphasis on the role of social interaction in language development (Bates, 1976; Bloom & Lahey, 1978; McLean & Snyder-

Feature	SICD	PLS	REEL	Denver	Birth to Three	Bayley Scales	ACLC	Ordinal Scales	Vineland	ELI
Assesses functions of communication	L	–	L	L	L	L	–	L	L	–
Analyzes preverbal communication	L	–	L	L	+	L	–	–	L	–
Assesses social-affective signaling	–	–	–	L	L	L	–	–	L	–
Profiles social, communicative, and symbolic abilities	–	–	–	–	+	–	–	–	L	–
Uses caregivers as informants and assesses child directly	+	–	+	+	L	–	–	–	L	–
Uses spontaneous child-initiated communicative interactions	L	–	–	–	–	–	–	–	–	+
Uses caregivers as active participants	–	–	–	L	–	–	–	–	–	L

Assessment instrument

Figure 1. Ten routinely used assessment instruments for developmentally young children, rated for characteristics of assessment content and strategies. The assessment instruments are listed from left to right in descending order by number of university programs in speech-language pathology that use each instrument routinely (Crais & Leonard, 1990). (SICD = Sequence Inventory of Communication Development; PLS = Preschool Language Scale; REEL = Receptive-Expressive Language Scale; Denver = Denver Developmental Screening Test; Birth to Three = Birth to Three Checklist of Learning and Language Behavior; Bayley Scales = Bayley Scales of Infant Development; ACLC = Assessment of Children's Language Comprehension; Ordinal Scales = Ordinal Scales of Psychological Development; Vineland = Vineland Adaptive Behavior Scales; ELI = Environmental Language Inventory; + = characteristic addressed to a limited extent; L = characteristic addressed in depth; – = characteristic not addressed.)

220

McLean, 1978). Children are viewed as active participants who learn to affect the behavior and attitudes of others through active signaling, and gradually learn to use more sophisticated and conventional means to communicate through caregivers' contingent social responsiveness (Dunst, Lowe, & Bartholomew, 1990). The quality and nature of the contexts in which interaction occurs is considered to have a great influence on the successful acquisition of language and communicative behavior. Proponents of pragmatic theory state that development can be understood only by analysis of the interactive context, not simply by focusing solely on the child or the caregivers. They have emphasized that successful communication involves reciprocity and mutual negotiation and that preverbal turn-taking provides the foundation for later conversational abilities (Bates, 1976; Bruner, 1978).

Recent literature has examined the relationship between communication and other aspects of development. Tronick (1989) discussed the relationship between the development of emotion and affective communication in infancy. He noted that the early affective expressions and displays of infants serve as signals to regulate interactions that help the caregiver read an infant's emotional state. Stern (1985) identified socioemotional achievements that appear prior to intentional communication. According to Stern, infants make deliberate attempts to share experiences with caregivers by sharing attention and affective states before communicating specific intentions. Based on the formulations of Tronick and Stern, Prizant and Wetherby (1990) emphasized the need for early interventionists to form an integrated view of socioemotional development and language and communication development.

During the 1980s, the child language literature emphasized the importance of prelinguistic communicative development for the acquisition of language (Bates, 1979; Bruner, 1981; Dore, 1986; McLean & Snyder-McLean, 1978). Prelinguistic or preverbal communication refers to gestures and/or sounds that are used as signals to communicate but are not referential or symbolic. Research indicates that communication development involves continuity from preverbal communication through linguistic communication, and the development of preverbal communication is a necessary precursor to the development of the intentional use of language to communicate (Bates, 1979; Harding & Golinkoff, 1979).

Along with the social and communicative bases, the cognitive bases of language acquisition have received continuing attention in the literature. In the first few years of life, a child's behavior becomes increasingly more deliberate and goal directed, shows increased evidence of foresight, and culminates with the ability to plan behavior through symbolic thought. Piaget (1952) hypothesized that the child's sensorimotor cognitive knowledge provides the basis for the emergence of language, as well as other symbolic abilities (i.e., deferred imitation, play, drawing, mental imagery). There is some evidence to suggest that cognitive development sets the pace for language acquisition (Sinclair, 1975; Slobin, 1973), and that impairments in the acquisition of language may stem from deficits in specific cognitive attainments (Leonard, 1978). However, several hypotheses about the relationship between language and cognition that differ from that of Piaget have been proposed (see Rice, 1983, for a review). The major issues addressed in the various theories are the extent to which language is influenced by cognition and whether or not language can influence cognition. Cromer (1976) offered a "weak cognition hypothesis" in stating that certain cognitive achievements are necessary but not sufficient to explain normal language acquisition. More recently, Cromer (1981) renewed interest in the nativist position and emphasized the interaction of an innate potential specific to language with environmental influences.

Curtiss, Yamada, and Fromkin (1979) have argued more strongly that grammatical aspects of language have unique organizing principles that are independent of general cognition. They demonstrated the dissociation of grammar and cognition in a group of children with mental retardation by providing evidence that for some of these children, grammar was more advanced than nonverbal combinatorial abilities, whereas for other children, nonverbal combinatorial actions, were more advanced than grammatical abilities. Although cognition may not account for the grammatical aspects of language, there is accumulating evidence of parallels between cognition and the emergence of preverbal communication, first words, and first-word combinations (see Bates & Snyder, 1987; Rice, 1983). In a review of research on the association between language and cognition, Bates and Snyder (1987) concluded that there are meaningful associations between specific achievements in communication/language and cognition, but that these relationships change from the prelinguistic stage to the acquisition of syntax.

In an attempt to account for the parallels between language and cognition, Bates (1979) formulated an explanatory theory of the origins of the human symbolic capacity. Bates hypothesized that the symbolic capacity evolved in phylogeny as a "new product" built from the interaction of available "old parts." That is, specific cognitive and social components evolved for purposes unrelated to language functions. When the relative proportions of available cognitive-social components reached a certain threshold level, new interactions among the components resulted, creating the new capacity for symbols. Based on a cross-sectional study of 25 children without disabilities, Bates (1979) isolated three cognitive-social components that contribute to the symbolic capacity: imitation, tool use, and communicative intent. The symbol-using capacity is manifest in the development of both language and play. Thus, the "new product," the symbolic capacity, was constructed in phylogeny and is reconstructed in ontogeny from the interactions of at least three "old parts"—imitation, tool use, and communicative intent. This theoretical construct suggests that assessment of the symbolic capacity should address a child's skill level in language and play. If the child shows deficiencies in these symbolic skills, then further assessment should explore the component skills that form the foundation for symbol use (i.e., communicative intent, imitation, tool use).

Current theories on the social and cognitive bases of language acquisition offer new perspectives on the assessment of language in children with communicative impairments. One implication is that profiles of a child's social-affective, communicative, cognitive, and linguistic abilities are essential components of the assessment of a developmentally young child's communicative competence. Assessment practices need to go beyond measures of language form or placement of a child in the role of respondent. The child's communicative abilities need to be examined in natural communicative exchanges, with the child's cognitive abilities serving as a developmental frame of reference. The next section examines how a child's profile of communicative and symbolic abilities has important implications for assessment and early identification of children with communication impairments.

LITERATURE SUPPORTING
THE POTENTIAL FOR EARLIER IDENTIFICATION

A developmental communication disorder may reflect a specific impairment within the linguistic domain or may stem from a more pervasive impairment in cognitive and/or social development. Assessment for the early identification of a communication impairment should therefore focus on two major content areas: the child's profile of communicative and social-affective abilities, and the child's symbolic level across verbal and nonverbal domains. Literature on children with and children without communication impairments suggests that information about a child's early communicative and symbolic development has important implications for early identification. This literature is reviewed briefly here.

Communication Development
in Children without Disabilities

Children without disabilities use prelinguistic gestures and vocalizations beginning as early as 8–9 months of age to communicate for a variety of purposes prior to the emergence of words (Bates, 1979; Coggins & Carpenter, 1981; Harding & Golinkoff, 1979; Wetherby, Cain, Yonclas, & Walker, 1988). Bruner (1981) suggested that there are three "innate communicative intentions" that emerge during the first year of life: 1) *behavior regulation* (i.e., acts used to regulate the behavior of another for purposes of obtaining or restricting environmental goals, 2) *social interaction* (i.e., acts used to direct the attention of another to oneself for affiliative purposes, and 3) *joint attention* (i.e., acts used to direct the attention of another for purposes of sharing the focus on an entity or event). Children without disabilities use intentional communicative signals for these three major functions during the prelinguistic stage (Wetherby et al., 1988). Thus, before the emergence of words, children without disabilities are able to use signals to communicate intentionally for a broad range of purposes.

Developmental progressions have been identified in the communicative means (i.e., behaviors used to express intentions) used by children without disabilities. Children first use contact gestures (e.g., giving an object, showing an object, and pushing an adult's hand) at about 9 months of age. Distal gestures (e.g., open-hand reaching, distant pointing, waving) emerge at about 11 months (Bates, O'Connell, & Shore, 1987). Children without disabilities show an increase in the sophistication of vocalizations from the prelinguistic stage through the multiword stage by using more vocalizations without gestures and more vocalizations that contain consonant and vowel combinations (Carpenter, Mastergeorge, & Coggins, 1983; Kent & Bauer, 1985; Wetherby et al., 1988). They also use a substantial proportion of consonants in their vocal communicative acts during the prelinguistic stage and the proportion of consonants and multisyllabic utterances increases between the prelinguistic and the one-word stage.

Communication Development in Children with Communication Impairments

School-age and older preschool children with identified communicative impairments have been found to differ from children without impairments in terms of the pattern of communicative functions and means. The range of communicative functions expressed by children with specific language impairments has been found to be restricted relative to children without disabilities with the same chronological age but commensurate with children without disabilities with the same language age (Fey, Leonard, Fey, & O'Connor, 1978; Leonard, Camarata, Rowan, & Chapman, 1982; Rom & Bliss, 1981). Children with autism in the prelinguistic and early stages of language development have been found to use a disproportionately high ratio of communicative acts to regulate the behavior of others and a disproportionately low ratio (or absence) of acts to engage in social interaction and to reference joint attention relative to children at the same language stage without disabilities (Wetherby, 1986; Wetherby & Prutting, 1984; Wetherby, Yonclas, & Bryan, 1989). A similar pattern was found in nonverbal institutionalized adolescents with profound mental retardation who displayed a low rate of intentional communication (Cirrin & Rowland, 1985). Such differences in the use of communicative functions may be evident in young prelinguistic children, which may be useful in early identification and differential diagnosis of at-risk infants and preschool children.

By definition, children with communication impairments show delays or differences in the acquisition of communicative means, that is, in the forms used to express communicative intentions. Children with specific language impairments and autism have been found to use fewer vocalizations and more gestures to express intentions during the prelinguistic and early one-word stage compared to language-age matched children without disabilities (Rowan, Leonard, Chapman, & Weiss, 1983; Snyder, 1978; Wetherby & Prutting, 1984; Wetherby et al., 1989). Few investigations have studied the quality of prelinguistic communicative vocalizations by children with communication impairments. Wetherby et al. (1989) found that children with specific language impairments and autism showed a deficiency in vocalizations containing consonants. Thus, reliance on gestures and a limited consonantal repertoire appear to be typical for children with communication impairment, and should be apparent in younger children during early communication development.

Symbolic Development in Children without Disabilities

In normal development, preverbal intentional communication provides a foundation for the emergence of symbols, seen in the child's use of language and play (Bates, 1979). Much attention has been given to the relationship between language and play. Fewell and Kaminski (1988) defined play as "spontaneous activity that involves interaction with objects in a pleasurable manner" (p. 147). Development in symbolic play progresses along three dimensions: 1) *decontextualization*, which is the ability to produce an action scheme using objects that are not realistic or are in a different context from that in which the action usually occurs; 2) *decentration*, which is the ability to use others as agents and recipients of actions; and 3) *sequential organization*, which is the ability to organize action schemes in sequence (Fewell & Kaminski, 1988; Westby, 1988). In normal development, some achievements in language have been found to parallel those in play (McCune-Nicolich & Carroll, 1981; Shore, O'Connell, & Bates, 1984). For example, as children begin to produce single words they use single action schemes in play. As they begin to use word combinations, they display multiple action schemes in play.

Symbolic Development in Children with Communication Impairments

Children who have communication impairments may also have impairments in other aspects of symbolic development. A large number of studies have demonstrated that children with autism show significant deficits in symbolic play (Dawson & Adams, 1984; Sigman & Ungerer, 1984; Wetherby & Prutting, 1984; Wing, Gould, Yeates, & Brierly, 1977). Compared to language-age matched children without disabilities, children with autism perform at lower levels on symbolic play (i.e., using pretend action schemes with objects), but at higher levels on combinatorial play (i.e., combining objects in ordinal relations) (Wetherby & Prutting, 1984). This is presumably because the social demands associated with symbolic play are greater than those associated with combinatorial play. In contrast, performance of young children with specific language impairments in symbolic play is deficient compared to chronological-age matched children without disabilities, but commensurate with or higher than language-age matched children without disabilities (Terrell & Schwartz, 1988; Terrell, Schwartz, Prelock, & Messick, 1984). Thus, a comparison of a child's ability to use symbols in language and play provides important information for identifying a communication impairment and differentiating along a continuum of more specific language delays to more pervasive social-communicative impairments.

In summary, the literature reviewed here suggests that a child's profile of communicative development, even prior to the emergence of words, may be a sensitive indicator of the likelihood of subsequent difficulties in language acquisition. Additionally, patterns of strengths and weaknesses in different aspects of play compared to language may be predictive of a communicative impairment.

PROPOSED MODEL FOR COMMUNICATION ASSESSMENT

Since 1980, we have been developing a framework for assessing communicative, symbolic, and social-affective abilities of developmentally young children. This work has culminated in the development of the Communication and Symbolic Behavior Scales (CSBS) (Wetherby & Prizant, 1990). The CSBS is an assessment instrument designed to examine communicative, social-affective, and symbolic abilities of children whose functional communication abilities range from prelinguistic intentional communication to early stages of language acquisition (i.e., between 8 months and 2 years in communication and language). The major purpose of this assessment instrument is twofold. First, it can be used for the early identification of children with communication impairments. Second, it can be used to establish a communicative and symbolic profile to provide directions for further assessment, to plan intervention goals, and to chart changes in these abilities over time.

The procedures used in the CSBS were originally conceived as informal procedures to sample communication abilities of children with autism at preverbal and early verbal stages (Wetherby & Prutting, 1984). The need for communication sampling procedures arose from the limited utility of available formal language and communication measures. What was needed was a means to gather information about children's abilities in spontaneous communicative interactions that was more efficient than naturalistic observations. Of particular concern was providing ample opportunity for a child to initiate communication without relying on the child's comprehension of or compliance with verbal instructions. The CSBS sampling procedures are, in part, an expansion and refinement of the procedures described by Wetherby and Prutting (1984) and Wetherby et al. (1988).

The CSBS uses a standard but flexible format for data gathering through a variety of procedures. The sampling procedures allow for direct assessment of children using a continuum from structured to unstructured contexts. Rather than setting up discrete trials with expected responses, the sampling procedures were designed to resemble natural ongoing adult–child interactions and to provide opportunities for use of a variety of communicative behaviors. The procedures also enable the examiner to assess the parent's interactions with the child directly in addition to using the parent as a source of information about the child.

The CSBS yields data that are converted to scores on 20 five-point rating scales of communicative, social-affective, and symbolic behaviors. A total score is computed from the 20 parameters, with a total possible score of 100. Seven cluster scores are derived from the 20 scales: 1) communicative functions; 2) gestural communicative means; 3) vocal communicative means; 4) reciprocity; 5) social-affective signaling; 6) verbal symbolic behavior; and 7) nonverbal symbolic behavior. Definitions of the communication and symbolic parameters measured in the 20 scales are presented in Table 1. A profile summary listing the 20 scales and the values of the points on each scale is provided in the appendix.

The growing body of literature on developmental pragmatics provided the theoretical constructs from which the scales were derived. Determination of the 20 scales was based on pilot studies of the CSBS of children with and children without communication impairments (Wetherby, Prizant, & Kublin, 1989). The scales included on the CSBS were selected because they were able to differentiate children without impairments, children with specific language impairments, and children with more pervasive social-communicative impairments. It is expected that the scales will continue to be refined after national field testing and further research investigations.

The scales were designed so that children without impairments would achieve a score close to the highest point (5) on the communication scales (i.e., scales 1–16) by 18 months, and close to the highest point (5) on the symbolic scales (i.e., scales 17–20) by 24 months.

Preliminary Field Test Data

National field testing on a sample of approximately 450 children without impairments between 8 and 24 months of age is currently being conducted. The field test sites were selected on the basis of responses to a questionnaire mailed to several hundred individuals and agencies (e.g., university clinics, hospitals, early intervention programs) that expressed interest in participating in the study. Responses to the questionnaire established whether the respon-

Table 1. Definitions of the communication and symbolic parameters measured by the Communication and Symbolic Behavior Scales (CSBS)

Term	Definition
Communicative functions	
Range of functions	Variety of specific purposes for which a child communicates (e.g., request object, protest, call, show off, comment)
Behavioral regulation	Communicative acts used to regulate the behavior of another person to obtain or restrict an environmental goal
Joint attention	Communicative acts used to direct the attention of another person to an object, event, or topic of a communicative act
Gestural communicative means	
Conventional gestures	Gestural communicative acts whose meaning is shared by a general community (e.g., giving, showing, pushing away, open-handed reaching, pointing, waving, head nodding, head shaking)
Distal gestures	Gestural communicative acts in which the child's hand does not touch a person or object (e.g., open-handed reaching, pointing at a distance, waving)
Coordination of gesture and vocal acts	Communicative acts that are composed of a gesture and a vocalization produced simultaneously or that overlap in time
Vocal communicative means	
Isolated vocal acts	Transcribable vowels or vowel and consonant combinations that are used as a communicative act and are not accompanied by a gesture
Inventory of consonants	Total number of different consonants produced as part of communicative acts
Syllable shape	Vocal communicative acts that are transcribable vowel plus consonant combinations (i.e., syllables must contain at least one consonant)
Multisyllables	Vocal communicative acts that contain two or more syllables. Syllables may be made up of vowels only or vowels and consonants.
Reciprocity	
Discourse structure: Respondent acts	Communicative acts that are in response to the adult's conventional gesture or speech
Rate	Frequency of communicative acts displayed per minute
Repair strategies	Persistence in communication, measured by repetition and/or modification of a previous communicative act when a goal is not achieved
Social-affective signaling	
Gaze shifts	Alternating eye gaze between a person and an object and back. It may be either a person-object-person or an object-person-object gaze shift.
Positive affect with eye gaze	Clear facial expressions of pleasure or excitement, which may or may not be accompanied by a vocalization that is directed toward the adult with eye gaze

(continued)

Table 1. (continued)

Term	Definition
Episodes of negative affect	Clear vocal expressions of distress or frustration that commence when the vocalization begins and continue until the child has recovered and has displayed a neutral or positive affect
Verbal symbolic behavior	
Expressive language	Measure of the number of different words used (i.e., spoken or signed) and the number of multiword combinations produced. A word or word approximation must be used to refer to a specific object, action, or attribute and only that word class.
Language comprehension	Measure of comprehension of contextual cues, single words, and multiword utterances
Nonverbal symbolic behavior	
Symbolic play	Measure of the child's use of agents and actions with objects in pretend play
Combinatorial play	Measure of the child's ability to use one object in combination with another object or group of objects to construct a product (e.g., a tower)

dent was qualified to administer the CSBS and whether the respondent had access to sufficient numbers of children without impairments. Approximately 30 sites were selected in order to provide a sample stratified by region of the country and age, race, population density, and socioeconomic status within each site. Each field test site was provided with the CSBS-Research Edition (Wetherby & Prizant, 1990), including the manual, assessment materials, and training videotapes on the sampling and scoring procedures. Each field test site was required to provide a minimum of 15 videotaped samples and was given specific feedback on the sampling procedures from one of the authors after submitting the first videotaped sample. All of the samples were completed by December, 1990. The authors are providing individualized training to a small number of clinicians to score the field test videotapes. Normative data obtained from national field testing are expected to be published by August, 1991.

Preliminary field testing of the CSBS has been completed on 33 children without communication impairments at prelinguistic, single-word, and multiword stages of expressive language and communication development (Wetherby & Prizant, 1990). Determination of reliability with this sample included examining internal consistency and interrater agreement. The internal consistency coefficient (alpha coefficient), computed for the CSBS total score based on the sample of children without impairments, was .93, indicating that performance on one scale corresponded with performance on other scales. Interrater reliability was examined by comparing ratings of videotapes of 30% of the children without impairments made by two independent raters. It was calculated by determining the number of agreements (i.e., exact matches of ratings) on each of the 20 scales for each subject divided by the total number of agreements plus disagreements, and then multiplying this value by 100 to determine the percentage of agreement. Overall agreement was 95% of the 200 comparisons (20 CSBS scales for each of the 10 children); agreement on each of the scales ranged from 80% to 100%.

The preliminary field testing results of the CSBS are presented in Figures 2, 3, and 4, for children without impairments functioning in the prelinguistic, single word, and multiword stages, respectively. The results of the CSBS for 17 children without impairments who are functioning in the prelinguistic stage are presented in Figure 2. The average scores on the communication scales

Prelinguistic Stage (n=17, 9-14 months)	1	2	3	4	5
Communicative Functions	■	■	■		
1. Range of Functions			●		
2. Behavioral Regulation				●	
3. Joint Attention			●		
Communicative Means: Gestural	■	■	■		
4. Conventional Gestures		●			
5. Distal Gestures			●		
6. Coordination of Gesture and Vocal Act				●	
Communicative Means: Vocal	■	■	■		
7. Isolated Vocal Acts		●			
8. Inventory of Consonants			●		
9. Syllable Shape			●		
10. Multisyllables			●		
Reciprocity	■	■			
11. Discourse Structure			●		
12. Rate		●			
13. Repair Strategies			●		
Social/Affective Signalling	■	■	■	■	
14. Gaze Shifts				●	
15. Positive Affect			●		
16. Negative Affect				●	
Verbal Symbolic Behavior	■				
17. Expressive Language	●				
18. Language Comprehension		●			
Nonverbal Symbolic Behavior	■	■			
19. Symbolic Play		●			
20. Combinatorial Play		●			

Figure 2.   CSBS results for seventeen 9- to 14-month-old children without impairments functioning in the prelinguistic stage. Solid circles represent average scores on the 20 individual scales. Solid bars represent average cluster scores.

generally fell between 2 and 3, with scores nearing 5 on behavioral regulation, conventional gestures, gaze shifts, and negative affect. The average scores on the symbolic scales were near 2, except for expressive language, which was 1. The results of 11 children without impairments who were functioning in the one-word stage are presented in Figure 3. The average scores on the communication scales generally fell between 3 and 5. On the symbolic scales the average scores were near 3, except for expressive language, which was 1.5. The results for five children without impairments who were functioning in the multiword stage are presented in Figure 4. The average scores on the communication scales as well as the symbolic scales generally fell near 5.

One Word Stage (n=11, 13-18 months)	1	2	3	4	5
Communicative Functions					
1. Range of Functions			•		
2. Behavioral Regulation				•	
3. Joint Attention				•	
Communicative Means: Gestural					
4. Conventional Gestures				•	
5. Distal Gestures				•	
6. Coordination of Gesture and Vocal Act				•	
Communicative Means: Vocal					
7. Isolated Vocal Acts			•		
8. Inventory of Consonants			•		
9. Syllable Shape				•	
10. Multisyllables				•	
Reciprocity					
11. Discourse Structure			•		
12. Rate			•		
13. Repair Strategies			•		
Social/Affective Signalling					
14. Gaze Shifts				•	
15. Positive Affect			•		
16. Negative Affect				•	
Verbal Symbolic Behavior					
17. Expressive Language	•				
18. Language Comprehension			•		
Nonverbal Symbolic Behavior					
19. Symbolic Play			•		
20. Combinatorial Play		•			

Figure 3.   CSBS results for eleven 13- to 18-month-old children without impairments functioning in the one-word stage. Solid circles represent average scores on the 20 individual scales. Solid bars represent average cluster scores.

Multiword Stage (n=5, 19-24 months)	1	2	3	4	5
Communicative Functions	▬▬▬▬▬▬▬▬				
1. Range of Functions				●	
2. Behavioral Regulation					●
3. Joint Attention					●
Communicative Means: Gestural	▬▬▬▬▬▬▬				
4. Conventional Gestures				●	
5. Distal Gestures				●	
6. Coordination of Gesture and Vocal Act					●
Communicative Means: Vocal	▬▬▬▬▬▬▬▬				
7. Isolated Vocal Acts				●	
8. Inventory of Consonants					●
9. Syllable Shape					●
10. Multisyllables					●
Reciprocity	▬▬▬▬▬▬				
11. Discourse Structure					●
12. Rate				●	
13. Repair Strategies				●	
Social/Affective Signalling	▬▬▬▬▬▬				
14. Gaze Shifts				●	
15. Positive Affect				●	
16. Negative Affect				●	
Verbal Symbolic Behavior	▬▬▬▬▬▬▬				
17. Expressive Language				●	
18. Language Comprehension				●	
Nonverbal Symbolic Behavior	▬▬▬▬▬▬▬				
19. Symbolic Play				●	
20. Combinatorial Play				●	

Figure 4. CSBS results for five 19- to 24-month-old children without impairments functioning in the multiword stage. Solid circles represent average scores on the 20 individual scales. Solid bars represent average cluster scores.

Case Examples and Clinical Profiles

In order to demonstrate how the CSBS can be used to generate profiles for young children, five case examples of prelinguistic children will be presented. The case examples include two very low birth weight premature children, one child with a history of abuse and neglect, one child demonstrating an early profile of autistic disorder, and one child with a profile of pervasive developmental disorder who does not demonstrate a social impairment of the severity associated with autistic disorder. The names used are fictitious. CSBS profiles for each of these cases are displayed in Figures 5–9.

Case 1

Mary was a very low birth weight premature child whose communication development was advanced for her corrected age. Mary was assessed at 12 months, 12 days corrected age as part of a follow-up study on very low birth weight premature infants. Mary was born at 28 weeks gestational age, with a birth weight of 1,147 grams. Her health in the first year of life was reported to be unremarkable, except for a cold with a minor ear infection.

Mary was living with her parents and a 2-year-old brother. On the CSBS Caregiver Questionnaire, Mary's mother reported that Mary communicated through pointing, sounds, gestures, and emerging single words. Her mother noted that she started pointing at about 10 months of age, and at the time of assessment produced a wide variety of sounds accompanying points and other gestures. When Mary was frustrated or upset, she reportedly first attempted to communicate through sounds and gestures, but frequently screamed to bring attention to herself. She was reported to be responsive to social games and to respond primarily to speech accompanied by gestures. Her mother indicated that she was beginning to point to her nose during social games when she heard the word "nose" and to stop her activity and look when she was told "no."

Mary presented as an alert and engaging child with a positive disposition. She was able to complete the full CSBS, and showed excellent attention and interest during the assessment. As can be seen in Figure 5, Mary's performance on all CSBS clusters was equal to or exceeded mean scores for children at a prelinguistic stage. Mary communicated for a range of functions across behavioral regulation, social interaction, and joint attention categories. Acts to establish joint attention exceeded those for behavioral regulation, indicating a high degree of social motivation and sociability in communication. Mary used four different conventional gestures, including pointing, showing, reaching, and giving. She also demonstrated the use of five distal gestures in the form of a symbolic point. She produced a variety of consonant sounds in her communicative acts. Reciprocity was extremely high. She demonstrated a high rate of communicative acts for a prelinguistic child (3.0 per minute), and repeated and modified communicative acts to repair breakdowns. She consistently regulated the interaction with her mother and the evaluator through the use of gaze shifts and expression of positive affect, with no observed instances of negative affect.

Mary produced only one early word form (i.e., "uh-oh"), which she used to establish joint attention. She did not demonstrate comprehension of words without accompanying gestures. She was able to demonstrate a few single-action schemes in play toward others, but showed little interest in combinatorial play (i.e., she combined only two objects without regard for order). Her mother indicated that her behavior was typical in reference to her

Mary (12 months corrected age)
Prelinguistic

	1	2	3	4	5
Communicative Functions					
1. Range of Functions			●	✗	
2. Behavioral Regulation				●	✗
3. Joint Attention			●		✗
Communicative Means: Gestural					
4. Conventional Gestures			●	✗	
5. Distal Gestures			● ✗		
6. Coordination of Gesture and Vocal Act				●	✗
Communicative Means: Vocal					
7. Isolated Vocal Acts		● ✗			
8. Inventory of Consonants			● ✗		
9. Syllable Shape			●		✗
10. Multisyllables			● ✗		
Reciprocity					
11. Discourse Structure			●	✗	
12. Rate		●		✗	
13. Repair Strategies			●		✗
Social/Affective Signalling					
14. Gaze Shifts				●	✗
15. Positive Affect		● ✗			
16. Negative Affect				●	✗
Verbal Symbolic Behavior					
17. Expressive Language	✗				
18. Language Comprehension		● ✗			
Nonverbal Symbolic Behavior					
19. Symbolic Play		●	✗		
20. Combinatorial Play		✗			

Figure 5. CSBS results for Mary, age 12 months, 12 days (corrected age). Xs represent scores on the 20 individual scales. Unfilled bars with diagonal lines represent average cluster scores. Solid circles and bars represent CSBS results for prelinguistic children without impairments.

alertness, emotional reaction, level of interest and attention, comfort level, level of activity, overall level of communication, and play behavior.

Mary's profile is indicative of a child at a preverbal intentional level who is advanced across virtually all developmental parameters compared to other prelinguistic children. Evidence of emerging symbolic play and transition to referential words was apparent. Her performance on the communication scales, however, was commensurate with children of her approximate chronological age (i.e., 15 months) rather than her corrected age or language stage. Such variability in development of very low birth weight premature infants has been observed in a variety of studies, including those documenting advanced development relative to corrected age (Vohr & Garcia-Coll, 1988).

Case 2

Teddy is a child whose communication development is delayed for his corrected age. Teddy, who was assessed at 12 months, 17 days corrected age, was a very low birth weight premature infant born at 29 weeks gestational age with a birth weight of 1,090 grams. His health in the first year of life was reported to be good.

Teddy was living with his parents and a 4-year-old brother, who was also born prematurely. On the CSBS Caregiver Questionnaire, Teddy's mother reported that Teddy communicated through sounds, pointing, and other gestures. He had just begun to vocalize more, and had just started to point. However, when asked how Teddy communicated basic needs for requesting, rejecting, or attempting to attract attention to self, Teddy's mother provided no description of specific gestural communication. Teddy enjoyed playing social games, and demonstrated frustration by crying. He was able to understand gestures, words, and short phrases with accompanying gestures that were needed to aid in comprehension.

Teddy presented as an alert, but somewhat wary and cautious child. He was able to complete the full CSBS, although he demonstrated minimal intentional communication and appeared to tire toward the end of the assessment. In general, his attention was good and he appeared interested in actively exploring materials. As can be seen in Figure 6, Teddy's performance on all CSBS cluster and individual scale scores was below mean scores for children at a prelinguistic stage, except for scores on social-affective signaling, which was roughly commensurate. Teddy produced only seven communicative acts in categories of behavioral regulation and joint attention. Conventional gestures were limited to giving and showing, and no distal gestures were used. Vocalizations were not coordinated with gestural communicative acts, although some intonated vowel-like forms were noted during object exploration. Teddy's rate of communication was very low (approximately 0.3 acts per minute), indicative of an emerging intentional communication level. He did not persist or modify acts to repair breakdowns. Teddy showed strength in social-affective signaling, where he demonstrated a relatively high frequency of gaze shifts, and shared positive affect at a level typical for prelinguistic children. No episodes of negative affect were noted.

No language forms were observed, nor did Teddy respond to language even when accompanied with gestures. Play primarily involved use of a variety of sensorimotor schemes for exploration of materials, and Teddy was able to combine two objects in play without regard for order. Teddy's mother indicated that in areas of overall level of communication, play behavior, level of activity, level of interest and attention, and alertness, Teddy's behavior was typical. However, she noted that he was a bit more reserved than usual and somewhat more cautious.

Teddy (12 months corrected age) *Prelinguistic*	1	2	3	4	5
Communicative Functions	▨▨▨▨				
1. Range of Functions			•X		
2. Behavioral Regulation		X		•	
3. Joint Attention		X	•		
Communicative Means: Gestural	▨▨				
4. Conventional Gestures		X•			
5. Distal Gestures	X	•			
6. Coordination of Gesture and Vocal Act	X		•		
Communicative Means: Vocal	▨				
7. Isolated Vocal Acts	X	•			
8. Inventory of Consonants	X	•			
9. Syllable Shape	X		•		
10. Multisyllables	X	•			
Reciprocity	▨				
11. Discourse Structure	X	•			
12. Rate	X •				
13. Repair Strategies	X	•			
Social/Affective Signalling	▨▨▨▨▨▨			▨	
14. Gaze Shifts				•	X
15. Positive Affect			•X		
16. Negative Affect				•	X
Verbal Symbolic Behavior	▨				
17. Expressive Language	X				
18. Language Comprehension	X •				
Nonverbal Symbolic Behavior	▨				
19. Symbolic Play	X	•			
20. Combinatorial Play		X			

Figure 6.   CSBS results for Teddy, age 12 months, 17 days (corrected age). Xs represent scores on the 20 individual scales. Unfilled bars with diagonal lines represent average cluster scores. Solid circles and bars represent CSBS results for prelinguistic children without impairments.

Teddy's profile is indicative of a child at emerging intentional levels of communication functioning at a presymbolic level in all areas assessed. When compared to other prelinguistic children, he clearly demonstrated delays in communication and verbal and nonverbal symbolic abilities. However, clear strengths were apparent in social-affective signaling, which is a positive prognostic factor for further language and communicative growth. Although his mother described higher level communicative functioning on the caregiver questionnaire, she rated his behavior on the CSBS as typical, for the most part. However, her indication of greater cautiousness probably indicates that observed abilities on the CSBS represented a conservative estimate. Although the pattern was clearly one of delay given Teddy's corrected age, the great variability observed in development of premature children and the tendency for some children to "catch up" later speak against a long-term prognostic statement. This was especially true considering Teddy's good attention, and positive social-affective behavior. Clearly, a child like Teddy needs to receive early intervention services considering his at-risk status and the delays observed.

Case 3

The first two case examples are of young children who were biologically at risk for developmental delays due to prematurity. Mary displayed communicative abilities that were advanced for her corrected age while Teddy displayed communication that was somewhat delayed. Both children displayed relative strengths in social-affective signaling. In contrast, Adam was environmentally at risk for developmental delays. Adam, a child with a traumatic psychosocial history, has limited use of communication for social interaction and flat expression of affect.

Adam, a twin who was removed from his biological parents at age 1 because of documented neglect and abuse, was assessed at 23 months of age. Adam had been separated from his twin sister, and placed in a foster home that included three other foster children and two adopted children. Referral for the communication evaluation was made by a child psychiatrist, who expressed concern over Adam's communication functioning. Adam was originally referred to the child psychiatrist by his foster parents, who were concerned about his lack of developmental progress in the 11 months since he had been placed in their home. According to his foster mother, Adam was extremely passive and lethargic and had to be "pushed to perform even if he was wet or hungry." Adam's medical and developmental history in the first year of life was unknown to his foster parents. However, they indicated that upon entrance to their home at 12 months of age, Adam was a healthy child of appropriate size and weight and was walking independently. The Bayley Scales of Infant Development (Bayley, 1969) was administered prior to the CSBS, and Adam was found to have a mental development index of 104.

Adam's foster parents reported that Adam had developed some imitative speech at approximately 18 months, but that such development had stopped, and that words were used only infrequently. Adam communicated primarily through pointing and reaching, and his passivity had resulted in adults anticipating his needs. He typically either sat passively or attempted to obtain objects by himself, rather than request assistance. He had not been observed to seek comfort in appropriate situations, and did not greet others or indicate any awareness of entrances or departures of others. His affect was reported to be generally flat, although he smiled during enjoyable activities. He was reported to become frustrated easily over intrusion by other children, with much whining and some self-abusive behavior, including scratching at his legs and face on occasion. For the most part, Adam was reported to be a silent

child who refrained from interactions with other children but responded somewhat better in one-on-one situations with adults.

Adam presented as a lethargic but alert child. He demonstrated a clear air
of cautiousness, even though he demonstrated interest in materials presented
during the CSBS. He became noticeably more interested in interacting approximately halfway into the evaluation when looking at books, but did not
complete the full CSBS due to active rejection of symbolic and combinatorial
play materials.

As can be seen in Figure 7, Adam demonstrated a scatter of abilities
relative to children in a prelinguistic stage. He clearly demonstrated delays in
all areas except the communicative function scales compared to children at his
age, who would be in the multiword stage, as well as to younger children at
the single-word stage. Adam communicated for functions of behavioral regulation and joint attention, with a rate of communicative acts of 1.3 per
minute. Communicative acts for joint attention primarily involved using a
contact point (i.e., his finger touching the item of reference) to establish joint
attention to materials and pictures in books. He did not demonstrate any acts
for social interaction, and displayed wariness about and actively rejected
activities involving face-to-face interaction. Adam used two conventional gestures, pointing and giving, and demonstrated two instances of distal pointing.
Coordination of gestural and vocal acts occurred primarily during joint attention activities, and this did not occur until later in the evaluation, and under
only limited circumstances (i.e., sharing books, pointing at desired objects).
Complexity of vocalizations was limited to a few protoword forms (i.e.,
approximations of "there," "what's that?") heard during the book sharing
activity. Adam did demonstrate the ability to persist through repeating communicative acts to repair breakdowns.

Social-affective signaling was characterized by use of gaze shifts for
social referencing. However, no instances of positive affect and only one
expression of negative affect was noted. This resulted in an overall picture of
an extremely limited range of affect, giving an impression of extreme cautiousness. Face-to-face interaction appeared to be stressful for Adam. As
noted, expressive language was limited to two protoword forms and Adam
responded only to speech accompanied by gestures or situational cues. No
symbolic or combinatorial play was observed as Adam rejected these materials. However, he was observed to be able to combine at least two objects in
play, and to use single schemes directed toward others on the Bayley Scales.

Adam's profile is indicative of a child who is clearly demonstrating
developmental delays in specific areas of functioning. However, significant
involvement of socioemotional development is clear. Of particular interest
was his ability to communicate for shared attention, and his use of gaze shifts
for social referencing, indicating clear awareness of others, and the presence
of basic social competence. However, Adam's history of neglect and abuse

Adam(23 months) *Prelinguistic*	1	2	3	4	5
Communicative Functions	▨▨▨▨▨▨				
1. Range of Functions		✗ ●			
2. Behavioral Regulation				● ✗	
3. Joint Attention			●	✗	
Communicative Means: Gestural	▨▨▨▨▨				
4. Conventional Gestures		✗●			
5. Distal Gestures		✗ ●			
6. Coordination of Gesture and Vocal Act			✗ ●		
Communicative Means: Vocal	▨▨▨▨▨				
7. Isolated Vocal Acts		● ✗			
8. Inventory of Consonants			● ✗		
9. Syllable Shape			●✗		
10. Multisyllables		✗ ●			
Reciprocity	▨▨▨▨				
11. Discourse Structure		✗ ●			
12. Rate		● ✗			
13. Repair Strategies			●	✗	
Social/Affective Signalling	▨▨▨▨▨▨				
14. Gaze Shifts				✗ ●	
15. Positive Affect	✗	●			
16. Negative Affect				✗ ●	
Verbal Symbolic Behavior	▨▨				
17. Expressive Language	✗				
18. Language Comprehension		●✗			
Nonverbal Symbolic Behavior	▨▨				
19. Symbolic Play	✗	●			
20. Combinatorial Play	✗	●			

Figure 7. CSBS results for Adam, age 23 months. Xs represent scores on the 20 individual scales. Unfilled bars with diagonal lines represent average cluster scores. Solid circles and bars represent CSBS results for prelinguistic children without impairments.

appears to be evident in his clear rejection of face-to-face interaction during social games, and his extremely limited range of affect, giving the impression of cautiousness and wariness of others. These observations are consistent with reports by his foster parents. These findings are also consistent with research on children with a history of neglect and abuse, which has found language and developmental delays attributed to neglectful and abusive experiences in early childhood (Cicchetti, 1989).

Case 4

Case 3 illustrates the possible secondary effects of abuse and neglect on a child's social-communicative profile. This profile was characterized primarily by a limited range of affect and lack of communication to engage in social interaction. Although Adam was delayed in language development, he was able to communicate with gestures and vocalizations for behavior regulation and joint attention. Case 4 exemplifies a very different communication and symbolic profile due to a social impairment characteristic of children with autism.

Billy was assessed at 24 months, 9 days on referral by an audiologist who was concerned about communication and social development. Billy was living with his parents and 4-year-old brother. His medical history was reported to be unremarkable. Billy was the product of a full-term pregnancy and normal delivery. Billy's mother indicated that motor milestones were normal, but that Billy had not yet acquired speech for communication. Words had been heard infrequently, some without clear communicative intent. His parents felt that little improvement in communication had been noted in the 6 months prior to the evaluation.

Billy presented as a somewhat alert and attractive child, who appeared to be aware of others, but demonstrated limited positive affect and eye contact. He was able to complete the full CSBS, although attention varied with the materials used and situations presented. He demonstrated a clear object focus when given objects, with some difficulty coordinating attention between persons and objects. As shown in Figure 8, Billy demonstrated a highly skewed profile of communicative functions, communicating primarily for behavioral regulation functions of requesting or protesting. Only one form of conventional gesture (i.e., giving) was observed and no distal gestures were observed during the evaluation. Billy often manipulated his mother's hand or the evaluator's hand to request. In a few instances, he was able to coordinate gestural and vocal acts. Vocal communicative means were limited to a few instances of vowel-like vocalizations accompanying gestural acts. Billy was more vocal during noninteractive play, but vocalizations primarily involved vowel-like intonated utterances.

Billy demonstrated a rate of 0.5 communicative acts per minute, and was able to repair breakdowns by repeating acts. Social-affective signaling was limited but not absent. Gaze shifting for social referencing occurred most often prior to requests and protests, and a few instances of sharing of positive affect were noted, with one episode of negative affect. No expressive language forms were heard.

Billy demonstrated the use of comprehension strategies by responding inconsistently to language accompanied by gestural cues. He explored objects primarily for their sensory properties and demonstrated no instances of functional object use toward self or symbolic play. He was able to combine four objects in combinatorial play without regard to order.

Billy's profile is indicative of a child with delays in most areas compared to children at a prelinguistic level. Exceptions include reciprocity, where a high score in repair strategies due to persistence in signaling was noted.

Billy (24 months)
Prelinguistic

	1	2	3	4	5
Communicative Functions	bar				
1. Range of Functions		X •			
2. Behavioral Regulation			X •		
3. Joint Attention	X	•			
Communicative Means: Gestural	bar				
4. Conventional Gestures	X	•			
5. Distal Gestures	X	•			
6. Coordination of Gesture and Vocal Act		X	•		
Communicative Means: Vocal	bar				
7. Isolated Vocal Acts	X •				
8. Inventory of Consonants	X	•			
9. Syllable Shape	X	•			
10. Multisyllables	X	•			
Reciprocity	bar				
11. Discourse Structure		X •			
12. Rate	X •				
13. Repair Strategies			•	X	
Social/Affective Signalling	bar				
14. Gaze Shifts				X •	
15. Positive Affect			• X		
16. Negative Affect				X •	
Verbal Symbolic Behavior	bar				
17. Expressive Language	X				
18. Language Comprehension		• X			
Nonverbal Symbolic Behavior	bar				
19. Symbolic Play	X	•			
20. Combinatorial Play		• X			

Figure 8. CSBS results for Billy, age 24 months. Xs represent scores on the 20 individual scales. Unfilled bars with diagonal lines represent average cluster scores. Solid circles and bars represent CSBS results for prelinguistic children without impairments.

Extreme limitations were noted in communicative functions and gestural and vocal means. Cluster scores on verbal and nonverbal symbolic behavior were roughly commensurate with those of other prelinguistic children, with combinatorial play significantly higher than symbolic play, which was absent. When compared to other children within his chronological age range, Billy revealed even more significant delays in all areas.

Thus, Billy's profile is characterized by an absence of joint attention, a predominance of intentional communication for behavioral regulation, the use of relatively primitive gestures, a limited use of gaze shifts and range of affect, and greater abilities in play of a relatively nonsocial nature (combinatorial play) relative to play dependent upon social experiences (symbolic play). This profile is characteristic of children who meet criteria of autistic disorder (American Psychiatric Association, 1987), although such a diagnosis is not warranted at this young age (Prizant & Wetherby, 1988; Wetherby et al., 1989; Wetherby & Prutting, 1984).

Case 5

Jimmy is a child with social impairments. He was referred by his mother and speech-language pathologist at 32 months, 16 days in order to obtain specific information regarding his level of communication and play abilities. Jimmy was born at full term with no remarkable pre- or perinatal history. He had a history of recurrent otitis media beginning at 6 months of age with a reported extreme fluctuation of hearing acuity and perforated tympanic membrane. He regularly received medication for his ear infections, which reportedly responded to the medication. Two hearing tests, performed 3 and 9 months prior to the evaluation, indicated thresholds at 25 dB for speech. Both the otolaryngologist and the audiologist believed that Jimmy's speech delay was not primarily attributable to his recurrent otitis media.

Jimmy was living at home with his parents and 5-year-old brother. His mother and early intervention personnel provided information for the CSBS Questionnaire. They indicated that Jimmy communicated through a variety of means, including sounds, gestures, pointing (which emerged only recently), and single words used infrequently. Significant changes had been observed in Jimmy's communication 6 months prior to the evaluation, including the appearance of words and word approximations, and increased social orientation and motivation to communicate. At the time of assessment, Jimmy demonstrated deficiencies in social behavior, including infrequent eye contact and infrequent requests for assistance. Reportedly, social interest had increased prior to the evaluation, with Jimmy demonstrating greater interest in engaging in social games. Response to speech was reported to be inconsistent, but occurred when Jimmy was highly motivated by objects, actions, or people in the immediate environment. Jimmy responded most consistently when gestures accompanied speech. At other times, he did not orient or respond to speech at all. Jimmy's mother and his early interventionists reported that he demonstrated little interest in symbolic play, and had clear strengths in dealing with visually and spatially organized materials, such as nesting cups and form boards. He reportedly did not initiate interaction with other children, but was beginning to demonstrate an increased interest by observing them in play.

Jimmy presented as a very pleasant and positive child. However, he did not establish eye contact and did not demonstrate greeting behavior. His behavior was somewhat inconsistent throughout the evaluation, ranging from clear attention and interest to less goal-directed exploratory behavior. When focused, his affect was extremely positive with evidence of clear social orientation. His parents indicated that across areas of alertness, emotional reaction, level of interest and attention, comfort, overall level of communication, and play behavior, Jimmy demonstrated greater abilities than are typically observed. Jimmy's parents noted that he never "turned off" during the evaluation, and that in general, he was much more attentive and alert in one-on-one interactions.

On the CSBS, shown in Figure 9, Jimmy demonstrated abilities commensurate with or greater than children without impairments at prelinguistic levels. One exception includes a slightly depressed score in social-affective signaling. Compared to children at multiword stages who are at significantly younger chronological ages (see Figure 4), Jimmy showed clear delays in all areas of ability. Jimmy's communicative function profile demonstrated a sig-

Jimmy (32 months)
Prelinguistic

	1	2	3	4	5
Communicative Functions					
1. Range of Functions			•X		
2. Behavioral Regulation				•	X
3. Joint Attention		X•			
Communicative Means: Gestural					
4. Conventional Gestures			• X		
5. Distal Gestures	X	•			
6. Coordination of Gesture and Vocal Act				•	X
Communicative Means: Vocal					
7. Isolated Vocal Acts			• X		
8. Inventory of Consonants			•	X	
9. Syllable Shape			•		
10. Multisyllables			X •		
Reciprocity					
11. Discourse Structure			X •		
12. Rate		• X			
13. Repair Strategies			•		X
Social/Affective Signalling					
14. Gaze Shifts			X	•	
15. Positive Affect			•	X	
16. Negative Affect				X •	
Verbal Symbolic Behavior					
17. Expressive Language	X				
18. Language Comprehension		•X			
Nonverbal Symbolic Behavior					
19. Symbolic Play		X•			
20. Combinatorial Play		•			X

Figure 9. CSBS results for Jimmy, age 32 months. Xs represent scores on the 20 individual scales. Unfilled bars with diagonal lines represent average cluster scores. Solid circles and bars represent CSBS results for prelinguistic children without impairments.

nificantly greater proportion of behavioral regulation acts compared to joint attention acts, indicative of a social communicative impairment. However, increased social interests had reportedly emerged, as evidenced by increasing acts for social interaction and joint attention. Jimmy's parents reported that such behavior had been absent 3 months prior to this evaluation. Jimmy's communicative acts included combinations of gestures used with vocalizations or protowords. However, conventional gestures were limited to giving, reaching, and contact pointing. Vocalizations accompanying communicative acts were characterized by a number of different consonant forms, some multisyllabic productions, and a few protowords (i.e., "boo" to request "peek-a-boo," "do it" to request objects or assistance). Jimmy's rate of communicative acts was 1.1 per minute, and he demonstrated the ability to repeat and modify acts in persisting to repair communication breakdowns. Social-affective signaling was characterized by limited gaze shifts for social referencing, with a relatively high level of shared positive affect. As noted, fewer than four protowords were observed, and language comprehension was limited to utterances produced with gestural cues. Nonverbal symbolic behavior was characterized by an extreme discrepancy between combinatorial play strengths (i.e., stacking five rings in order) and very limited symbolic play (i.e., only single schemes directed toward self).

Jimmy's profile is indicative of a child with a significant social-communicative impairment (i.e., pervasive developmental disorder). It also indicates a shift from a more significant social-communicative impairment toward a more specific language impairment and developmental delay without significant social impairments. Given Jimmy's history of a virtual absence of eye contact and limited social-affective signaling as recent as 3 months prior to the evaluation, it appeared as if Jimmy was "blossoming" socially. This was evidenced by an increase in gaze shifts and shared positive affect, and the beginning use of communicative acts for social interaction and joint attention functions. Jimmy's parents indicated that he has just begun to "show them things" and to initiate social games, something that is commensurate with the findings of this evaluation. Increased interest in other children in the early intervention program is an additional indicator. It is likely that structured opportunities for learning and socialization in the early intervention program have contributed significantly to recent social growth.

EDUCATIONAL AND CLINICAL IMPLICATIONS

Professionals have come a long way from the traditional practice of waiting until a child is talking to evaluate that child for a language impairment. In this chapter, we have described procedures for sampling communication and symbolic abilities in children who are not yet talking or are at early language stages. Five cases of prelinguistic children were presented to illustrate that children functioning in the prelinguistic stage show very diverse communication and symbolic abilities. A child's profile of communication and symbolic abilities can contribute to the early identification of a language impairment as well as provide guidelines for the design of an early intervention program. With educational services for preschool children now mandated for younger children, the ability to apply systematic assessment techniques is increasingly important.

The CSBS provides a profile of a child's strengths and weaknesses to be used in designing the *context* of intervention programs, which may be implemented in a home-based and/or center-based educational program. The child's communicative behavior displayed during the different contexts used in the assessment procedures provides information about the degree of structure needed in the language-learning context. Intervention should provide contexts with the optimal degree of structure and adult "scaffolding" needed to foster successful interactions. Activities with greater communicative demands should be planned in contexts of relative strengths (e.g., during combinatorial rather than symbolic play, serving behavioral regulation rather than joint attention functions). Activities involving multiple experiences should be provided to enhance learning in areas of weaknesses (e.g., types of play, communicative functions), while minimizing communicative demands and providing models of developmentally appropriate communication.

The child's profile of strengths and weaknesses in communicative and symbolic abilities should also be used for decision making regarding the *content* of intervention programs. The child's weaknesses on the communication parameters relative to his or her symbolic development level should be high-priority goals in intervention. If social-affective signaling or reciprocity is low, opportunities should be provided to increase social referencing, rate of communication, and repair strategies. If the child's range of communicative functions is limited, it should be expanded. For children who show strengths in social-affective signaling, reciprocity, and communicative functions, more sophisticated gestural, vocal, and verbal communicative means should be targeted. For children showing weaknesses in one or both aspects of play, activities should be planned to provide models and to engage the child in the use of objects in play at appropriate developmental levels.

While the CSBS sampling procedures resemble natural adult–child interactions, the focus of this instrument is on profiling the child's strengths and weaknesses. Assessment of developmentally young children should also include a measure of the quality of teacher–child and caregiver–child interactions. Dunst et al. (1990) have suggested that "caregiver social responsiveness to infant behavior is a major determinant of a child's acquisition of communicative competence" (p. 39). Having the caregiver present and participating in the CSBS assessment process may help the caregiver understand the child's developmental level and identify the child's communicative attempts. Additionally, this may be a first step toward improving the caregiver's responsiveness to the child's communicative initiations.

DIRECTIONS FOR FUTURE RESEARCH

The recent proliferation of research on infant communication and the national priority of early identification and intervention of developmental disorders has expanded the potential application of the CSBS. The CSBS was designed to be used in clinical settings by professionals from a variety of disciplines as an evaluation tool to identify children with communication impairments between 8 and 24 months of age or to chart progress and plan intervention for children with communication impairments at these communication ages. Additionally, this instrument is well suited as a measure of communication for research studies of young children. It may be used to explore longitudinal relationships vis à vis socioemotional, communication, language, and symbolic development. Because the CSBS measures aspects of communication that are not assessed on most currently used formal assessment tools, it may prove to be instrumental as a measure of a child's communicative competence in research studying the effectiveness of various approaches to early intervention. The utilization of videotape recording may be helpful to compare parents' perceptions of their child with their child's actual abilities displayed during the assessment.

Future research should be directed toward generating profiles of communication and symbolic abilities in specific high-risk populations, such as children born prematurely, children born to teenage mothers, children exposed prenatally to drugs or alcohol, and children experiencing recurrent middle ear infections. Our current research efforts are directed at generating communication and symbolic profiles that differentiate along a continuum of specific language impairments to more pervasive social-communicative impairments. Our future research plans include the empirical derivation of a screening version of the CSBS based on results with young children with communicative impairments. A screening measure will be designed for use in the home, day care center, or pediatrician's office for the early identification of children with the potential for a communication and/or language problem.

CONCLUSION

The passage of P.L. 99-457 has provided the impetus for the early identification of children with communication impairments leading to appropriate interventions. Literature on children without disabilities and children with communication impairments suggests that information about a child's early communicative, social-affective, and symbolic development has important implications for early identification. This chapter presents a framework for assessing communicative, social-affective, and symbolic abilities of developmentally young children with a recently developed instrument, the CSBS, which is currently undergoing national standardization. The five case examples presented in this chapter demonstrate how the CSBS can be used to generate developmental profiles of young children. Profiling young children's communicative competence and symbolic capacity can provide important information for the early identification of children with communication impairments and for differentiating language learning problems of children along a continuum of more specific language delays to more pervasive social-communicative impairments. This information should lead to the development of more specific approaches for working with young children and their caregivers in planning early intervention programs.

REFERENCES

American Psychiatric Association. (1987). *Diagnostic and statistical manual of mental disorders* (3rd ed., rev.). Washington, DC: Author.

Aram, D., & Hall, N. (1989). Longitudinal follow-up of children with preschool communication disorders: Treatment implications. *School Psychology Review, 18,* 487–501.

Aram, D., & Nation, J. (1980). Preschool language disorders and subsequent language and academic difficulties. *Journal of Communication Disorders, 13,* 159–170.

Baker, L., & Cantwell, D. (1987). A prospective psychiatric follow-up of children with speech/language disorders. *Journal of the American Academy of Child and Adolescent Psychiatry, 26,* 546–553.

Bangs, T. (1986). *Birth to three checklist of learning and language behavior.* Allent, TX: DLM Teaching Resources.

Bates, E. (1976). *Language and context: The acquisition of pragmatics.* New York: Academic Press

Bates, E. (1979). *The emergence of symbols: Cognition and communication in infancy.* New York: Academic Press.

Bates, E., O'Connell, B., & Shore, C. (1987). Language and communication in infancy. In J. Osofsky (Ed.), *Handbook of infant development* (pp. 149–203). New York: John Wiley & Sons.

Bates, E., & Snyder, L. (1987). The cognitive hypothesis in language development. In I. Uzgiris & J. Hunt (Eds.), *Infant performance and experience* (pp. 168–204). Urbana: University of Illinois Press.

Bayley, N. (1969). *Manual for the Bayley Scales of Infant Development.* New York: Psychological Corporation.

Beitchman, J., Nair, R., Clegg, M., & Patel, P.G. (1986). Prevalence of speech and language disorders in five-year-old kindergarten children in the Ottawa-Carlton region. *Journal of Speech and Hearing Disorders, 51,* 98–110.

Bloom, L., & Lahey, M. (1978). *Language development and language disorders.* New York: John Wiley & Sons.

Bristol, M., & Schopler, E. (1984). A developmental perspective on stress and coping in families of autistic children. In J. Blacher (Ed.), *Families of severely handicapped children* (pp. 91–134). New York: Academic Press.

Bruner, J. (1978). From communication to language: A psychological perspective. In I. Markova (Ed.), *The social context of language*. Chichester: John Wiley & Sons.

Bruner, J. (1981). The social context of language acquisition. *Language and Communication, 1,* 155–178.

Bzoch, K., & League, R. (1971). *Receptive-Expressive Language Scale*. Baltimore: University Park Press.

Carpenter, R., Mastergeorge, A., & Coggins, T. (1983). The acquisition of communicative intentions in infants eight to fifteen months of age. *Language and Speech, 26,* 101–116.

Cichetti, D. (1989). How research on child maltreatment has informed the study of child development. Perspectives from developmental psychopathology. In D. Cichetti & V. Carlson (Eds.), *Child maltreatment: Theory and research on causality and consequences of child abuse and neglect*. Cambridge: Cambridge University Press.

Cirrin, F., & Rowland, C. (1985). Communicative assessment of nonverbal youths with severe/profound mental retardation. *Mental Retardation, 23,* 52–62.

Coggins, T., & Carpenter, R. (1981). The communicative intention inventory: A system for observing and coding children's early intentional communication. *Applied Psycholinguistics, 2,* 235–251.

Crais, B., & Leonard, C. (1990). PL 99-457: Are speech-language pathologists trained and ready? *American Speech-Language-Hearing Association Journal, 32,* 57–61.

Cromer, R. (1976). The cognitive hypothesis of language acquisition and its implications for child language deficiency. In D. Morehead & A. Morehead (Eds.), *Normal and deficient child language* (pp. 283–333). Baltimore: University Park Press.

Cromer, R. (1981). Reconceptualizing language acquisition and cognitive development. In R. Schiefelbusch & D. Bricker (Eds.), *Early language: Acquisition and intervention* (pp. 51–137). Baltimore: University Park Press.

Curtiss, S., Yamada, J., & Fromkin, V. (1979). How independent is language? On the question of formal parallels between grammar and action. *UCLA Working Papers in Cognitive Linguistics, 1,* 131–157.

Dawson, G., & Adams, A. (1984). Imitation and social responsiveness in autistic children. *Journal of Abnormal Child Psychology, 12,* 209–226.

Dore, J. (1986). The development of conversational competence. In R. Scheifelbusch (Ed.), *Language competence: Assessment and intervention* (pp. 3–60). San Diego: College-Hill Press.

Dunst, C., Lowe, L.W., & Bartholomew, P.C. (1990). Contingent social responsiveness, family ecology, and infant communicative competence. *National Student Speech Language Hearing Association Journal, 17,* 39–49.

Fewell, R., & Kaminski, R. (1988). Play skills development and instruction for young children with handicaps. In S. Odom & M. Karnes (Eds.), *Early intervention for infants and children with handicaps: An empirical base* (pp. 145–158). Baltimore: Paul H. Brookes Publishing Co.

Fey, M., Leonard, L., Fey, S., & O'Connor, K. (1978). *The intent to communicate in language-impaired children*. Paper presented at the third annual Boston University Conference on Language Development, Boston.

Foster, R., Fiddan, J., & Stark, J. (1973). *Assessment of children's language comprehension*. Austin, TX: Learning Concepts.

Frankenburg, W., & Dodds, J. (1969). *Denver Developmental Screening Test*. Denver: University of Colorado Medical Center.

Guralnick, M.J., & Bennett, F.C. (Eds.). (1987). *The effectiveness of early intervention for at-risk and handicapped children*. New York: Academic Press.

Hall, P., & Tomblin, J. (1978). A follow-up study of children with articulation and language disorders. *Journal of Speech and Hearing Disorders, 43,* 227–241.

Harding, C., & Golinkoff, R. (1979). The origins of intentional vocalization in prelinguistic infants. *Child Development, 50,* 33–40.

Hedrick, D., Prather, E., & Tobin, A. (1984). *Sequenced inventory of communication development* (2nd ed.). Los Angeles: Western Psychological Service.

Howlin, P., & Rutter, M. (1987). The consequences of language delay for other aspects of development. In W. Yule & M. Rutter (Eds.), *Language development and language disorders* (pp. 271–294). Philadelphia: J.B. Lippincott.

Kent, R., & Bauer, H. (1985). Vocalizations of one-year-olds. *Journal of Child Language, 12,* 491–526.

Leonard, L. (1978). Cognitive factors in early linguistic development. In R. Schiefelbush (Ed.), *Bases of language intervention* (pp. 67–96). Baltimore: University Park Press.

Leonard, L., Camarata, S., Rowan, L., & Chapman, K. (1982). The communicative functions of lexical usage by language impaired children. *Applied Psycholinguistics, 3,* 109–127.

MacDonald, J.D. (1978). *The Environmental Language Inventory.* Columbus, OH: Charles E. Merrill.

McCune-Nicolich, L., & Carroll, S. (1981). Development of symbolic play: Implications for the language specialist. *Topics in Language Disorders, 2,* 1–15.

McLean, J., & Snyder-McLean, L. (1978). *A transactional approach to early language training.* Columbus, OH: Charles E. Merrill.

Miller, J. (1983). Identifying children with language disorders and describing their language performance. In J. Miller, D. Yoder, & R. Schiefelbusch (Eds.), *Contemporary issues in language intervention. Asha Reports, 12,* 61–74.

Piaget, J. (1952). *The origins of intelligence in children.* New York: Basic Books.

Prizant, B., Audet, L., Burke, G., Hummel, L., Maher, S., & Theadore, G. (1990). Communication disorders and emotional/behavioral disorders in children. *Journal of Speech and Hearing Disorders, 55,* 179–192.

Prizant, B., & Wetherby, A. (1988). Providing services to children with autism (0–2) and their families. *Topics in Language Disorders, 9,* 1–23.

Prizant, B., & Wetherby, A. (1990). Toward an integrated view of early language and communication development and socioemotional development. *Topics in Language Disorders, 10,* 1–16.

Rice, M. (1983). Contemporary accounts of the cognition/language relationship: Implications for speech-language clinicians. *Journal of Speech and Hearing Disorders, 48,* 347–359.

Rom, A., & Bliss, L. (1981). A comparison of verbal communicative skills of language impaired and normal speaking children. *Journal of Communication Disorders, 14,* 133–140.

Rossetti, L. (1990). *Infant-toddler assessment: An interdisciplinary approach.* Boston: College-Hill Press.

Rowan, L., Leonard, L., Chapman, K., & Weiss, A. (1983). Performative and presuppositional skills in language-disordered and normal children. *Journal of Speech and Hearing Research, 26,* 97–106.

Shonkoff, J., & Hauser-Cram, P. (1987). Early intervention for disabled infants and their families: A quantitative analysis. *Pediatrics, 80,* 650–658.

Shore, C., O'Connell, B., & Bates, E. (1984). First sentences in language and symbolic play. *Developmental Psychology, 20,* 872–880.

Sigman, M., & Ungerer, J. (1984). Cognitive and language skills in autistic, mentally retarded and normal children. *Developmental Psychology, 20,* 293–302.

Sinclair, H. (1975). The role of cognitive structures in language acquisition. In E.H. Lenneberg & E. Lenneberg (Eds.), *Foundations of language development* (Vol. 1, pp. 223–238). New York: Academic Press.

Slobin, D. (1973). Cognitive prerequisites for the development of grammar. In C. Ferguson & D. Slobin (Eds.), *Studies of child language development.* New York: Holt, Rinehart & Winston.

Snyder, L. (1978). Communicative and cognitive abilities and disabilities in the sensorimotor period. *Merrill-Palmer Quarterly, 24,* 161–180.

Sparrow, S., Balla, D., & Cichetti, D. (1984). *The Vineland Adaptive Behavior Scales* (Interview ed.). Circle Pines, MN: American Guidance Service.

Stern, D. (1985). *The interpersonal world of the infant.* New York; Basic Books.

Terrell, B.Y., & Schwartz, R.G. (1988). Object transformations in the play of language-impaired children. *Journal of Speech and Hearing Disorders, 53,* 459–466.

Terrell, B.Y., Schwartz, R.G., Prelock, P., & Messick, C.K. (1984). Symbolic play in normal and language impaired children. *Journal of Speech and Hearing Research, 27,* 424–429.

Tronick, E. (1989). Emotions and emotional communication in infants. *American Psychologist, 44,* 112–119.

U.S. Department of Education. (1987). *Ninth Annual Report to Congress on the Implementation of the Education of the Handicapped Act.* Prepared by the Division of Innovation and Development, Office of Special Education Programs. Washington, DC: Author.

Uzgiris, I., & Hunt, J. (1975). *Assessment in infancy: Ordinal scales of psychological development.* Urbana: University of Illinois Press.

Vohr, B., & Garcia-Coll, C. (1988). Follow-up study of high-risk low birthweight infants. In H. Fitzgerald, B. Lester, & M. Yogman (Eds.), *Theory and research in behavioral pediatrics* (Vol. 4). New York: Plenum Press.

Warren, S.F., & Kaiser, A.P. (1988). Research in early language intervention. In S.L. Odom & M.B. Karnes (Eds.), *Early intervention for infants and children with handicaps: An empirical base* (pp. 89–108). Baltimore: Paul H. Brookes Publishing Co.

Westby, C. (1988). Children's play: Reflections of social competence. *Seminars in Speech and Hearing, 9,* 1–14.

Wetherby, A. (1986). Ontogeny of communicative functions in autism. *Journal of Autism and Developmental Disorders, 16,* 295–316.

Wetherby, A., Cain, D., Yonclas, D., & Walker, V. (1988). Analysis of intentional communication of normal children from the prelinguistic to the multi-word stage. *Journal of Speech and Hearing Research, 31,* 240–252.

Wetherby, A., & Prizant, B. (1989). The expression of communicative intent: Assessment guidelines. *Seminars in Speech and Language, 10,* 77–91.

Wetherby, A., & Prizant, B. (1990). *Communication and Symbolic Behavior Scales-Research Edition.* Chicago: Riverside Publishing.

Wetherby, A., Prizant, B., & Kublin, K. (1989). *Assessing infants and toddlers with an eye toward intervention.* Short course presented at the annual convention of the American Speech-Language-Hearing Association, St. Louis, MO.

Wetherby, A., & Prutting, C. (1984). Profiles of communicative and cognitive-social abilities in autistic children. *Journal of Speech and Hearing Research, 27,* 364–377.

Wetherby, A., Yonclas, D., & Bryan, A. (1989). Communicative profiles of handicapped preschool children: Implications for early identification. *Journal of Speech and Hearing Disorders, 54,* 148–158.

Wing, L., Gould, J., Yeates, S., & Brierly, L. (1977). Symbolic play in severely mentally retarded and in autistic children. *Journal of Child Psychology and Psychiatry, 18,* 167–178.

Zimmerman, I., Steiner, V., & Evatt, R. (1969). *Preschool language scale.* Columbus, OH: Charles E. Merrill.

Appendix

Communication and Symbolic Behavior Scales

■ COMMUNICATION SCALES

COMMUNICATIVE FUNCTION

1. Range of Communicative Functions
Variety of behavioral regulation, social interaction, and joint attention

1	2	3	4	5
absence of differentiated functions		1 function in each major category		at least 6 functions in 3 major categories

2. Proportion of Functions
Behavioral regulation

1	2	3	4	5
no behavioral regulation acts		4-9 behavioral regulation acts		at least 15 behavioral regulation acts

3. Proportion of Functions
Joint attention

1	2	3	4	5
no joint attention acts		4-9 joint attention acts		at least 15 joint attention acts

COMMUNICATIVE MEANS

4. Gestural Means
Variety of conventional gestures

1	2	3	4	5
no conventional gestures		3 different conventional gestures		at least 5 different conventional gestures

5. Gestural Means
Distal hand gestures

1	2	3	4	5
no distal gestures		4-6 distal gestures		at least 10 distal gestures

6. Gestural and Vocal Means
Coordination of gestures and vocalizations

1	2	3	4	5
no coordinated gest. + voc. acts		4-9 coordinated gest. + voc. acts		at least 15 coordinated gest. + voc. acts

7. Vocal Means
Isolated vocal acts

1	2	3	4	5
no isolated acts		4-9 isolated acts		at least 15 isolated acts

8. Vocal Means
Inventory of consonants

1	2	3	4	5
no consonants		4-6 different consonants		at least 10 different consonants

9. Vocal Means
Syllable shape

1	2	3	4	5
no consonants		4-9 syllables with a consonant		at least 15 syllables with a consonant

10. Vocal Means
Multisyllables

1	2	3	4	5
no multisyllables		4-9 multisyllables		at least 15 multisyllables

RECIPROCITY

11. Respondent Acts
Response to conventional gestures
or speech

1	2	3	4	5
no respondent acts		4-9 respondent acts		at least 15 respondent acts

12. Rate of Communicative Acts
Acts per minute

1	2	3	4	5
1 act per minute		2 acts per minute		at least 4 acts per minute

13. Repair Strategies
Persistence & ability to modify act

1	2	3	4	5
no persistence		2 repeated acts to persist		2 modified acts to persist

SOCIAL/AFFECTIVE SIGNALLING

14. Gaze Shifts
Alternating eye gaze between
person & object

1	2	3	4	5
no gaze shifts		4-9 gaze shifts		at least 15 gaze shifts

15. Display of Affect
Positive affect with eye gaze

1	2	3	4	5
no pos. affect		4-9 displays of pos. affect		at least 15 displays of pos. affect

16. Display of Affect
Episodes of negative affect

1	2	3	4	5
at least 15 displays of neg. affect		4-9 displays of neg. affect		no neg. affect

■ SYMBOLIC BEHAVIOR SCALES

VERBAL SYMBOLIC BEHAVIOR

17. Symbolic Level
Expressive lexicon & utterance length

1	2	3	4	5
less than 4 lexical forms		at least 15-word lexicon		at least 15 multiword combinations

18. Symbolic Level
Language comprehension

1	2	3	4	5
no response strategy		comprehends 3 body parts or 2 agents		comprehends 3 possessive combinations

NONVERBAL SYMBOLIC BEHAVIOR

19. Symbolic Level
Symbolic play

1	2	3	4	5
no action schemes		uses 4 single-action schemes toward others		uses at least 1 triple-action scheme in sequence

20. Symbolic Level
Combinatorial play

1	2	3	4	5
no combinatorial actions		combines 4 unordered objects		combines at least 5 ordered objects

10

Getting Children with Developmental Disabilities to Talk to Adults

Paul J. Yoder, Betty Davies, and Kerri Bishop

T HE PURPOSE OF THIS CHAPTER is to review the literature and present new data on the reciprocal effect of conversational recruiting strategies and children's early conversational participation. First, we describe the problems caused by infrequent talking by children with developmental disabilities. Second, we review the literature regarding three conversational recruiting strategies. Third, we present the results of a recent study of parental use of the recruiting strategies with children with developmental disabilities. Finally, we discuss the clinical and research implications of what we do and do not know about conversational recruiting strategies.

IMPORTANCE OF TALKING

Many children with developmental disabilities talk less often than other children of the same linguistic level (Rosenberg, 1982). Language intervention, language assessment, and parent–child interactions are all affected when children with developmental disabilities fail to speak when they are able to do so.

Children who converse often with adults may develop language more quickly than children who do so less often for two reasons. First, adults use several techniques that effectively model new language structures immediately after the child talks. For example, it is widely accepted that continuing the child's spoken topic while modeling slightly more advanced ways to communicate the child's message (e.g., expansions and recasts) facilitates the acquisition of new language structures (Nelson, 1989; Snow et al., 1987). Second, immediate feedback on language use may help the child test hypotheses about underlying linguistic rules and concepts (Hoff-Ginsberg & Shatz, 1982). For example, in the one-word stage of language learning (i.e., early in

This research was supported by Grant No. HD22812 from the National Institute of Child Health and Development (HD22812).

Brown's Stage I [Brown, 1973]), children without language impairment improve the accuracy of their receptive and productive noun category labels when adults correct inaccurate use of the noun labels and point out the functional distinction between the referent for the overextended term and the inappropriately named object (Chapman, Leonard, & Mervis, 1986). In short, conversational involvement with adults may be particularly important to young children's ability to avail themselves of adult input for language learning purposes.

Developmentally young children who converse infrequently present the diagnostician with a challenge. Tasks designed to elicit child talking often fail to elicit the language behaviors that are the focus of the assessment, even though the children demonstrate the ability to produce the target linguistic structure in a language sample (Lahey, Launer, & Schiff-Myers, 1983; Prutting, Gallagher, & Mulac, 1975). Children who speak infrequently generate meager language samples, thereby casting doubt on the representativeness of the samples. Without methods for eliciting language use in the context of conversation, language assessment methods for developmentally young, infrequent speakers is likely to be inaccurate.

Finally, when children do not talk often, parents often work hard to initiate and maintain the interaction. For example, parents tend to use more directives when their children are not engaged in the interaction (Tannock, 1988). The greater interactive burden that parents of infrequent talkers carry affects parents' use of recruiting strategies, such as topic continuations, and may result in less frequent or strained parent–child interaction over time (Yoder, 1990).

Although simply conversing with adults is important, multiword replies are more desirable than single-word replies for several reasons. Multiword replies provide the adult with more information about the child's intended message (Snow et al., 1987). The additional information provides the adult with a better basis for: 1) providing expansions that accurately encode the child's message, 2) analyzing child grammatical structures, and 3) carrying on a conversation that is closely matched to the child's conversational interest.

Therefore, it is important to identify strategies that adults may use with children with developmental delays that elicit the children's single-word and multiword conversational replies. In this chapter, such verbal interactional strategies will be called *conversational recruitment strategies*.

A REVIEW OF THE LITERATURE ON THREE CONVERSATIONAL RECRUITMENT STRATEGIES

Topic Continuations

Continuing a conversation on a topic about which a child is currently talking may elicit further child conversation for two reasons. First, children are likely to be interested in topics about which they choose to talk; their interest may provide incentive and reinforcement for further exploration of the topic. Second, it may be easier for children to understand adult speech on the child's topic because the information-processing load may be less for topic continuations than for topic initiations (Bloom, Rocissano, & Hood, 1976; Hoff-Ginsberg, 1987a, 1987b; Landry & Chapieski, 1989). Empirically, child replies have been found to follow adult topic continuations more often than topic initiations in samples of young children without disabilities (Chapman, Miller, MacKenzie, & Bedrosian, 1981) and in children with hearing impairment (Kenworthy, 1986).

Questions

To simplify the exposition, the term *questions* will subsequently refer to the larger category of prompts for verbal information. As used in this chapter, questions refers to all verbal utterances that explicitly ask the child to provide verbal information. It should be noted that not all utterances that have an interrogative syntactic form request information (e.g., "Can you close the door?") and not all requests for verbal information are questions (e.g., "Tell me what you want."). The term *comments* will be used to refer to adult utterances that are not requests for verbal information (e.g., directives, questions that do not request information, declaratives).

Questions may elicit child talk because they generally carry a relatively heavy social obligation for the child to respond (Olsen-Fulero & Conforti, 1983). Questions are frequently used to allocate speaker turn in conversations with young children (Blount, 1977, Ervin-Tripp & Miller, 1977). Utterances with a rising intonational curve, such as some questions, appear to command the child's attention (Garnica, 1977). Children without disabilities in Brown's first two stages of language learning respond more frequently to questions than to comments (Bloom et al., 1976; Howe, 1981). However, questions differ in their probability of eliciting child replies. A combination of behavioral and information-processing models may predict which question types the child is most likely to address. Simply put, the child will respond to a question when his or her motivation to respond is greater than the cost of formulating an appropriate answer. Questions that continue the child's topic may be particularly powerful elicitors of child replies for two reasons. First, responding to these types of questions is associated with a relatively high payoff because the child may be interested in the content of the conversation. Second, topic-continuing questions may be relatively easy for the child to understand because of the relatively low information-processing load compared to topic-initiating questions.

In a similar vein, questions that continue the child's topic may be particularly likely to elicit multiword replies. As mentioned above, topic-continuing questions may be particularly likely to be understood by the child. Additionally, it would seem logical to assume that a child would have or would seek more information about a topic of interest to him or her. Therefore, children's replies to adult requests for more information about the topic may be particularly informative. In Brown's late Stage I, the length of the utterance increases as the amount of information conveyed by the child's utterance increases (Brown, 1973).

Unsolicited contingent queries represent a subset of questions that continue the topic. A contingent query is a request for clarification or confirmation of an earlier utterance. In this chapter, unsolicited contingent queries are adult requests for clarification or confirmation that are used after a child utterance that has some intended effect other than the elicitation of the adult query (Garvey, 1977).

When prelinguistic children and children in Brown's Stage I produce ambiguous communicative messages, adults are most likely to use requests for confirmation (i.e., a type of yes/no topic continuing question) or general requests for repetition (e.g., "What?", "Huh?") (Gallagher, 1981; Golinkoff, 1986). Parents and therapists request clarification of specific parts of children's ambiguous utterances (e.g., Child: I want X. Adult: You want what?) with increasing frequency after their children regularly combine words into early semantic relations and simple sentences (Gallagher, 1981).

Stage I children without disabilities respond to most of the contingent queries they receive (Gallagher, 1981; Golinkoff, 1986). However, the type and length of the response is influenced by the child's developmental level and the type of unsolicited contingent query. In response to general requests for repetition, Stage I children with small vocabularies (i.e., fewer than 70 words) tend to repeat their message after general repetition requests, whereas children with large vocabularies (i.e., more than 90 words) tend to reduce, add, or substitute words in their initial message (Wilcox & Webster, 1980). Stage I children using high-level syntax (i.e., two or more productive semantic rules) are more likely to respond to repetition requests with multiword elaborations or multiword substitutions than are children using low-level syntax (i.e., no more than one productive semantic rule) (Wilcox & Webster, 1980).

The type of response the contingent query requests also influences the type and length of the child's reply. For example, the social obligation of a request for confirmation (i.e., a type of yes/no question) can be fulfilled with a single-word reply or nonlinguistic response strategy (e.g., nodding). Therefore, questions that seek yes/no answers may not elicit child replies as often as other questions, or if they do, they may not elicit multiword replies. Gallagher (1981) found that Stage I children without disabilities tended to give confirmation responses to confirmation requests and repetitions to repetition requests. By Stage II, children without disabilities specify or elaborate their earlier message more often following adult specification requests than after general requests for repetition (Anselmi, Tomasello, & Acunzo, 1986).

Verbal Routines

Verbal routines, as used in this chapter, are conversations that: 1) recur frequently, 2) have a predictable and recognizable sequence, 3) have at least one spoken turn for each speaker, and 4) have content that is limited to a small set of variations. In addition, the child is required to fulfill his or her role in the routine consistently as evidence of child knowledge of the routine "script." Examples of common verbal routines include culturally defined early games (e.g., nursery rhymes), common question-answer exchanges (e.g., "What is this?"), play scripts around familiar toys (e.g., talking about what to eat and drink while playing with a tea set), and tutorial exchanges (e.g., counting together).

Several researchers have used an information-processing argument to predict and explain why verbal routines may aid the child in participating in conversations (e.g., Peters, 1983). These well-practiced verbal games may allow a child to participate in adult–child dialogues more often than is usual because the predictability and, in some cases, the rhyme and rhythm may reduce the information-processing load needed to understand the adult's speech and the child's role in dialogue (Shatz, 1983). Additionally, the mnemonic support of many routines may provide an adequate basis for correct performance based on delayed imitation of previously heard forms (Snow et al., 1987). Empirically, 18- to 24-month-old children without disabilities have been found to exhibit more utterances in routinized interactions than in non-routinized ones (Conti-Ramsden & Friel-Patti, 1987; Snow et al., 1987).

THE PRESENT STUDY

We know from 2 decades of research on parent child interaction that children and parents have a reciprocal effect on each other (Bell & Harper, 1981). However, there is almost no information concerning which aspects of children's speech and language affect parents' use of conversational recruiting strategies or the quality of parent–child routines.

Identifying child behaviors that affect parental use of conversational recruiting strategies or the quality of routines may reduce the probability that professionals will implicitly blame some parents of children with developmental delays for not using the recruiting strategies as often or for not using the routines as well as other parents. Additionally, knowing the conversational context of recruiting strategies in naturally occurring conversations may improve the naturalness and effectiveness of conscious use of the strategies.

To begin uncovering the conversational context of recruiting strategies, we tested the immediate effect of topic relatedness and length of utterances by children with developmental delays on adult use of the recruiting strategies. On the basis of previous work (Yoder & Davies, 1990), we predicted that child talk would elicit adult use of topic-continuing recruiting strategies and suppress the use of topic-initiating recruiting strategies. We also expected that child replies would elicit adult continuing recruiting strategies better than child topic initiations, because parents could identify the topic of child replies more readily than that of child initiations.

Within routines, the study determined whether the amount of verbal child participation in routines was negatively related to the average length of the adult conversational turn during routines. Short maternal turns may allow more time for the child to participate in the conversation than do long maternal turns (Olsen-Fulero, 1982). Therefore, parents who use shorter turns (i.e., few utterances per turn) in routines may be more likely to allow greater child participation. Additionally, less child participation in routines may elicit longer parental turns because parents may feel obliged to fill the conversational space. Although the correlational design used here does not allow the direction of effect to be specified, testing the magnitude of the relationship is valuable to future research and clinical work.

Purposes of the Study

The purpose of the study described in the next several sections was threefold. First, it tested whether the obligation level and topic relatedness of the parents' utterances elicited replies of any length and, more specifically, whether they elicited multiword replies from their children with developmental delays. Second, it tested whether the routineness of parent–child conversations affected the amount of verbal participation by the child. Third, it explored whether the presence and type of preceding child utterances affected the presence of adult conversational recruiting strategies and the quality of parent–child routines. The developmental period of the children investigated was the stage in which children are just learning to produce multiword utterances (i.e., Brown's Stage I [Brown, 1973]). We investigated these recruiting strategies in parent–child pairs. Observing parent–child interaction allows identification of naturally occurring recruiting strategies used by adults who are likely to know the children's abilities.

Design of the Study

Subjects

The selection criteria for the children in the study were: 1) mean length of utterances between 1.01 and 2.00, 2) at least 50 intelligible utterances per 30-minute sample, 3) no noticeable sensory impairments, and 4) evidence of cognitive delay. Nineteen children with developmental delay at Brown's Stage I and the parent who reportedly spent the most time with the child participated in the study. The children ranged from 36 to 76 months old. However, their average expressive level was at the 25-month level and their average receptive level was at the 27-month level. The average mean length of utterance in morphemes was 1.50 and ranged between 1.2 and 2.01. Eighteen mothers and one father participated. The average participating parent was middle class, as indicated by years of education and occupational status. Table 1 provides additional information about the subjects.

Interactive Context

Parents and children engaged in a typical freeplay interaction session for 30 minutes with age-appropriate toys provided by the investigator. We asked the parents to play with their children as they normally would at home. Sessions were videotaped through a one-way mirror and audiotaped by means of a wireless microphone worn by the child and a microphone suspended from the ceiling.

Parent Identification of Routines

By definition, routines are idiosyncratic to individual parent–child pairs. Alone, the staff could not identify routines from ongoing freeplay because we

Table 1. Profile of parents and children participating in the study

	Mean	Range
Parent		
Participating parent's years of education	13.4 yrs.	8–17 yrs.
Mother's occupational status[a]	40.9	16–69
Father's occupational status[a]	44.57	22–78
Child		
Chronological age	50 mos.	36–76 mos.
Productive age[b]	25 mos.	16–36 mos.
Mean length of utterance	1.50	1.2–2.01
Receptive age[b]	27 mos.	16–36 mos.
Mental age[c]	29 mos.	18–42 mos.
Productive developmental quotient[b]	0.55	0.31–0.76
Receptive developmental quotient[b]	0.60	0.31–1.01
Cognitive developmental quotient[b]	0.63	0.40–0.88

[a]Occupational status scores derived from the *International Standard of Classification of Occupations* (1968). Mean = 43.3; standard deviation = 16.9; range = 2–90. Data are reported for parent(s) with whom the child lived.

[b]Productive and receptive age equivalency scores from the Sequenced Inventory of Communication Development-Revised (Hedrick, Prather, & Tobin, 1984) and the Receptive-Expressive Emergent Language Scale (Bzoch & League, 1971). Developmental quotients are calculated by dividing age equivalency by chronological age at time of test. They index degree of delay with respect to chronological age.

[c]Mental ages from the Bayley Scales of Infant Development (Bayley, 1969) and the Merrill-Palmer Scale of Mental Tests (Stutsman, 1948).

could not know which exchanges seen in the laboratory were similar to what the parent–child dyads usually did in their routines. Other researchers have used familiar picture books (Snow et al., 1987) or familiar toys (Conti-Ramsden & Friel-Patti, 1987) to elicit routines from children. Pilot data indicated that many of the families with low socioeconomic status had no routines centered around picture books or small toys that they could bring to the lab. Therefore, we worked with parents to identify routines that occurred in the freeplay sessions. Such an approach allowed identification of routines that were not specific to particular toys or activities, thus providing more potential for greater generalizability of the results to many types of parent–child interactions.

After the freeplay session, the parent was taught the five defining characteristics of routines. These defining characteristics were that the interaction: 1) contains at least one spoken adult and one spoken child turn in the exchange, 2) occurs at least once per week, 3) has a predictable and recognizable sequence, 4) has a limited set of options for appropriate role fulfillment, and 5) contains at least one child turn in which the child fulfills his or her role consistently. After several examples and feedback to parent-generated examples, the parent viewed the middle 20 minutes of the freeplay session, stopping the tape to discuss a possible routine. At every potential routine, it was determined whether the specific exchange fit the criteria and whether the child was participating in the routine as he or she usually did at home. If so, we recorded the beginning and ending times and utterances for later coding of routine boundaries. Two weeks later, the parent returned to repeat the procedure. After the second session, the parent made a final decision about any exchanges that were identified in one session but not in the other. Later, coders verified the routine boundaries using parent-indicated times and utterances and the topic coding conventions.

Preparation of Data for Analysis

From the audio- and videotaped sessions, trained transcribers recorded the content and sequence of spoken utterances and of pauses that were 2 seconds long or longer. Pauses were included as relevant events in order to represent accurately the way parents and children used the conversational time. We verified all transcripts by viewing the videotaped session while checking the veracity of the transcript before coding. Independent reliability checks on the middle 15 minutes of three randomly selected transcripts yielded point-by-point agreement averaging .94 (standard deviation = .081) on five aspects of transcription: 1) presence of event, 2) identification of major event type, 3) segmentation of utterances, 4) glossing the meaning of the adult utterances, and 5) glossing the meaning of at least partially intelligible child utterances.

We coded adult utterances for topic relatedness (i.e., continuation versus initiation versus other), obligation level (i.e., questions versus comments), and type of question (i.e., yes/no versus other). We coded child utterances for topic relatedness and length (i.e., single word versus multiword). Reliability analyses of the coded variables was assessed on 34% of the data and yielded an average reliability index of .84.

We defined topic by the referent object and ongoing actions or events. In the rare occurrence that the subject matter of the conversation was an abstract entity (e.g., a song) or an absent entity (e.g., a friend), the sentence subject or object was the topic of the conversation (Chapman et al., 1981; Kenworthy, 1984). In the case of unintelligible utterances, we coded the topic from non-verbal behaviors showing attention to an entity, activity, or event (Kenworthy, 1984). Once a topic was continued by the noninitiating partner, either partner could unilaterally continue the topic within that exchange. In this way, each code could follow itself, thus preventing a necessary dependency between categories (Kenworthy, 1984).

We defined questions as adult utterances that oblige the child to give a verbal response regardless of the syntactic form of the adult utterance. Questions included the adult utterance types that Olsen-Fulero and Conforti (1983) found to have a high summoning power and that occurred most frequently in their sample of mother–child interaction sessions. We further distinguished questions by the type of response requested (i.e., yes/no versus other) be-cause logically, such information should covary with the length of the child reply received. Comments included directives in any form, including yes/no questions that serve a directive function (e.g., "Can you close the door?"); comments in any form, including tag questions (e.g., "You are closing the door, aren't you?"); praise or feedback to the child's actions (e.g., "Thanks for closing the door."); and responses to child questions.

Results of the Study

Utterance Types that Immediately Affect Child Conversation

Unlike summary level analyses, sequential analyses require that the input data reflect the sequence of events (e.g., whether a child reply immediately fol-lowed an adult continuation). Such analyses are necessary to test hypotheses about the immediate effect of one behavior on another. The given behavior is the proposed eliciting behavior (e.g., adult questions) and the target behavior is the proposed elicited behavior (e.g., child replies).

One type of behavior is said to elicit another in this report when the average difference between the obtained sequential frequency (i.e., the num-ber of times the target behavior follows the given behavior) and the expected sequential frequency is greater than expected by chance. The need to compare obtained and expected sequential counts is apparent if one considers that a relatively high proportion of adult topic continuations will be followed by child replies when an adult consistently inserts topic continuations in the pauses left by a gregarious child who is carrying on a monologue. Fortunately, the frequency with which one would expect child replies to follow adult topic continuations given the total frequency with which these two behaviors occur in the session can be estimated. In sequential analysis, expected sequential frequency is defined as the probability of the target behavior (e.g., number of child replies/total number of event pairs in the analysis) times the total number of instances of the given behavior (e.g., number of times the adult continues the topic) (Bakeman & Gottman, 1986). Paired t-tests were used to test the statistical significance of the difference between obtained and expected frequencies in order to establish whether chance selection of an unrepresentative sample (i.e., sampling error) was a likely explanation for the size of the mean difference.

Table 2 presents the adult utterance types that had an immediate effect on the general category of child replies or the subcategory of child multiword replies. No adult utterances had an inhibiting effect on child replies in general. In fact, all adult utterances except initiating comments elicited child replies. With regard to multiword replies, only adult continuing non-yes/no questions and adult continuing comments elicited multiword replies. In contrast, adult initiating comments inhibited multiword replies.

For the most part, we expected these results. We expected continuations to elicit child replies because the child is likely to be interested in a topic he or she initiated and it may be relatively easy to understand adult talk in the exchange. Moreover, we hypothesized that the social obligation to respond to questions would motivate children to reply. Finally, we posited that the potentially greater salience of questions over comments (e.g., rising intonation) would serve to signal the child that it was his or her turn to speak. It should be

Table 2. Adult utterances that immediately affect child replies

Reply	Mean of obtained sequential frequency	Mean of expected sequential frequency
Any reply		
Continuing yes/no questions	23.95	13.10
Continuing non-yes/no questions	33.47	15.12
Continuing comments	114.42	84.04
Initiating yes/no questions	2.15	1.21
Initiating non-yes/no questions	3.42	2.05
Multiword reply		
Continuing non-yes/no questions	6.00	3.45
Continuing comments	27.00	20.59
Initiating comments	1.37	2.74

Note: Only variables with significant mean differences between obtained and expected sequential frequencies are included in the table: $N = 19$.

noted that the general category of child replies is composed mostly of single-word replies (mean proportion of replies that are single word = .72; standard deviation = .13). This is a relevant point because the adult utterances that elicit multiword replies are different from those eliciting conversational replies.

A few of the results were surprising. We did not expect continuing comments to elicit multiword replies. Although not predicted, the topic-continuing aspect of these comments may have elicited multiword replies because these adult utterances are relatively understandable to the child and show interest in a topic in which the child has recently engaged. Additionally, continuing comments, unlike continuing yes/no questions, show interest in the child's topic without placing constraints on the child's expected response. We did not predict that initiating comments would inhibit multiword replies. In retrospect, the result makes sense because topic initiations are more difficult to understand than topic continuations and comments do not obligate the child to exert the mental energy needed to decode the topic initiation.

Effect of Different Types of Elicitors of Child Conversation

Repeated measures MANOVA indicated differences in the transitional probability of child replies following one or another of the aforementioned elicitors of child replies (multivariate $F = 31.30$; $p = .000$). Table 3 presents specific comparisons among the recruiting strategies. Specifically, continuing non-yes/no questions (mean = .58), continuing yes/no questions (mean = .52), and initiating yes/no questions (mean = .51) were stronger elicitors of child replies (Duncan's Multiple Range Test critical differences = .136; $p < .05$) than were continuing comments (mean = .35) and initiating non-yes/no questions (mean = .37).

Table 3.   Relative summoning power of elicitors of child replies and multiword replies

Reply	Mean transitional probability
Any reply	
Continuing non-yes/no questions	.58
Continuing yes/no questions	.52
Initiating yes/no questions	.51
Initiating non-yes/no questions	.37
Continuing comments	.35
Multiword reply	
Continuing non-yes/no questions	.11
Continuing comments	.08

Note: Homogeneous sets are indicated by same number. Significant differences are indicated by different numbers.

We expected, and found, that continuing questions would elicit child replies more often than continuing comments because: 1) questions carry a greater social obligation to respond, 2) they may be more salient than comments, and 3) they signal the child's turn in the conversation. As predicted, continuing questions elicited child replies more than initiating questions. We anticipated this result, reasoning that continuations would be easier for children to understand than initiations.

We did not anticipate the specific nature of the interaction between response type requested and topic relatedness in predicting the summoning power on child replies. It appears that merely responding to yes/no questions is sufficiently easy that these Stage I children could respond to initiating yes/no questions as easily as they could respond to continuing non-yes/no questions. It may be that children respond more to yes/no questions than to non-yes/no questions only if the questions initiate a new topic because responding to yes/no questions requires less comprehension of the adult's utterance than does appropriate responding to *wh-* or two-choice questions. In contrast, children may respond equally to yes/no and non-yes/no questions when the question continues the topic because the children understand both sufficiently well to respond.

With regard to multiword replies, continuing non-yes/no questions (mean $= .11$) were more likely to elicit child multiword replies (paired $t = 2.64$; $p = .02$) than were continuing comments (mean $= .08$). Continuing non-yes/no questions elicited multiword replies more often than any other adult utterance type. We anticipated this finding because continuing utterances were thought to be easier to understand than initiating ones and because non-yes/no questions demand responses other than yes/no replies from the child, many of which may be multiword replies.

Effects of Child Speech on Adult Use of Recruiting Strategies

Using a procedure analogous to that used to identify adult conversational strategies that recruit child replies, we compared the observed and expected sequential frequency for these recruiting strategies when they followed single word replies, multiword replies, and initiations. This procedure was used to identify the aspects of child speech that elicited or inhibited adults' use of recruiting strategies. All coded adult utterance types were investigated except initiating comments, which did not elicit either child replies or child multiword replies.

Table 4 indicates which aspects of child speech immediately elicited or inhibited adult recruiting strategies. Child talk, regardless of how it was coded, elicited adult continuing yes/no questions such as confirmation questions (e.g., "Did you say ball?"). Child replies elicited adult continuing comments and inhibited initiating adult questions. Child single word replies and topic initiations elicited continuing non-yes/no questions (e.g., "What?", "What do you want?").

Table 4.　Immediate effects of child speech on adult use of recruiting strategies

Adult reply	Single-word reply by child	Multi-word reply by child	Topic initiation by child
Continuing			
Non-yes/no questions	Elicitor	Neutral	Elicitor
Yes/no questions	Elicitor	Elicitor	Elicitor
Comments	Elicitor	Elicitor	Neutral
Initiating			
Non-yes/no questions	Inhibitor	Inhibitor	Neutral
Yes/no questions	Inhibitor	Inhibitor	Neutral

The pattern of results is more complex than was predicted. As posited, all child speech elicited adult use of continuing yes/no questions. However, we expected child talk to elicit all continuing recruiting strategies, including continuing non-yes/no questions and continuing comments. We had assumed that adults would be motivated to continue the child's topic for as long as the child wished to do so. Child talk may elicit continuing yes/no questions because such questions provide confirmation about the adult's understanding of the young child's message and are highly likely to elicit a child response (Olsen-Fulero & Conforti, 1983). Additionally, confirmation requests are the most common type of contingent query given to Stage I children without disabilities (Gallagher, 1981). Single-word replies and topic initiations are likely to be incomplete messages. The incomplete messages in single-word replies may have elicited the less common, but often more informative, types of contingent queries (i.e., general repetition requests and requests for specification [Gallagher, 1981]), which were coded here as continuing non-yes/no questions. That is, the adult may need more information about the child's intended message to interpret many single-word utterances. Child replies may elicit adult continuing comments because the child's message may be sufficiently clear for the adult to continue without requesting more information as long as the child continues the ongoing topic.

We also predicted, and confirmed, that child replies would inhibit adult recruiting strategies that initiated the topic, because we assumed that most parents would want to continue the child topic, not intrude upon it. Perhaps child initiations did not inhibit adult initiating questions because the child's topic-initiating message may not have been sufficiently clear to continue, thereby setting up the conditions for the adult's secondary goal of keeping the child engaged in some sort of play or conversation without conflicting with the presumed primary goal of continuing the child's topic.

Effects of Different Types
of Child Speech on Adult Use of Recruiting Strategies

Multiword replies elicited adult continuing comments (mean = .55) more often than single-word replies (mean = .47; paired $t = 3.07; p < .01$). Single-word replies elicited adult continuing yes/no questions (mean = .14) more often than did multiword replies (mean $= .10$) or child initiations (mean $=$ .08; multivariate $F = 4.86$; $p < .02$; Duncan's Multiple Range test's critical difference $= .032$; $p < .05$). There were no significant differences in the extent to which child single-word replies, multiword replies, and initiations elicited other adult recruiting strategies.

We did not anticipate the relative summoning power of single-word child replies, multiword child replies, and child initiations on adult recruiting strategies. Looking at the data now, we can make sense of them. Child multiword replies may elicit continuing comments more than child single-word replies because multiword replies provide sufficient information to the adult so as to alleviate the need to ask the competing topic-continuing recruiting strategies, questions. Similarly, single-word replies by the child may elicit continuing yes/no questions more often than multiword replies because the adult needs more information about the child's message when the message is conveyed with single-word utterances. The request for confirmation, a type of continuing yes/no questions, is the most frequently used type of contingent query in Stage I children without disabilities (Gallagher, 1981). Finally, single-word replies by the child may elicit continuing yes/no questions more often than do topic initiations by the child because the adult may have had more difficulty identifying the topic from a child initiation, which was likely to have been a single word.

Effect of Parent and Child Participation in Routine Conversations on Child Speech

The children participated in routine conversations (mean rate $= .24$ utterances per minute, or about one utterance per 4-minute interval) more than they participated in nonroutine conversations (mean rate $= .16$ utterances per minute, or one utterance per 6-minute interval; paired $t = 3.11$; $p < .01$). We predicted this difference for several reasons. First, the predictable dialogue structure and familiar content of routines may aid children in understanding adult speech and in recognizing when it is their turn to speak. Second, the frequent adult modeling in routines may teach children how to respond when it is their turn to speak. Third, the predictable nature, frequent occurrence, and, in some cases, rhythm of routines may aid the child's memory of past models and successful responses, which may in turn help the child respond in the future.

As predicted, parents of children who participated in routines more often tended to use relatively short spoken turns during routines ($r = -.50$; $p < .05$). We were interested in turn length because it has been hypothesized that short turns allow the child more time to talk than do long turns and thus may be a desirable interactional style (Olsen-Fulero, 1982). We also posited that when children talk frequently, their parents do not have the need, or sometimes even the opportunity, to talk.

Validity of the Study's Results

The measurement context in the study was a freeplay session in a laboratory setting. The study does not adequately address whether the results would generalize to nonplay interactions. However, there is little reason to doubt that many of these same relations would also hold true in freeplay sessions occurring outside the laboratory.

Because this study is one of the first to examine recruiting strategies and routines with children with developmental delays, it is important to state the extent to which the results are likely to be replicated. The confidence with which one can generalize any study's results depends partly on whether the obtained effects were predicted from theory and past empirical literature (Kerlinger, 1979). Those results that were predicted before data collection should elicit greater confidence than those that were not predicted. Future replication of unpredicted results should improve one's confidence in their generalizability.

Before the results of this study can be generalized to similar subjects and situations, it must be established that the study was internally valid. A causal inference does not mean that the causal behavior (e.g., recruiting strategies) is the only cause of the affected behavior (e.g., child replies) or that the affected behavior will always occur when the causal behavior occurs. When one attributes causation to a relationship, it means that presence of the causal behavior or factor increases the probability that the affected behavior will occur.

Sequential analyses, such as those used in this study, allow very specific hypotheses to be tested, thereby reducing the number of alternative explanations to obtained sequential relationships. However, the present results should not be interpreted as strong support for the inference that the recruiting strategies caused the children to reply. For example, more removed events (e.g., previous child replies) could reliably cause the adult to use a recruiting strategy and the child to talk. Even more detailed or exhaustive sequential analyses, such as using longer lags or multiple lags when predicting the presence of child replies, would not allow as much confidence as an experimental design allows for inferring that the given behaviors (e.g., recruiting strategies) caused the target behaviors (e.g., child replies) to occur. However, the sequential analysis of naturally occurring conversations can be used to identify the likely causal agents and the contexts of most effective use of these potential causal agents.

In comparison to the sequential analysis results, one can have even less confidence that the results of the routine–nonroutine comparison or the summary level correlation between child talk and parental turn length in routines indicate causal relationships. In the context of nonexperimental research designs, such as the one used here, summary level analyses allow more unanticipated explanations for the results than do sequential analyses. For example, many variables may covary with the conversations called routines (e.g., content of the conversation), which could in turn influence the amount of child talking. Additionally, the association between child routine participation and adult turn could be a child effect (e.g., children who talk frequently do not allow opportunities for their parents to talk much) or an adult effect (e.g., adults who use short turns leave time for their children to talk). Additionally, a third variable (e.g., the presence of a question-answer routine) could cause both child conversational participation and short adult turn length. Finally, a combination of parent, child, and third variable explanations could account for the summary level relationships.

All of this may be discouraging. It is important to remember, however, that many experimental studies have failed to produce interpretable results because the intricacies of social interaction were not sufficiently understood before the presumed causal variable was manipulated experimentally. Studying naturally occurring routines and recruiting strategies can help in designing future experimental studies that improve the empirical basis for the notion that routines and recruiting strategies facilitate more frequent child language use.

EDUCATIONAL AND CLINICAL IMPLICATIONS

It should be noted that the data presented here address effects on child language use, not language development. Many researchers have posited that conversational styles that recruit child conversations indirectly facilitate language development (Hoff-Ginsberg, 1990; Kaye & Charney, 1980; McDonald & Pien, 1982; Olsen-Fulero & Conforti, 1983) because child conversational participation may elicit adult behaviors, such as expansions (Snow et al., 1987), that past research has demonstrated facilitate language development. Currently, there is no strong evidence that getting children with language delay to talk more often with adults who frequently use conversational recruiting strategies helps the children to talk more with nontrainers using different interaction styles. There is correlational evidence that children who talk frequently tend to develop language quickly (Hart & Risley, 1980; Nelson, 1973). However, no study has demonstrated that facilitating more frequent child talk will affect future language development.

Even if recruiting strategies and routines do not result in generalized conversation with untrained adults, recruiting strategies may "scaffold" the interaction so that it is easier for the child to continue talking about the same conversational topic. Doing so may help the child attend to and comprehend the adult language models occurring in the conversation (Bloom et al., 1976). Empirical support that naturally occurring use of conversational recruiting strategies and routines facilitates language development is restricted to significant longitudinal and concurrent correlational studies with children without disabilities (Barnes, Gutfreund, Satterly, & Wells, 1983; Conti-Ramsden &

Friel-Patti, 1987; Hoff-Ginsberg, 1986; Snow et al., 1987; Yoder & Kaiser, 1989) and children with language impairment (Yoder, 1989).

Despite the lack of experimental evidence supporting the causal relationship between recruiting strategies and language use or development, two frequently used approaches of language intervention depend, in part, on such strategies to get children to talk during intervention sessions: the Milieu Model and the Responsive Interactive Model, described in Chapters 2 and 3, respectively. Although some representatives of the responsive interaction approach do not recommend using questions to elicit child talk (Manolson, 1985; Weiss, 1981), routines are recommended in some form or another by most interactive programs. The incidental teaching technique of the milieu models (Hart & Risley, 1975) uses questions that continue the child's topic as a critical component of the teaching episode. Such interventions have been found to be particularly useful for helping many types of children with developmental disabilities in using language that was understood but infrequently used (Warren & Kaiser, 1986). It is not yet clear to what extent these interventions facilitate generalized language use in conversations with people not using the recruiting strategies.

Finally, the results have implications for assessing children with developmental delays who are functioning in Brown's Stage I. The present study found that questions about a topic begun by the child are much more likely to be addressed than are questions that initiate a new topic. Several studies have documented cases in which children have used more complex language during language samples than in elicited production tests (Lahey et al., 1983; Prutting et al., 1975). Most elicited production language tests are essentially a series of unrelated questions and activities. The noted discrepancy between language sample performance and elicited production performance could occur because the children did not understand questions that initiated a new topic during the elicited production tests. Elicited production testing methods may be more effective when test questions are embedded within a conversational context because the children appear to understand conversationally embedded questions more often than the typical test questions.

DIRECTIONS FOR FUTURE RESEARCH

At least three experiments are logical extensions of the previously discussed studies on eliciting child conversation. First, the recruiting strategies could be manipulated experimentally to determine whether doing so aids the child in conversing more often and in longer utterances. Mothers naturally ask more questions they know their children can answer. When clinicians or experimenters deliberately use an interaction style designed on the basis of our sequential analysis results, attention to the types of *wh*-questions to which Stage I children are likely to respond is particularly important. Research on children without disabilities (see Clancy, 1989, for a review) and children with language delays (Lee & Ashmore, 1983) shows that children respond to "where," "what," and "what do" questions before they respond to "why," "when," and "how" questions. Second, "routineness" of an interaction could be manipulated while keeping the content of the interaction constant by building a routine with the child and observing changes in the child's language use as the interaction became more routinized. Finally, the confidence with which one can reasonably infer that children's speech influences their parents' interaction style would be increased if one observed whether the parents' interaction with the children (e.g., turn length to routines and use of recruiting strategies) changed as a function of experimentally manipulated changes in the children's generalized amount of talking.

The theoretical rationale for the responsive interaction and milieu methods of language intervention lacks two critical pieces of support. We still do not know whether use of scaffolding interactions such as those investigated here results in more frequent child conversation with people using untrained interaction styles. Furthermore, we still do not know whether talking more frequently will indirectly affect future child language development. More frequent use of the recruiting strategies could be manipulated while assessing the generalized effects on frequency of child conversation with untrained adults. If the untrained adults use more frequent language facilitating techniques (e.g., expansions), and if the children develop language relatively more quickly than children with whom the recruiting strategies are not used, the support for language intervention methods that use questions to elicit child talk will be greatly enhanced.

CONCLUSION

The research described here represents a step toward supporting the intervention models that encourage language interventionists to use recruiting strategies and routines to elicit child talk that can then be expanded or corrected to facilitate the child's language development (e.g., milieu language teaching; activity-based teaching). Because of concern, raised by Fey (1986) and Mahoney and Powell (1988), that frequent use of questions may encourage the child to become dependent on questions to signal his or her turn to talk, we recommend that questions be used only when the child will not talk at a sufficient rate unless prompted to do so, and that they be faded as the child becomes more assertive. We also suggest that embedding test questions within a conversational context may prove more effective at eliciting Stage I children's language use than the typical testing method, which uses many questions that initiate new topics frequently.

REFERENCES

Anselmi, D. Tomasello, M., & Acunzo, M. (1986). Young children's responses to neutral and specific contingent queries. *Journal of Child Language, 13*, 135–144.

Bakeman, R., & Gottman, J.M. (1986). *Observing interaction: An introduction to sequential analysis.* Cambridge: Cambridge University Press.

Barnes, S., Gutfreund, M., Satterly, D., & Wells, G. (1983). Characteristics of adult speech which predict children's language development. *Journal of Child Language, 10*, 65–84.

Bayley, N. (1969). *Bayley Scales of Infant Development.* New York: Psychological Corporation.

Bell, R.Q., & Harper, L.V. (1981). *Child effects on adults.* Lincoln: University of Nebraska Press.

Bloom, L., Rocissano, L., & Hood, L. (1976). Developmental interaction between information processing and linguistic knowledge. *Cognitive Psychology, 8*, 521–552.

Blount, B.G. (1977). Ethnography and caretaker–child interaction. In C.E. Snow & C.A. Ferguson (Eds.), *Talking to children: Language input and acquisition* (pp. 297–308). Cambridge: Cambridge University Press.

Brown, R. (1973). *First language: The early stages.* Cambridge: Harvard University Press.

Bzoch, K., & League, R. (1971). *Receptive-Expressive Emergent Language Scale.* Gainesville, FL: Anhinga Press.

Chapman, K.L., Leonard, L.B., & Mervis, C.B. (1986). The effect of feedback on young children's inappropriate word usage. *Journal of Child Language, 13*, 101–117.

Chapman, R.S., Miller, J.F., MacKenzie, E.H., & Bedrosian, J. (1981). *The development of discourse skills in the second year of life.* Paper presented at the Second International Congress for the Study of Child Language, Vancouver.

Clancy, P.M. (1989). Form and function in the acquisition of Korean wh-questions. *Journal of Child Language, 16*(2), 323–348.

Conti-Ramsden, G., & Friel-Patti, P. (1987). Scriptedness: A factor in children's variation in language use? In K. Nelson & A. van Kleeck (Eds.), *Children's language* (Vol. 6). Hillsdale, NJ: Lawrence Erlbaum Associates.

Ervin-Tripp, S., & Miller, W. (1977). Early discourse: Some questions about questions. In M. Lewis & L. Rosenblum (Eds.), *Interaction, conversation, and the development of language.* New York: John Wiley & Sons.

Fey, M.E. (1986). *Language intervention with young children.* San Diego: College-Hill Press.

Gallagher, T.M. (1981). Contingent query sequences within adult-child discourse. *Journal of Child Language, 8*, 51–62.

Garnica, O. (1977). Some prosodic and paralinguistic features of speech to young children. In C. Snow & C. Ferguson (Eds.), *Talking to children: Language input and acquisition.* Cambridge: Cambridge University Press.

Garvey, C. (1977). The contingent query: A dependent act in conversation. In M. Lewis & L.A. Rosenblum (Eds.), *Interaction, conversation, and the development of language* (pp. 63–93). London: John Wiley & Sons.

Golinkoff, R. (1986). 'I beg your pardon?': The preverbal negotiation of failed messages. *Journal of Child Language, 13*, 455–476.

Hart, B., & Risley, T. (1975). Incidental teaching of language in the preschool. *Journal of Applied Behavior Analysis, 8*, 411–420.

Hart, B., & Risley, T. (1980). In vivo language intervention: Unanticipated general effects. *Journal of Applied Behavior Analysis, 13*, 407–432.

Hedrick, D.L., Prather, E.M., & Tobin, A.R. (1984). *Sequenced Inventory of Communication Development Test Manual.* Seattle: University of Washington Press.

Hoff-Ginsberg, E. (1986). Function and structure in maternal speech: The relation to the child's development of syntax. *Developmental Psychology, 22*(2), 155–163.

Hoff-Ginsberg, E. (1987a, April). *Conversation as a resource-limited process for two-year-olds.* Paper presented at the Society for Research in Child Development, Baltimore.

Hoff-Ginsberg, E. (1987b). Topic relations in mother–child conversations. *First Language, 7*, 145–158.

Hoff-Ginsberg, E. (1990). Maternal speech and the child's development of syntax: A further look. *Journal of Child Language, 17*(1), 85–100.

Hoff-Ginsberg, E., & Shatz, M. (1982). Linguistic input and the child's acquisition of language. *Psychological Bulletin, 92*, 3–26.

Howe, C. (1981). Acquiring language in a conversational context. In R. Schaffer (Ed.), *Behavioral development: A series of monographs* (pp. 81–141). London: Academic Press.

International Standard Classification of Occupations. (1968). Geneva: International Labor Office.

Kaye, K., & Charney, R. (1980). How mothers maintain "dialogue" with two-year olds. In D.R. Olsen (Ed.), *The social foundations of language and thought* (pp. 191–206). New York: Norton.

Kenworthy, O.T. (1984). *The influence of selected discourse and auditory factors upon the language acquisition of hearing-impaired children.* Unpublished doctoral dissertation, University of Wisconsin, Madison.

Kenworthy, O.T. (1986). Caregiver–child interaction and language acquisition of hearing impaired children. *Topics in Language Disorders, 6*(1), 1–11.

Kerlinger, F.N. (1979). *Behavioral research: A conceptual approach.* New York: Holt, Rinehart, & Winston.

Lahey, M., Launer, P.B., & Schiff-Myers, N. (1983). Prediction of production: Elicited imitation and spontaneous speech productions of language disordered children. *Applied Psycholinguistics, 4*, 317–343.

Landry, S.H., & Chapieski, M.L. (1989). Joint attention and infant toy exploration: Effects of Down syndrome and prematurity. *Child Development, 60*, 103–118.

Lee, R., & Ashmore, L. (1983). Receptive and expressive wh-question performance by language-delayed children. *Journal of Child Language, 16*, 99–109.

Mahoney, G., & Powell, A. (1988). Modifying parent–child interaction: Enhancing the development of handicapped children. *Journal of Special Education, 22*(1), 82–96.

Manolson, A. (1985). *It takes two to talk: A Hanen early language parent guidebook.* Toronto: Hanen Early Language Resource Centre.

McDonald, L., & Pien, D. (1982). Mother conversational behavior as a function of interactional intent. *Journal of Child Language, 9*, 337–358.

Nelson, K. (1973). Structure and strategy in learning to talk. *Monograph of the Society for Research in Child Development, 38* (1–2, Serial No. 149).

Nelson, K.E. (1989). Strategies for first language teaching. In M. Rice & R. Schiefelbusch (Eds.), *The teachability of language* (pp. 263–310). Baltimore: Paul H. Brookes Publishing Co.

Olsen-Fulero, L. (1982). Style and stability in mother conversational behavior: A study of individual differences. *Journal of Child Language, 9*, 543–564.

Olsen-Fulero, L., & Conforti, J. (1983). Child responsiveness to mother questions of varying type and presentation. *Journal of Child Language, 10,* 495–520.

Peters, A. (1983). *The units of language acquisition.* Cambridge: Cambridge University Press.

Prutting, C.A., Gallagher, T.M., & Mulac, A. (1975). The expressive portion of the NSST compared to a spontaneous language sample. *Journal of Speech and Hearing Disorders, 40,* 40–47.

Rosenberg, S. (1982). The language of the mentally retarded: Development, processes, and intervention. In S. Rosenberg (Ed.), *Handbook of applied psycholinguistics.* Hillsdale, NJ: Lawrence Erlbaum Associates.

Shatz, M. (1983). Communication. In P.H. Mussen (Ed.), *Handbook of child psychology: Vol III. Cognitive development.* New York: John Wiley & Sons.

Snow, C.E., Perlmann, R., & Nathan, D.C. (1987). Why routines are different: Toward a multiple-factors model of the relation between input and language acquisition. In K. Nelson & A. van Kleeck (Eds.), *Children's language* (Vol. 6). Hillsdale, NJ: Lawrence Erlbaum Associates.

Stutsman, R. (1948). *Merrill-Palmer Scale of Mental Tests.* Chicago: C.H. Stoelting Co.

Tannock, R. (1988). Mothers' directiveness in their interactions with their children with and without Down syndrome. *American Journal of Mental Retardation, 93,* 154–165.

Warren, S., & Kaiser, A. (1986). Incidental language teaching: A critical review. *Journal of Speech and Hearing Disorders, 51,* 291–299.

Weiss, R. (1981). INREAL intervention for language handicapped and bilingual children. *Journal of the Division of Early Childhood, 4,* 40–51.

Wilcox, M.J., & Webster, E.J. (1980). Early discourse behavior: An analysis of children's responses to listener feedback. *Child Development, 51,* 1120–1125.

Yoder, P.J. (1989). Maternal question use predicts later language development in specific language disordered children. *Journal of Speech and Hearing Disorders, 54,* 347–355,

Yoder, P.J. (1990). The theoretical and empirical basis of early amelioration of developmental disabilities: Implications for future research. *Journal of Early Intervention, 14*(1), 27–42.

Yoder, P.J., & Davies, B. (1990). Do parental questions and topic continuations elicit replies from developmentally delayed children?: A sequential analysis. *Journal of Speech and Hearing Research, 33*(3), 563–573.

Yoder, P.J., & Kaiser, A.P. (1989). Alternative explanations for the relationship between maternal verbal interaction style and child language development. *Journal of Child Language, 16*(1), 141–161.

11

Evaluating Outcomes with Children with Expressive Language Delay

Grover J. Whitehurst, Janet E. Fischel,
David S. Arnold, and Christopher J. Lonigan

THIS CHAPTER IS ABOUT CHILDREN who are slow to learn to talk. Technically, this is called *specific* expressive language delay (ELD), a condition characterized by a substantial delay in the development of spoken language compared with receptive language and nonverbal intelligence (American Psychiatric Association, 1987). We stress the qualifier *specific* to distinguish ELD from *nonspecific* expressive language delay, which refers to a level of expressive delay that is in keeping with a child's level of cognitive or receptive language delay. For example, a child with a tested IQ of 70 and an expressive language quotient of 65 would have a nonspecific expressive delay and would probably receive a primary diagnosis of mental retardation, whereas a child with an IQ of 90 and an expressive language quotient of 65 would probably be diagnosed as having ELD. This distinction is important because there is evidence that the etiology and developmental course of ELD are substantially different from the etiology and developmental course of the type of non-specific expressive delay that occurs as part of other syndromes (e.g., mental retardation, pervasive developmental disorder, general language impairment). When we use the acronym ELD, we refer to specific expressive language delay. In cases where expressive delay is or may be nonspecific, we use the term *general expressive delay* or *language impairment*.

Nothing in our definition of ELD prevents a child with ELD from having another diagnosis, such as mental retardation. However, in such a case the child's level of expressive delay would have to be substantially greater than his or her level of nonverbally measured intelligence and receptive language

Portions of this research were supported by grants to Grover Whitehurst and Janet Fischel by the National Institute of Child Health and Human Development (Grant No. HD19245) and by the National Institute of Mental Health (Grant No. MH41603). Preparation of this chapter was aided by a grant to Grover Whitehurst by the Smith Richardson Foundation.

ability to justify the ELD label. This approach defines ELD in terms of the gap between expressive and other abilities. Arbitrariness is inescapable, as are serious measurement issues. These are topics to which we shall turn shortly.

This chapter seeks to answer the following questions: 1) How should ELD be measured? 2) How can the child with ELD be characterized? 3) What is the developmental course of ELD? 4) What causes ELD? 5) Should ELD be treated, and if so, how? Some of our findings—such as the fact that no evidence supports the belief that treatment for ELD is efficacious in the long term—may be surprising and provocative.

DEFINING AND MEASURING ELD

The essence of ELD as a diagnostic category is the gap between the development of expressive language and other skills: the child is badly behind in expressive development and normal in other areas, or much farther behind in expressive development than in other areas. How should this gap be measured?

Absolute Approach

One approach that is intuitively appealing but inappropriate and misleading is to compare absolute levels of linguistic knowledge measured in the expressive and receptive modes. The problem is that expressive language is more difficult to acquire than receptive language. For example, Bates, Bretherton, and Snyder (1988) report that among toddlers, receptive knowledge exceeds expressive ability by a factor of 3 to 4. Anyone who has tried to learn a second language or who has taken multiple choice tests knows this directly—we can understand more than we can produce. Thus, if we were to compare expressive skill to receptive skill on an absolute scale, all children would be diagnosed as having ELD.

Normative Approach

Given the natural gap between receptive and expressive skills, the appropriate approach is normative. We need to compare the child's level of expressive skill assessed using norms for expressive development with the child's level of receptive and cognitive skills assessed using norms for receptive and cognitive development. In this way, we are comparing what is normal for expressive development with what is normal for receptive and cognitive development.

Assessment Instruments

The normative approach depends on the availability of standardized, normed assessment instruments that distinguish among expressive language, receptive language, and cognitive development. These instruments must be appropriate to the age at which ELD first becomes identified as a problem—around 24 months of age—and they must continue to be appropriate throughout the preschool period.

Although there are many tests of language and cognitive development that are appropriate to the preschool period (see Cantwell & Baker, 1987), very few extend down to 24 months of age; separate expressive, receptive, and cognitive abilities; are based on child performance rather than parent report; and have acceptable psychometric properties (i.e., norms, standardization, reliability, validity). None of these tests is ideal. We have used the Expressive One-Word Picture Vocabulary Test (Gardner, 1981) as a test of expressive ability. It is most appropriate for the younger (e.g., 2-year-old) child with ELD whose expressive skills are limited to a few single words. We have used the Peabody Picture Vocabulary Test-Revised (Dunn & Dunn, 1983) as a test of receptive ability. Although the standardization sample for the Peabody Picture Vocabulary Test-Revised extends down to 30 months of age, the manual allows the determination of language age in children as young as 21 months. We have used the Leiter International Performance Scales (Leiter, 1976) to assess cognitive development in children with ELD. The Leiter scales are weak psychometrically, but the instrument is attractive to young children and easily administered.

Other assessment instruments can also be used with younger children. For example, the Reynell Developmental Language Scales, second revision (Reynell, 1985) separate expressive and receptive development and are attractive to young children. However, the norm group is English and some of the test items reflect English culture. The Reynell scales become a useful language assessment instrument for older children because they include a normed scale of grammatical development. The copying, bead memory, and pattern analysis subtests from the Stanford-Binet Intelligence Scale, fourth edition (Thorndike, Hagen, & Sattler, 1986) are appropriate tests of cognitive development that can be given with minimal verbal interaction and that extend down to 24 months of age. The verbal expression subscale of the Illinois Test of Psycholinguistic Ability (Kirk, McCarthy, & Kirk, 1968) is a sensitive test of expressive descriptive abilities. However, it has a floor effect that makes it inappropriate until a child is at least 30 months of age. Among older children with ELD who have developed a reasonable repertoire of expressive vocabulary, the Templin-Darley Tests of Articulation, second edition (Templin & Darley, 1968) provide a means of separating phonological from vocabulary skills. Evidence that ELD is first manifest in vocabulary delay and later in articulation difficulties is presented later in this chapter.

Diagnosis of ELD should rule out severe hearing loss and pervasive developmental disorder. Severe hearing loss is extremely unlikely in a child who performs well on a test of receptive language, but milder hearing losses are frequent in children with ELD (Fischel et al., 1990; Lonigan, Fischel,

Whitehurst, Arnold, & Valdez-Menchaca, 1991). An assessment by a trained audiologist experienced with young children is advisable for any child with a language delay.

Pervasive developmental disorder is not at issue for a child whose tested receptive language and nonverbal cognitive abilities are within normal limits. It becomes a concern, however, in the child who is difficult to test. In these cases, the examiner may be unable to separate ability from compliance: the child may be able to perform but unwilling to do so. Careful questioning of the parents is often useful (e.g., "Can the child carry out complex verbal instructions such as 'Go to my room and get the keys from the dresser and we'll go to MacDonalds'?"). In general, parents are reliable sources of information about their children's general levels of verbal ability. In cases in which an examiner is unable to obtain the child's cooperation but the parent believes the child is able to perform some items on tests of cognitive or receptive language, it can be useful to schedule another appointment for assessment and to have the parent work on similar tasks with the child at home during the interim.

A more problematic situation concerns disruptive behavior disorders, including attention deficit hyperactivity disorder. Such conduct problems are functionally connected to the developmental course of ELD in many children (Caulfield, Fischel, DeBaryshe, & Whitehurst, 1989; Lonigan et al., 1991). Thus, we view conduct problems and expressive language delay as comorbidities.

There remains the question of the size of the gap between expressive and receptive skills, or expressive and cognitive skills to be used to determine a diagnosis of ELD. Any cut-off is arbitrary, and definitions in the literature vary widely. For example, Stevenson and Richman (1976) used a 6-month gap between language age and cognitive age at 30 months of age as a criterion for language delay. However, this degree of delay represents a difference of less than 1 standard deviation from the mean. We question whether a child whose expressive ability is within the normal range (i.e., within 1 standard deviation of the mean for his or her age) should be characterized as delayed, and whether a gap of less than 1 standard deviation is sufficient to diagnose a specific language impairment. Other investigators have used similar standards for defining ELD. Rescorla and Schwartz (1988) allowed children with as little as a 3-month gap in language age between receptive and expressive scores to be defined as having ELD. Silva (1980) employed what to us is a better approach. Children were first defined as having a language delay if they were at least 2 standard deviations below the mean for their age on either receptive or expressive tests. These children were then further characterized as to whether their delay was receptive, expressive, or both, and whether their language delay was accompanied by a cognitive delay.

Our approach has been to diagnose ELD in those cases in which a child's expressive score on the One-Word Picture Vocabulary Test is at least 2.33 standard deviations below the mean, with the corresponding receptive score and cognitive score within 1 standard deviation of the mean. This results in a defined population that is severely delayed expressively in both absolute and relative terms. The 2.33 standard deviation criterion on the One-Word Picture Vocabulary Test has the additional advantage that at 24–30 months it identifies children who typically are unable to label any object or picture on demand. We have found that 2-year-olds who can label a number of objects on request are likely to show very rapid spontaneous progress in expressive language, even though they may be substantially delayed when they are assessed (Fischel, Whitehurst, Caulfield, & DeBaryshe, 1989).

Determination of the size of the gap between expressive development and other development necessary for a diagnosis of ELD is arbitrary, but crucially important. We believe that researchers who are interested in expressive delay from a theoretical or process orientation might do well to establish lenient criteria, and then use the degree of delay as a process or predictor variable. Researchers or practitioners who are interested in ELD as a clinical disorder should use strict criteria for diagnosis if their work is to have relevance to children with the extreme delays that generate parental concern and professional attention.

PREVALENCE AND SIGNIFICANCE OF ELD

The question of whether specific ELD is primarily a theoretically interesting anomaly or is also a disorder is of considerable practical importance. Before a developmental delay is categorized as a disorder it must be determined that it is associated with significant distress for parent or child, or with impairment in important areas of current or future functioning. Poor progress in the growth of expressive language skill by 2-year-old children generates two sets of opinion—one favoring a wait-and-see approach: one favoring prompt intervention. At the heart of this controversy is an opposing set of views on whether early expressive delay is a disorder.

Taking the view that expressive language delay is a self-correcting problem, authors of one text on neuropsychological development ask, "Does he hear? Does he understand what is said to him? If the answers to these questions are 'yes,' the child will talk when what he wishes to communicate cannot be transmitted adequately by means of gestures and pantomime. The parents must avoid pressuring the child to talk. . . ." (Knobloch & Pasamanick, 1974, p. 290).

Evidence in favor of the view that early ELD is not a disorder tends to be anecdotal, and focuses on the rate of spontaneous remission of symptoms. For example, the *Diagnostic and Statistical Manual of Mental Disorders,* third edition, revised *(DSM-III-R)* reports that "as many as 50% of the children with this disorder may spontaneously catch up in their expressive language abilities before they reach school age and thus not require any specialized help" (American Psychiatric Association, 1987, p. 46).

The contrary view also has its adherents. A marked impairment of expressive language that is not associated with mental retardation or a neurologic condition is categorized as a disorder by the *DSM-III-R* (American Psychiatric Association, 1987). Consistent with this view, a popular developmental pediatrics text opens the chapter on speech and language evaluation by noting: "Talking is normal, and not talking is not. While this may seem obvious, too often a child with delayed speech is treated as if speech will begin when the child is ready. Few physicians, confronted by a boy who is old enough to walk but who isn't, would comfort the mother by saying, 'Well, he'll walk when he's ready.' " (Blager, 1981, pp. 81–82).

Support for treating expressive delay as a disorder comes from studies demonstrating that expressive delay is associated with a variety of undesirable developmental sequelae. Children with delayed onset of expressive language are more likely to have academic problems (Aram & Nation, 1980; Fundudis, Kolvin, & Garside, 1980; Klackenberg, 1980), behavioral and psychiatric problems (Baker & Cantwell, 1982a, 1982b; Beitchman, Nair, Clegg, Ferguson, & Patel, 1986), and later problems in speech and language (Aram & Nation, 1980; Klackenberg, 1980).

Unfortunately, it is difficult to choose rationally between the view that ELD is a disorder worthy of active intervention and the view that ELD represents normal individual variation, because there is no prospective study of a carefully defined sample of young children with ELD. None of the studies cited above, in which an association between language delay and concurrent or later problems is shown, has carefully separated specific subgroups of children with language impairment. None has employed a rigorous and exclusive definition of ELD. Such a definition includes only expressive language deficit, without any accompanying deficit in receptive language or general cognitive skills. In keeping with this point, Lenoard (1988), among others, has argued persuasively for the need to differentiate subtypes in research on children with language impairment.

A second problem is that virtually all studies of ELD have focused on children at least 3 years old, although ELD is manifest by 24 months or earlier, and is of considerable concern to parents by then. The *DSM-III-R,* for instance, notes that "severe forms usually occur before age three and are easily recognized" (American Psychiatric Association, 1987, p. 46).

Pediatricians and other professionals are faced with relatively large numbers of 2-year-olds who have very limited expressive skills. One survey, in which parents in pediatricians' waiting rooms were interviewed, placed the prevalence of severe expressive delay as high as 15% of poor children and 7% of middle-class children at age 24 months (Rescorla, 1984). As we have indicated, there is very little information that would allow parents or professionals to make informed decisions about such children.

The paucity of information about the young child with ELD extends to the effects of treatment. It is not clear that there are interventions for ELD that are effective. One typical method of treatment of ELD involves placing the child in a therapeutic preschool environment involving ongoing in-class efforts to enhance language skills and occasional one-on-one speech therapy. Another typical method of treatment involves weekly in-office treatment by a private speech clinician. We know of no systematic outcome study of such treatments. Few early interventions for disabling conditions have been the subject of outcome research (Fischel, 1985). There is thus nothing remarkable about the absence of data on the effectiveness of preschool-based treatment of ELD. However, several studies suggest caution in assuming that such treatment works. Aram and Nation (1980) found no relationship between involvement in preschool intervention for speech and language problems and the occurrence of problems in children during their school years. Bishop and Edmundson (1987) found that language outcome for a group of preschool children with language impairment could be predicted from the severity of the child's initial impairment, but not from the amount of therapy that the child had received. Cantwell (1987) reported similar findings. In terms of relatively long-term outcomes, we have found no correlation between progress in expressive language for 2-year-old children with ELD and involvement in typical speech therapy (Fischel et al., 1989). Many studies show that specific speech and language teaching procedures can lead to acquisition of particular language forms (see reviews by Leonard, 1981, and Warren & Kaiser, 1988). An important question, however, is whether such specific instruction has any measurable long-term benefit for the child.

DISCRIMINANTS OF ELD

The aim of this section is to describe how children with ELD and their families differ from children with normal language development and their families. Finding a difference between a diagnostic group and a normal control group does not mean, of course, that the difference caused the condition that is the basis of the diagnosis. For example, schizophrenics as a group dress less well than the normal population, but no one would conclude that poor clothing causes schizophrenia. At the same time, a search for causes needs to begin with a search for differences, because the causes must lie somewhere within the set of characteristics that differentiate the index group from the rest of the population.

Biological Conditions

Gender

Male children appear to suffer from virtually all maladies at greater rates than female children. This gender imbalance is marked with respect to ELD. Of the roughly 100 2- and 3-year-old children who have been diagnosed by us as having ELD, 84% have been male. Since nearly all of these children were brought in by parents as a result of newspaper announcements of a program for "children who are slow to talk," there is no reason to expect any referral bias toward males. Silva (1980) reports that 67% of 3-year-old children with all types of language delays are males. Paul (1989) found that 76% of her sample of 31 2-year-olds with expressive delay were male, while 82% of Bishop and Edmundson's (1987) sample of 4-year-olds with language impairment were male. These data indicate clearly and consistently that all types of specific language impairments, including ELD, occur at disproportionate rates among male preschool children.

Genetic Factors

The etiology and course of various psychological problems are affected by genetic factors. Genetic influences have been documented by means of twin and adoption studies in disorders such as schizophrenia (Fischer, 1973; Wender, Rosenthal, Kety, Schulsinger, & Welner, 1974) and antisocial behavior (Christiansen, 1974; Mednick, Schulsinger, Higgins, & Bell, 1974). It has been posited that language delay is similarly influenced by inherited factors (Ludlow & Cooper, 1983). This hypothesis cannot currently be evaluated directly. Little is known about the etiology of language problems, and no twin or adoption studies have been conducted to examine the possibility of a genetic influence in the transmission of language disorders. Consanguinity studies (also termed *family history studies*) are currently the most relevant source of information on assessing genetic hypotheses about language deficits. Consanguinity studies examine the amount of familial aggregation of disorders. Such studies cannot conclusively establish a genetic role in the etiology of a disorder because they confound shared genetics with shared environment. That is, high concordance rates within families could be due to genetic factors, but might also result from living conditions that are common to family members. Despite this inherent ambiguity in interpreting familial aggregation of disorders, such studies can inform etiological theories, and are quite cost effective compared to twin or adoption studies.

Two recent consanguinity studies provide the most convincing evidence of familial aggregation in language disorders. Bishop and Edmundson (1986) briefly reported family history data in the context of a study on the relation of hearing loss to language delay. Reports obtained from the parents of 56 children with language impairment indicated that these children were significantly more likely than a sample of control children to have relatives who had been treated for speech or language problems.

Through interviews with mothers, Tallal, Ross, and Curtiss (1989) collected family history data on 76 children with language disorders and without cognitive deficits and 54 matched control children. They found that the mothers of children with language disorders were far more likely than mothers of controls to report that family members had a history of language problems, were held back in school, and/or had poor writing ability.

The interpretation of these findings is restricted by a problem that has plagued much of the research on language delay. Studies of language problems have often aggregated groups of children that may in fact be quite heterogeneous. Specifically, language disorders (i.e., problems in using and understanding language) and speech disorders (e.g., stuttering, phonological problems) are often undifferentiated (Beitchman et al., 1986; Jenkins, Bax, & Hart, 1980). Moreover, receptive and expressive delays are often considered together (Cantwell & Baker, 1980; Cantwell, Baker, & Mattison, 1980).

Whitehurst, Arnold, et al. (in press) used questionnaire data to assess the family history of speech, language, and school problems in 62 young children with ELD, and 55 children without such problems. In contrast to previous studies of language and speech problems, no strong familial component of ELD was found. Furthermore, family history was not predictive of later language development in children with ELD. These findings argue against genetic and familial causes of ELD, and attest to the importance of differentiating subtypes of early language problems. Language impairments that involve receptive delays may have genetic determinants, while ELD may not.

Laterality

Brain laterality as indicated by handedness has often been viewed as related to language development, perhaps because of the connection between handedness and cerebral dominance and Broca's area of the brain. About 70% of speech in left-handers is localized in the left hemisphere; for right-handers the figure is about 95% (Springer & Deutsch, 1989). We compared handedness (as reported by mothers) in 93 children with ELD and 91 controls. The proportion of left-handers was virtually the same in both groups (ELD = .33, controls = .31). These data suggest that laterality is not related to ELD.

Prematurity, Birth Weight, and Birth Complications

Birth complications are known to affect later language development (Cohen, Parmelee, Sigman, & Beckwith, 1988). However, the evidence does not support such a relation for ELD. In our sample of 91 children with ELD and 91 controls, average birth weight was normal (ELD = 7.9 pounds, controls = 8.0 pounds), and rates of prematurity (i.e., 35 weeks gestation or less) were low (ELD = 7.5%, controls = 8.8%). Birth complications, defined as any abnormal condition in the neonate or the mother other than a Caesarean section (e.g., jaundice, prolapsed cord, bleeding during pregnancy) were also similar in the two groups (ELD = 24%, controls = 22%). These data suggest that prematurity, birth weight, and birth complications are not related to ELD.

Oro-motor Deficiencies

Children might be slow to talk because of neurological conditions that make it difficult for them to control the organs of speech. We examined this issue by asking mothers of children with ELD and mothers of controls whether their children ever experienced problems chewing, ever choked on their food, or ever drooled. Rates of problems in chewing were very low (about 1%) and did not differ in the two populations. However, evidence supporting oro-motor deficiencies in children with ELD came from drooling and choking. Some incidence of drooling occurred in 32% of the children with ELD versus 21% of the controls ($\chi^2 = 7.29$, degrees of freedom = 1, $p < .01$). Likewise, 23% of children with ELD were reported to choke on their food at least occasionally versus 9% of the controls ($\chi^2 = 22.05$, degrees of freedom = 1, $p < .001$). Although the proportion of children with ELD who experienced either of these problems was small, we believe that these data offer support for the hypothesis that oro-motor problems are connected with ELD in some children.

Otitis Media

Otitis media, or inflammation of the middle ear, is a common disease of infancy and early childhood. Approximately 50% of all children experience at least one episode of otitis media during the first year of life; by 3 years of age, approximately two thirds of all children experience at least one episode; and one third of all children experience three or more episodes of otitis media prior to age 3 (Howie, 1980). During the acute phase of otitis media, children may experience pain, fever, and other overtly expressed symptoms. Otitis media is often associated with fluid in the ear (effusion) that persists after the acute phase of the infection has passed (Teele, Klein, & Rosner, 1980). The occurrence of otitis media is often associated with conductive hearing loss of a transient nature, and may lead to chronic auditory impairment (Bess, 1983).

Several studies have found a relationship between an early history of otitis media and later problems in language development. For instance, Teele et al. (1980) followed a cohort of 205 children from birth to 3 years of age. The presence of otitis media was periodically assessed by otoscopic examination. Tests of speech and language were administered when the children were 3 years old. Children who had had prolonged episodes of otitis media had significantly lower language scores. The correlation between the cumulative duration of otitis media and language scores was strongest for children from the highest socioeconomic levels. The length of time spent with otitis media in the first 6–12 months of life was most strongly associated with poorer language scores.

Lonigan et al. (1991) compared medical records of middle ear disease occurring up to 30 months of age in a population of 65 children with ELD and a control group of 50 children. No differences in the frequency, duration, or timing of medically documented episodes of otitis media were found. However, longitudinal analyses with the children with ELD revealed a significant relationship between otitis media and expressive language improvement. The strongest positive predictor of language improvement between 2 and 3 years of age was the amount of time spent with otitis media between 12 and 18 months of age. In other words, children with ELD with an early history of otitis media were likely to show more rapid progress in the development of expressive language than children with ELD without a history of otitis media.

These findings suggest that children with ELD represent two etiological populations depending on a history of otitis media. When ELD is caused primarily by otitis media during a critical period for the development of expressive language, improvement is highly likely. However, in the absence of such a history, the causes of ELD are likely to be more central and longlasting. The absence of between-group differences, coupled with the predictive power of otitis media history within the ELD group, suggests either that another factor interacts with otitis media to cause ELD or that otitis media depresses language development for all children.

Summary

The findings reviewed suggest that ELD is, in part, a function of biological conditions. Specifically, males are much more likely to experience ELD than are females, children with ELD are more likely to experience oro-motor problems than children with normally developing language, and children with ELD and an early history of otitis media are much more likely to improve than children with ELD and no such history. Birth complications, genetic factors, and laterality to not appear to be related to ELD.

Social-Interactional Factors in ELD

Demonstrating a role for biological factors in ELD does not negate the importance of environmental factors. Indeed, one would expect biological variables and environmental variables to interact, as they appear to do in ELD.

Family Size and Birth Order

Data on the relationship between family size and ELD are sketchy. The only investigation that has employed epidemiological methods is that of Richman and Stevenson (1977). They found that language delay occurred significantly more often among children from large families. The study is marred by the fact that expressive and receptive delays were not distinguished, and no attempt was made to control statistically for potentially confounding factors, such as socioeconomic status. Nevertheless, we have collected data that are consistent with the Richman and Stevenson conclusions. We compared 94 2-year-olds with ELD to 91 controls of similar socioeconomic background. Parents of the controls had responded to newspaper announcements of various studies of language development. In that sense, the route of recruitment for the controls was similar to that for the children with ELD. Our study found a strong correlation between the incidence of ELD and the number of children in the family ($\chi^2 = 22.23$, degrees of freedom $= 5$, $p = .0001$). These data should be interpreted with caution. A mother who does not work outside the home and whose child is developing normally may be much more likely to volunteer herself and her 2-year-old child for a study of language development if the child is a first born or only child than if the child has siblings. If the family is small, the mother will have more time to volunteer herself and her child for a research program; if the child is her first, the mother is much more likely to be curious (or anxious) about the child's language status. The result would be that mothers of 2-year-old children with older siblings would be less likely to volunteer for studies of normal language development. Recruitment of children with ELD would not suffer from such a bias, in that the child's status would motivate the mother to seek professional advice regardless of convenience issues, such as those that are a function of the number of children in the family. This bias would thus be likely to affect the study's finding. Needed here is a properly designed epidemiological study that would examine the influence of factors such as family size on the incidence of various types of language impairments.

Socioeconomic Status

Rescorla (1984) reports an inverse relationship between socioeconomic status and ELD. Prevalence of ELD among 2-year-olds seen in five pediatric clinics was approximately 10% in private practice clinics and approximately 17% in a primary-care medical clinic serving inner-city families on public assistance, thus suggesting a relationship. Unfortunately, Rescorla did not measure receptive language or cognitive ability. Thus, these conclusions may not be relevant to ELD.

Family Stress

Caulfield et al. (1989) administered the Parenting Stress Index (Abidin, 1983) to 34 mothers of 2-year-olds with ELD and 34 mothers of controls matched on age, sex, and demographic characteristics. There were no differences between the two groups of mothers on the Parent Domain of the Parent Stress Index, which includes scales related to depression, restriction of roles, sense of competence, attachment, relationship with spouse, social isolation, and parent health. However, mothers of children with ELD in this study gave their children significantly less favorable ratings on the acceptability subscale of the child domain, which addresses parental expectations concerning the child's physical, intellectual, and emotional characteristics. Taken together, these findings suggest that family stress is not a root cause of ELD, but that, not unexpectedly, having a child with ELD can add to family stress.

Verbal Interactions in the Family

It is possible that parents of children with ELD provide a verbal environment that is not supportive of the development of expressive language. Indeed, anxiety about this is expressed by many parents of children with ELD. Several studies have attempted to describe the nature of parental speech to children with language impairment. The available research is inconclusive. Some studies have suggested that the linguistic environment of children with language impairment is qualitatively or quantitatively different from that of children without impairment (Buium, Rynders, & Turnure, 1974; Marshall, Hegrenes, & Goldstein, 1973; Petersen & Sherrod, 1982; Wulbert, Inglis, Kriegsmann, & Mills, 1975). In contrast, other studies have suggested that parental speech to children with language impairment is highly similar to that directed at children without impairment (Conti-Ramsden & Friel-Patti, 1983; Cunningham, Siegel, van der Spuy, Clark, & Bow, 1985).

As with so much other research on language impairment, research on verbal interactions suffers because various categories of language impairment are aggregated. It is not only possible, but likely, that verbal interactions are substantially different for children with receptive language delays and children with ELD or articulation difficulties. An additional problem with the research on verbal interactions is that verbal interactions per se have not been the target of study. Instead, investigators have typically measured only the frequency of various categories of maternal speech, ignoring child speech and the contingent relations between child and parental speech. Consider, for example, the difference between the sentence "Tom is coming Sunday" spoken by a mother to a child to initiate a conversation and the same sentence spoken to the child immediately after the child has said, "Tom come Sunday."

Yet another problem with existing research on parental speech is that language interactions with children with language impairment have typically been compared to interactions with controls of the same chronological age. However, as Leifer and Lewis (1983) have pointed out, a difference between maternal behavior with children with language impairment and maternal behavior with children of the same age without language impairment may represent nothing more than maternal adjustment to the linguistic deficits of the former. Adjusting one's language to the ability level of one's listener is expected among mature communicators (Whitehurst & Sonnenschein, 1985), and should not be taken as evidence that the mother's language style somehow caused the child's language impairment.

Whitehurst, Fischel, et al. (1988) attempted to remedy some of the problems in previous research on language interactions by using a three-group design. Children with ELD were compared with two other control groups: same-age peers with equivalent receptive skills and younger children with equivalent expressive skills. If aberrant language interactions are responsible, in part, for ELD, one would expect language interactions in families of children with ELD to be different from those in either of the comparison groups. Conversely, if language interactions involving children with ELD are driven by the child's limited expressive abilities, one would expect those interactions to be similar to those that occur with younger children without language impairment who also have limited expressive vocabularies. Comparing major categories of pragmatic interaction (e.g., directives, *wh*-questions, repetition, correction, expansions), we found that 28-month-old children with ELD experienced a verbal environment very much like that of 17-month-olds without language impairment and unlike that of 28-month-old children without impairment. These results demonstrate clearly that verbal interactions in families of children with ELD are driven by the child's deficiencies in expression. In other words, the child's delay causes parents to speak differently, not vice versa.

Behavior and Discipline in the Family

The association between language problems and behavioral disorders of childhood has been documented extensively (e.g., Baker & Cantwell, 1982a, 1982b; Beitchman et al., 1986; Cantwell & Baker, 1980; Jenkins et al., 1980; Richman & Stevenson, 1977). For example, in a group of 705 randomly sampled 3-year-olds, Richman and Stevenson (1977) reported a base rate prevalence of behavior problems of 14% as assessed by parental responses on a behavior screening interview. Of those children in the sample who exhibited language delay, 58% had concurrent behavior problems. In a sample of 418 preschool children, Jenkins et al. (1980) also found an association between low language scores and behavior problems. In this study, behavior problem ratings were obtained from a physician's evaluation of parental responses on a structured behavior interview.

In a well-designed study, Beitchman et al. (1986) compared the rates of behavioral and emotional problems in a group of 142 children with diagnosed speech and language disorders and in a control group. Frequency estimates of psychiatric disorders were based on a semistructured psychiatric interview with a subset of children from each group. The estimated frequency of psychiatric disorder (i.e., at least one *DSM-III* Axis I disorder) was 48.7% for the children with speech or language impairment and 12% for the control group.

Axis I diagnoses were then grouped into three categories: attention deficit disorder, emotional disturbance, and conduct disorder. The estimated prevalence rates for children in the test group were 30.4% for attention deficit disorder, 12.8% for emotional disturbance, and 5.5% for conduct disorder. The corresponding rates for the control group were 4.5%, 1.5%, and 6.0%, respectively.

Clinical reports have also suggested that early language delay is often associated with behavioral disturbance. Cantwell and Baker (1980) investigated the incidence of psychiatric disorders in 200 consecutive admissions to a community speech and language clinic. Fifty-three percent of the clinic sample were found to have at least one psychiatric disorder as diagnosed by *DSM-III* criteria. Thirty children (14% of the sample) received the diagnosis of attention deficit disorder with hyperactivity. Other common diagnoses were avoidant disorder (8%) and oppositional disorder (5%). Children in speech-oriented special education classes have also been rated by their teachers as having more problems than children in regular classrooms, as measured by the Quay Behavior Problem Checklist (Lindholm & Touliatos, 1979).

Although the correlation of language and behavior problems has been documented extensively, research on this relationship suffers from at least two important limitations. The first is the problem encountered repeatedly in research on language impairment, namely, the failure to differentiate significantly diverse types of speech and language disorders. When studies have differentiated types of language disorder, interesting results have emerged. For example, Baker and Cantwell (1982b) categorized children as exhibiting a pure speech disorder, a speech and language disorder, or a pure language disorder. The prevalence of diagnosed psychiatric disorder was much higher for the group with pure language impairment (95%) than for the group with pure speech impairment (29%), with the group with speech and language impairment (45%) falling in between. The distribution of developmental disorders, such as enuresis and mental retardation, followed the same pattern. Given the variation in the relationship between language and behavior problems shown here for broad groupings of speech and language problems, there is need for research that identifies the behavioral characteristics of carefully defined subgroups of children with language impairment. The nature of the relationship between language and behavior can then be examined within those subgroups.

The second shortcoming in the research on language delay and behavior problems is the primary reliance on parent and teacher report in assessing inappropriate behavior (Jenkins et al., 1980; Lindholm & Touliatos, 1979; Stevenson & Richman, 1976). The benefits of multimodal assessment of problems, and specifically, the importance of including behavioral observation in clinical assessment, has been emphasized in the recent literature on assessment (Barton & Ascione, 1984; Mash & Terdal, 1981; Nelson & Hayes,

1979). Barton and Ascione (1984) suggested that observation of child behaviors may be less subject to inferences and subjective criteria than parental report. In addition, direct observations that include the parent may allow the separation of child effects from parent effects (Barton & Ascione, 1984; Nelson & Hayes, 1979). Child behavior, adult behavior, and adult perception are all inextricably combined in parent or teacher reports.

Caulfield et al. (1989) examined parent–child interaction and behavior problems in 34 2-year-old children with ELD using behavioral observations. They predicted that children with ELD would exhibit more negative and noncompliant behavior than controls, and that parents would rate children with ELD as exhibiting more problematic behavior. Alternatively, if the association between language and behavior problems was not found in this group of children, a subgroup of children with language delay for whom behavior problems are not related to language delay would have been identified, or behavior problems in children with language delay could be posited to develop only later. Such findings would warrant longitudinal study of these children to establish whether behavior problems ever arise and, if so, at what point. A finding, for example, that the youngest children with ELD do not exhibit an elevated rate of behavior problems but do so later in development would be consistent with a causal model in which language delay produces behavior problems. Each of these potentially important lines of inquiry depends on establishing the relationship, if any, between ELD and behavior problems in 2-year-olds.

Parent–child interaction was observed in a semistructured play and clean-up situation modified from the paradigm used by Vaughn, Kopp, and Krakow (1984). The clean-up portion of the play session was videotaped and coded by independent observers. The behavior codes included categories of maternal directive and responsive behavior as well as child compliance and noncompliance. A MANOVA conducted on the child behavior data was significant ($F(7, 32) = 3.278$, $p < .01$). Univariate tests of individual child behavior categories showed several group differences. The delayed group engaged in higher rates of negative behaviors, including crying, screaming, hitting, and throwing toys. The delayed group also engaged in a higher rate of nonverbal communication. Univariate tests on the maternal behavior data showed that mothers of control children engaged in higher rates of non–task oriented conversation and mothers of children with ELD were more likely to use physical discipline. These results confirmed the hypothesis that children with ELD exhibit elevated rates of problem behaviors compared to matched controls.

Caulfield (1989) followed up on the finding of elevated rates of behavior problems in children with ELD by investigating two models of the relationship between language delay and behavior problems. The frustration model holds that a child with inadequate verbal skills for a given situation will exhibit negative behaviors out of frustration. These behaviors may function to communicate the child's needs to others, leading to reward for problem behavior. The self-control model suggests that expressive language is important in the development of self-control. Children with limited expressive language are less able to control their behavior and are more likely to behave impulsively.

A group of 23 2-year-old children with ELD and a group of 20 controls were observed in laboratory tasks that varied in communicative demands. For example, pointing was sufficient for the child to respond correctly in one task, naming was necessary in another task, and reading (which none of the children could do) was necessary in another task. Results showed an interaction of task and group: children with ELD and children without language impairment had very low rates of misbehavior in the nonverbal pointing task (which was communicatively easy for both groups), while both sets of children had elevated rates of misbehavior in the reading task (which was communicatively difficult for both). However, in the naming task (which was difficult for children with ELD and easy for the normal group), the children with ELD showed much higher rates of misbehavior such as tantruming and whining than did the control group. These results support the frustration model of problem behavior in children with language impairment by demonstrating that situations that are communicatively difficult generate misbehavior. The implication is that because of their limited vocabularies, children with ELD experience more communication difficulties than children without language impairment. Caulfield (1989) investigated this hypothesis by asking mothers of children with and children without ELD to estimate the number of times a week that their children experienced communicative situations that exceeded their verbal skills. This figure was 70.52 for children with ELD and 9.78 for children without ELD ($p < .001$).

Overall, the frustration model receives strong support from these findings. The self-control model was not supported. Individual measures of self-control (e.g., the ability to delay gratification in a laboratory waiting task) did not differ between the test and control groups and did not correlate with expressive skills within either group.

Summary

Our survey of research on social-interactional factors in the development of ELD identified family size, family socioeconomic status, and patterns of misbehavior and discipline as potential discriminants of children with ELD, with misbehavior and discipline being the most clearly established of these variables. In contrast, family stress as experienced by the mother exclusive of the stress associated with having an ELD child was not higher for the ELD group. Family verbal interactions for children with ELD are different from those of children of the same chronological age without ELD, but similar to those of younger children at the same level of expressive development. This suggests that the verbal environment in the family is affected by the child's language delay, rather than a root cause of that delay.

PRELINGUISTIC CHARACTERISTICS OF CHILDREN WITH ELD

Theorists have debated for decades whether infant babble is continuous with the development of early speech. Jesperson (1925) was among the first to make a strong argument for discontinuity, describing babble as a meaningless playful activity in which the infant does not intend to produce particular sounds. In contrast, Lorimer (1928) and Lewis (1951) conceived of the transition from babble to speech as a continuous process, the transformation of "bits of babble" into meaningful words. The continuity position fell out of favor with the English translation of Jacobson's monograph, *Child Language Aphasia and Phonological Universals* (1941/1968). Jacobson elaborated the earlier ideas of Jesperson (1925), citing as further evidence of discontinuity that some infants exhibit a "silent period" during the transition from babble to speech.

More recently, the pendulum of opinion seems to have swung back toward a continuity position, based on research showing that sounds that are favored during babble continue to predominate in early words. For example, Oller, Wieman, Doyle, and Ross (1975) found that infants' "favorite" sounds during babble were inserted where they did not belong in early words, and "nonfavored" sounds were omitted when they should have been uttered. Similarly, Vihman, Macken, Miller, Simmons, and Miller (1985) found that for individual children, the consonant distribution, vocalization length, and phonotactic structure of babbled sounds were virtually identical to those of first words.

Whitehurst, Smith, Fischel, Arnold, and Lonigan (in press) addressed issues of continuity between babble and language development for 2-year-olds with ELD. Within that population, they wanted to determine if the frequency, complexity, and/or social function of babble facilitates the later acquisition of expressive vocabulary. A facilitative relationship on all of these dimensions would mean that among a population of children with ELD at the very beginnings of acquisition of expressive vocabulary, those who babbled most frequently, with the greatest complexity, and with a greater social use of babble would acquire vocabulary faster than those who were at lower levels on these dimensions.

There is no relevant research on the relation between babble and speech in children with ELD. However, research on children without language impairment suggests that frequent, complex, pragmatically functional babble should facilitate expressive language. Vihman and Miller (1988), for instance, found continuity of form and function between babble, gestures, and words for children in the earliest stages of the acquisition of expressive vocabulary. Bates, Benigni, Bretherton, Camaioni, and Volterra (1979) have posited a mechanism for such continuity: the child's understanding of symbolic and pragmatic functions. Presumably, children who demonstrate that their babble and gestures can be used to make comments to and requests of adults have acquired a conceptual prerequisite for expressive vocabulary.

Alternatively, one might conceptualize babble and expressive vocabulary as becoming competitive communication systems by the time children are 2 years old. Children with ELD who produce frequent, complex, or pragmatically functional babble might have less motivation to acquire words than children who have less developed babble.

Clarification of this issue would have important clinical implications for children whose expressive language is delayed. For example, if frequent communicative babble is positively correlated with later acquisition of words, one might attempt to intervene so as to increase such babble in 2-year-olds who have not yet developed expressive vocabulary and who also babble at low rates. Knowing the relationship between babble and early words in children with ELD would also allow improved predictions of the course of language development for individual children. This could be very useful to practitioners and parents in deciding how to manage these children.

We examined the utterances of 37 2-year-old children with ELD while they were interacting with their mothers. Utterances were divided into words, which were recorded verbatim, and babble. Babble consisted of any non-vegetative, noncry utterance other than words. Babbled utterances were also coded for whether they contained consonants or consisted entirely of vowels. In addition, both words and babble were coded as to whether they were socially interactive, defined as produced in response to the mother or with visual attentiveness to her.

A hierarchical multiple regression approach was used to identify the best predictors of the children's expressive language scores, obtained 5 months after the natural language sample of words and babble. We found that two variables, rate of words and rate of vowel babble, were the best predictors of language progress and together accounted for much of the variance in outcome scores (multiple $R = .637$, $F(2, 34) = 11.62$, $p = .0003$). The beta weights for these two variables were similar in size and opposite in sign (rate of words, $\beta = .498$, $p = .0010$; rate of vowel babble, $\beta = -.470$, $p = .0016$). This means that children with the highest rate of words and the lowest rate of vowel babble showed the greatest gains in expressive language over the 5 months between assessment and follow-up.

One derived variable, the ratio of consonant babble to total babble, was also examined. This produced the highest simple correlation with language outcome of any single variable in the study ($r = .501$, $p = .0017$). This suggests that consonant babble is in function closer to words than to vowel babble, and that children who produce predominantly consonant babble are best able to handle the demands of vocabulary acquisition.

A developmental sequence of vowel babble to consonantal babble to words can be supported within the frequency domain by the data reported earlier. This is in line with classic continuity theory, and leads to the straight-forward prediction that children who are more advanced in the first two steps of this developmental sequence will reach the third step faster. However, this relationship is complicated substantially by the finding that the child's frequency of use of words and frequency of use of vowel babble at initial assessment *independently* predict expressive language 5 months later. Under the classic continuity position, one would expect a negative relationship between words and vowel babble at initial assessment (i.e., children who are producing a high frequency or proportion of vowel babble should be producing a low frequency of words and vice versa). However, there is essentially no relationship between words and vowel babble at the initial assessment: knowing the frequency of a child's vowel babble tells us nothing about the contemporaneous frequency of words or vice versa.

Our interpretation of these findings is that vowel babble and words represent functionally competitive communication systems for 2-year-old children with ELD. The screams, whines, and grunts that constitute vowel babble can be part of an effective social communication system—witness Caulfield's (1989) finding that children with ELD have much larger repertoires of nonverbal communication skills than do controls, with the typical communication pattern being a combination of grunting and pointing. High rates of vowel babble, particularly as a proportion of all babble, indicate that this system is working for the child. If the system is working, the child will be slower to develop expressive language, even if he or she has learned to use a few words. A successful communication system involving vowel babble does not prevent the child from learning words (hence the independence of words and vowel babble at the initial assessment), but it nevertheless undercuts the motivation for continued acquisition of words (hence the negative relationship between vowel babble and expressive language 5 months later). The situation is perhaps similar to that of the English-speaking tourist in Spain, who picks up a few words of Spanish but is unmotivated to learn more since the Spaniards whose livelihood depends on tourism are able to communicate in English. Whitehurst and Valdez-Menchaca (1988) have demonstrated exactly this effect with preschool children, who showed limited use of words in a second language as long as they could communicate successfully in their native language. By analogy, we view vowel babble as a native language for children with ELD who produce it at high rates. Conventional expressive language is a second language that will be acquired slowly because the child's native language is effective. Children who produce vowel babble at relatively low rates will have stronger motivation to acquire language because there is no competing communication system.

The clinical implications of this position are straightforward. First, interventions for children with ELD should withdraw support for attempts to communicate via vowel babble and gesturing. Removing the communicative rewards for babble serves as a motivational foundation for the child's acquisition and use of expressive vocabulary. The present research suggests a distinction between vowel and consonant babble: Consonant babble might be treated as protowords, since it is positively correlated with language progress, whereas vowel babble might be treated as gestural in function and no longer rewarded.

INTERVENING WITH CHILDREN WITH ELD

The research described in this chapter suggests but does not compel directions for treatment of children with ELD. The picture that emerges is as follows: children with ELD experience unusual difficulties in learning to talk for reasons that are largely biological. These reasons include oro-motor deficiencies, hearing problems resulting from middle ear disease, and perhaps a complex of genetic variables that predispose male children to language problems. Children with ELD and their families react to expressive inability in a number of ways. The child develops an extensive repertoire of gestures and vocalizations that serve his or her communicative needs. The parents, who are concerned about the child's delay and who need to communicate with the child, are all too ready to respond to and interpret these nonverbal communications. By the time the child is 30 months of age, these grunts and gestures have become a rich communicative system that competes with the development of normal expressive language. Because pointing and grunting are not as informative as words, children with ELD experience much communicative frustration. These frustrations are often accompanied by whining, crying, and other misbehavior, which often spur parents to discover what the child wants and provide it. This produces problem behaviors in children with ELD, which some parents may treat more leniently than they might if the child were not expressively delayed. Finally, because parents tailor their language to the child based on the child's level of expressive language, children with ELD typically generate a language environment that is more appropriate for younger children.

This model of the development of early ELD suggests that successful treatment will have to shift the pattern of reward for communication to expressive language and away from its competitor, gesturing and grunting. It suggests that misbehavior will have to be diminished as a part of the parent regaining control of the child's communications. And it suggests that because the child has biological difficulties in talking and is already far behind, an environment will have to be provided that is more supportive of expression and more intense than the normal environment for a 2-year-old learning language.

We previously mentioned that there is a paucity of research on the long-term efficacy of treatment of early language impairments, including the treatment of ELD. Positive conclusions in the literature about long-term effects of early language intervention do not appear to be justified. For instance, Huntley, Holt, Butterfill, and Latham (1988) concluded that the benefits of an early language intervention that they evaluated "were persisting 5 years after it ended" (p. 136). However, there was no control group to support this conclusion. Several studies that have examined the long-term adjustment of preschool children with language impairment have found no evidence supporting the efficacy of the types of treatment typically available in the community (Aram & Nation, 1980; Bishop & Edmundson, 1987; Cantwell, 1987).

We wanted to use a therapeutic approach that is different from the typical community-based alternative, and to assess the efficacy of that approach over the long term. We developed a parent training, home-based treatment for ELD. There are many reasons for preferring this type of milieu therapy over the more traditional situation in which a language therapist works one-on-one with a child (Warren & Kaiser, 1988), and detailed parent-training procedures have shown some success with children who suffer general language impairment (Zelazo, Kearsley, & Ungerer, 1984).

Our treatment program consisted of seven standard assignments that could be modified and tailored, where necessary, to individual families' needs. These assignments were delivered to parents in biweekly office visits that lasted about 30 minutes each. Typically, only one parent—the mother—attended training sessions, to which she brought her child. The child, however, was not involved directly in the training sessions. Usually, a research assistant kept the child involved in a separate play room while the mother met with the clinician.

The training sessions with the mother consisted of a discussion of the results of the previous assignment and delivery of the new assignment. The training session always ended with role play, with the trainer playing the role of the child, and the mother playing herself. The mother was given corrective feedback as necessary until she reacted consistently and as instructed to examples of child behavior.

The actual written assignments that were delivered to mothers are available from the authors. Table 1 outlines the principal goals and procedures of each assignment. We shall discuss two of the assignments to illustrate the treatment program.

Assignment 1, which we believe is critical, focuses on shifting motivation from gestural communication to vocal communication. All of the children with ELD with whom we have had contact communicate very successfully by pointing, nodding, grunting, and pulling their parents from place to place. As noted previously, children with ELD engage in such symbolic gestures at much higher frequencies than children of the same age without

Table 1. Biweekly assignments for children being treated for ELD

Assignment	Description	Purpose
1	Forced choice between favored and nonfavored objects with the favored object given to the child only if he or she tries to label it or imitates parent's labeling of it	Shift motivation from gesturing to talking
2	For a selected list of 20 words, parent asks wh-question when the child is interested in the corresponding referent and gives item or complies with child request only if child tries to label object or tries to imitate parent's labeling.	Establish a small working vocabulary of noun labels
3	Incidental teaching procedures in which parent asks child to label or imitate parent's labeling for any activity in which the child shows interest and over which the parent can control access	Extend the parent's teaching of noun labels to any target suggested by the child's behavior
4	Introduction of requirement of two-word combinations involving negation, recurrent, nonexistence, and verb-object requests	Increase grammatical complexity of language
5	Introduction of labeling exercise in which the child is rewarded with praise and attention rather than with receipt of the activity named	Teach the child to talk for attention rather than for specific reward
6	Introduction of descriptive task in the context of story time. The parent follows one-word labels by the child with specific wh-questions (e.g., "What does the duck say?").	Expand the child's descriptive skills and encourage spontaneous speech
7	Use by parent of open-ended questions in story time (e.g., "Tell me what is going on in this picture."). In addition, parent is given rules involving saying more to the child when the child initiates a conversation and getting the child to say more in response to parent-initiated turns.	Increase spontaneous language and give the parent strategies for continued stimulation of the child following the end of treatment

language impairment (Caulfield, 1989). We conceptualize symbolic gesturing in 2-year-olds with ELD as competitive with normal expressive language. Children with ELD might prefer symbolic gesturing to vocalization for a number of reasons, including oro-motor deficiencies and hearing problems. Whatever the reason, these children have developed a preference for nonverbal communication that we believe must be altered if the children are to benefit from any form of intervention.

We conducted a motivational assessment with the parents to determine objects, foods, and activities that the child either liked very much or did not prefer. These were then formed into pairs, each pair consisting of a preferred and a nonpreferred item. For example, a child might have preferred a toy car to a block from a block set. All the paired items were things the child could do without (i.e., items such as milk were not used). Several times a day the parent presented pairs of these items to the child and provided a choice (e.g., "This is a car and this is a block: Which do you want?") Initially, the child always pointed. The parent presented the choice again, telling the child that he or she must say which one he or she wanted. Again the child pointed. The parent feigned misunderstanding and gave the child the nonpreferred item. The child typically fussed or had a tantrum. The parents were trained to ignore this behavior. Later, the choice was presented again. Soon the child made an attempt to label the preferred object, which he or she immediately received with much praise.

In general, once the motivational issue was handled in Assignment 1, the later assignments were drawn from the literature on normal language development. They were designed to highlight and intensify what parents of children without language impairment do that seems to be helpful in acquiring more complex language. The aim was not to have the parents replicate the timing and frequency of stimulation that is characteristic of interaction between children without language impairment and their parents (we do not take that pattern as optimal), but rather to take the most effective elements of normal interaction and intensify them.

For example, in the last assignments, parents were trained to read to their child in ways that encouraged the child to express him- or herself verbally. For example, parents were instructed to ask the child open-ended questions, such as "What is going on in this picture?" The child's responses were then expanded by the parent. We have shown in related research that these book reading procedures have powerful effects on children's development of expressive language (Whitehurst, Falco, et al., 1988; Valdez-Menchaca, 1990).

Does Intervention Work?

A variety of data were gathered on children at each of four assessment periods. We focus on four of those measures that are most relevant to language progress: the Peabody Picture Vocabulary Test-Revised, the One-Word Picture Vocabulary Test, the expressive subscale of the Illinois Test of Psycholinguistic Abilities (ITPA), and the 50-item screening test of the Templin-Darley Tests of Articulation, second edition.

Results from these four tests can be presented in several forms. We chose to present standard scores on each of the three expressive language measures, corrected for each child's receptive language ability. Our measure of receptive language ability was the Peabody Picture Vocabulary Test-Revised. Thus, the child's standard score on the Peabody at each assessment period was subtracted from the child's standard scores on each of the three expressive tests. We did this to obtain a measure of specific expressive delay, which is, by definition, relative to receptive delay.

Figure 1 presents the test results for the treatment and control groups at four assessment periods: 28-month pretest (mean age = 27.95 months, standard deviation = 3.4), 34-month posttest (mean age = 33.9 months, standard deviation = 3.84), 44-month posttest (mean age = 43.7 months, standard deviation = 4.63) and 65-month posttest (mean age = 65.2 months, standard deviation = 4.34), where the months in each case are the average chronological age at which the children were assessed. All scores are expressed on a standard score scale in which the mean is 100 and the standard deviation is 15, (i.e., a typical IQ scale). The obtained standard deviations for each measure for each group at each age were slightly less than 15 (mean standard deviation = 13.48).

Figure 1a shows that the Peabody scores for the two groups were in the normal range at each assessment point. The groups began at equivalent levels but diverged at the 44-month and 65-month posttests. This was due to differential drop-out characteristics across the treatment and control groups. We did not expect treatment to affect the Peabody scores since the children had no deficiency in this area and the treatment was not directed to receptive language. The important point from Figure 1a is that the children in this study have normal receptive language and, by inference, normal intelligence at all assessment points. Normal intelligence was confirmed by formal assessments using the Leiter International Performance Scales at the pretest and the information and geometric forms subtests from the Wechsler Preschool and Primary Scale of Intelligence (Wechsler, 1967) at the 65-month posttest. For the entire sample, mean IQ based on the Leiter Scales was 126. Wechsler subscale IQ at the 65-month posttest was 108 for the entire sample. No child had Peabody or Wechsler scores below 85 at any assessment point.

Figure 1b displays progress in expressive vocabulary across time. Here the two groups differed significantly at the 34-month posttest. The treatment group had improved to a point at which they were only 11 language quotient points behind their receptive skills, while the control group was 22 points behind. This difference was mirrored in other dependent measures not repre-

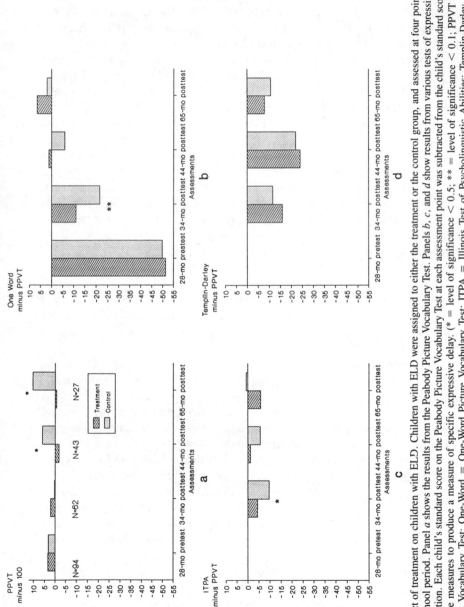

Figure 1.   Effect of treatment on children with ELD. Children with ELD were assigned to either the treatment or the control group, and assessed at four points during the preschool period. Panel *a* shows the results from the Peabody Picture Vocabulary Test. Panels *b*, *c*, and *d* show results from various tests of expressive skill and articulation. Each child's standard score on the Peabody Picture Vocabulary Test at each assessment point was subtracted from the child's standard score on the expressive measures to produce a measure of specific expressive delay. (* = level of significance < 0.5; ** = level of significance < 0.1; PPVT = Peabody Picture Vocabulary Test; One-Word = One-Word Picture Vocabulary Test; ITPA = Illinois Test of Psycholinguistic Abilities; Templin-Darley = Templin-Darley Tests of Articulation.)

sented in the figure: the treatment group was 7 months ahead of the control group on months of language age from the One-Word ($F = 10.08$, degrees of freedom $= 62$, $p = .003$), was 4 months ahead on months of language age from the ITPA ($F = 11.26$, degrees of freedom $= 60$, $p = .002$), showed an average change score across these two measures of 9.5 months of language age versus 2.2 months in the control group ($F = 26.69$, degrees of freedom $= 61$, $p < .001$), had an average expressive IQ across the One-Word and the ITPA of 94 versus 85 for the control group ($F = 5.50$, degrees of freedom $= 61$, $p = .021$), and had 72% of its members within the normal range (i.e., above 84) on the One-Word versus 41% of the members of the control group ($X^2 = 5.93$, $N = 62$, degrees of freedom $= 1$, $p = .014$). However, these strong and consistent differences were not maintained at later assessment points. The two groups were not statistically different at the 44-month and 65-month posttests, although the treatment group continued to surpass the control group in absolute terms, as shown in Figure 1b. Both groups were in the normal range at the last two posttests. Combining subjects in the treatment and control groups, only 12% had scores below 85 on the One-Word at 44 months, and only 4% had scores below 85 at 65 months.

Two important points emerge from Figure 1b. First, treatment worked by moving children into the normal range on expressive vocabulary as measured at the posttest. Second, by 44 months of age, the vocabulary skills of both groups of children had caught up with their receptive skills, and this continued to be true at 65 months. Thus, these children were no longer expressively delayed in vocabulary, whether or not they participated in our home treatment program.

Figure 1c displays results for the ITPA. No data are presented for the 28-month pretest because the ITPA has a floor for language age of 24 months. Thus, it is insensitive to the degree of delay in this population of children, whose expressive skills are in keeping with those of a nondelayed 13-month-old. Simple t-tests on the group differences at each assessment point are not significant. However, there is a significant difference favoring the experimental group at the 34-month posttest on the measure of months of language age on the ITPA. Furthermore, the corrected score at the 34-month posttest that is the basis for Figure 1c is statistically significant if a more sensitive test is employed by covarying out chronological age at 34 months and One-Word score at 28 months ($t = 2.43$, degrees of freedom $= 57$, $p = .017$). Finally, 83% of the treatment group and 57% of the control group fell within the normal range ($\chi^2 = 5.82$, $N = 61$, degrees of freedom $= 1$, $p < .05$). As with the One-Word scores, performance on the ITPA for both groups was well within the normal range and not different from the level of receptive ability at the previous two posttests. In terms of individual subjects, 16% were below the normal range at 44 months, and 7% were below normal at 65 months.

Figure 1d displays the results from the Templin-Darley Tests of Articulation. This test of articulation was not administered at the 28-month pretest. No differences between groups were expected on the Templin-Darley, since the treatment intervention had no content that was relevant for articulation skills. The data are consistent with this expectation. The interesting and important point to draw from Figure 1d concerns the degree of articulation problems at 44 months. The entire sample averaged 23 standard score points below the mean receptive level (i.e., 1.53 standard deviations) at this assessment point, and 35% of the children were below the normal range. Their average Templin-Darley raw score of 16.6 fell below the cut-off score for the test, suggesting inadequate articulation skills for their age. Articulation skills actually decreased relative to receptive skills between 34 and 44 months, at a time when expressive vocabulary skills were improving to within the normal range.

Figure 1d indicates that the phonological errors that are evident at 44 months had diminished by 65 months, at which point average articulation skills were within the normal range and only 0.6 standard deviations behind receptive skills. In terms of individual subjects, 78% fell within the normal range. These findings are remarkably consistent with those of Bishop and Edmundson (1987), who also found that 78% of a sample of children with exclusively phonological problems at age 4 had no measurable speech or language difficulties by 5.5 years. Whether this means that children with ELD are entirely normal by 5.5 years of age, or have developed other problems, is an issue to which we shall return.

What Other Clinical Services
Did the Children Receive and with What Effects?

We did not accept children into the treatment program who were receiving other speech and language services. Parents of children in treatment were free to seek other services for their children after our intervention had ended. Parents of control group children were free to seek speech and language services at any time. We collected data on use of therapeutic services at each of the three posttest periods. Services were defined as regular clinical contact with a speech and language professional either in or out of school. Parents in both groups sought speech or language therapy for their children at high rates. At 34 months, 31% of the control group was receiving special services. By 44 months, this figure had risen to 65% for the control group and 56% for the treatment group. At the 65-month posttest, parents of 64% of the children in the control group reported that their child had received special speech or language services during the period since their 34-month posttest, compared to 42% in the treatment group.

Our records on service utilization allow for an interesting quasiexperiment on the effects of preschool speech and language interventions other than our own. We conducted t-tests on a variety of dependent variables at 34, 44, and 65 months as a function of whether the child was reported to have been receiving clinical services at each of those assessments. We excluded children in our home-based treatment group from these tests at 34 months, but included them at the later assessment points. There were no effects that would support the efficacy of the community-based services the children received. Generally, there were no statistically significant differences between children who were and children who were not receiving community-based clinical services. The few exceptions to this generalization were all in a direction that favored children who had not received clinical services: children who were reported to have been receiving clinical services at 34 months scored lower on the Templin-Darley at 65 months ($t = 2.40$, degree of freedom = 9, $p = .042$); children who were reported to have been receiving clinical services at 44 months scored lower on the One-Word at 65 months ($t = 2.73$, degrees of freedom = 18, $p = .014$). The first of these effects may reflect the fact that the children who were tested at 65 months and who were receiving clinical services at 34 months had significantly lower scores on the ITPA at 34 months. However, such a confound was not present in the negative relationship between clinical services at 44 months and One-Word scores at 65 months.

We examined this issue from a slightly different perspective by identifying eight children who never received clinical speech and language services, and comparing them at each assessment point with all other children on all measures of language and cognition. There were no differences that approached significance between these two groups on any measure, including the initial severity of their language problems.

EDUCATIONAL AND CLINICAL IMPLICATIONS

Home-Based Intervention Is Effective in Treating Severe Delay in Expressive Vocabulary

Several important conclusions emerge from these results. Severe delay in expressive vocabulary can be treated successfully with a home-based intervention that uses the parents as therapists. Success is defined as substantial increases in expressive language skills during and immediately after treatment, compared with a control group.

Different Symptoms Are Associated with ELD at Different Ages

ELD among 2-year-olds is primarily manifest as delay in expressive vocabulary, while ELD in 3- and 4-year-olds is primarily manifest as errors in phonology.

ELD May Be Self-Correcting

By 5–6 years of age, there were no measured abnormalities among children who were diagnosed as having ELD at 2 years of age. Three caveats are necessary. First, there were no measures of pragmatic or syntactic development in this study at later follow-ups. It is possible that the children who were included at the 65-month posttest had deficiencies in those areas of language or in other areas of development, such as social interactions. If so, the deficiencies were subtle and not apparent in our examination of the children. Second, it is possible that problems will emerge later in the development of these children. Scarborough and Dobrich (1990) have reported the later occurrence of reading disabilities in a small sample of children with early language delays who appeared to catch up in their language development by 5 years of age. Third, it is possible that the developmental course of ELD may be different in children reared in poverty. The subjects in the present study were from middle-class families.

Phonological Problems Are Not Affected by Intervention that Improves Vocabulary Skills

A home-based intervention for 2-year-olds with ELD, while effective in accelerating vocabulary skills, did not decrease the likelihood of later phonological problems. Such an intervention had no measurable effects by 5–6 years of age. The failure to obtain significant effects at later follow-ups may have been due in part to low statistical power as a result of reduced sample size. However, all the differences that were statistically nonsignificant were also small in absolute terms, suggesting that any long-term effects of the intervention were not clinically important.

Community-Based Intervention Is Not Effective in Treating ELD

Traditional community-based special services for children with ELD had no demonstrable effects at any point in time. By combining many types of community-based services in our analysis we may have masked positive effects from a subset of those types of services. However, since the vast majority of ELD children in this sample had no demonstrable cognitive or linguistic deficiencies by the time they were 5½ years old, issues of the efficacy of community-based therapy may be moot.

DIRECTIONS FOR FUTURE RESEARCH

Most large-scale research projects raise as many questions as they answer. Our work on ELD is no exception. The following are among the many research issues that arise from the work reviewed in this chapter:

1. We found (from parent reports) that children with ELD were more likely to choke on food and drool than controls. Could more sensitive measures of oro-motor development serve as clinically useful risk factors for general or specific ELD?

2. We found that children with ELD with an early history of otitis media showed more rapid progress in expressive language than children with ELD without a history of otitis. Does otitis media serve to depress language development in all children, including those with ELD? Or does it interact with other variables that are unique to the child with ELD to potentiate problems in expressive development? Why does otitis media affect expressive development? Does it distort the child's ability to compare his or her verbal productions with those of adult models, does it affect parental stimulation of the child, or does it function through a more central mechanism?

3. In two studies, family size has been shown to be a simple correlate of ELD. Would family size remain a correlate of ELD if potentially confounding variables such as social class were controlled? If so, does this suggest that deficits in parent–child verbal interactions play a causal role in the development of expressive delay in at least some children?

4. What is the relationship between ELD and social class? Does ELD vary inversely with social class, or is expressive delay among children of low-income parents more likely to be accompanied by receptive delay?

5. We demonstrated that communicative frustration was a source of behavior problems in children with ELD. Are individual differences in parenting skills related to the extent to which behavior problems develop in children with language delays? Should behavior problems be treated along with language problems, or can language therapy work effectively in isolation from the child's other problems?

6. We demonstrated that consonant babble was positively associated with subsequent expressive growth in children with ELD, while the opposite was true of vowel babble. Is this also true for children with general language delay, or for children without language impairment? Since consonant babble may be a marker for articulation skills, might effective therapy for expressive delay incorporate measures for increasing a child's articulatory fluency?

7. We demonstrated that there were few lasting effects of early ELD through 5½ years of age. Are children with a history of early ELD at risk for school-related problems even though they appear to catch up to other children by kindergarten? If so, what distinguishes those children who do not have later problems from those who do?

8. Might the intervention program that was shown to be effective over the short term with children with ELD also be effective with children with more general language impairments?

CONCLUSION

Specific ELD is a complex phenomenon with many determinants. At least in middle-class children, its onset appears to be related to biological variables. However, children with ELD create environments that exacerbate their condition because nonverbal forms of communication become successful competitors with normal expressive language. A parent training, home-based intervention has substantial short-term effects on expressive language, but these effects do not endure over a several year follow-up. By 5½ years of age, children who were diagnosed as having ELD at age 2 appear to have normal language in most respects regardless of their treatment history, although a minority (22%) continue to experience problems in articulation.

Given that ELD is a self-correcting problem for most children and that an intensive home-based intervention does not generate long-term effects, one might argue that the research that we have reported has limited relevance. We think that would be a mistaken view. First, research on ELD has considerable relevance for our understanding of normal language development. It shows, among other things, that expressive language and receptive language are modular, that they develop independently, and are functions of different sets of biological and environmental variables. This research also shows conclusively that expressive language can be affected significantly by characteristics of the social environment. This is a useful antidote to biologically oriented theories of language development (Pinker, 1984). Second, the research is likely to be relevant to understanding and treatment of more general language impairment. Finally, it is important to remember that the transitory nature of ELD for most children is measured in years. During the time the child experiences delays in expressive vocabulary and has articulation difficulties, the parents are likely to be unhappy and the child may experience social consequences, such as peer rejection. Parents may be reluctant to enroll the child in preschool programs and other potentially valuable experiences until the child can talk normally. In this context, a treatment program may be quite valuable. We should remember that a variety of medical conditions are also usually self-correcting (e.g., the common cold, viral influenza), but treatment is considered justified because it reduces stress and discomfort. Should months to years of language difficulties for a child be viewed as any less a proper candidate for treatment than the common cold?

REFERENCES

Abidin, R. (1983). *Parental stress index (PSI): Clinical manual, form 6*. University of Virginia, Author.

American Psychiatric Association. (1980). *Diagnostic and statistical manual of mental disorders* (3rd ed.). Washington, DC: Author.

American Psychiatric Association. (1987). *Diagnostic and statistical manual of mental disorders* (3rd ed., rev.). Washington, DC: Author.

Aram, D.M., & Nation, J.E. (1980). Preschool language disorders and subsequent language and academic difficulties. *Journal of Communication Disorders, 13,* 159–170.

Baker, L., & Cantwell, D.P. (1982a). Developmental, social and behavioral characteristics of speech and language disordered children. *Child Psychiatry and Human Development, 12,* 195–206.

Baker, L., & Cantwell, D.P. (1982b). Psychiatric disorders in children with different types of communication disorders. *Journal of Communication Disorders, 15,* 113–126.

Barton, E.J., & Ascione, F.R. (1984). Direct observation. In T.H. Ollendick & M. Hersen (Eds.), *Child behavior assessment: Principles and procedures* (pp. 166–194). Elmsford, NY: Pergamon.

Bates, E., Begnini, L., Bretherton, I., Camaioni, L., & Volterra, V. (1979). *The emergence of symbols: Cognition and communication in infancy.* New York: Academic Press.

Bates, E., Bretherton, I., & Snyder, L. (1988). *From first words to grammar: Individual differences and dissociable mechanism.* Cambridge: Cambridge University Press.

Beitchman, J.H., Nair, R., Clegg, M., Ferguson, B., & Patel, P.G. (1986). Prevalence of psychiatric disorders in children with speech and language disorders. *Journal of the American Academy of Child Psychiatry, 25,* 528–535.

Bess, F.H. (1983). Hearing loss associated with middle ear effusion. In Workshop on effects of otitis media on the child. *Pediatrics, 71,* 639–652.

Bishop, D.V.M., & Edmundson, A. (1986). Is otitis media a major cause of specific developmental language disorders? *British Journal of Disorders of Communication, 21,* 321–338.

Bishop, D.V.M., & Edmundson, A. (1987). Language-impaired 4-year-olds: Distinguishing transient from persistent impairment. *Journal of Speech and Hearing Disorders, 52,* 156–173.

Blager, F.B. (1981). Speech and language evaluation. In W.K. Frankenburg, S.M. Thornton, & M.E. Cohrs (Eds.), *Pediatric developmental diagnosis* (pp. 79–93). New York: Thieme-Stratton.

Buium, N., Rynders, J., & Turnure, J. (1974). Early maternal linguistic environment of normal and Down's syndrome language-learning children. *American Journal of Mental Deficiency, 79,* 52–58.

Cantwell, D.P. (1987, November). *Children with communication disorders—a group at psychiatric risk.* Presented at Psychiatry Grand Rounds, State University of New York, Stony Brook.

Cantwell, D.P., & Baker, L. (1980). Psychiatric and behavioral characteristics of children with communication disorders. *Journal of Pediatric Psychology, 5,* 161–178.

Cantwell, D.P., & Baker, L. (1987). *Developmental speech and language disorders.* New York: Guilford Press.

Cantwell, D.P., Baker, L., & Mattison, R. (1980). Psychiatric disorders in children with speech and language disorders. *Child Psychiatry and Development, 12,* 195–206.

Caulfield, M.B. (1989). Communication difficulty: A model of the relation of language delay and behavior problems. *SRCD Abstracts, 7,* 212.

Caulfield, M.B., Fischel, J.E., DeBaryshe, B.D., & Whitehurst, G.J. (1989). Behavioral correlates of developmental expressive language disorder. *Journal of Abnormal Child Psychology, 17,* 187–201.

Christiansen, K.O. (1974). The genesis of aggressive criminality. Implications of a study of crime in a Danish twin study. In J. deWit & W.W. Hartup (Eds.), *Determinants and origins of aggressive behavior* (pp. 233–254). Paris: Mouton & Co.

Cohen, S.E., Parmalee, A.H., Sigman, M., & Beckwith, L. (1988). Antededents of school problems in children born preterm. *Journal of Pediatric Psychology, 13,* 493–508.

Conti-Ramsden, C., & Friel-Patti, S. (1983). Mothers' discourse adjustments to language-impaired and nonlanguage-impaired children. *Journal of Speech and Hearing Disorders, 48,* 360–367.

Cunningham, C.E., Siegel, L.S., van der Spuy, H.I.J., Clark, M.L., & Bow, S.J. (1985). The behavioral and linguistic interactions of specifically language-delayed and normal boys with their mothers. *Child Development, 56,* 1389–1403.

Dunn, L.M., & Dunn, L.M. (1983). *Peabody Picture Vocabulary Test—Revised (PPVT-R).* Circle Pines, MN: American Guidance Service.

Fischel, J.E. (1985). Infant intervention: An examination of methods and efficacy. In G.J. Whitehurst (Ed.), *Annals of child development* (Vol. 2, pp. 161–194). Greenwich, CT: JAI Press.

Fischel, J.E., Whitehurst, G.J., Caulfield, M.B., & DeBaryshe, B.D. (1989). Language growth in children with expressive language delay. *Pediatrics, 82,* 218–227.

Fischel, J.E., Whitehurst G.J., Lonigan, C.J., et al. (1990). In reply to Ruben: The role of hearing loss in the development of expressive language delay. *Pediatrics, 85,* 1130–1131.

Fischer, M. (1973). Genetic and environmental factors in schizophrenia: A study of schizophrenic twins and their families. *Acta Psychiatrica Scandinavica,* Suppl. 238.

Fundudis, T., Kolvin, I., & Garside, R.F. (1980). A follow up of speech retarded children. In L.A. Hersov, M. Berger, & A.R. Nichol (Eds.), *Language and language disorders in childhood* (pp. 97–113). New York: Pergamon.

Gardner, M.F. (1981). *Expressive One-Word Picture Vocabulary Test.* Novato, CA: Academic Therapy Publications.

Howie, V.M. (1980). Developmental sequelae of chronic otitis media: A review. *Developmental and Behavioral Pediatrics, 1,* 34–38.

Huntley, R.M.C., Holt, K.S., Butterfill, A., & Latham, C. (1988). A follow-up study of a language intervention programme. *British Journal of Disorders of Communication, 23,* 127–140.

Jacobson, R. (1968). *Child language aphasia and phonological universals* (A.R. Keiler, Trans.). The Hague: Mouton. (Original work published in 1941 as *Kindersprache, aphasie und allgemeine lautgesetze.* Uppsala: Almqvist and Wiksell.)

Jenkins, S., Bax, M., & Hart, H. (1980). Behaviour problems in pre-school children. *Journal of Child Psychology and Psychiatry, 21,* 5–17.

Jesperson, O. (1925). *Language.* New York: Holt, Rinehart,& Wilson.

Kirk, S.A., McCarthy, J.J., & Kirk, W.D. (1968). *Illinois Test of Psycholinguistic Abilities.* Urbana: University of Illinois Press.

Klackenberg, G. (1980). What happens to children with retarded speech at 3? Longitudinal study of a sample of normal infants up to 20 years of age. *Acta Paediatrica Scandinavica, 69,* 681–685.

Knobloch, H., & Pasamanick, B. (1974). *Gesell and Amatruda's developmental diagnosis* (3rd ed.) New York: Harper & Row.

Leifer, J.S., & Lewis, M. (1983). Maternal speech to normal and handicapped children: A look at question-asking behavior. *Infant Behavior and Development, 6,* 175–187.

Leiter, R. (1976). *Supplement to general instructions for the Leiter International Performance Scale.* Chicago: Stoelting Co.

Leonard, L.B. (1981). Facilitating linguistic skills in children with specific language impairment. *Applied Psycholinguistics, 2,* 89–118.

Leonard, L.B. (1988). Is specific language impairment a useful construct? In S. Rosenberg (Ed.), *Advances in applied psycholinguistics* (pp. 1–39). Cambridge: Cambridge University Press.

Lewis, M.M. (1951). *Infant speech: A study of the beginnings of language.* New York: Humanities Press.

Lindholm, B.W., & Touliatos, J. (1979). Behavior problems of children in regular classes and those diagnosed as requiring speech therapy. *Perceptual and Motor Skills, 49,* 459–463.

Lonigan, C.J., Fischel, J.E., Whitehurst, G.J., Arnold, D.S., & Valdez-Menchaca, M.C. (1991). *The role of otitis media in the development of expressive language delay.* Unpublished manuscript.

Lorimer, F. (1928). *The growth of reason: A study of the role of verbal activity in the growth of the structure of the human mind.* London: Kegan Paul, Trench, & Trubner.

Ludlow, C.L., & Cooper, J.A. (Eds.). (1983). *Genetic aspects of speech and language disorders.* New York: Academic Press.

Marshall, N., Hegrenes, J., & Goldstein, S. (1973). Verbal interactions: Mothers and their retarded children versus mothers and their nonretarded children. *American Journal of Mental Deficiency, 77,* 415–419.

Mash, E.J., & Terdal, L.G. (1981). Behavioral assessment of childhood disturbances. In E.J. Mash & L.G. Terdal (Eds.), *Behavioral assessment of childhood disorders* (pp. 3–78). New York: Guilford Press.

Mednick, S.A., Schulsinger, F., Higgins, J., & Bell, B. (1974). *Genetics, environment, and psychopathology.* Amsterdam: North Holland/Elsevier.

Nelson, R.O., & Hayes, S.C. (1979). Some current dimensions of behavioral assessment. *Behavioral Assessment, 1,* 1–16.

Oller, D.K., Wieman, K.A., Doyle, W., & Ross, C. (1975). Infant babbling and speech. *Journal of Child Language, 3,* 1–11.

Paul, R. (1989). Profiles of toddlers with delayed expressive language. *SRCD Abstracts, 7,* 94.

Petersen, G.A., & Sherrod, K.B. (1982). Relationship of maternal language to language development and language delay of children. *American Journal of Mental Deficiency, 86,* 391–398.

Pinker, S. (1984). *Language learnability and language development.* Cambridge: Harvard University Press.

Rescorla, L. (1984, April). *Language delay in two-year-olds.* Paper presented at the International Conference on Infant Studies, New York.

Rescorla, L., & Schwartz, E. (1988, April). *Outcome of specific expressive language delay.* Paper presented at the International Conference on Infant Studies, Washington, DC.

Reynell, J.K. (1985). *Reynell developmental language scales* (2nd rev.). Windsor, England: NFER-Nelson.

Richman, N., & Stevenson, J. (1977). Language delay in 3-year-olds. *Acta Pediatrica Belgica, 30,* 213–219.

Scarborough, H.S., & Dobrich, W. (1990). Development of children with early language delay. *Journal of Speech and Hearing Disorders, 33*, 70–83.

Silva, P.A. (1980). The prevalence, stability and significance of developmental language delay in preschool children. *Developmental Medicine and Child Neurology, 22*, 768–777.

Springer, S.P., & Deutsch, G. (1989). *Left brain, right brain.* New York: W.H. Freeman.

Stevenson, J., & Richman, N. (1976). The prevalence of language delay in a population of three-year-old children and its association with general retardation. *Developmental Medicine and Child Neurology, 18*, 431–441.

Tallal, P., Ross, R., & Curtiss, S. (1989). Familial aggregation in specific language impairment. *Journal of Speech and Hearing Disorders, 54*, 167–173.

Teele, D.W., Klein, J.O., & Rosner, B.A. (1980). Epidemiology of otitis media in children. *Annals of Otology, Rhinology and Laryngology, 89*, 5–6.

Templin, M., & Darley, F. (1968). *Templin-Darley Tests of Articulation* (2nd ed.). Iowa City: University of Iowa Bureau of Educational Research and Service.

Thorndike, R.L., Hagen, E.P., & Sattler, J.M. (1986). *Stanford-Binet Intelligence Scale* (4th ed.). Chicago: Riverside Publishing Company.

Valdez-Menchaca, M.C. (1990). *Child effects on maternal language: Their implications for long-term maintenance of early intervention effects.* Unpublished doctoral dissertation, State University of New York, Stony Brook.

Vaughn, B.E., Kopp, C., & Krakow, J. (1984). The emergence and consolidation of self-control from eighteen to thirty months of age: Normative trends and individual differences. *Child Development, 55*, 990–1004.

Vihman, M.M., Macken, M.A., Miller, R., Simmons, H., & Miller, J. (1985). From babbling to speech: A reassessment of the continuity issue. *Language, 61*, 397–445.

Vihman, M.M., & Miller, R. (1988). Words and babble at the threshold of language acquisition. In M.D. Smith & J.L. Locke (Eds.), *The emergent lexicon: The child's development of linguistic vocabulary* (pp. 151–184). San Diego: Academic Press.

Warren, S.F., & Kaiser, A.P. (1988). Research in early language intervention. In S.L. Odom & M.B. Karnes (Eds.), *Early intervention for infants and children with handicaps: An empirical base* (pp. 89–108). Baltimore: Paul H. Brookes Publishing Co.

Wechsler, D. (1967). *Wechsler Preschool and Primary Scale of Intelligence.* New York: Psychological Corporation.

Wender, P.H., Rosenthal, D., Kety, S.S., Schulsinger, F., & Welner, J. (1974). Crossfostering: A research strategy for clarifying the role of genetic and experiential factors in the etiology of schizophrenia. *Archives of General Psychiatry, 30*, 318–325.

Whitehurst, G.J., Arnold, D.S., Smith, M., Fischel, J.E., Lonigan, C.J., & Valdez-Menchaca, M.C. (in press). Family history of children with and without expressive language delay. *Journal of Speech and Hearing Research.*

Whitehurst, G.J., Falco, F.L., Lonigan, C., Fischel, J.E., Valdez-Menchaca, M.C., Debaryshe, B.D., & Caulfield, M. (1988). Accelerating language development through picture-book reading. *Developmental Psychology, 24*, 552–559.

Whitehurst, G.J., Falco, F.L., Menchaca, M.C. DeBaryshe, B.D., & Caulfied, M.B. (1988). Verbal interaction in families of normal and expressive language delayed children. *Developmental Psychology, 24*, 690–699.

Whitehurst, G.J., Fischel, J.E., Lonigan, C.J., Valdez-Menchaca, M.C., DeBaryshe,

B.D., & Caulfield, M.B. (1988). Verbal interaction in families of normal and expressive language delayed children. *Developmental Psychology, 24,* 690–699.

Whitehurst, G.J., Smith, M., Fischel, J.E., Arnold, D.S., & Lonigan, C.J. (in press). The continuity of babble and speech in children with expressive language delay. *Journal of Speech and Hearing Research.*

Whitehurst, G.J., & Sonnenschein, S. (1985). The development of communication: A functional analysis. In G.J. Whitehurst (Ed.), *Annals of child development* (Vol. 2, pp. 1–48). Greenwich, CT: JAI Press.

Whitehurst, G.J., & Valdez-Menchaca, M.C. (1988). What is the role of the reinforcement in early language acquisition? *Child Development, 59,* 430–440.

Wulbert, M., Inglis, S., Kriegsmann, E., & Mills, B. (1975). Language delay and associated mother-child interaction. *Developmental Psychology, 11,* 61–70.

Zelazo, P.R., Kearsley, R.B., & Ungerer, J.A. (1984). *Learning to speak: A manual for parents.* Hillsdale, NJ: Lawrence Erlbaum Associates.

12

Measuring Children's Conversational Language

Thomas Klee

THE STUDY OF CHILD LANGUAGE acquisition has benefited from the wide variety of research methods by which data have been gathered. Language sample analysis has arguably had the greatest single impact on the study of children's language acquisition of any data-gathering technique. This is true both of the study of normal language acquisition and the study of children with language impairment.

The purpose of this chapter is to explore several methods used in research and clinical practice to quantify and evaluate the spontaneous language production of young children and to discuss various problems that have arisen in the use of such methods. The emphasis is on the nature of the transcript itself, as well as on numerical summary measures that are often derived from transcripts of the expressive language of preschool children. The scope of the paper is confined to the span of development between Brown's Stage 1 (i.e., two-word combinations) and the early stages of syntactic development.

The chapter focuses on language produced in (quasi-) naturalistic contexts as opposed to language produced in response to test items, such as that produced in formal elicitation procedures and tests. First, various methods that have been used to segment the continuous stream of speech into discrete units for analysis are examined and their effect on the resulting dependent variables is discussed. Next, data are presented on the variability that inevitably arises as a consequence of having different individuals transcribing naturalistic data. Finally, some observations on one commonly used metric of spontaneous language, mean length of utterance in morphemes (MLU), is offered, particularly with respect to the validity of the measure.

TRANSCRIPTIONAL METHODS AND PROBLEMS

Much of the knowledge about children's language production has been acquired from data gathered and later interpreted from audiotaped conversations.

The audiotaped sample provides the raw data from which the child language researcher works. The nature and quality of these raw data are influenced by whom the child was talking to, what the child was talking about, where the interaction took place, how the child and his or her interlocutor felt about being observed and recorded, and many other social and cultural factors.

Before any systematic analysis can be conducted on these data, however, the information preserved on the tape must be transformed in such a way that linguistic measurements can be carried out on it. This transformation takes on various forms depending on the analysis intended for it.

In the case of acoustic analysis of the speech signal, the transformation involves converting an auditory signal to a visual representation of that signal—a graphic display of a spectrum, for example—from which acoustic measurements can be made. In the case of phonological analysis of the same signal, the transformation involves listening to the tape, making judgments about which phonetic properties are involved, and representing those judgments with a system of conventional graphic symbols (e.g., symbols of the International Phonetic Alphabet [International Phonetic Association, 1979] or the Phonetic Representation of Disordered Speech [PRDS] group [Phonetic Representation of Disordered Speech Working Party, 1983]).

In the case of grammatical, semantic, or pragmatic analyses, a similar level of human intervention is involved in transforming the spoken data. A trained individual must listen to the recorded sample and make what will inevitably be subjective judgments about what was spoken by a child who may not be fully intelligible. The transcriber's decisions are codified using a transcriptional format that is likely to be unique to a particular research laboratory and the research questions being asked. This collection of judgments, or observations, is known as a transcript. (For a general discussion of the issues involved in transcription format, see Ochs, 1979. For examples of computer-based transcriptional systems, see Johnson, 1986, MacWhinney, 1987, and Miller & Chapman, 1985.)

If we focus on one of these areas of linguistic inquiry, that of children's emerging grammatical skills, we find that there are at least three distinct areas of transcription methodology that must be addressed if the resulting data are to be reliable and replicable. Decisions must be made with regard to: 1) segmenting the continuous speech stream into discrete units for analysis (i.e., *utterances*), 2) segmenting utterances into words and determining the productivity of these units (see, for example, Ingram, 1981, and Peters, 1983), and 3) segmenting words into morphemes.

The construct of utterance—its definition, identification, and organization—is at the core of linguistic analysis, yet less may have been written about this important analytical unit than about any other segmental feature of children's language. This linguistic unit plays an obvious role in such broadly used measures of children's language production as mean length of utterance (MLU), mean number of utterances per speaker turn, and type–token ratios (TTR).

The definitional problem of what exactly constitutes an utterance in orally produced language (Huddleston, 1984) is encountered at all levels of development, from the earliest instances of word combination (e.g., whether a "stage of successive single-word utterances" exists [Bloom, 1973] or not [Branigan, 1979]) to later points in development, during which multiple clauses are conjoined by various connective elements (e.g., *and*). The problem of definition is complicated even further when considerations are given to language varieties that depart from the standard form, examples of which are to be found in the language of children who have been termed "language disordered" and in the language of many adult aphasic speakers.

When they have been given any formal definition at all, utterances have been defined in various ways by various investigators. To illustrate the diversity of definitional approaches, let us begin with several examples of utterances that might be found in a language sample:

1. the boy can go if he wants to
2. the boy sang and the girl danced
3. the boy sang and he danced
4. the boy ate his dinner and went out

The Reading MRC Project has developed explicit criteria for segmenting conversational speech into units for analysis (Fletcher & Garman, 1988; Garman, 1989a, 1989b; Johnson, 1986). Four types of *text-units* are first recognized: 1) minor elements, 2) lexical elements, 3) phrasal elements, and 4) clausal elements. Type 4 text-units are defined on the basis of the main verb plus all of the clause elements associated with it, such as subject, complement, object, and adverbial. Any connectives are placed at the beginning of the text-unit. In this way, clausal text-units are comprised of single clauses, each containing a single main verb. An analysis of the four examples above would produce the following eight clausal text-units:

1a. the boy can go
1b. if he wants to
2a. the boy sang
2b. and the girl danced
3a. the boy sang
3b. and he danced
4a. the boy ate his dinner
4b. and went out

Since the definition of text-units does not allow for complex sentences to appear in the data set, additional criteria were set forth for combining certain clausal text-units into higher-order analysis-units (A-units). The A-unit is an adaptation of Hunt's (1965, 1970) T-unit construct, which was defined as a main clause together with any subordinate clause attached to it. Using Hunt's procedure, the four examples above may be divided into the following seven T-units:

1. the boy can go if he wants to
2a. the boy sang
2b. and the girl danced
3a. the boy sang
3b. and he danced
4a. the boy ate his dinner
4b. and went out

Segmented using the Reading criteria, the same corpus would result in five A-units, with the main departure from Hunt's procedure having to do with how coordinating connectives and the subjects within the clauses they conjoin are treated:

1. the boy can go if he wants to
2a. the boy sang
2b. and the girl danced
3. the boy sang and he danced
4. the boy ate his dinner and went out

One obvious reason for defining utterance boundaries in this way is to keep independent clauses having different subjects and conjoined by *and* from being counted as single utterances, and thus inflating indices such as MLU.

Although there is as yet no consensus among researchers regarding the definitional parameters of the utterance as it is produced by children who are in the process of development, it is clear that the science must progress beyond the level of the transcriber's intuition.

EFFECT OF THE LISTENER ON LANGUAGE MEASURES

The process of transcription is by its nature a subjective endeavor. Because of this, we might expect that different transcribers would produce different transcriptions after listening to the same sample of speech. The cumulative effect of decisions regarding utterance, word, and morpheme segmentation can be compared across individual transcribers in order to estimate just how variable trained people might be on this task. For this purpose, we have looked at various linguistic measures resulting from the transcriptions of 12 transcribers, all of whom listened to the same language sample.

The transcribers chosen for this demonstration were first-semester graduate students studying for the master's degree in communication disorders. All were enrolled in a graduate course in child language development. Prior to enrolling in this course, the students had varying levels of experience with transcribing, ranging from no experience at all in the case of three students to formal instruction in phonetic transcription in the case of nine students. None of the 12 had any previous training or experience in the type of transcription system used in this study, which had a computer-based, broad morphemic-based format (Klee, 1985).

The students were given the task of listening to a 10-minute audiotaped sample of a mother–child interaction recorded in the child's home while the mother and child were engaged in freeplay with toys that were familiar to both. The child was a girl of 3 years, 7 months with speech and language appropriate for her age. The child was fitted with a wireless FM transmitter and microphone, which produced a high-fidelity audio recording.

All of the students had been trained in the use of the SALT computer program (Miller & Chapman, 1986) and its associated transcription format (Miller & Chapman, 1985). Transcription was done independently by each student by listening to the tape on a transcription machine and typing utterances directly into a computer file using a text editor program. The data presented here represent the results of the students' efforts on their first transcription of a language sample using this system.

Language production measures used in the comparison were selected on the basis of their quantitative nature, since we were interested in judging how similar or different the students' transcriptions were in terms of such aspects as numbers of utterances and words, utterance length, and intelligibility. The variables evaluated were: mean length of utterance in morphemes (MLU), total number of utterances produced by the child (TOTUTT-C), total number of utterances produced by the mother (TOTUTT-M), total number of complete and intelligible utterances produced by the child (TOTCI-C), total number of complete and intelligible utterances produced by the mother (TOTCI-M), total number of words produced by the child (TNW), and the number of different words (NDW) produced by the child. The language production measures were calculated using the SALT1 computer program (Miller & Chapman, 1986).

To illustrate the kind of variability that might be expected in such a listening task, the students' interpretations of one of the first utterances in the conversation are presented. The child who was recorded was the author's daughter; naturally, her speech pattern, vocabulary, and grammatical usage were quite familiar to the author, who transcribed the first utterance as

(can) can you help me put this one in?

The auxiliary verb was spoken twice, the first instance being represented in the transcript as a repetition (as such it has been set apart from the rest of the utterance by parentheses). How was this same utterance interpreted by the students?

Table 1 sets out the transcriptions of the 12 students. Only one student (3) produced a transcription identical to that of the author. The transcription most commonly offered (1) was one in which the repeated auxiliary was not noted. Four of the students represented what they heard in this way. Two of the

Table 1.   Various transcriptions of "can you help me put this one in?"

Transcription	Number of transcriptions
1. can you help me put this one in?	4
2. X can you help me put this one in?	2
3. (can) can you help me put this one in?	1
4. Xcan you help me put this one in?	1
5. X you help me put this one in?	1
6. X will you help me put this one in?	1
7. X *will you help me put this one in?	1
8. do you know how they put this one in?	1

Note: X = unintelligible segment; Xcan = indicates doubt about transcriptional accuracy; *will = omitted word; ( ) = repeated segment.

students indeed heard the child utter something prior to the word *can*, but were uncertain about how to interpret the segment(s). This can be seen in (2), with the unintelligible element(s) being coded as an "X." One student (4) produced a transcription in which only a single instance of the auxiliary was represented, and indicated some uncertainty about this. Another student (5) was unwilling to codify this uncertainty with a word, instead transcribing an "X" in its place. The transcriptions of one student (6) contained the auxiliary *will* instead of *can*, another student (7) indicated that *will* should have been used but was omitted. Finally, one student's interpretation (8) was altogether different from the rest, indicating *do you know how they* . . . rather than *can can you help me*. . . . Note that this student preserved the same number of words and syllables in the sequence preceding *put this one in?*, but came up with an entirely different set of words.

This is, admittedly, a selective look at one utterance, but it is representative of a general characteristic of transcription: that of inherent variability across transcribers. We now consider the consequences of this intertranscriber variation on the set of quantitative measures that often serve as outcome variables in research and in the clinic.

Table 2 presents a summary of each of the outcome variables resulting from the 12 students' transcriptions as well as the mean and standard deviation of the group on each of the measures. On the MLU measure, the students' transcriptions ranged from 3.66 to 4.09, with a mean MLU of 3.90. This amount of variation—nearly half a morpheme—represents nearly one stage of language development defined in terms of Brown's (1973) stages.

The total number of utterances transcribed (TOTUTT), which is considered here as a test of how consistent the students were in applying utterance segmentation rules, ranged from 100 to 123, with a mean of 114 utterances. The same 23% difference between the minimum and maximum is seen in the total number of complete and intelligible utterances (TOTCI), which ranged

Table 2. Comparison of 12 transcribers on a 10-minute audiotaped sample of conversational speech

Transcriber	Child					Mother	
	MLU	TOTUTT	TOTCI	TNW	NDW	TOTUTT	TOTCI
1	3.66	112	80	253	87	94	85
2	3.74	115	98	321	106	100	92
3	3.77	120	82	269	94	104	89
4	3.79	123	89	296	96	99	91
5	3.88	115	86	291	97	97	88
6	3.90	115	83	281	92	98	88
7	3.94	108	82	278	92	92	87
8	3.97	115	95	336	116	96	94
9	3.97	122	98	337	108	99	91
10	3.99	100	83	291	98	90	83
11	4.04	110	92	327	109	100	86
12	4.09	112	96	342	103	93	88
M	3.90	114	89	302	100	97	89
SD	0.13	6	7	30	9	4	3

Note: MLU = mean length of utterance in morphemes; TOTUTT = total number of utterances; TOTCI = total number of complete and intelligible utterances; TNW = total number of words; NDW = number of different words; M = mean; SD = standard deviation.

from 80 to 98, with a mean of 89 utterances. TOTCI, of course, functions as the denominator in the MLU computation, and any transcriber variation here will introduce variability into MLU. Less utterance variability is seen in the transcription of both the mother's TOTUTT and the mother's TOTCI, with a 16% and 13% difference, respectively, between the minimum and maximum values.

Total number of words (TNW) and number of different words (NDW), resulted in even greater transcriber variation than the utterance counts. The transcribers having the highest values on TNW and NDW logged 35% and 33% more words, respectively, in their transcripts on these measures than the students with the lowest values. It bears repeating here that all the transcribers were listening to the same sample of mother–child conversation. Thus the variation we are pointing out is not variation within the child (although variability within the child does exist), but is variation within the listener.

There are two concerns here. The first relates to the reliability of the measures; the second relates to their validity. First, if the clinician were to compare this child's MLU against a set of age norms (e.g., Miller & Chapman, 1981) for the purpose of determining the age appropriateness of the measure, the interpretation might be very different depending upon who did the transcription. In the case of this 43-month-old child, all 12 MLU values exceeded the cutoff of 1 standard deviation below the mean for her age group. All of the transcribers would thus have come to the same conclusion regarding age appropriateness. However, had this child been 53 months old, for example, the 1 standard deviation cutoff would be 3.87. The first four transcribers would have concluded that her MLU was below that expected for her age, whereas the other eight would have concluded that it was within normal limits.

The second concern has to do with the validity of these measures. The assumption that is often made that because certain linguistic traits can be measured readily (e.g., utterance length as an approximation of the construct of grammatical complexity) and because the measurements take the form of numerical quantities (e.g., MLU), the higher a particular value, the greater the representation of the underlying linguistic construct. One must be very cautious with this sort of logic. The question of validity must be addressed. Where are the data that support the assumption of a linear relationship between these values and linguistic behavior? This point will be developed in the following sections.

USE OF MEAN LENGTH OF UTTERANCE (MLU) AS A MEASURE OF LINGUISTIC COMPLEXITY

Researchers are constantly attempting to capture the richness and diversity of human behavior—whether cognitive, social, or linguistic—by proposing constructs thought to represent these complex behaviors and by devising methods for measuring the constructs. As in any of the sciences, the process of measurement in the social sciences entails representing a particular construct with a set of numerical values. The variables used to measure behaviors or constructs must be examined by evaluating their validity and reliability.

One aspect of the reliability of several measures of children's language production—that of transcription agreement between listeners—has been discussed. In this section the validity of MLU as a measure of linguistic complexity is examined. MLU is widely used as a measure of children's developing language by researchers studying both normal development and language impairment (see Bennett-Kastor, 1988, for a critical review). MLU has seen service as an independent variable (e.g., in matching groups of normal and impaired subjects), as a dependent variable (e.g., in judging treatment efficacy), and as a subject selection variable. One standard type of study compares some aspect of language development in two or more groups of children without impairment, each group differing in terms of MLU. Another type of study looks at linguistic differences between children with language impairment and children without language impairment who have been matched on MLU. (Limitations that have resulted from devising research based on using MLU-matched groups may have restricted the characterization of language disorder, a point developed in Miller, 1987.)

Often, the reasons for using MLU to make group comparisons are not made explicit by the researcher. One might assume that MLU has been used, at least in part, because of Brown's observation that "two children matched for MLU are much more likely to have speech that is, on internal grounds, at the same level of constructional complexity than are two children of the same chronological age" (1973, p. 55). However, the empirical support for this supposition is not very convincing beyond MLUs of about 3.00 (Klee & Fitzgerald, 1985; Rondal, Ghiotto, Bredart, & Bachelet, 1987).

Two illustrations should illuminate the nature of the problem in making assumptions about the construct validity of MLU beyond Brown's Stage I and II of development.

Illustration I: Longitudinal Data and MLU

Brown's (1973) advocacy of the use of MLU rather than chronological age as a metric by which to make predictions about children's language acquisition stemmed from studying three children who were in the process of acquiring English. Eve was followed from 18 to 27 months; Adam and Sarah were followed from 27 to 43 months. However, Brown's 1973 study dealt mainly with their language development during MLU Stages I and II (MLU range of 1.50–2.50).

In noting that "children develop language at widely varying rates," Brown sought a metric that would be independent of age. He settled on MLU, since, in his view, "MLU is an excellent simple index of grammatical development because almost every new kind of knowledge increase length" (1973; p. 53). Interestingly, later research has found a significant correlation between MLU and age in groups of middle- and upper–middle class children (Miller & Chapman, 1981), working class children (Klee, Schaffer, May, Membrino, & Mougey, 1989), and in a group of children with specific language impairment (Klee et al., 1989).

Brown's claim of an isomorphism between utterance length and utterance complexity has been disputed by a number of investigators (Crystal, 1974; Johnston & Kamhi, 1984; Klee & Fitzgerald, 1985; Rondal et al. 1987). One of the problems with linking utterance length and grammatical complexity or in using MLU as even a "simple index of grammatical development" can be illustrated with the following longitudinal comparison. The data in this example come from the author's recordings of one of his own children, Gillian, over the course of the preschool period. Two samples of Gillian's conversational language are presented, one from age 2;9, the other from age 3;2. Both samples were collected under similar conditions. Gillian and her mother were recorded for 20 minutes while playing with a set of familiar toys in the home.

The data were transcribed by the author and verified by an independent judge. So that the frequency of occurrence of linguistic constructions could be compared between samples, the corpora were equated in terms of the number of major utterances. From each of the 20-minute samples, 100 consecutive major utterances were analyzed in terms of their clause, phrase, and morphological structure using the analytical framework developed by Crystal, Fletcher, and Garman (1989; Crystal, 1979, 1982) known as LARSP (Language Assessment, Remediation and Screening Procedure). A major utterance was an utterance that was Stage I major or higher. Thus, Stage I minor utterances and all section A utterances (i.e., those that represented symbolic noise or were partly or wholly unintelligible, deviant, incomplete, ambiguous, or stereotypical) were excluded from the count of 100.

Gillian's profile at age 2;9 contained some evidence of Stage V clause structure (Table 3). That is, complex sentences had come to be used in addition to the simple sentences characteristic of Stages II–IV. This sample of 100 major utterances contained 3 complex sentences, all of which involved coordination (e.g., "I take that off and put this one on.").

Phrase structure at 2;9 had progressed to Stage IV, with both noun phrases and verb phrases containing elaboration. Noun phrases contained various combinations of determiner, adjective, preposition, pronoun, and coordinated noun phrases (XcX), with two instances of a combination of four of these elements— "on the other ear" and "at the book store." Verb phrases were marked with the copula and auxiliary verb forms, as well as catenative verbs, verb particles, verb negation, and complex verb phrases.

At the word level, there is evidence of inflection usage in both the noun phrase and the verb phrase by age 2;9. Verb phrase morphology included the simple past tense form and the third person singular inflection. Noun phrase morphology included the plural form and the genitive inflection. Gillian's use of certain grammatical features was not yet fully mastered, with "errors" noted in clause element omission; word order; concord; and determiner, preposition, auxiliary, and copula omissions.

By age 3;2, Gillian's grammatical capabilities were more advanced, as might be expected from a child who is 5 months older. At the clause level, there was a greater use of complex sentences, not only in number but also in syntactic variety. Both coordination (the only type of complex sentence represented in the data of 2;9) and subordination were used. Four sentences contained adverbial elements that were themselves clauses (e.g., "because they hurt me *when they're there*"), one sentence included a comparative clause, and another sentence included a clause embedded within the object of the

Table 3. Comparison of speech of child without disabilities at 2 years, 9 months and 3 years, 2 months

Age of child	Stage I utterances[a]	Simple sentences[b]	Complex sentences[b]	Mean length of utterance
2 yrs., 9 mos.	27	97	3	3.74
3 yrs., 2 mos.	51	90	10	2.94

[a]As percentage of all utterances.
[b]As percentage of major utterances.

sentence. Thus, Gillian's use of complex sentences increased from 3% at age 2;9 to 10% at age 3;2.

Phrase development also showed evidence of continued maturation. Not only were the frequencies of occurrence higher in the later transcript for most of the constructions used in the earlier transcript, but new structures were also employed in the later transcript.

Regarding morphological development, all of the bound morphemes occurring in the earlier transcript were also present in the later one. In addition, two new forms—the present participle and the past participle—occurred in the later transcript.

Did the advancements in clause, phrase, and word structure coincide with an increase in MLU between transcripts? Gillian's MLU was 3.74 at age 2;9 and 2.94 at age 3;2, an average decrease of 0.8 morphemes per utterance. In terms of Brown's (1973) stages of development, this represented a drop of two stages, from late Stage IV/early Stage V at the earlier age to Stage III at the later age (Miller, 1981). The advancements made in grammatical development over this 5-month period, as evidenced on the LARSP profiles, were not reflected in increased MLU.

One reason for this was that more single-word utterances were produced during the later transcript (82 out of 160 utterances, or 51%) than during the earlier transcript (32 out of 119 utterances, or 27%). With respect to MLU, the presence of single-word utterances in transcripts of children beyond the single-word stage of development can be thought of as noise in the sense that they often reflect the pragmatic constraints of the conversation (e.g., "yes" and "no" responses to the adult interlocutor's questions) and have the undesired effect of depressing the numerical value of the index, as indeed they did here. The proportion of such utterances in the transcripts of 2- and 3-year-old children without impairment is not insignificant. In one study, they accounted for an average of 31% (range = 16%–47% across children) of the utterances in the corpus (Klee & Fitzgerald, 1985). In a second sample of children without impairment of the same age, they accounted for an average of 34% of all utterances, while in a sample of children the same age with specific language impairment, they averaged 50% of all utterances (see Klee et al., 1989).

Illustration II: Cross-Sectional Data and MLU

The second illustration examines two children exhibiting similar MLUs. The two cases were part of a larger study of the relationship between MLU and age in children with and children without specific language impairment (Klee et al., 1989). They are referred to by subject number (M34 and M70) throughout this discussion. Both these children were considered by their parents to be developing normally. The children's development was confirmed as normal by a speech-language pathologist following a formal evaluation of their language and speech development. Both subjects were boys and both demonstrated similar MLUs, as measured from all complete and intelligible utterances occurring in a 20-minute language sample with their mothers. Subject M34 was age 2;9 and had an MLU of 3.29; subject M70 was age 2;10 with an MLU of 3.26. Both MLUs were within the normal range (Miller & Chapman, 1981).

When the language samples were equated for 75 major utterances (in the manner described for Gillian's samples) and compared with one another, differences in the two grammatical profiles emerge. M34 displays evidence of clause structure up through Stage III, with only one additional clause type (SVOA) characteristic of Stage IV. There is no evidence in the M34 sample of complex sentences. In contrast, M70 produced two complex sentences (Stage V), one containing coordinated clauses and another containing a comparative clause. M70 also exhibited a more extensive variety of Stage IV clause types (SVOA, SVCA, SVOO, SVOC, letXY+, and QVS) compared with M34's single Stage IV clause type (SVOA).

A similar picture emerges at phrase level. While both M34 and M70 display Stage II–IV phrase constructions, there is a quantitative difference between the two transcripts, especially with respect to the verb phrase. M34 exhibits more of the earlier developing catenative verb forms than M70, but only an emerging capability with the copula and auxiliary verb forms. Both children had created ample linguistic opportunities to display use of these forms by producing utterances in which copulas and obligatory auxiliaries were called for, but M34 produced only a single copula and three auxiliaries, whereas M70 produced 28 copulas and 12 auxiliaries in these sentences.

Finally, M70 demonstrated more advanced morphology than M34. M70 produced a variety of inflections (e.g., present and past participles, third-person singular, plural), whereas M34 produced only a single inflectional type, the simple past tense.

Neither of these illustrations supports Brown's contention that MLU is an "excellent simple index of grammatical development." In the first illustration, it was shown that Gillian's patterns of grammatical development were more advanced at age 3;2 than at age 2;9, despite the decrease in MLU between the two samples. This departure from the normal pattern of monotonic increase in MLU with age could be dismissed as sampling variability. However, when longitudinal data on MLU are plotted over time, it is not unusual to find MLU following a nonmonotonic path (see, e.g., the MLU profiles of Adam and Sarah in Brown, 1973).

The second illustration shows that preschool children with similar MLU can have significantly different profiles of grammatical production. The presumption that children with similar MLUs are developmentally similar was not borne out when more extensive analyses of grammatical usage were performed.

EDUCATIONAL AND CLINICAL IMPLICATIONS

These conclusions have several implications for assessing and remediating children's language problems. First, MLU should not be used as a substitute for more comprehensive analyses when evaluating the language production skills of children suspected of having linguistic difficulties. Beyond Brown's Stage II, grammatical level and MLU are not highly correlated, as the examples cited have illustrated. This is not to say that MLU should not be used as a developmental indicator of children's language level. Rather, MLU should be recognized for what it is: a measure of average utterance length, not a measure of the global linguistic status or overall linguistic "health" of the child. An abnormally low MLU may or may not indicate associated language difficulties, just as an MLU within the normal range may or may not indicate language normality (Klee, Schaffer, May, Membrino, & Mougey, 1987). The length of the child's utterances is obviously not as important as the communicative ability of the child and the linguistic means employed by the child to convey a message verbally.

In our clinical work, we routinely begin our assessment of the child's language production by computing MLU. We then compare it with what would be expected for the child's age. The computation is done by the SALT1 computer program (Miller & Chapman, 1986). The MLU value generated by the computer is then compared to data collected on children without language impairment using equations for predicting MLU from the child's age (Klee et al., 1989; Miller & Chapman, 1981). This is only the first step in analyzing a transcription of the child's conversational language, however. The second, and by far more important, step is to conduct a thorough evaluation of the child's language production. The nature of this evaluation varies depending on the clinician's judgment of the child's linguistic difficulties, but it invariably results in the application of an analytical method based on the language sample from which clinical decisions can be made (see Klee, 1985, for a discussion of some of these procedures.)

Having made the commitment to use a particular clinical method, the researcher must adopt standard, replicable procedures. The application of clinical linguistic tools must be standardized (e.g., in determining how to segment the language sample into utterances, words, and morphemes) such that the outcome variables represent as nearly as possible the child's linguistic behavior rather than variance contributed by the examiner.

DIRECTIONS FOR FUTURE RESEARCH

Conversational language samples have been employed for the past several decades in research aimed at producing ecologically valid descriptions of children's language production. The process of transcription itself and the development of psychometrically sound measures of language production have come to be focused upon as important components of the study of language development and language disorder. It is clear that many of the methods and measures that once were employed without question have, over time, come under scrutiny, and that new approaches are called for.

As Miller (1987) has observed, the MLU comparison group strategy has directed research on language disorders since the 1970s. If it has directed the way research studies are designed—and it has—then it has also directed the way we conceive of language impairment, for our conception is based, in part, on the outcome of the studies we design. This strategy continues to be used as the method of choice for comparing children with and children without language impairment, despite the fact that the research questions have changed over the years. The question we must pose is, on what language characteristics are children with and children without language impairment comparable when matched on MLU? Are two groups of children with identical MLUs equivalent in terms of grammatical level? If a between-groups research design calls for children with and children without language impairment to be matched on grammatical level, why not match directly on grammatical level? This will, of course, require forthcoming innovations in developmental language indices, which will contend with and ultimately supplant MLU as the measure of choice.

It is hoped that the issues raised in this chapter will encourage researchers to begin exploring new avenues and proposing fresh methods for comparing groups of children. Studying the reliability and validity of language production measures is an important component of the study of child language and applications within the remedial setting.

CONCLUSION

The conclusions we may draw from the research on child language development, and in particular, from comparisons between children with and children without language impairments are limited by the methods and measures employed in the research. The same limitations apply to the methods and measures we use in the clinic to characterize children with language impairment. Remediation relies, at least in part, on the information supplied by the measures we use to assess these children. In this chapter, we have argued for the need to establish better the psychometric properties (i.e., validity and reliability) of the language production measures we employ in our work as clinicians, educators, and researchers. Inevitably this will lead us to explore new and better ways of assessing, and thus characterizing, the language and communication abilities of children.

REFERENCES

Bennett-Kastor, T. (1988). *Analyzing children's language: Methods and theory.* Oxford: Basil Blackwell.

Bloom, L. (1973). *One word at a time*. The Hague: Mouton.

Branigan, G. (1979). Some reasons why successive single word utterances are not. *Journal of Child Language, 6*, 411–421.

Brown, R. (1973). *A first language: The early stages*. Cambridge: Harvard University Press.

Crystal, D. (1974). Review of R. Brown, *A First Language*. *Journal of Child Language, 1*, 289–307.

Crystal, D. (1979). *Working with LARSP*. London: Edward Arnold.

Crystal, D. (1982). *Profiling linguistic disability*. London: Edward Arnold.

Crystal, D., Fletcher, P., & Garman, M. (1989). *Grammatical analysis of language disability* (2nd ed.). London: Cole and Whurr.

Fletcher, P., & Garman, M. (1988). LARSPing by numbers. *British Journal of Disorders of Communication, 23*, 309–321.

Garman, M. (1989a). The role of linguistics in speech therapy: assessment and interpretation. In P. Grunwell & A. James (Eds.), *The functional evaluation of language disorders* (pp. 29–57). London: Croom Helm.

Garman, M. (1989b). Syntactic assessment of expressive language. In K. Grundy (Ed.), *Linguistics in clinical practice* (pp. 92–117). London: Taylor & Francis.

Huddleston, R. (1984). *Introduction to the grammar of English*. Cambridge: Cambridge University Press.

Hunt, K.W. (1965). *Grammatical structures written at three grade levels*. National Council of Teachers of English, Research Report No 3. Champaign, IL: National Council of Teachers of English.

Hunt, K.W. (1970). Syntactic maturity in school children and adults. *Monographs of the Society for Research in Child Development, 35*.

Ingram, D. (1981). Early patterns of grammatical development. In R.E. Stark (Ed.), *Language behavior in infancy and early childhood*. New York: Elsevier.

International Phonetic Association. (1979). *The principles of the international phonetic association*. London: International Phonetic Association.

Johnson, M. (1986). *A computer-based approach to the analysis of child language data*. Unpublished Ph.D. thesis, University of Reading.

Johnston, J.R., & Kamhi, A.H. (1984). Syntactic and semantic aspects of the utterances of language-impaired children: The same can be less. *Merrill-Palmer Quarterly, 30*, 65–85.

Klee, T. (1985). Clinical language sampling: analysing the analyses. *Child Language Teaching and Therapy, 1*, 182–198.

Klee, T., & Fitzgerald, M.D. (1985). The relation between grammatical development and mean length of utterance in morphemes. *Journal of Child Language, 12*, 251–269.

Klee, T., Schaffer, M., May, S., Membrino, I., & Mougey, K. (1987). *Sensitivity and specificity of MLU in preschool children*. Paper presented at the annual meeting of the American Speech-Language-Hearing Association, New Orleans.

Klee, T., Schaffer, M., May, S., Membrino, I., & Mougey, K. (1989). A comparison of the age–MLU relation in normal and specifically language-impaired preschool children. *Journal of Speech and Hearing Disorders, 54*, 226–233.

MacWhinney, B. (1987). CHAT Manual. *Transcript Analysis, 4*.

Miller, J.F. (1981). *Assessing language production in children: Experimental procedures*. Baltimore: University Park Press.

Miller, J.F. (1987). A grammatical characterization of language disorder. *Proceedings of the First International Symposium on Specific Speech and Language Disorders in Children*. London: AFASIC.

Miller, J.F., & Chapman, R.S. (1981). The relation between age and mean length of utterance in morphemes. *Journal of Speech and Hearing Research, 24*, 154–161.

Miller, J.F., & Chapman, R.S. (1985, September). *SALT user's manual* (rev. ed.). Madison: University of Wisconsin, Language Analysis Lab.

Miller, J.F., & Chapman, R.S. (1986). *Systematic Analysis of Language Transcripts (SALT1)* (Computer software, VAX/VMS version 1.1a). Madison: University of Wisconsin, Language Analysis Lab.

Ochs, E. (1979). Transcription as theory. In E. Ochs & B.B. Schieffelin (Eds.), *Developmental pragmatics* (pp. 43–72). New York: Academic Press.

Peters, A.M. (1983). *The units of language acquisition*. Cambridge: Cambridge University Press.

Phonetic Representation of Disordered Speech Working Party. (1983). *The phonetic representation of disordered speech*. London: The King's Fund.

Rondal, J.A., Ghiotto, J., Bredart, S., & Bachelet, J-F. (1987). Age-relation, reliability and grammatical validity of measures of utterance length. *Journal of Child Language, 14,* 433–446.

13

Linguistic Communication in Persons with Mental Retardation

Leonard Abbeduto and Sheldon Rosenberg

How well do persons with mental retardation function as speakers and listeners in their everyday social interactions? This is a major question facing those who conduct language assessments or implement language interventions with this population. Language assessments should be intended to predict an individual's language behavior in everyday social encounters; language interventions should be designed to promote the use of more effective and appropriate language behaviors in those encounters. Meeting these goals requires information on the effectiveness with which persons with mental retardation deal with the requirements of communication through language and the factors that might limit their ability to do so. This chapter summarizes the research in these areas and outlines the implications for assessment and intervention. We also suggest directions for future research that may facilitate the development of effective assessment and intervention protocols for persons with mental retardation.

We have limited the literature reviewed in three ways. First, for the most part, we examine research on communication through spoken language only (i.e., linguistic communication). Thus, we do not review studies of prelinguistic communication or nonlinguistic aspects of communication in persons who have some facility with spoken language. Second, by limiting the review to research on spoken language, we have in effect limited it to research on persons with borderline to moderate mental retardation. The conclusions reached in our review, therefore, are not necessarily generalizable to persons with more severe disabilities. Third, we have focused on the communicative behaviors of persons with mental retardation, and on the knowledge and skills

Preparation of this manuscript was supported by Grant No. HD24356 from the National Institute of Child Health and Human Development to the first author and by Grant No. 03352 from the National Institute of Child Health and Human Development to the Waisman Center on Mental Retardation.

underlying those behaviors, rather than on the ways in which the environments of these persons may contribute to their problems in linguistic communication. We do not deny that the environment plays a role in the acquisition and use of the skills and knowledge underlying effective linguistic communication. Rather, the focus reflects our own research interests and the belief that an in-depth treatment of both organismic and environmental factors in linguistic communication was not possible within a single chapter.

PERFORMANCE IN FUNDAMENTAL AREAS OF LINGUISTIC COMMUNICATION

In this section, we review research findings on the effectiveness with which persons with mental retardation meet the requirements of communication through spoken language. We focus on the four areas of communication that have been most frequently studied by researchers interested in mental retardation: 1) establishing referents, 2) managing speech acts, 3) repairing breakdowns in communication, and 4) organizing conversation. The aim of this section is to describe the adequacy of the performance of persons with mental retardation in each of these areas. The factors that limit the adequacy of their performance are considered in a subsequent section. We point out here only that a deficit in linguistic competence (i.e., knowledge of the syntactic, semantic, and phonological components of language) is only one of the factors that can limit performance in linguistic communication.

Establishing Referents

A fundamental task in any type of communicative interaction is to establish clearly the persons, places, and things being referred to in a participant's utterance (Whitehurst & Sonnenschein, 1985). Unless the participants recognize the referents of a speaker's utterance, the conversation will not progress very far. Consider, for example, the problems that would arise if a participant began the conversation with "She said it again." and gave no clue as to who "she" was and to what "it" referred. Consider the problems that would result if a listener who heard "He quit this morning." simply guessed at the referent of "he" rather than taking advantage of the information contained in the speaker's prior utterance ("Did you hear about Bob?"). Because of the impact of referential failures on social interaction, referential communication has been a popular topic in the field of mental retardation.

Early studies involved the use of a procedure originally developed by Glucksberg and Krauss (1967) in their work with children without disabilities. In this procedure, two people, a speaker and listener, are separated by an opaque partition. The speaker is shown a set of stimuli (e.g., abstract geometric designs), one of which is arbitrarily designated as the referent. The same stimuli are presented to the listener, who is not informed as to the identity of the referent. The speaker's job is to produce a message that fits the referent but none of the other stimuli. The listener's job is to select the referent on the basis of the speaker's message.

Speaker–listener dyads of adolescents with mental retardation perform poorly at establishing referents in this type of non–face-to-face situation. Their efforts seldom lead to selection of the referent by the listener (Beveridge & Tatham, 1976; Longhurst, 1974; Rueda & Chan, 1980). This is true whether the stimuli are abstract geometric patterns (Longhurst, 1974); pictures of simple scenes, such as a girl cutting a cake (Beveridge & Tatham, 1976; or pairs of common objects differing on only a single dimension, such as a clown with a hat and a clown without a hat (Rueda & Chan, 1980). Although IQ is correlated with performance in this type of task, even dyads of adolescents with borderline retardation (i.e., IQs between 70 and 90) have been found to achieve selection of the referent by the listener only about half of the time (Longhurst, 1974).

The referential failures of dyads of persons with mental retardation result from the inadequate messages of speakers rather than from the inadequate responses of listeners. This is indicated by the finding that adults without disabilities are seldom able to select the referent on the basis of a message that has been produced by a speaker with mental retardation (Longhurst, 1974; Rueda & Chan, 1980), whereas listeners with mental retardation perform well when given fully informative messages (Longhurst, 1974; Rueda & Chan, 1980). Although 10-year-old children without disabilities do well as speakers in the Glucksberg and Krauss task (Glucksberg, Krauss, & Higgins, 1975; Robinson & Whittaker, 1986), persons with mental retardation who have mental ages near 10 years produce inadequate messages at a high rate (Longhurst, 1974). Thus, the speaker role in the task of establishing referents may be especially problematic for adolescents with mental retardation, at least in non–face-to-face interactions.

More recent research on the speaker side of dyadic referential communication has focused on face-to-face encounters, but the results have not always been particularly informative. Kernan and Sabsay (1987) found that when retelling the story line of a recently viewed film, adults with mild to moderate retardation made more errors in their use of definite and indefinite articles to introduce referents than did college students without disabilities. The fact that adults with mental retardation make these referential errors infrequently in conversation (Rosenberg & Abbeduto, 1987), however, suggests that the Kernan and Sabsay results may reflect more about their subjects' ability to encode and retrieve the story from memory than about their referential ability. In a study by Loveland, Tunali, McEvoy, and Kelly (1989), subjects explained a game to an experimenter, who asked questions (e.g., "What happens next?") when the subject failed to provide critical information spontaneously. Although the 10- to 30-year-olds with Down syndrome who were tested provided the necessary information without extensive questioning, the lack of a comparison group without disabilities makes it difficult to interpret the adequacy of their performance. (In fairness to Loveland et al., it should be noted that they were interested in the referential abilities of persons with mental retardation and autism relative to the referential abilities of persons with mental retardation only. For their purposes, no comparison group of people without disabilities was necessary.) Clearly, more work on reference making in face-to-face interaction is needed.

In the Glucksberg and Krauss procedure, the speaker's utterance is intended to be the only source of information about the referent. That is, a dyad can succeed on a consistent basis only if the speaker produces utterances that unambiguously specify his or her intended referents and the listener relies only on what the speaker says to select a referent. In everyday conversation, in contrast, speakers frequently produce utterances that are ambiguous if considered in isolation (Levinson, 1983). Listeners are usually able to resolve such ambiguity with little difficulty by relying on the context in which the utterance occurs, and are expected to do so by speakers (Clark, Schreuder, & Buttrick, 1983).

A recent investigation by Abbeduto, Davies, Solesby, and Furman (1991) demonstrated that 8- to 11-year-olds with mild to moderate mental retardation were as skilled as mental age–matched children without disabilities at using contextual information to resolve referential ambiguities in the language they heard. If the context made clear that the speaker was looking for a gift for a child, for example, the children in both groups reacted to a request such as "Show me that cup." by selecting a child's cup over an adult's cup as the speaker's intended referent.

Summary and Implications

To summarize, persons with mental retardation reveal the greatest delays in establishing referents in their performance as speakers. The speaker role is particularly problematic in non–face-to-face situations. Because of the importance of establishing one's referents to the success of even the simplest communicative exchange, assessment and intervention efforts with this population should target referential performance, particularly its productive aspects. However, before assessment instruments and intervention procedures can be developed, several questions about the referential performance of persons with mental retardation must be answered:

1. Do the referential difficulties of persons with mental retardation extend to all types of face-to-face exchanges? There is no guarantee that the results of studies involving the Glucksberg and Krauss procedure will generalize to face-to-face situations (Abbeduto & Rosenberg, 1987). The results of studies of face-to-face referential communication have been difficult to interpret. In fact, it remains to be determined whether performance in the

Glucksberg and Krauss situation predicts referential problems in non–face-to-face interactions associated with different information processing and social demands (e.g., conversing about familiar topics over the telephone). What is needed is a careful analysis of the environments in which individuals with mental retardation normally engage in referential communication. Their performance should then be examined in a representative sample of those environments.

2. What is the developmental course of referential skills in persons with mental retardation? With one exception (Abbeduto et al., 1991), research on referential communication has focused on adolescents and adults. Early intervention, which is certainly the preferred approach to communication problems, requires data on the referential performance of children with mental retardation, particularly in light of the fact that deficits in communication have been observed for persons with mental retardation even during the prelinguistic period (Greenwald & Leonard, 1979).

Managing Speech Acts

By producing a linguistic expression, a participant in a social interaction performs a social act. In the right circumstances, for instance, the utterance of "It's nine o'clock." would be an act of assertion, the utterance "Move over." an act of requesting. Austin (1962) coined the term *speech act* to refer to the social acts that are performed through language. Researchers in mental retardation have become interested in speech acts on the assumption that problems in this area will limit an individual's ability to participate in social interaction, and can adversely affect how he or she is perceived by others (Abbeduto & Benson, in press).

Producing Speech Acts

Much of the work in this area has focused on whether persons with mental retardation use language to perform the same types of speech acts, with the same relative frequencies, as do persons without developmental disabilities. The approach in such studies has been first to record an individual's language as he or she interacts with one or more persons (e.g., peer, parent, teacher) in a loosely structured setting such as mealtime or freeplay. Each of the individual's intelligible utterances is then classified as falling into one or more categories of speech acts on the basis of the words spoken, the context (e.g., the activities in which the participants are physically engaged), and the ways in which the other participant(s) in the interaction react to the utterance. The categories of speech acts have differed across studies, but in all cases the categories were thought to be those expressed by children and/or adults without disabilities. A listing of the speech act categories employed in three of these studies (Abbeduto & Rosenberg, 1980; Coggins, Carpenter, & Owings, 1983; Owens & MacDonald, 1982) is provided in Table 1 for illustration.

Table 1.   Examples of categories of speech acts used in research on mental retardation

Coggins, Carpenter, & Owings (1983)[a]	Owens & MacDonald (1982)[a]	Abbeduto & Rosenberg (1980)[b]
Question	Request for information	Assertion
Naming an entity	Request for object	Commissive
Declaration (i.e., assertion)	Comment on object	(i.e., commitment to a future action)
Practice with language (e.g., singing, rhyming)	Answer to another's request for information	Request for action/object
Suggestions/commands (i.e., for actions/objects)	Protest	Expressive (i.e., evaluation of a proposition/entity, as in "I hate her")
Continuants (i.e., acknowledgments, such as "oh," "mmhmm")		Question

Note: Not all of the categories used in each study are listed.
[a]Subjects were children.
[b]Subjects were adults.

This line of inquiry suggests that many children with mental retardation reveal developmental delays in their expression of speech acts. In particular, when interacting with a parent, 2- to 7-year-olds with Down syndrome produce the same types of speech acts and at approximately the same relative rates as do much younger children without developmental disabilities (Coggins et al., 1983; Owens & MacDonald, 1982). Although it seems probable that children with retardation due to factors other than Down syndrome would also reveal delays in this area, we are aware of no published studies involving such children.

Little is known about the speech acts expressed by persons with mental retardation who are of school age or older. Several studies (Abbeduto & Rosenberg, 1980; Owings & McManus, 1980; Owings, McManus, & Scherer, 1981; Zetlin & Sabsay, 1980) have indicated that adults and adolescents with borderline to severe mental retardation produce the same types of speech acts as adults without developmental disabilities. However, comparison groups of adults without developmental disabilities were not included in these studies, thus making it impossible to determine if the frequencies with which the subjects with mental retardation expressed the various types of speech acts are similar to those typical for speakers without disabilities.

In addition to allowing the expression of a wide range of social acts, natural language allows any particular act to be encoded in a number of different forms (Levinson, 1983). Although the imperative is the prototypical form for requesting an action, for instance, there are numerous other forms a speaker can use when making such a request (e.g., "I want you to sign this.", "Could you sign this?", "Could I ask you to sign this?"). In fact, as research on communication in prelinguistic children without disabilities has demonstrated (e.g., Snyder, 1978; Sugarman, 1984), nonlinguistic and even nonverbal routes are available for the expression of many speech acts. Response generalization, then, is an important part of effective speech act management. Language users must not only master the forms of language, they must learn the range of forms associated with particular speech acts (Abbeduto & Benson, in press).

This facet of speech act management was examined by Abbeduto (1984), who used hypothetical situations to prompt the production of requests by children with borderline to moderate retardation. Abbeduto found that these children did not rely exclusively on the imperative, but used interrogative forms as well (e.g., "Do you wanna play?"). This suggests that children with mental retardation have fairly sophisticated knowledge of the social acts that can be performed by the linguistic forms in their productive repertoires. Abbeduto (1984) also suggested, however, that the range of linguistic forms that persons with mental retardation use for requesting decreases with age, perhaps because of the high frequency with which adult caregivers model imperative requests when interacting with these children (Cardoso-Martins & Mervis, 1985).

Although language makes available to speakers a number of forms for expressing any given speech act, speakers do not select forms at random (Levinson, 1983). Instead, they are guided by, among other things, a desire to maintain good social relations with the other participants in the interaction (Brown & Levinson, 1978). That is, not all of the linguistic forms that can be used for a particular speech act are equivalent in terms of social acceptability. For instance, "I want another." and "Do you have another?" convey the same request, but the former does so impolitely and the latter, politely (Gordon, Budwig, Strage, & Carrell, 1980). Thus, a speaker who wished to maintain good social relations would more often than not opt for "Do you have another?" over "I want another."

There is evidence that the language behavior of persons with mental retardation may not be conducive to the maintenance of good social relations. In a study by Nuccio and Abbeduto (in press), school-age children with mild to moderate mental retardation and children without disabilities matched to them on mental age were prompted to request objects from an adult experimenter who always complied. These researchers found that the subjects with mental retardation relied heavily on impolite, noninterrogative forms (e.g., "Another toy.") when requesting an object from an adult experimenter, whereas their mental age peers without disabilities used polite interrogative forms (e.g., "Can I have another toy?") almost exclusively. This was true despite the fact that the subjects with mental retardation were able to produce many of the interrogative forms used by the children without disabilities. Bliss (1985) elicited requests to hypothetical situations from school-age children and adolescents with mental retardation, and found, among other things, that compared to mental age matches without disabilities, they made greater

338 / Abbeduto and Rosenberg

use of forms that mentioned their needs (e.g., "I want you to keep this puppy that I found.") and less use of forms that mentioned the benefits of compliance (e.g., "If you keep this puppy, you'll be happy."). Requests of the former type are less polite than are those of the latter type (Gordon et al., 1980). Thus, persons with mental retardation are less adept at selecting socially acceptable forms for their speech acts than would be expected on the basis of their levels of cognitive functioning.

In selecting among the potential linguistic forms that a speech act could take, speakers must also consider the context in which that act will occur. For example, a speaker who wishes to maintain good social relations might select an extremely polite request form (e.g., "May I please have another?") for a listener who is angry or upset but a moderately polite form (e.g., "Can you give me another?") for a listener who is not angry or upset. That is, maintaining good social relations requires more politeness in some contexts than in others. Moreover, speakers may not care about maintaining good social relations in some contexts. For instance, a speaker might use the impolite "I want that back." to make clear that he or she is not interested in maintaining good relations with an addressee who has just taken the speaker's property.

Persons with mental retardation attend to important dimensions of the context when selecting forms for their speech acts, although they come to do so at a later age than do persons without developmental disabilities. School-age children with borderline to moderate retardation select linguistic forms for their requests according to characteristics of the addressee, such as his or her age (Abbeduto, 1984), emotional state (Nuccio & Abbeduto, in press), level of familiarity (Bliss, 1985), and level of activity when the request is made (Nuccio & Abbeduto, in press). Children and adolescents with mental retardation also base their choice of request forms on a consideration of the nature of the act they are requesting (Abbeduto, 1984; Bliss, 1985). For instance, their requests are in a more polite form when they seek a favor than when they seek to end a violation of their rights. In all of the studies in this area, however, the subjects with mental retardation revealed a sensitivity to context that was more appropriate for their mental ages than for their chronological ages (Abbeduto, 1984; Bliss, 1985; Nuccio & Abbeduto, in press).

Comprehending Speech Acts

Not only the expression of speech acts, but also their comprehension poses a challenge for the participants in a social interaction (Abbeduto & Benson, in press). The challenge for listeners arises because many linguistic expressions can be used to perform different speech acts in different contexts; thus, a listener cannot rely solely on what a speaker says. For example, "That's mine." would function as a request for the return of an object if addressed to someone who was using one of the speaker's prized possessions without permission. This sentence would function merely as an assertion, however, if uttered by a wealthy business person while giving a tour of the properties he or she had amassed. Listeners, then, must use the context to help them decide which of the speech acts that an utterance could convey is actually intended (Abbeduto & Benson, in press).

Several observational studies suggest that many persons with mental retardation can understand speech acts in at least some circumstances. In the context of naturally occurring activities, such as clean-up and mealtime, for example, adolescents and adults with mild to moderate retardation typically respond appropriately to the speech acts performed by their peers and caregivers (Abbeduto & Rosenberg, 1980; Bedrosian & Prutting, 1978; Zetlin & Sabsay, 1980). In one study (Abbeduto & Rosenberg, 1980), for example, the adults with mental retardation responded in an appropriate manner to more than 90% of the utterances addressed to them that required responses (e.g., requests for information).

The results of these studies, however, should not be taken to indicate that persons with mental retardation have no problems in the domain of speech act comprehension. First, these studies have sampled the performance of persons with mental retardation only in situations in which they interacted with familiar peers or caregivers within the context of fairly routinized activities. The speech acts performed in such interactions may be so highly predictable from the context that listeners need conduct only cursory analyses of the speaker's words. Alternatively, the linguistic expressions used in such interactions may be highly transparent, in that they afford few alternative interpretations, thus minimizing the need to use context. This raises the possibility that listeners with mental retardation may fail to understand speech acts in situations in which in-depth analyses of the context and of the speaker's words are required. They may have comprehension problems, for example, if the speaker is not familiar to them, or if the talk is not embedded in a highly routinized activity. Second, although the subjects in these studies correctly responded to the speech acts of others at a seemingly high rate (but at less than 100%), it is difficult to interpret their level of performance because comparable data on mental age matches without disabilities were not provided.

In fact, studies in which comprehension has required a careful consideration of both context and utterance or in which a comparison group without disabilities was included have demonstrated that the development of speech act comprehension is delayed in individuals with mental retardation. Abbeduto, Davies, and Furman (1988) included comparison groups without disabilities, and tested comprehension under unfamiliar experimental conditions. Moreover, the materials and procedures used ensured that accurate comprehension could be achieved only by considering both the speaker's words and the context in which they were embedded. These investigators found below chronological age–level comprehension of speech acts by children and adolescents with mild to moderate retardation. Leifer and Lewis (1984) found that preschool children with Down syndrome were less adept at responding to the speech acts of their mothers during freeplay than expected on the basis of their chronological ages. Other studies indicate that children with a variety of forms of mental retardation comply with maternal suggestions and commands at a rate equivalent to that seen for mental age matches without disabilities (Hanzlik & Stevenson, 1986; Sigman, Mundy, Sherman, & Ungerer, 1986). Thus, persons with mental retardation reveal developmental delays in their comprehension of speech acts, although they may eventually become skilled at listening in familiar, highly predictable situations associated with minimal communicative demands.

Summary and Implications

Persons with mental retardation reveal delays in all aspects of their speech act performance. In the role of speaker, they use language to perform the same social acts performed by younger children without disabilities. Speakers with mental retardation also reveal delays in their use of contextual information to make decisions about the linguistic forms their speech acts should take. They have even greater difficulty, however, limiting their selection to socially acceptable linguistic forms. Persons with mental retardation also reveal delays in understanding speech acts, although as they enter adulthood they may become quite good at comprehending language when it is embedded in highly familiar types of interaction. Because of the importance of the task of speech act management to the exchange of information and the maintenance of good social relations, assessment and intervention efforts involving this population should target speech act performance. Before this can be done, however, two questions need to be answered:

1. What is the relationship between speech act performance and aging in persons with mental retardation? The suggestion by Abbeduto (1984) that some aspects of performance decline with age points out the need for longitudinal studies of speech act development in this population. Data provided by such studies would be useful in identifying the causes of the communicative difficulties experienced by persons with mental retardation and in identifying ages at which intervention is needed most.

2. Can persons with mental retardation deal effectively with the full range of situations in which speech acts must be expressed and understood? There are many different types of contextual information that can be relevant to the decisions that speakers and listeners make about speech acts (Bach & Harnish, 1979). For example, decisions about how polite a request should be depend on, among other things, the relative age, status, and power of speaker and listener (Gordon & Ervin-Tripp, 1984); the affect and activity level of the listener (Nuccio & Abbeduto, in press); the reason or cause of the request (Abbeduto, 1984); the nature of the activity or object requested (Wilkinson & Spinelli, 1983); the formality of the setting (Gor-

don & Ervin-Tripp, 1984); and whether the request is embedded within a conversation or task-oriented episode (Abbeduto & Nuccio, 1989). Only a few of these dimensions of context have been represented in studies of the requesting behavior of persons with mental retardation. Moreover, investigations into the influence of context on the linguistic forms selected by persons with mental retardation have involved an examination of only the speech act of requesting. Expression of any speech act, however, requires choosing a linguistic form. For example, decisions about the form an answer to a question should take depend on factors such as the closeness of the relationship between the participants and their relative status (Holtgraves, 1986). In sum, there are many important aspects of speech act management for which there is simply a lack of data on the performance of individuals with mental retardation.

Repairing Breakdowns in Communication

Communication does not always proceed in a troublefree manner. For example, listeners may fail to attend to a speaker's utterance, or err in their decisions about how to interpret the speaker's words. Speakers may misarticulate their utterances, or assume that the referents of their utterances can be determined when they cannot. When problems such as these occur, the participants can apply a number of repair devices. For instance, a listener can use "Huh?" to signal a need for the speaker to repeat an utterance and "Which one?" to gain more information about an ambiguous referential expression (Garvey, 1977). Repair devices play an important role in the process of linguistic communication: listeners who fail to indicate the need for repair can miss much of the information the speaker is trying to convey and may inadvertently respond to the speaker in socially unacceptable ways, whereas speakers who ignore indications of a problem may not get their message across, and may appear self-centered to their partners.

Persons with mental retardation have been found to produce repair devices. Zetlin and Sabsay (1980), for instance, found that adolescents with organically caused moderate retardation produced a variety of repair devices (e.g., "Where?" in response to "There's an apple right there."). In their study of the mealtime conversations of adults with borderline to moderate retardation, Abbeduto and Rosenberg (1980) found that 5% of the subjects' responses to a prior conversational turn were verbal requests for repair. It is difficult to interpret the results of these studies, however, without a careful analysis of the conditions under which the repair devices were (and were not) used. For example, there is no way of determining how often the subjects should have but did not produce a request for repair. Nevertheless, these studies do suggest that by adulthood, many persons with mental retardation are willing to use the repair devices in their repertoires, at least in familiar, nondemanding interactions.

Studies that have involved an analysis of the conditions under which repair devices are and are not used have shown that many persons with mental retardation often fail to produce linguistic repair devices when they are called for. Abbeduto et al. (1991), for instance, found that when faced with an ambiguous request that could refer to either of two physically present objects, children with mild to moderate retardation seldom produced requests for clarification (i.e., "Which one?"). Instead, these children usually selected and acted on one of the objects, seemingly at random. This contrasted with the frequent production of clarification requests by the children of the same mental age without disabilities. Adults with moderate mental retardation also sometimes fail to request clarification of inadequate referential expressions (Rueda & Chan, 1980).

The problems that persons with mental retardation have using repair devices, however, are less pronounced in some circumstances than in others. In particular, Warne and Bedrosian (cited in Bedrosian, 1988) found that three of their four adult subjects with moderate retardation were more likely to request clarification when an experimenter spoke about a physically absent referent that was unrelated to the current topic of conversation than when he or she spoke about an absent referent related to the topic.

Taken together, the studies on the production of repair devices demonstrate that persons with mental retardation use repair devices only under a rather limited set of circumstances. One possible interpretation of this result is that these persons have limited knowledge about repair devices and the conditions under which they can be used. Alternatively, performance factors, rather than limited knowledge, may explain their failure to use repair devices. For instance, the information-processing demands associated with some situations (e.g., talking about absent referents) may be so high as to exceed the cognitive resources of persons with mental retardation, which results in deterioration in many facets of their communicative performance, including their use of repair devices (Shatz, 1983).

Research on the ability of persons with mental retardation to respond to requests for repair of their own inadequate messages suggests that this may be an area in which they are relatively strong. Coggins and Stoel-Gammon (1982) and Scherer and Owings (1984), for instance, found that 5- to 6-year-olds with Down syndrome responded to nearly all of the requests for repair directed to them by an adult during a variety of loosely structured activities. Moreover, these children more often than not responded by revising their original, problematic utterance rather than by simply repeating it verbatim. Paul and Cohen (1984) also provide evidence that persons with mental retardation deal effectively with a number of different types of requests for repair. They found that their subjects, whose average age was near 30 and average performance IQ was 68, responded in some way to all of the experimenter's requests for confirmation (e.g., "You watched 'Dynasty'?"), for repetition (e.g., "What?"), and for repetition of a specific constituent (e.g., "You left what?"). Paul and Cohen also found that their subjects' responses were tailored appropriately to the type of request addressed to them.

Although response to requests for repair appears to be an area of relative strength, there is reason to believe that persons with mental retardation do reveal some developmental delay in this area. For example, Gallagher (1977) and Garvey (1977) found that preschool children without disabilities responded appropriately to repair requests at a rate similar to that of the 5- to 6-year-olds with Down syndrome studied by Coggins and Stoel-Gammon (1982) and Scherer and Owings (1984). In addition, some individuals with mental retardation find some types of repair requests more difficult to process and respond to than others. This was evident in a study by Longhurst and Berry (1975), who investigated the ability of children and adolescents with borderline to moderate mental retardation to respond to three types of requests for repair: nonverbal (i.e., a puzzled facial expression), explicit verbal (i.e., "Tell me something else about the picture."), and implicit verbal (i.e., "I don't understand."). Longhurst and Berry found that most of their subjects responded appropriately at a high rate to explicit verbal requests, which make the response requirements clear. Only the highest functioning subjects in the sample, however, were able to deal effectively with the other repair devices, which did not make explicit what course of action the subject was to take. It is possible that the information-processing demands of the nonverbal and implicit verbal repairs exceeded the cognitive capabilities of the subjects with more severe disabilities.

Summary and Implications

Assessment and intervention with persons with mental retardation must focus on performance in repairing communicative breakdowns, with particular emphasis on the area of greatest delay, namely, the production of repair devices. Before this can be done, however, additional information is needed on the conditions that lead to better and worse performance in the production of repair devices. The research performed to date suggests that persons with mental retardation are more likely to produce repair requests in some situations than in others. However, performance has been examined in only a limited set of circumstances. Abbeduto et al. (1991) and Warne and Bedrosian (cited in Bedrosian, 1988) examined requests for clarification only in response to ambiguous referential expressions. There are many other types of communication problems. For example, speakers can produce messages that: 1) do not allow the listener to identify any referent at all (Beal, 1987; Sonnenschein, 1986), 2) contain unfamiliar words (Lempers & Elrod, 1983), or 3) are acoustically poor (Lempers & Elrod, 1983). No research has been done on the ability of persons with mental retardation to use repair devices to resolve these types of problems. Finally, although several intervention procedures have been shown to increase the use of repair devices by young children without disabilities (Whitehurst & Sonnenschein, 1985), the applicability of these procedures to persons with mental retardation has yet to be evaluated.

Organizing a Conversation

A conversation is more than a collection of individual utterances or even pairs of utterances (i.e., initiations and responses). The utterances comprising a conversation fit together in systematic ways. First, conversations are organized by principles of turn-taking. The participants in a conversation do not all talk at once, but take turns talking (Sacks, Schegloff, & Jefferson, 1974). Second, conversations are organized into topics. The participants in a conversation typically produce utterances that relate to and help develop one or more themes or issues (Dorval & Eckerman, 1984). Third, conversations are organized according to interpersonal principles. Each participant tries to control the conversation so that it moves in a direction that will lead to the fulfillment of his or her social goals (e.g., a participant may try to bring the discussion back to a topic of interest to him or her). Failure to produce utterances that conform to these principles of organization can limit the transmission of information among participants, frustrate the participants in their attempts to achieve important goals, and lead to negative evaluations of participants who are the source of organizational problems. Consider, for example, how little information would be exchanged if the participants in a conversation all talked at once rather than taking turns. Consider, too, the reaction of the participants to a person who constantly interrupted their talk. Despite the importance of these principles of organization to communication and to social functioning, little work has been done on the performance of persons with mental retardation in this area.

Turn-Taking Organization

Observational studies have typically shown that dyadic conversations between children with mental retardation and their caregivers display turn-taking organization. That is, there are few instances in which the utterances of the two participants overlap or in which one participant interrupts the other (Davis & Oliver, 1980; Davis, Stroud, & Green, 1988). In some studies (e.g., Davis et al., 1988), the rate of turn-taking errors in interactions between parents and their children with mental retardation has been found to be similar to that expected on the basis of the children's level of linguistic competence. In other studies (e.g., Tannock, 1988), these interactions have been found to contain more turn-taking errors than would be expected on the basis of the children's linguistic competence, but even in these studies the rate of such errors was low.

Such findings, however, should not be taken to mean that children with mental retardation intend to engage in, or understand, turn-taking in the way that adults without disabilities do (Sacks et al., 1974). It may be that like parents of children without disabilities (Snow, 1972), parents of children with disabilities control the interaction to ensure that there is an orderly transition between turns despite the limited turn-taking capabilities of their children (Tannock, 1988).

The difficulties of interpretation inherent in caregiver–child observational studies can be avoided by studying the peer interactions of subjects with mental retardation. This is possible, of course, only for subjects whose language and communicative skills are developed to a point that allows them to engage in meaningful peer interaction. Such an approach was taken by Abbeduto and Rosenberg (1980), who observed mealtime conversations among triads of adults with borderline to moderate mental retardation. These investigators found that the majority of the speaker changes were managed appropriately. Overlaps of different speakers or interruptions of one speaker by another occurred in only 10% of the speaker changes. This is somewhat higher than the 5% error rate that has been reported for the conversations of adults without disabilities (Levinson, 1983). Although this may indicate that adults with mental retardation are less adept at turn-taking than are adults without disabilities, the fact that the data for the two types of speakers were not collected under identical conditions makes such a conclusion tentative at best. Moreover, even if this conclusion is correct, the relatively low rate of errors observed by Abbeduto and Rosenberg suggests that failure to take turns is not a major communicative problem for many adults with borderline to moderate mental retardation.

Topical Organization

Children with mental retardation reveal delays in their ability to contribute to the topic of conversation. In particular, Tannock (1988) observed interactions between children with Down syndrome and their mothers, and found that topic length (measured by number of turns) for these interactions was similar to that seen for interactions between younger children without disabilities and their mothers. The extent of the delay was thus no greater than the extent of delay in cognitive functioning.

Studies of adults with mental retardation have focused on the extent to which subjects stay on topic and on the nature of their contributions to the topic. Abbeduto and Rosenberg (1980) found that the mean number of consecutive turns on the same topic ranged from 7 to 21 for their three triads of subjects with mental retardation. The greatest number of consecutive turns spent on a topic by each triad ranged from 36 to 157. Although this would seem to imply highly developed topic skills in these subjects, the results of a study by Warne and Bedrosian (cited in Bedrosian, 1988) suggest that this may not be the case. Warne and Bedrosian found that although the adults with moderate retardation they studied stayed on topic, their utterances often did not seem to help in the progression of the topic. For example, their subjects often continued the topic by producing an acknowledgment, such as "mm-hmm." Acknowledgments allow the topic to be maintained without the addition of any semantic content (Dorval & Eckerman, 1984). Together these studies suggest that although adults with mental retardation can sustain a topic over substantial spans of conversational space, they have problems developing the topic in the ways that adults without disabilities do. Topic length, therefore, may not be a good indicator of topic-related skills when dealing with older children and adults.

Interpersonal Organization

The organization of conversation at an interpersonal level also appears to be a problem for some adults with mental retardation. Bedrosian and Prutting (1978) analyzed the conversations of four adults with severe retardation for the occurrence of *arching* and *chaining,* two devices for controlling the direction of the conversation. In arching, a participant responds to a question with another question (Mishler, 1975). Answering "Do you like the hamburger?" with "Yes, do you?" is an instance of arching. Chaining occurs when a participant, in acknowledging a response to his or her question, asks another question. An example of chaining would be a response of "Oh, I see. Why?" to a conversational partner's response of "yes" to the question "Do you like the hamburger?" Bedrosian and Prutting found that three of the four subjects they studied used chaining and arching. However, the frequency with which these devices were used and thus the degree of control exerted by these subjects was low.

Summary and Implications

Research findings on the ability of persons with mental retardation to organize their talk is limited, especially regarding the level of interpersonal organization. The research that has been done, however, suggests that assessment and intervention with this population may need to focus on the ability to make meaningful, substantive contributions to the conversational topic and on the ability to be assertive and exercise control over the direction of the talk. Turn-taking is not a major problem for persons with mental retardation because the rate of turn-taking errors is low throughout development, but even here there is some delay. Before the appropriate assessments and interventions can be designed, two questions must be addressed:

1. How well do persons with mental retardation manage conversational organization in the full range of interactions in which they must participate? The research findings on turn-taking, topical organization, and interpersonal organization come almost entirely from situations in which the subjects with mental retardation conversed with familiar people in familiar, loosely structured situations. A different picture might emerge

from observations of their interactions with less familiar partners or in more structured situations.

2. What types of information do persons with mental retardation use when deciding whether or not and when to take a speaking turn? Adults without disabilities attend to a number of different cues to make such decisions (Duncan, 1972). For example, a drop in pitch, the completion of a hand gesture, and the boundary of a grammatical unit are cues that adults without disabilities use to identify points at which a change in speaker can occur. Identification of the types of cues to which persons with mental retardation attend would allow the situations in which such persons would be likely to have trouble with turn-taking to be predicted.

FACTORS CONTRIBUTING TO POOR LINGUISTIC COMMUNICATION

Success in linguistic communication can be limited by impairments in any of several areas of mental and behavioral functioning (Abbeduto & Rosenberg, 1987). A lack of linguistic competence (i.e., facility with the phonological, syntactic, and semantic aspects of language) can adversely affect linguistic communication. For example, because so many of the linguistic forms used to make polite requests are interrogative (Brown & Levinson, 1978), persons who fail to master interrogative syntax may have no recourse but to make their requests through impolite, noninterrogative forms. Linguistic communication can also be adversely affected by limitations in basic information-processing abilities, conceptual knowledge, and other cognitive skills (Shatz, 1983). Consider, for example, speakers whose cognitive problems include poor organization of and retrieval from long-term memory. When making a request, such speakers may select a linguistic form at random, because they are unable to retrieve information about their addressee (e.g., his or her status). Poorly developed interpersonal goals and motives, a lack of knowledge about other people's intentions and beliefs, and other limitations in social competence or knowledge of and reasoning about the social world can limit the effectiveness of linguistic communication as well (Abbeduto & Benson, in press). For instance, persons with problems in the domain of social competence may fail to make polite requests because their poor perspective-taking skills prevent them from anticipating the reaction of their addressees to an impolite request. Linguistic communication will also be constrained by impairments in pragmatic competence (Abbeduto & Rosenberg, 1987). Pragmatic competence refers to knowledge about linguistic communication per se, and includes recognition of the social uses of language and of the dimensions of context relevant to particular speaking and listening choices (Abbeduto & Rosenberg, 1987). For example, a speaker who fails to recognize that request forms differ in terms of politeness or that relative status has specific implications for linguistic politeness would have a pragmatic problem that would be manifested in his or her requesting behavior. (Although pragmatic competence makes reference to concepts within the domain of social competence [e.g., social status], the two types of knowledge are not identical. For example, one could recognize differences among people in terms of their social status, but fail to recognize that those differences in status should determine the linguistic forms that should be used when making requests. In this case, the limitation would be in the domain of pragmatic competence, not social competence. Alternatively, one could recognize that people who differ in status should be talked to differently, but have limited knowledge about the relative status of different people. In this case, the problem would be in the area of social competence, not pragmatic competence.)

This analysis demonstrates that the problems with linguistic communication that persons with mental retardation experience may have a number of sources. Persons with mental retardation have impairments in language (Rosenberg, 1982), cognition (Brooks, McCauley, & Merrill, 1987), and social competence (Simeonsson, Monson, & Blacher, 1984). Limitations in pragmatic knowledge and skill have also been posited (Abbeduto & Nuccio, 1989; Abbeduto & Rosenberg, 1987). In the next several sections, we review research on the ways in which the cognitive, linguistic, social, and pragmatic impairments of persons with mental retardation may contribute to their problems in linguistic communication.

Cognitive Contributions

Cognitive development appears to place strong constraints on the linguistic communication of persons with mental retardation. Evidence for this claim comes largely from studies that have compared persons with mental retardation and children without mental retardation matched to them in terms of cognitive ability (as indexed by mental age or some other summary measure). All four of the areas of linguistic communication considered in this chapter are represented in these studies: establishing referents (Abbeduto et al., 1991), managing speech acts (Abbeduto, 1984; Abbeduto et al., 1988; Bliss, 1985; Hanzlik & Stevenson, 1986; Nuccio & Abbeduto, 1991; Sigman et al., 1986), repairing communicative breakdowns (Abbeduto et al., 1991), and organizing the conversation (Davis et al., 1988; Tannock, 1988). Performance in both the speaker (Abbeduto, 1984; Bliss, 1985; Davis et al., 1988; Nuccio & Abbeduto, in press; Tannock, 1988) and listener (Abbeduto et al., 1988, 1991; Hanzlik & Stevenson, 1986; Sigman et al., 1986) roles were investigated in this set of studies as well. Different measures of cognitive functioning were used across studies. The mental age range of the subjects in these investigations was about 1-12 years, and the level of retardation of the subjects was borderline to moderate.

Although these studies examined a range of tasks, cognitive measures, and ability levels, the results are similar. In no study did the level of linguistic communication of the group with mental retardation exceed that of the comparison group. This contrasts with studies involving groups matched on measures of functioning in other domains (e.g., productive linguistic competence), in which persons with mental retardation performed better than the comparison group. Such findings suggest that there may be certain cognitive developments that function to place an upper bound on performance in linguistic communication (Abbeduto & Benson, in press). Unfortunately, these cognitive prerequisites for effective linguistic communication cannot be identified, because researchers have examined communicative performance only in relation to mental age or other measures that summarize performance across numerous cognitive skills and domains of conceptual knowledge.

Although there may be cognitive abilities that are prerequisites for linguistic communication, it is unlikely that such abilities are sufficient for effective communication through language (Abbeduto & Rosenberg, 1987). Consistent with this claim is the finding that persons with mental retardation perform worse in some areas of linguistic communication than would be expected on the basis of their levels of cognitive functioning. For example, persons with mental retardation have been found to be less likely to use clarification requests (Abbeduto et al., 1991) and to select polite forms for their requests than are children without disabilities matched on mental age (Bliss, 1985; Nuccio & Abbeduto, in press). Thus, cognitive impairments represent only one of several types of impediments to mature communicative performance.

Linguistic Contributions

Many persons with mental retardation have impairments in linguistic competence that are more severe than their impairments in the cognitive domain (Abbeduto, Furman, & Davies, 1989; Chapman, 1981; Miller & Chapman, 1984; but see Curtiss, 1988, and Curtiss & Yamada, 1981, for some interesting exceptions). They sometimes perform better in linguistic communication than would be expected on the basis of their linguistic competence, however. Leifer and Lewis (1984), for example, found that relative to children without disabilities who were matched to them on mean length of utterance (MLU), preschool children with Down syndrome were advanced at understanding and responding to the speech acts of adult caregivers. The fact that the children with mental retardation probably had higher mental ages than their language-level matches may account for the differences in their communicative performance. Other studies have indicated that school-age children with mild to moderate mental retardation were as adept at using context to establish referents (Abbeduto et al., 1991) and to manage speech acts (Abbeduto et al., 1988) as were their mental age matches without disabilities despite the fact that the measured receptive linguistic (i.e., syntactic-semantic) competence of the former was significantly below that of the latter. Such findings suggest that impairments in linguistic competence may not limit performance in linguistic communication as strongly as cognitive development in persons with mental retardation.

We are not claiming that impairments in linguistic competence do not affect the development of linguistic communication. Linguistic communication logically requires some facility with the linguistic system (Abbeduto & Benson, in press). A participant needs to have mastered the syntax and semantics of at least two request forms, for example, in order to face a choice on whether to use a relatively polite or impolite linguistic form for an intended request. Our claim is that not all achievements in linguistic competence are essential for successful linguistic communication, and thus not all impairments in linguistic competence invariably result in a diminished capacity to communicate. Despite especially severe impairments in linguistic competence, therefore, many persons with mild to moderate mental retardation acquire the linguistic prerequisites for many everyday communicative tasks. We do not know, however, which achievements in linguistic competence are essential for success in specific areas of linguistic communication. This is so because, for the most part, researchers have examined linguistic communication only in relation to MLU, receptive language age, or other measures that summarize performance across numerous aspects of linguistic competence.

Social Contributions

Expertise in the domain of social functioning is crucial to linguistic communication (Abbeduto & Benson, in press; Astington, Harris, & Olson, 1988; Shantz, 1981). For example, there is evidence that among children without disabilities, perspective-taking skill is related to the use of polite forms of request (Nippold, Leonard, & Anastopoulus, 1982) and to the production of unambiguous messages in referential communication tasks (Roberts & Patterson, 1983). Aspects of social competence other than perspective taking are also thought to be involved in linguistic communication. For example, a student whose social deficits include a lack of knowledge of the difference in status between a student and a teacher would see no reason to be polite when making a request of a teacher (Rice, 1984). This would be true even if the student was pragmatically competent and knew that high-status speakers warranted linguistic politeness. As another example, consider a listener whose social deficits included a limited knowledge of age and gender differences in object preferences. When faced with a choice between a little girl's wallet and a man's wallet, such a listener might be unable to identify the referent of "I am shopping for a little girl. Show me that wallet." (Abbeduto et al., 1991). Additional examples of the relationship between social knowledge and reasoning and linguistic communication can be found in Bach and Harnish (1979).

There have been only a few attempts to account for the linguistic communication problems of persons with mental retardation in terms of impaired social functioning. These attempts have for the most part failed to find a relationship between functioning in these domains (Abbeduto & Nuccio, 1989). This may be due, however, to limitations in the measures of social competence employed (Benson, Abbeduto, Short, Nuccio, & Maas, 1990). Recent evidence of serious perspective-taking problems in children and adolescents with mild to moderate mental retardation (Benson et al., 1990) suggests that there is a need for additional work on social contributions to the linguistic communication problems of this population.

Pragmatic Contributions

Some of the problems that persons with mental retardation experience in linguistic communication are partly the result of a lack of knowledge about the process of linguistic communication itself. The high rate of inadequate messages produced by speakers with mental retardation in referential tasks, for example, is due in part to limitations in their pragmatic knowledge. In particular, many of these individuals do not recognize the importance of the speaker's words to the success of the exchange (Beveridge, Spencer, & Mittler, 1979) and, therefore, their criteria for what constitutes an adequate message are less stringent than is appropriate. The failure of listeners with mental retardation to use clarification requests (e.g., "Which one?") to resolve referential ambiguity may also be the result of limited pragmatic knowledge. Abbeduto et al. (1991) have suggested that persons with mental retardation may not recognize that "Which one?" will get them the information they need to resolve an ambiguity. Thus, the referential performance of persons with mental retardation as speakers and listeners may reflect, in part, limited pragmatic knowledge.

The influence of pragmatic deficits may extend to other areas of linguistic communication as well. Groups with and without mental retardation that are matched on measures of cognitive, linguistic, or social competence sometimes differ in their levels of performance in linguistic communication, and some measures of linguistic communication in these groups correlate moderately, if at all, with measures of their functioning in these other domains. Differences in pragmatic knowledge may account for some of this unexplained variation. Testing this possibility directly, however, would require examining the relationship between linguistic communication and measures of linguistic, cognitive, social, and pragmatic competence within the same study. This has yet to be done.

Summary and Implications

The research reviewed here suggests that the problems in linguistic communication experienced by persons with mental retardation are not the result of a simple failure to master the linguistic system. In fact, the research suggests that cognitive impairments may place stronger constraints on many aspects of linguistic communication than do linguistic impairments. Although the role of deficits in social competence has not yet been examined in sufficient detail, it is likely that such deficits will also be found to constrain some aspects of linguistic communication. Limited knowledge about the process of linguistic communication itself also contributes to the poor performance of persons with mental retardation in this area. Understanding the nature of any client's difficulties in communication, therefore, will require assessments in all four domains (Abbeduto & Nuccio, 1989). Depending on the results of such an assessment, intervention will need to target one or more of these domains.

We are a long way, however, from being able to apply this multidomain approach to assessment and intervention in linguistic communication. Such an approach requires information on relationships between specific cognitive, linguistic, social, and pragmatic competencies, on the one hand, and narrowly defined aspects of linguistic communication, on the other. This has not always been the approach. Instead, linguistic communication has typically been examined in relation to gross measures, which, like mental age, summarize performance across a number of very different skills. Although such summary measures have provided useful data, we must now move on and test hypotheses about the specific skills and knowledge underlying particular aspects of linguistic communication.

EDUCATIONAL AND CLINICAL IMPLICATIONS

Language assessments and interventions involving persons with mental retardation must be designed to deal with asynchronous performance across different facets of linguistic communication. In all four of the areas of linguistic communication we have considered, the speaker role has often been found to be more problematic than the listener role for persons with mental retardation. For example, although adults with mental retardation fail to request repair of other speaker's problematic messages in many of the situations in which repair is called for, they tend to be skilled at responding to a variety of requests for repair of their own messages. Even within the speaker or the listener roles, however, there is asynchronous development. Children with mild to moderate mental retardation, for example, are less adept at using clarification requests than at using context to resolve referential ambiguity. Asynchronous developments such as these suggest that assessments that target one aspect of linguistic communication may tell us little about other aspects of a client's performance, and that an intervention that leads to improvements in one facet of linguistic communication may have no effect on other facets. Thus, the current focus of most interventionists on speaking performance (Warren, 1987) must be expanded to include the listener role.

Assessment and intervention have traditionally placed the greatest emphasis on linguistic contributions to a client's communicative difficulties (Abbeduto & Benson, in press; Abbeduto & Nuccio, 1989; Wollner, 1983). The research reviewed suggests that the cognitive constraints on linguistic communication are stronger than those imposed by linguistic impairments, at least for persons with borderline to moderate mental retardation, who have some facility with language. Traditional assessment protocols and programs of intervention, therefore, will need to be expanded to include an increased emphasis on cognition. Pragmatic and, perhaps, social knowledge and skill will need to be included in this expanded approach as well.

DIRECTIONS FOR FUTURE RESEARCH

There is much work to be done before assessment of and intervention in linguistic communication can be expanded in the way we have suggested. In the studies reviewed, linguistic communication was examined in relation to gross measures that, like mental age, summarize performance across a number of very different skills. Effective assessment and intervention, however, must be predicated upon relationships between specific cognitive, linguistic, social, and pragmatic competencies and narrowly defined aspects of linguistic communication. Researchers will need to rely on theories about the nature of linguistic communication and its development to guide their search for such specific relationships.

Even once the specific cognitive, linguistic, social, and pragmatic competencies underlying performance in a given area of linguistic communication have been identified, additional research will be needed to determine the best methods for assessing and teaching those competencies. Although these methods will depend in part on the nature of the skills and knowledge identified, it seems certain that these methods must be embedded within the context of linguistic communication. Previous attempts to measure or train linguistic behaviors and cognitive skills outside of the contexts in which those skills will be used have failed (Butterfield & Belmont, 1977; Warren, 1987). Use of a skill in a therapeutic setting does not predict the degree to which it will be used in appropriate naturalistic settings. Thus, researchers will need to devise ways of measuring and training behaviors such as retrieving information about a listener's characteristics from long-term memory, producing interrogative forms, anticipating other people's reactions to different request forms, and recognizing variations in linguistic politeness within the context of naturalistic interactions involving spoken linguistic communication.

Additional research is needed on environmental contributions to the development of pragmatic competencies in persons with mental retardation. There is a large body of literature attesting to the role of the environment in the development of pragmatic knowledge and skills in children without disabilities. For example, the extent to which parents expose their preschool children to the printed word affects the rate at which the latter acquire knowledge about speech act comprehension (Reeder, 1990). Formal instruction in reading and writing facilitates schoolage children's attention to characteristics of speaker's messages when making decisions about referential adequacy (Beal & Flavell, 1984). Parents of children without disabilities also instruct their children in the importance and use of politeness markers, about rules of turn taking, and about the role of context in communication (Becker, 1990). No study has examined the extent to which parents of persons with mental retardation display similar instructional strategies with their children. Were it found that parents or teachers of children with disabilities failed to instruct their children in similar ways, interventions could be designed to modify parental behavior and educational practices.

Persons with mild to moderate mental retardation have been treated as a homogeneous group in the studies described in this chapter. There is a need to examine the possibility that there are subgroups within this group that reveal different profiles of strengths and weaknesses—and thus require different interventions—in linguistic communication. Comparisons among persons with different etiologies may prove a good beginning in the search for such subgroups. This is suggested by recent evidence of differences between persons with Down syndrome and persons with other forms of mental retardation in terms of nonverbal communication (Mundy, Sigman, Kasari, & Yirmiya, 1988).

CONCLUSION

Throughout this chapter, we have stressed the idea that linguistic communication depends on competencies in other domains (e.g., cognition). It is important to note in conclusion that problems in linguistic communication can also function as causes of problems in these other domains. One example of this is provided by recent work on the precursors to differences in sociometric status among intellectually average children. This research has suggested that deficits in linguistic communication, including the inappropriate use of context, may be responsible in part for some children being rejected or ignored by their peers (Black & Hazen, 1990; Hazen & Black, 1989). Such treatment by peers is likely to be associated with further problems in the social domain later in development (Gottman & Parkhurst, 1980). Treatment of the problems in linguistic communication experienced by persons with mental retardation, therefore, may help to alleviate some of their problems in the domains of social, cognitive, and linguistic competence.

REFERENCES

Abbeduto, L. (1984). Situational influences on mentally retarded and nonretarded children's production of directives. *Applied Psycholinguistics, 5,* 147–166.

Abbeduto, L., & Benson, G. (in press). Speech act development in nondisabled children and individuals with mental retardation. In R. Chapman (Ed.), *Child talk: Performance processes in child language development.* Chicago: Year Book Medical Publishers.

Abbeduto, L., Davies, B., & Furman, L. (1988). The development of speech act comprehension in mentally retarded individuals and nonretarded children. *Child Development, 59,* 1460–1472.

Abbeduto, L., Davies, B., Solesby, S., & Furman, L. (1991). Identifying the referents of spoken messages: The use of context and clarification requests by children with mental retardation and by nonretarded children. *American Journal on Mental Retardation, 95,* 551–562.

Abbeduto, L., Furman, L., & Davies, B. (1989). Relation between the receptive language and mental age of persons with mental retardation. *American Journal on Mental Retardation, 93,* 535–543.

Abbeduto, L., & Nuccio, J. (1989). Evaluating the pragmatic aspects of communication in school-age children and adolescents: Insights from research on atypical development. *School Psychology Review, 18,* 498–508.

Abbeduto, L., & Rosenberg, S. (1980). The communicative competence of mildly retarded adults. *Applied Psycholinguistics, 1,* 405–426.

Abbeduto, L., & Rosenberg, S. (1987). Linguistic communication and mental retardation. In S. Rosenberg (Ed.), *Advances in applied psycholinguistics: Vol. 1. Disorders of first language development* (pp. 76–125). Cambridge: Cambridge University Press.

Astington, J.W., Harris, P.L., & Olson, D.R. (Eds.), (1988). *Developing theories of mind.* Cambridge: Cambridge University Press.

Austin, J.L. (1962). *How to do things with words.* Oxford: Oxford University Press.

Bach, K., & Harnish, R.M. (1979). *Linguistic communication and speech acts.* Cambridge: MIT Press.

Beal, C.R. (1987). Repairing the message: Children's monitoring and revision skills. *Child Development, 58,* 401–408.

Beal, C.R., & Flavell, J.H. (1984). Development of the ability to distinguish communicative intention and literal message meaning. *Child Development, 55,* 920–928.

Becker, J.A. (1990). Processes in the acquisition of pragmatic competence. In G. Conti-Ramsden & C. Snow (Eds.), *Children's language* (Vol. 7, pp. 7–24). Hillsdale, NJ: Lawrence Erlbaum Associates.

Bedrosian, J.L. (1988). Adults who are mildly to moderately mentally retarded: Communicative performance, assessment and intervention. In S.N. Calculator & J.I. Bedrosian (Eds.), *Communication assessment and intervention for adults with mental retardation* (pp. 265–307). Boston: College-Hill Press.

Bedrosian, J.L., & Prutting, C.A. (1978). Communicative performance of mentally retarded adults in four conversational settings. *Journal of Speech and Hearing Research, 21,* 79–95.

Benson, G., Abbeduto, L., Short, K., Nuccio, J., & Maas, F. (1990). *Perspective-taking skills of persons with mental retardation: Recognizing ignorance and false belief.* Paper presented at the biennial convention of the Society for Research in Child Development, Seattle.

Beveridge, M., Spencer, J., & Mittler, P. (1979). Self-blame and communication failure in retarded adolescents. *Journal of Child Psychology and Psychiatry and Allied Disciplines, 20,* 129–138.

Beveridge, M., & Tatham, A. (1976). Communication in retarded adolescents: Utilization of known language skills. *American Journal of Mental Deficiency, 81,* 96–99.

Black, B., & Hazen, N.L. (1990). Social status and patterns of communication in acquainted and unacquainted preschool children. *Developmental Psychology, 26,* 379–387.

Bliss, L.S. (1985). The development of persuasive strategies by mentally retarded children. *Applied Research in Mental Retardation, 6,* 437–447.

Brooks, P., McCauley, C., & Merrill, E. (1987). Cognition and mental retardation. In F. Menolascino & J.A. Stark (Eds.), *Preventive and curative intervention in mental retardation* (pp. 295–318). Baltimore: Paul H. Brookes Publishing Co.

Brown, P., & Levinson, S. (1978). Universals in language usage: Politeness phenomena. In E. Goody (Ed.), *Questions and politeness* (pp. 356–389). Cambridge: Cambridge University Press.

Butterfield, E.C., & Belmont, J.M. (1977). Assessing and improving the executive cognitive functions of mentally retarded people. In I. Bialer & M. Sternlicht (Eds.), *Psychological issues in mental retardation.* New York: Psychological Dimensions.

Cardoso-Martins, & Mervis, C.B. (1985). Maternal speech to prelinguistic children with Down syndrome. *American Journal of Mental Deficiency, 89,* 451–458.

Chapman, R. (1981, April). *A clinical perspective on individual differences in language acquisition among mentally retarded children.* Paper presented at the biennial meeting of the Society for Research in Child Development, Boston.

Clark, H.H., Schreuder, R., & Butterick, S. (1983). Common ground and the understanding of demonstrative reference. *Journal of Verbal Learning and Verbal Behavior, 22,* 245–258.

Coggins, T.E., Carpenter, R.L., & Owings, N.O. (1983). Examining early intentional communication in Down's syndrome and nonretarded children. *British Journal of Disorders of Communication, 18,* 99–107.

Coggins, T.E., & Stoel-Gammon, C. (1982). Clarification strategies used by four Down's syndrome children for maintaining normal conversational interaction. *Education and Training of the Mentally Retarded, 18,* 65–67.

Curtiss, S. (1988). Abnormal language acquisition and the modularity of language. In F.J. Newmeyer (Ed.) *Linguistics: The Cambridge survey* (Vol. 2, pp. 96–116). Cambridge: Cambridge University Press.

Curtiss, S., & Yamada, J. (1981). Selectively intact grammatical development in a retarded child. *UCLA Working Papers in Cognitive Linguistics, 3,* 61–91.

Davis, H., & Oliver, B. (1980). A comparison of aspects of the maternal speech environment of retarded and nonretarded children. *Child: Care, Health and Development, 6,* 135–145.

Davis, H., Stroud, A., & Green, L. (1988). Maternal language environment of children with mental retardation. *American Journal on Mental Retardation, 93,* 144–153.

Dorval, B., & Eckerman, C.O. (1984). Developmental trends in the quality of conversation achieved by small groups of acquainted peers. *Monographs of the Society for Research in Child Development* (Serial No. 206).

Duncan, S. (1972). Some signals and rules for taking speaking turns in conversations. *Journal of Personality and Social Psychology, 23,* 283–292.

Gallagher, T. (1977). Revision behaviors in the speech of normal children developing language. *Journal of Speech and Hearing Research, 20,* 303–318.

Garvey, C. (1977). The contingent query: A dependent act in conversation. In M. Lewis & L.A. Rosenblum (Eds.), *Interaction, conversation, and the development of language* (pp. 63–93). New York: John Wiley & Sons.

Glucksberg, S., & Krauss, R.M. (1967). What do people say after they have learned how to talk? Studies of the development of referential communication. *Merrill-Palmer Quarterly, 13,* 309–316.

Glucksberg, S., Krauss, R., & Higgins, E.T. (1975). The development of referential communication skills. In F.D. Horowitz (Ed.), *Review of child development research* (Vol. 4, pp. 305–345). Chicago: University of Chicago Press.

Gordon, D.P., Budwig, N., Strage, A., & Carrell, P. (1980, October). *Children's requests to unfamiliar adults: form, social function, age variations.* Paper presented at the Boston University Conference on Language Development, Boston.

Gordon, D., & Ervin-Tripp, S. (1984). The structure of children's requests. In R.L. Schiefelbusch & J. Pickar (Eds.), *The acquisition of communicative competence.* (pp. 295–321). Baltimore: University Park Press.

Gottman, J.M., & Parkhurst, J. (1980). A developmental theory of friendship and acquaintanceship processes. In W.A. Collins (Eds.), *Development of cognition, affect, and social relations; Minnesota Symposia on Child Psychology* (Vol. 13, pp. 197–253). Hillsdale, NJ: Lawrence Erlbaum Associates.

Greenwald, C.A., & Leonard, L.B. (1979). Communicative and sensorimotor development of Down's syndrome children. *American Journal of Mental Deficiency, 84,* 296–303.

Hanzlik, J.R., & Stevenson, M.B. (1986). Interaction of mothers with their infants who are mentally retarded, retarded with cerebral palsy, or nonretarded. *American Journal of Mental Deficiency, 90,* 513–520.

Hazen, N.L., & Black, B. (1989). Preschool peer communication skills: The role of social status and interaction context. *Child Development, 60,* 867–876.

Holtgraves, T. (1986). Language structure in social interaction: Perceptions of direct and indirect speech acts and interactants who use them. *Journal of Personality and Social Psychology, 51,* 305–314.

Johnston, J. (1988). Specific language disorders in the child. In N.J. Lass, L.V. McReynolds, L.J. Northern, & D.E. Yoder (Eds.), *Handbook of speech-language pathology and audiology* (pp. 685–715). Toronto: B.C. Decker.

Kernan, K.T., & Sabsay, S. (1987). Referential first mention in narratives by mildly mentally retarded adults. *Research in Developmental Disabilities, 8,* 361–369.

Leifer, J.S., & Lewis, M. (1984). Acquisition of conversational response skills by young Down syndrome and nonretarded young children. *American Journal of Mental Deficiency, 88,* 610–618.

Lempers, J.D., & Elrod, M.M. (1983). Children's appraisal of different sources of referential communicative inadequacies. *Child Development, 54,* 509–515.

Levinson, S.C. (1983). *Pragmatics.* Cambridge: Cambridge University Press.

Longhurst, T.M. (1974). Communication in retarded adolescents: Sex and intelligence level. *American Journal of Mental Deficiency, 78,* 607–618.

Longhurst, T.M., & Berry, G.W. (1975). Communication in retarded adolescents: Response to listener feedback. *American Journal of Mental Deficiency, 80,* 158–164.

Loveland, K.A., Tunali, B.M. McEvoy, R., & Kelly, M.L. (1989). Referential communication and response adequacy in autism and Down's syndrome. *Applied Psycholinguistics, 10,* 301–313.

Miller, J.F., & Chapman, R. (1984). Disorders of communication: Investigating the development of language of mentally retarded children. *American Journal of Mental Deficiency, 88,* 536–545.

Mishler, E. (1975). Studies in dialogue and discourse: II. Types of discourse initiated by and sustained through questioning. *Journal of Psycholinguistic Research, 4,* 99–121.

Mundy, P., Sigman, M., Kasari, C., & Yirmiya, N. (1988). Nonverbal communication skills in children with Down syndrome. *Child Development, 59,* 235–249.

Nippold, M.A., Leonard, L.B., & Anastopoulos, A. (1982). Development in the use and understanding of polite forms in children. *Journal of Speech and Hearing Research, 25,* 193–202.

Nuccio, J., & Abbeduto, L. (in press). Dynamic contextual variables: Directives of persons with mental retardation. *American Journal on Mental Retardation.*

Nuccio, J., & Abbeduto, L. (1990b). *Dynamic contextual variables: Influences on directive production in persons with mental retardation and in nondisabled children.* Unpublished manuscript.

Owens, R.E. Jr., & MacDonald, J.D. (1982). Communicative uses of the early speech of nondelayed and Down syndrome children. *American Journal of Mental Deficiency, 86,* 503–510.

Owings, N.O., & McManus, M.D. (1980). An analysis of communication functions in the speech of a deinstitutionalized adult mentally retarded client. *Mental Retardation, 18,* 4, 309–314.

Owings, N.O., McManus, M.D., & Scherer, N. (1981). A deinstitutionalized retarded adult's use of communication functions in a natural setting. *British Journal of Disorders of Communication, 16,* 2, 119–128.

Paul, R., & Cohen, D.J. (1984). Responses to contingent queries in adults with mental retardation and pervasive developmental disorders. *Applied Psycholinguistics, 5,* 349–357.

Reeder, K. (1990). Text or context: The influence of early literate experience upon preschool children's speech act comprehension. In G. Conti-Ramsden & C.E. Snow (Eds.) *Children's language* (Vol: 7, pp. 305–326). Hillsdale, NJ: Lawrence Erlbaum Associates.

Rice, M. (1984). Cognitive aspects of communicative development. In R.L. Schiefelbusch & J. Pickar (Eds.), *The acquisition of communicative competence* (pp. 141–189). Baltimore: University Park Press.

Roberts, Jr., R.J., & Patterson, C.J. (1983). Perspective taking and referential communication: The question of correspondence reconsidered. *Child Development, 54,* 1005–1014.

Robinson, E.J., & Whittaker, S.J. (1986). Learning about verbal referential communication in the early school years. In K. Durkin (Ed.), *Language development during the school years.* London: Croom Helm.

Rosenberg, S. (1982). The language of the mentally retarded: Development, processes, and intervention. In S. Rosenberg (Ed.), *Handbook of applied psycholinguistics: Major thrusts of research and theory* (pp. 329–392). Hillsdale, NJ: Lawrence Erlbaum Associates.

Rosenberg, S., & Abbeduto, L. (1987). Indicators of linguistic competence in the peer group conversational behavior of mildly retarded adults. *Applied Psycholinguistics, 8,* 19–32.

Rueda, R., & Chan, K.S. (1980). Referential communication skills levels of moderately mentally retarded adolescents. *American Journal of Mental Deficiency, 85,* 45–52.

Sacks, H., Schegloff, E., & Jefferson, G. (1974). A simplest systematics for the organization of turn-taking in conversation. *Language, 50,* 696–735.

Scherer, N.J., & Owings, N.O. (1984). Learning to be contingent: Retarded children's responses to their mothers' requests. *Language and Speech, 27,* 255–267.

Shantz, C.U. (1981). The role of role-taking in children's referential communication. In W.P. Dickson (Ed.), *Children's oral communication skills* (pp. 85–102). New York: Academic Press.

Shatz, M. (1983). Communication. In J. Flavell & E.M. Markman (Eds.), *Cognitive development.* P. Mussen (Gen. Ed.), *Carmichael's manual of child psychology* (4th ed). New York: John Wiley & Sons.

Sigman, M., Mundy, P., Sherman, T., & Ungerer, J. (1986). Social interactions of autistic, mentally retarded and normal children and their caregivers. *Journal of Child Psychology and Psychiatry, 27*, 647–656.

Simeonsson, R.J., Monson, L.B., & Blacher, J. (1984). Social understanding and mental retardation. In P. Brooks, R. Sperber, & C. McCauley (Eds.), *Learning and cognition in the mentally retarded* (pp. 389–417). Hillsdale, NJ: Lawrence Erlbaum Associates.

Snow, C.E. (1972). Mother's speech to children learning language. *Child Development, 43*, 549–565.

Snyder, L. (1978). Communicative and cognitive abilities and disabilities in the sensorimotor period. *Merrill-Palmer Quarterly, 24*, 161–180.

Sonnenschein, S. (1986). Development of referential communication: Deciding that a message is uninformative. *Developmental Psychology, 22*, 164–168.

Sugarman, S. (1984). The development of preverbal communication: Its contribution and limits in promoting the development of language. In R.L. Schiefelbusch & J. Pickar (Eds.), *The acquisition of communicative competence* (pp. 24–67). Baltimore: University Park Press.

Tannock, R. (1988). Mothers' directiveness in their interactions with their children with and without Down syndrome. *American Journal on Mental Retardation, 93*, 154–165.

Warren, S.F. (1987, November). *Recent trends in language intervention research: Children and adolescents with mental retardation.* Paper presented at the 1987 Convention of the American Speech-Language-Hearing Association, New Orleans.

Whitehurst, G.J., & Sonnenschein, S. (1985). The development of communication: A functional analysis. In G.J. Whitehurst (Ed.), *Annals of child development* (Vol. 2, pp. 1–48). Greenwich, CT: JAI Press.

Wilkinson, L.C., & Spinelli, F. (1983). Using requests effectively in peer-directed instructional groups. *American Educational Research Journal, 20*, 479–501.

Wollner, S.G. (1983). Communicating intentions: How well do language-impaired children do? *Topics in Language Disorders, 4*, 1–14.

Zetlin, A.G., & Sabsay, S. (1980, March). *Characteristics of interaction among moderately retarded peers.* Paper presented at the Gatlinburg Conference on Research in Mental Retardation, Gatlinburg, TN.

14

The Changing Nature
of Communication
and Language Intervention

Diane Bricker

THE INTENT OF THIS CHAPTER is to discuss selected themes addressed by the other contributors to this volume. The goal has been to tease those themes that examine important intervention issues from the broad array of information presented. Many of the themes recur throughout the book, suggesting their importance to the field. I have taken the liberty of reformulating a number of the selected themes so that they more directly focus on intervention. A variety of other issues raised by the volume's contributors are not addressed in this chapter, reflecting my own bias toward work that has some relevance for intervention. I have become increasingly antagonistic toward communication research that has little to contribute to intervention efforts; I have become increasingly disenchanted with carefully controlled laboratory work that does not replicate the realities facing children who are trying to develop communication skills. Such work has little to offer parents, interventionists, or clinicians who are striving to improve the communicative repertoires of people with disabilities.

It is promising that the contributors to this volume have genuinely tried to address intervention issues. Many authors report on their investigations of innovative intervention strategies. For example, Yoder, Davies, and Bishop examine the effect of various adult recruitment strategies on child communicative output. Goldstein and Kaczmarek describe a series of investigations that examined the effectiveness of peer-mediated strategies. Whitehurst, Fischel, Arnold, and Lonigan discuss the effectiveness of intervention efforts

Preparation of this manuscript was supported, in part, by Grant Nos. H029D90110, H029B90254, and H029Q90086 from the U.S. Office of Special Education Programs to the Center on Human Development, University of Oregon.

with children who have expressive language delays. Romski and Sevcik describe their interesting work on using an augmentative approach to enhance communicative skills in children with severe mental retardation. Klinger and Dawson offer a set of intervention principles designed to improve the social communication of preschool children with autism. Kaiser, Yoder, and Keetz focus on examining the efficacy of a specific set of intervention procedures they call milieu teaching. Reichle, Mirenda, Locke, Piché, and Johnston discuss a variety of variables that can potentially affect the success of acquiring an initial augmentative communication system.

In contrast, the University Park Press Language Intervention Series, published in the 1970s and 1980s, contained little material that dealt directly with intervention strategies and even fewer chapters that presented empirically based approaches to improving the language skills of children with communication impairments. For example, in the volume entitled *Early Language: Acquisition and Intervention* (1981), edited by Richard Schiefelbusch and Diane Bricker, only five chapters directly addressed intervention issues, and none of these chapters presented work on the empirical verification of specific intervention techniques. The chapters that did address intervention did so by describing global programmatic approaches and outcomes (e.g., Kysela, Hillyard, McDonald, & Ahlsten-Taylor, 1981).

The content of the Schiefelbusch and Bricker volume reflected state-of-the-art language intervention for young children in the early 1980s. The present volume reflects the state of the art in the early 1990s. The contrast is important and revealing. The field of language intervention has made a number of significant changes, including devising and studying more specific intervention strategies and embedding training in children's social environments. The culmination of these changes can be seen in the Warren and Reichle thesis that communication and language intervention research has come of age. We are witnessing the advent of a new and exciting field that is multidisciplinary, problem driven, and yet committed to the evolution of theory that ultimately will assist in improving intervention efforts for people with communication impairments.

This volume heralds a new era for the field of communication and language intervention research. This volume, and the series of which it is a part, will help legitimize the field. In addition, this volume provides a focal point for researchers and clinicians who, although they represent an array of disciplines, share the common goal of improving communication in those whose communication skills are absent or deficient.

To highlight the intervention focus of this volume, I have extracted several important and recurring themes. These themes can be categorized under two major headings: reformulating of intervention approaches and changing assessment and evaluation procedures.

REFORMULATING INTERVENTION APPROACHES

Most of the preceding chapters examine ways in which intervention efforts should be reformulated. Five categories of reformulations have been identified that, if adopted by practitioners in the field, will produce significant shifts in communication intervention programs. These reformulations include: 1) shifting to learner-oriented approaches, 2) attending to the learner's social context, 3) embedding training into meaningful activities, 4) broadening the focus to prelinguistic behavior, and 5) adopting more comprehensive and cohesive intervention approaches.

Using Learner-Oriented Approaches

One of the more important changes in the field of communication intervention is the move away from intervention efforts that are adult focused and adult directed and that rely primarily on individual or small group didactic instruction. Investigators and interventionists are proposing strategies that more carefully and purposefully follow the lead and interests of the learner, particularly the younger child. Although the use of naturalistic training strategies that depend heavily on following the learner's cues is not new (see for example, Bricker, 1989; Duchan & Weitzner-Lin, 1987; Hart & Risley, 1975; Hart & Rogers-Warren, 1978; Koegel & Johnson, 1989; Warren & Rogers-Warren, 1985), the chapters in this volume reflect the growing support for using such approaches.

There are powerful reasons why the field of language intervention is shifting to learner-oriented teaching in which work on goals and objectives is embedded in activities of interest to learners, particularly young learners. First, focusing training on targets removed from the learner's experience and interest will likely lack meaning (Brown, Collins, & Duguid, 1989). For example, teaching children with language impairments to label zoo animals from pictures may do little to improve their ability to communicate their needs. Providing children appropriate words while they engage in daily and meaningful activities (e.g., getting ready for school) may do much to improve their communication ability. This approach is reflected in the augmentative training strategy reported by Romski and Sevcik. Second, the use of artificial contingencies has not been shown to maintain a behavior once those contingencies are removed, a point well made by Goldstein and Kaczmarek. The results of interventions that require praising children to maintain their responding (e.g., "Good talking") will likely not last when the learner is required to communicate in a social environment that does not provide that type of artificial feedback (e.g., when interacting with peers). As Reichle, Mirenda, Locke, Piché, and Johnston note, focusing training on activities of interest to the learner in large measure removes the need for artificial contingencies. If a child wishes to have a toy and communicates this need, receiving the toy is likely to be an adequate reward, thus obviating the need to tell the child that he or she is talking well.

Attending to Social Context

A second reformulation of intervention efforts is the expanded use of the learner's social environment. This position is not new, but reflects the impact of such theorists as Vygotsky. As Olswang, Bain, and Johnson as well as others (e.g., Uzgiris, 1981) have noted, Vygotsky's emphasis on the importance of the social environment for the development of language in the young child has made a significant contribution to theories of language acquisition.

Children are raised in social environments in which other social agents have great saliency (Beckwith, 1990). Social agents provide models and react to the communicative and motoric initiations of children. The interactions between children and their social environment provide at the very least the necessary information for breaking the language code, or more broadly, for coming to understand the social rules that govern particular language milieus. Although the underlying neurological system contains the necessary information for the development of species-specific behavior, the child's social environment provides the stimulation and feedback that permit the development of expected skills. To ignore the child's social context in the formulation and delivery of intervention is to ignore our understanding of learning in the human organism, and likely will not lead to the efficient development of appropriate social communication.

Several chapters in this volume support the need to conduct intervention efforts that incorporate the social context of the learner. As Whitehurst, Fischel, Arnold, and Lonigan suggest, the acquisition of expressive vocabulary among persons with severe expressive language delays can result from a home-based intervention. Tannock and Girolametto also indicate that parents are in a pivotal position to assume the role of primary intervention agent with infants and preschool children. The use of naturally occurring peer interactions clearly involves the learner's social environment as a vehicle for intervention. Goldstein and Kaczmarek indicate that the possible benefits of such a naturalistic approach include: reinforcement of appropriate communication behaviors in daily interactions, less expensive training because these behaviors tend to occur frequently throughout interactions, and enhanced maintenance and generalization because behaviors are reinforced through naturally occurring contingencies. Wetherby and Prizant also address this issue by arguing for the importance of actively involving the child in the learning process to improve the effects of language intervention. Romski and Sevcik also argue for conducting training in environments in which activities are meaningful and experience based. Klinger and Dawson suggest that for children with autism, aspects of the child's social environment may need to be emphasized and made explicit in the intervention process.

Embedding Training in Daily Activities

A third important reformulation is the shift in intervention efforts toward embedding children's goals and objectives into daily activities that occur as natural routines (e.g., changing diapers, washing hands) or as a function of children's interests (e.g., playing with a pet, taking a bath). The embedding of training targets in daily activities can naturally accompany intervention efforts that are child focused and recognize the child's social milieu.

As pointed out by Romski and Sevcik, early language training programs have tended to rely on structured teacher-selected activities to teach targeted goals and objectives. For example, to improve vocabulary skills, children are asked to name pictures or objects repeatedly as the teacher points to pre-selected items. Under such approaches, little attempt is made to assist children in learning the pragmatic or semantic dimensions of specific words. Training strategies that embed training in daily activities proceed differently. Names of words are taught as children interact with objects, people, or activities. For example, while engaging in water play the names of objects and actions the children use for pouring, splashing, filling, emptying, and moving can be emphasized. Another example, suggested by Klinger and Dawson, is the use of "naturally occurring patterns of early social interaction," during which the adult imitates the child's behaviors in order to reinforce the targeted behaviors.

Goldstein and Kaczmarek discuss the possible benefits of using naturally occurring peer interactions as training vehicles. Interestingly, Yoder, Davies, and Bishop report that in their subject sample the amount of talking by young children increased when they were engaged in routine conversations. These routines appear to provide children with the support or structure necessary to permit the production of more frequent verbal responses.

Examining Prelinguistic Behavior

A fourth reformulation or refocusing of intervention strategies identified in this volume is associated with prelinguistic behavior. There is increasing acceptance of the importance of early communicative, social, and cognitive behavior for the development of more sophisticated symbolic skills. Language does not spring from the child full blown. Rather, it evolves through the coordination of several systems, each affected by the social and physical environment. Many authorities are convinced that the early cooing and babbling interactions between infants and their caregivers provide the foundation or substance from which increasingly more sophisticated communicative behavior evolves. Acceptance of this position reinforces the importance of early intervention. As Anastasiow (1990) has recently speculated, there may be developmental periods during which the child is optimally prepared—from a neurological perspective—to learn particular skills. To permit these periods to slip by without providing children the appropriate stimulation may result in less than optimal development for children with disabilities.

A second important reason exists for intervention programs to begin early and to target a broad range of social, communicative, and cognitive repertoires. As Klinger and Dawson and Wetherby and Prizant suggest, it seems likely that early forms of behavior are necessary for the development of more advanced or complex response forms. That is, children will likely not be able to produce words requiring the sequencing of multiple sounds if they cannot produce single sounds. The vocalization and babbling produced by most children likely serves an important function of helping children tune their phonological system. Likewise, understanding the need to search for lost articles is unlikely unless the child has the concept of object permanence. The work of Romski and Sevcik suggests that comprehension may underlie the development of symbol production. Thus, from an intervention perspective, it seems important that infants and young children who are identified as having communicative delays or impairments be provided with intervention at the point of detection, and that the intervention include attention to all systems necessary to develop an adequate communication repertoire. Interestingly and appropriately, Wetherby and Prizant have adopted this position in reference to assessment and evaluation, an area addressed in the next section of this chapter.

Adopting a Comprehensive Approach

A fifth and final reformulation is the need to move away from fragmented intervention efforts toward more comprehensive approaches. Most children with communication problems do not have isolated disabilities. This is particularly true for younger children and children with more severe disabilities, a point emphasized by Romski and Sevcik and Abbeduto and Rosenberg.

Comprehensive efforts include a generalized plan of action that takes into account the important elements of children's repertoires that will enhance their total communicative ability. The child with no productive language, for example, will likely have problems in other areas, such as social interactions and cognitive functioning. To develop an intervention program that focuses exclusively on the language production deficit will probably not be optimal. Intervention targets may need to include enhancing the child's social and cognitive skills as well. Rather than developing and implementing intervention plans that target only one problem or an aspect of a problem, intervention plans should be developed that address all critical areas of need for the child.

Several of the contributors to this volume acknowledge the need for broad, comprehensive approaches to language intervention with children, in particular those with severe disabilities. Intervention techniques suggested by Klinger and Dawson for children with autism and by Romski and Sevcik for children with severe mental retardation emphasize the importance of using these strategies in conjunction with other coordinated treatment regimes.

Summary

It is heartening to see that the contributors to this volume agree on the need to move language intervention strategies away from those that rely on contrived and meaningless structures toward those that integrate training within daily social routines. Perhaps the only concern with this shift is that interventionists or clinicians may interpret this change to mean that careful planning and organization of intervention efforts are unnecessary. Just the opposite is true. The use of more naturalistic approaches requires more planning and more vigilance in monitoring children's progress over time. Without ensuring that children are given ample opportunity to learn new and more complex communication, naturalistic approaches will fail. The only mechanism to ensure that the necessary learning is occurring is to monitor the type of experiences being offered children by their social environment, and to monitor children's communicative responses to those experiences.

CHANGING ASSESSMENT AND EVALUATION PROCEDURES

The second set of themes extracted from the preceding chapters is the widespread call for change in the assessment and evaluation strategies used to monitor change as a result of intervention efforts. As Abbeduto and Rosenberg note, many instruments used to assess linguistic behaviors are not particularly good predictors of linguistic performance in social interactions.

Techniques derived from laboratory research tend to be difficult to employ in naturalistic situations, while field-based methods tend to lack sufficient control to demonstrate functional relationships between dependent and independent variables. As noted by many of the contributors to this volume, these problems are of paramount importance.

Olswang, Bain, and Johnson discuss the need to shift from static models of assessment and evaluation to dynamic models for certain purposes. The most important difference between these approaches is that the static model of assessment indicates what the child has achieved to date while the dynamic model is designed to indicate what the child is potentially capable of learning. As Olswang and her colleagues suggest, dynamic assessment purports to provide information on children's "potential for learning." The assessment instrument described in this volume by Wetherby and Prizant is an example of a dynamic approach designed to be used for the early identification of children with language problems and to develop a communication profile that can be used to design intervention programs.

As recognized by most contributors, new models or approaches to language assessment and evaluation are needed. However, development of these approaches faces major challenges. These challenges are reflected in three major themes that recur throughout this volume: 1) the need to formulate assessment and evaluation procedures so that they present an accurate reflection of children's communication skills, 2) the need to formulate assessment and evaluation procedures that can be used by practitioners across people and environments, and 3) the need to connect assessment outcomes more directly with intervention and evaluation. Each of these themes is discussed in the following sections.

Embedding Assessment and Evaluation in Daily Activities

Just as there is a trend toward embedding communication intervention in children's daily activities, there is growing awareness of the need to conduct assessment and evaluation activities in conjunction with routine child-directed activities as opposed to assessing fragmented skills in strange and unfamiliar settings. Rather than determine children's speaking vocabulary by having them label a set of predetermined objects, there is a need to ascertain what words children use and where and how those words are used throughout their daily transactions.

Language samples may more closely approximate the goal of embedding assessment within daily activities than other available techniques. Unfortunately, language samples are saddled with a number of serious problems. They are expensive to collect and even more expensive to analyze. As Klee suggests, often the type of analysis performed does not yield outcomes that permit an understanding of how children use or do not use their communication skills. In addition, as Klee's research demonstrates, outcomes can be affected by the listener and by the type of analysis used. Perhaps most unsettling is that information generated from language samples does not necessarily lead to the formulation of sound and appropriate intervention efforts.

The field of language intervention has yet to develop reliable and valid measures of current status and future progress that can be woven into children's daily activities. This goal remains unmet.

Developing More Functional Assessment and Evaluation Strategies

A second theme, discussed by Yoder, Davies, and Bishop, among others, is the need to develop assessment and evaluation strategies that can be used by practitioners in the field. Most interventionists appear to have little time to conduct even traditional assessments and evaluations. The majority of early intervention programs appear to administer pre–post standardized tests from which IEPs are developed and judgments of progress made. Some practitioners indicate that even the use of traditional assessment models may exceed their staff resources. Dynamic assessment and evaluation models are likely to involve the use of more frequent and more complicated assessment and evaluation measures. This often makes dynamic models unappealing to interventionists who already find it difficult to manage the many activities required by intervention programs for children and parents.

More functional and dynamic assessment procedures need to be developed that can be used across settings, people, and activities. These procedures should be user friendly and must be acceptable to the majority of communication interventionists. A successful solution will likely require the development of assessment procedures that can be more easily and reliably incorporated into programmatic activities. Success will also require the training (or retraining) of interventionists to understand how to use such assessment and evaluation techniques as well as the crucial contribution of assessment and evaluation to the intervention enterprise.

Linking Assessment, Intervention, and Evaluation

Development of more facilitative intervention content is highly dependent upon directly linking assessment, intervention, and evaluation efforts. Although a linked approach seems straightforward and the strategy of choice, most current models do not use assessment outcomes to formulate intervention plans. This occurs largely because the types of assessment measures used do not generate information that can be used to develop intervention content.

It is interesting to note the longevity of intervention models that have done little to relate assessment information to the formulation of intervention efforts. Traditionally, prior to intervention, children have been given a standardized test that purportedly identifies strengths and weaknesses and provides the basis from which to judge the effects of treatment. (An exception to this approach is investigators or practitioners who employ time series designs.) As many writers have noted (e.g., Bagnato & Neisworth, 1981; Bricker, 1989; Fewell, 1983) the use of standardized tests in a pre–post format is not satisfactory for the development of an adequate information base from which to formulate an appropriate IEP or IFSP. Most standardized tests were not developed to provide programming information for interventionists. Rather, their goal is to provide comparative information on children's performances. In addition, the administration of a test twice yearly is hardly adequate for the monitoring of change over time. To meet intervention needs, measures and procedures are required that yield information with direct relevance to programming and intervention efforts, and that can be administered frequently to monitor change.

The test-teach-test model, or curriculum-based assessment, is not new, but these models have, until recently, seen limited application (Notari, Slentz, & Bricker, 1990). There is growing interest in employing models that permit a direct connection between assessment findings and intervention efforts. One reason these more functional approaches have been slow to be adopted is that many practitioners do not clearly distinguish the various purposes of assessment instruments. For example, the use of a screening tool to conduct an initial assessment does not provide the necessary information to design an intervention program. As interventionists and researchers more clearly define the purpose of instruments for screening, identification, eligibility, program assessment, and evaluation, major changes in instrument choice will occur. Standardized instruments of language behavior are generally useful to establish eligibility for services, to compare children with a norm group, and to provide a general index of change over time. Such instruments provide neither the detail or content for the formulation of IEPs or IFSPs nor the information for writing daily program plans.

The need for tools to permit the sensible and useful connection between assessment, intervention, and evaluation is the problem that served to prompt the development of the Communication and Symbolic Behavior Scales, described by Wetherby and Prizant. Romski and Sevcik also describe an assessment system that provides a range of functional and programmatically relevant information on their subjects' progress toward the acquisition and subsequent use of communication skills.

Summary

A revolution is needed in the area of assessment and evaluation of communication skills. The move from traditional to more functional models of assessment and evaluation is overdue. The development of measurement strategies that link assessment, intervention, and evaluation and that are acceptable to interventionists presents major challenges to the leaders and innovators in the field of language intervention.

The improvement of intervention efforts hinges, in large measure, on the successful development of assessment and evaluation procedures that yield functional information about children's communication repertoires. Fundamental to the development of new assessment and evaluation approaches are research efforts to answer the many questions surrounding the development and implementation of functional models.

REEVALUATING INVESTIGATIVE NEEDS

The contributors to this volume have addressed a broad range of problems and concerns facing communication and language interventionists. Contributors have posed interesting questions and generated helpful outcomes. However, the findings presented underline the need for continued empirical work to provide the foundation for change in assessment, intervention, and evaluation. As Warren and Reichle note, "the field is more or less ready to move beyond its historic (and reductive) emphasis on the description and documentation of problems toward an increasing emphasis on intervention and treatment research" (p. 6).

Many intervention and treatment topics need to be pursued. However, three areas—establishing outcome measures, collecting field data, and generalizing learned behaviors—have particular saliency for the 1990s.

Establishing Outcome Measures

A pervasive problem addressed by contributors is the need for changes in outcome measures because of problems with reliability, validity, and methodological weaknesses. This problem is manifested by the need for measures that reflect the functional repertoires used for communicative transactions, the need for collecting information in the social context in which it typically occurs, and the need for reliable measures that accurately reflect the language performance of the learner rather than the bias of the data collector.

Measuring functional language skills while individuals with language problems engage in daily communicative exchanges is difficult for at least three reasons. First, it is considerably more costly to collect field data than to collect information in a contrived setting. Second, collection of information from the field gives the investigator little control, whereas collecting information using a standard task following specific procedures in an isolated setting allows considerable control. Third, collecting data while learners conduct their daily business may be intrusive. This problem is probably of greater concern for older subjects than for very young children. However, even young children may be affected by having an adult follow them around observing and recording their activities. Peers may also notice and respond.

Much of the credible language data (e.g., data that have been reliably collected with the necessary controls) have been obtained in controlled situations involving the administration of standardized measures. Although, as Klee points out, this is an appropriate strategy for some research questions, the appropriateness of such procedures for determining the effects of intervention is questionable. The primary concern is whether the behavior produced in controlled and unfamiliar settings reflects the user's repertoire in daily interactions. If measures of language are changed to examine functional repertoires, the examination occurs within the social context in which responses are generally used. Thus, outcome measures and settings must change if we are to measure functional language skills in their social contexts. It seems an obvious shift if we wish to determine the effect of intervention efforts on children's ability to communicate throughout their daily social interactions.

Collecting Field Data

How can functional repertoires be examined in their social contexts in ways that are, if not economical, at least affordable? A major reason that data are not collected by observing the learner in daily interactions is the financial cost involved. Tannock and Girolametto wonder if many of the caregiver–child interactive intervention regimes do not also extract too dear a cost from parents, who are often faced with an array of other demands. Thus, it is important to understand that the concept of cost refers to time as well as resources.

Many intervention programs are funded primarily to develop and offer services to children with disabilities and their families (e.g., HCEEP, local programs funded with P.L. 99-457 monies). Evaluation of the effect of the program is likely to be a secondary issue. In addition, intervention program budgets usually contain inadequate funds for evaluating the effect of the intervention. The best many intervention personnel can do is to administer pretests and posttests that require limited time and resources. If we wish to examine the effect of intervention efforts on children's daily communication skills, we must develop some creative options for evaluating the effect of these interventions.

Procedures that reflect children's functional communication skills are simple to use and relatively inexpensive. A strategy that might prove useful is the piggy-backing of research and intervention efforts. That is, systematic data collection by research teams could be done within the context of ongoing intervention programs. Such a strategy would seem to have significant benefits for both practitioners and researchers but will require compromise by both groups. Interventionists must be willing to make some adjustments to ensure that data collection is reliable. For example, classroom schedules can be maintained until a data collection phase is completed; children can be grouped in ways that meet the requirements of the research, and those groups maintained until the data collection is completed. Research personnel will also have to compromise and develop procedures that can be reliably used without disruption of daily classroom or home routines.

Ensuring Generalization and Maintenance

The issues of generalization and maintenance have nagged us for years (Stokes & Baer, 1977). Most researchers discuss the need to examine the generalization and maintenance of language training effects, but, as noted by Kaiser, Yoder, and Keetz, few investigators have collected systematic information that might indicate whether these effects transfer across settings, people, events, and conditions. Nor has the longevity of the effects been studied often. Yoder, Davies, and Bishop speculate about the generalizability of the recruiting strategies used in their study. However, their comments are speculative, and their findings need to be replicated.

Investigators and practitioners know that it is not sufficient to teach children communicative behaviors that depend upon specific cues since the individual may be unable to produce the communicative response in the absence of such cues. Years ago when working with young children with autism, we attempted to teach a nonverbal 4-year-old selected word–object associations. Using a two-choice discrimination paradigm, the child was verbally instructed which object to select. If the verbal cues were used for object selection, the child's response would always be correct (100%) across trials. If the verbal cue were not used to guide object selection, the child's responses would be random over time. Over hundreds of training trails, the child learned consistently to select a small green car when told "Take car." One day the green car was removed and a red car substituted. To our horror, the child did not select the car when asked to do so. This was a painful revelation about generalization, but it is unlikely that our pain equalled the child's in enduring such silly, nonfunctional, communication training.

If communication is to be functional for children, responses must be able to transcend changes in conditions, people, and activities. The use of a greeting can appropriately occur under an array of conditions and settings. To teach a child to say "Hi" when entering a classroom is only the beginning in helping the child learn that such a greeting can be used appropriately under countless conditions. This realization, which is reflected throughout this volume, emphasizes the need to investigate the use of more naturalistic intervention approaches (e.g., milieu language training [Kaiser, Hendrickson, & Alpert, in press] activity based–intervention [Bricker & Cripe, 1989]).

Summary

The road between research and practice has been full of barriers, detours, and often bottomless pits (Baumeister, 1981; Bricker, 1982; Butterfield, 1978). However, with the advent of volumes such as this, a resurfacing is occurring that will do much to facilitate the exchange of information between investigators and clinicians. Just a clinicians must appreciate the need for investigative work, researchers must recognize the needs and constraints facing parents and interventionists. Such mutual recognition and tolerance will do much to advance this new and important field.

CONCLUSIONS

Approaches that embed training in the daily routines of life are the goal of language and communication intervention. Such approaches superimpose communication instruction on interactive social transactions and encourage the use of communicative responses across varied settings, activities, and people. The structure of these approaches requires that children's communication address genuine needs and desires difficult to replicate in specifically designed training settings.

The promise of naturalistic intervention approaches must be fulfilled through systematic investigation of their effectiveness with people with communicative disabilities. As Warren and Reichle point out, theory must either mesh with empirical outcomes or change.

REFERENCES

Anastasiow, N. (1990). Implications of the neurobiological model for early intervention. In S. Meisels & J. Shonkoff (Eds.), *Handbook of early childhood intervention* (pp. 196–216). Cambridge: Cambridge University Press.

Bagnato, S., & Neisworth J. (1981). *Linking developmental assessment and curricula.* Rockville, MD: Aspen Publications.

Baumeister, A. (1981). Mental retardation policy and research: The unfulfilled promise. *American Journal of Mental Deficiency, 85,* 449–456.

Beckwith, L. (1990). Adaptive and maladaptive parenting: Implications for intervention. In S. Meisels & J. Shonkoff (Eds.), *Handbook of early childhood intervention* (pp. 53–77). Cambridge: Cambridge University Press.

Bricker, D. (1982). From research to application. In D. Bricker (Ed.), *Intervention with at-risk and handicapped infants.* Baltimore: University Park Press.

Bricker, D. (1989). *Early intervention for at-risk and handicapped infants, toddlers and preschool children* (pp. 1–9). Palo Alto, CA: VORT Corp.

Bricker, D., & Cripe, J. (1989). Activity-based intervention. In D. Bricker (Ed.), *Early intervention for at-risk and handicapped infants, toddlers and preschool children* (pp. 251–274). Palo Alto, CA: VORT Corp.

Brown, J., Collins, A., & Duguid, P. (1989). Situated cognition and the culture of learning. *Educational Researcher, 17* (1), 32–42.

Butterfield, E. (1978). Behavioral assessment of infants: From research to practice. In R. Minifie & L. Lloyd (Eds.), *Communicative and cognitive abilities: Early behavioral assessment* (pp. 575–586). Baltimore: University Park Press.

Duchan, J., & Weitzner-Lin, B. (1987). Nurturant-naturalistic intervention for language-impaired children. *Asha, 29*(7), 45–49.

Fewell, R. (1983). Assessing nandicapped infants. In G. Garwood & R. Fewell (Eds.), *Educating handicapped infants* (pp. 257–297). Rockville, MD: Aspen Publications.

Hart, B., & Risley, T. (1975). Incidental teaching of language in the preschool. *Journal of Applied Behavioral Analysis, 8,* 411–420.

Hart, B., & Rogers-Warren, A. (1978). A milieu approach to teaching language. In R. Schiefelbusch (Ed.), *Language intervention strategies* (pp. 193–235). Baltimore: University Park Press.

Kaiser, A., Hendrickson, J., & Alpert, C. (in press). Milieu language teaching: A second look. In R. Gable (Ed.), *Advances in mental retardation and developmental disabilities* (Vol. 4). London: Jessica Kingsley Publications.

Koegel, R., & Johnson, J. (1989). Motivating language use in autistic children. In G. Dawson (Ed.), *Autism* (pp. 310–325). New York: Guilford Press.

Kysela, G., Hillyard, A., McDonald, L., & Ahlsten-Taylor, J. (1981). Early intervention, design and evaluation. In R. Schiefelbusch & D. Bricker (Eds.), *Early language: Acquisition and intervention* (pp. 341–388). Baltimore: University Park Press.

Notari, A., Slentz, K., & Bricker, D. (1990). Assessment-curriculum systems of early childhood/special education. In R. Brown & D. Mitchell (Eds.), *Early intervention for disabled and at-risk infants* (pp. 160–205). London: Croom-Helm.

Schiefelbusch, R., & Bricker, D. (Eds). (1981). *Early language: Acquisition and intervention.* Austin, TX: PRO-ED.

Stokes, T., & Baer, D. (1977). An implicit technology of generalization. *Journal of Applied Behavior Analysis, 10,* 349–367.

Uzgiris, I. (1981). Experience in the social context. In R. Schiefelbusch & D. Bricker (Eds.), *Early language: Acquisition and intervention* (pp. 139–168). Baltimore: University Park Press.

Warren, S., & Rogers-Warren, A. (1985). *Teaching functional language: Generalization and maintenance of language skills.* Austin, TX: PRO-ED.

Author Index

Ladd, G. W., 101, 109
Lahey, M., 53, 73, 219, 247, 256, 271, 274
Lamb, M., 158, 178
Landesman, S., 125, 128
Landry, S. H., 257, 274
Langdell, T., 158, 161, 177
Lapenta-Neudeck, R., 116, 127
Latham, C., 298, 310
Launer, P. B., 256, 271, 274
Layton, T., 116, 130
League, R., 261, 273
Lee, L. C., 86, 110
Lee, R., 272, 274
Leet, H. E., 51, 73
Leifer, J. S., 339, 349, 357
Leiter, R., 279, 311
Lempers, J. D., 343, 357
Leonard, C. B., 202, 213, 218, 219, 220, 222, 224, 225, 248, 249, 256, 273, 282, 283, 335, 350, 357
Leslie, A., 162, 175, 176
Levinson, S. C., 334, 336, 337, 345, 347, 356, 357
Lewis, M., 56, 57, 58, 61, 62, 63, 64, 65, 66, 70, 76, 79, 289, 294, 311, 339, 349, 357
Lewis, V., 128
Lewy, A., 158, 159, 163, 164, 165, 176
Liddell, C., 71, 75
Lidz, C., 193, 194, 195, 213
Liefer, J. S., 289, 311
Light, J., 131, 154
Light, P., 116, 127
Lightbown, P., 202, 212
Lincoln, A., 164, 176
Lindgren, A., 144, 145, 155
Lindholm, B. W., 291, 311
Locke, P., 131, 144, 145, 154, 362, 363
Longhurst, T. M., 333, 343, 357
Lonigan, C. J., 277, 279, 280, 285, 287, 290, 294, 311, 312, 313, 361, 364
Lord, C., 174, 178
Lorimer, F., 294, 311
Lloyd, L. L., 3, 8, 114, 115, 116, 128, 129, 145, 154
Lobato-Barrera, D., 140, 153
Lovaas, O., 172, 178

Loveland, K. A., 333, 357
Lowe, L. W., 221, 245, 248
Ludlow, C. L., 284, 311
Luftig, R. L., 145, 155
Luria, A. R., 189, 191, 193, 213

Maas, F., 351, 355
MacDonald, J., 52, 53, 55, 56, 57, 58, 61, 62, 64, 66, 67, 68, 69, 74, 77, 335, 336, 358
Macken, M. A., 294, 312
MacKenzie, E. H., 257, 262, 273
MacWhinney, B., 316, 329
Maher, S., 218, 249
Mahoney, G., 49, 52, 54, 55, 56, 57, 58, 60, 61, 62, 64, 65, 68, 69, 74, 78, 167, 178, 272, 274
Malatesta, C., 160, 164, 166, 178
Manolson, A., 271, 274
Manolson, H. A., 49, 50, 52, 55, 56, 57, 58, 70, 75, 78
Marfo, K., 51, 75
Marinelli, B., 165, 178
Marshall, A. M., 9, 11, 12, 14, 25, 26, 27, 46
Marshall, N., 289, 311
Martyn, M., 115, 130
Mash, E. J., 291, 309
Mastergeorge, A., 224, 248
Mattison, R., 285, 309
Maurer, H., 69, 75
May, S., 323, 325, 327, 329
McCarthy, J. J., 279, 310
McCauley, C., 348
McClannahan, L. E., 13, 24, 25, 27, 29, 31, 35, 37, 39, 46
McConkey, R., 50, 56, 59, 70, 75
McCune-Nicolich, L., 225, 249
McDonald, K., 119, 125, 129
McDonald, L., 270, 274, 362, 374
McEvoy, M. A., 81, 92, 109
McEvoy, R., 333, 357
McGee, G. G., 13, 24, 25, 27, 29, 31, 35, 37, 46
McGrew, P. L., 86, 109
McLean, J., 52, 53, 75, 114, 117, 124, 128, 130, 207, 214, 219, 221, 249
McLean, M., 81, 109
McManus, M. D., 336, 358
McNew, S., 71, 72

Subject Index

Abuse, child with history of, CSBS case example involving, 237–239
Acceptability, social, of idiosyncratic gestures, 135–138
ACLC, *see* Assessment of Children's Language Comprehension
Acoustic analysis, in conversational language measurement, 316
Actions, toys drawing attention to, 186
Activation band model, 165
Activities
  assessment and evaluation embedded in, 368
  training activities embedded in, 365
Activity-oriented view, Vygotsky and, 189
Adults
  actions of, toys drawing attention to, 186
  effects of, on children's communicative behaviors, 87
  getting children to talk with, *see* Conversational recruitment
  prompting by
    in autism intervention, 171, 184–185
    in peer-mediated intervention, 98
  see also Parent(s)
Affective communication, emotional development and, 221
Affective sharing, as precursor to language, 162–163
Age
  expressive language delay and, symptoms of, 306
  zone of proximal development and, 197
Alternative communication systems, *see* Augmentative communication systems

American Sign Language (ASL)
  guessability of signs in, 144
  similarity of signs in, 146
American Speech-Language-Hearing Association (ASHA), 2, 7
Analog assessment tasks, challenging behavior and, 138, 139
Antecedents, in milieu teaching, 10
Arousal regulation, in autism, 164–165, 168
Articulation, stimulability testing in, 192
ASHA, *see* American Speech-Language-Hearing Association, 2, 7
ASL, *see* American Sign Language
Assessment
  of challenging behavior, 138, 139
  changing nature of, 367–373
  of conversational language, *see* Conversational language, measurement of
  curriculum-based, 369–370
  dynamic, 187–211
    see also Dynamic assessment
  early, *see* Early assessment
  embedded in daily activities, 368
  of expressive language delay, 278–281
  functional strategies for, development of, 368–369
  linkage of, with intervention and evaluation, 369–370
  of milieu teaching effects, 18, 19
  generalization, 22–28
  global language development, 32–35
Assessment of Children's Language Comprehension (ACLC), 220
Attention
  challenging behavior and, 138, 139

389

Speech output device
  learning and, 122
  see also Augmented language; Aug-
    mentative communication
    systems
Speech signal, acoustic analysis of, 316
Standardized tests
  language development and, 16
  problems with, 369
  see also Assessment; *specific tests*
Stanford-Binet Intelligence Scale, in ex-
    pressive language delay, 279
Static assessment
  dynamic assessment versus, 193–195
  of two-term utterances, 204–205
Stimulability testing, 192
Stimulation, optimal levels of
  autism and, 165–166, 168
  individual differences in, 165–166
Stimuli
  novel, attention to, 159, 164, 183
  social, development of contingency
    and, 158–160
Stimulus class generalization, 29–32
  communicative intent and, 134–135
Stress, family, expressive language de-
    lay and, 288–289
SuperWolf, in augmented language
    learning, 118
Symbol(s)
  gestures as, 190–191
  guessability of, 144–145
  motoric complexity of, 147
  opportunities for use of, 145
  similarity of, 146–147
  specificity of, 145–146
Symbol acquisition, augmented lan-
    guage learning and, 118–125
Symbolic behavior, in CSBS assess-
    ment, 229
Symbolic capacity, origins of, 222–223
Symbol learning, augmented language
    and, 122–124
Symbolic play, development of
  in children with communication im-
    pairments, 225–226
  in children without disabilities, 225
Symbol production
  comprehension and, 116–117
  see also Graphic mode techniques
Synthetic speech output, *see* Augmenta-
    tive communication systems;
    Augmented language

Systematic Analysis of Language Tran-
    scripts (SALT), 121
Systematic commenting, 15

Task(s)
  in LPAD, 200–202
  presentation of, modality of, 201–202
Task demands, challenging behavior
    and, 138, 139
Teacher/Parent Questionnaire (QUEST),
    augmented language learning
    and, 120
Teaching
  communicative intents for, selection
    of, 133–135
  milieu, *see* Milieu teaching
  of tasks, LPAD and, 201
  transactional, naturalistic approach
    and, 52
  see also Intervention(s)
Templin-Darley Tests of Articulation, in
    expressive language delay, 279,
    301, 302, 304
Test(s), *see* Standardized tests; *specific
    tests*
Test-teach-test paradigm, 194, 369–370
  see also Dynamic assessment;
    Zone of proximal development
    (zpd)
Text units, in Reading MRC Project,
    317
Therapy, *see* Intervention(s); *specific type*
Thought
  creative, 4–5
  ecological, 5
  reductive, 4
Toddlers, *see* Early *entries*
Topic continuations, as conversational
    recruitment strategy, 256–257,
    259–260
  see also Conversational recruitment
Topical organization, mental retardation
    and, 345–346
Toys, facilitating social interaction, au-
    tism and, 186
Trained responses, in milieu teaching,
    11, 14
Trainers, generalization across, milieu
    teaching and, 22–28
Training
  need for, augmentative communica-
    tion systems and, 150